General Sir Richard Dannatt (since January 2011 General the Lord Dannatt GCB CBE MC DL) is one of the most respected British Generals of modern times. He stepped down from the position of Chief of the General Staff in August 2009. In the same year he was appointed by the Queen to the position of Constable of the Tower of London. In January 2011 he entered the House of Lords as a Crossbench Peer.

LEADING FROM THE FRONT

The Autobiography

GENERAL SIR RICHARD DANNATT

CORGI BOOKS

TRANSWORLD PUBLISHERS
61–63 Uxbridge Road, London W5 5SA
A Random House Group Company
www.rbooks.co.uk

LEADING FROM THE FRONT
A CORGI BOOK: 9780552162616

First published in Great Britain
in 2010 by Bantam Press
an imprint of Transworld Publishers
Corgi edition published 2011

Addresses for Random House Group Ltd companies outside the UK
can be found at: www.randomhouse.co.uk
The Random House Group Ltd Reg. No. 954009

The Random House Group Limited supports The Forest Stewardship
Council® (FSC®), the leading international forest certification organisation. All
our titles that are printed on Greenpeace approved FSC® certified paper carry
the FSC® logo. Our paper procurement policy can be found at
www.randomhouse.co.uk/environment

Typeset in 11/14.5pt Times New Roman by
Falcon Oast Graphic Art Ltd.
Printed in the UK by CPI Cox & Wyman, Reading, RG1 8EX.

2 4 6 8 10 9 7 5 3 1

This book is dedicated to my own amazing family
and all our incredible military families everywhere.
Thank you.

Contents

Foreword

This is a timely book. There has scarcely been a moment in the Army's long history when soldiers, serving or retired, have constituted so small a proportion of our nation's population. For all the reportage of fighting in Iraq and now Afghanistan we have rarely understood less about the young men – and, increasingly, young women too – who do what Richard Dannatt calls 'most of the heavy lifting, the fighting and the dying' in the wars that have come to characterize our age. On the one hand, it is encouraging to see how Help for Heroes has touched a resonant chord of national gratitude; how the unofficial ceremonies in the Wiltshire town of Wootton Bassett represent respect and gratitude for service personnel who have paid the ultimate price; and how units returning from their tours of duty now march with pride through their home towns. But on the other, we have been paying private soldiers less than traffic wardens, routinely saving money in an overstretched defence budget by postponing long-overdue repairs to military accommodation, and being shamefully laggardly in ensuring that the families of the seriously wounded do not have to scramble for bed and breakfast accommodation to be close to their loved ones in hospital. We have been sapping our Army's willingness to serve in a dangerous world where operational tours run on thick and fast, essential equipment is too often lacking and there are rarely enough helicopters.

It is received wisdom that politicians are ultimately to blame for this, and indeed, Richard Dannatt argues that 'if war is too important to be left to generals, then the funding of war is too important to be left to politicians'. But he goes a good deal farther, arguing that in 2006 the Military Covenant between the Army and the society it serves was 'badly out of kilter', and that 'the real lack was in leadership and drive at the highest levels'. At least part of the difficulty lay in the tension between the corporate and single-service tasks of the heads of the three individual armed services, for 'the tribal chief function inevitably sits at odds with a service chief's more corporate roles'. Although he is charged with responsibility for the overall fighting effectiveness of the Army, 'today the Chief of the General Staff . . . owns so few of the decision-making levers pulled and pushed by his predecessors. Alanbrooke and Templer would have shaken their heads at my inability to determine and decide.'

The book's title reflects its author's conviction that 'looking after individuals should naturally be a principal duty of the chain of command', for leadership is every bit as important in Whitehall corridors as it is on mean streets or parched hillsides. In the first half of the book Richard Dannatt describes his career from officer cadet to general, and it is easy to see the influences that helped shape him, for his views are much more a reflection of wide experience than of any abstract reasoning. We forget just how dangerous Northern Ireland was in the 1970s and 1980s: in his first four-month tour of duty in Belfast in 1971 his battalion of Green Howards lost five killed, twenty seriously wounded and seventy-five injured. He writes with palpable affection for 'these wonderfully dependable private soldiers on which the British Army is built' and admits that he had much to learn – not just from his superiors: his platoon sergeant whacked him in the chest when he left camp without a radio, saying: 'That will teach you to risk my soldiers' lives . . .' On another tour Major Peter Willis, his company commander, was killed with three others by an IRA bomb, leading Dannatt to insist that the legitimate way of achieving political change is through the ballot box, not the gun: 'That is a principle worth dying for.'

Richard Dannatt married Philippa Gurney in Norwich in 1977, and 'my wonderful wife, Pippa' is never far from his thoughts, whether in moving house twenty-three times in thirty-three years of marriage or in having a husband who managed to be unavoidably absent for so many of the crucial events of family life. They have three sons and a daughter: one of the boys followed his father into the Army and has fought in Iraq and Afghanistan. If serving as a junior officer in the infantry gave Richard Dannatt an enduring respect for soldiers, then his own experience of supportive family life underlined the pivotal importance of the military family, for so very much depends upon it. Scarcely less important is his religious belief, deeply rooted in the Essex farming stock from which he comes, and accentuated by a major stroke at the age of twenty-six that has 'had a vast impact on what I think and do'.

Dannatt was at the Staff College during the Falklands War, and like so many of his generation he was sorry to miss it, although the narrow margin of victory emphasized that the country was taking risks with defence. 'If you want to do it,' he writes, 'you have to be prepared to pay for it – muddling through on the good-will of our servicemen and women is immoral.' As a young lieutenant colonel he served as Military Assistant to the Minister of State for the Armed Forces, and reflects on the fact that in his three years in the minister's private office he worked with three ministers, three private secretaries and seven assistant private secretaries: a lack of continuity that did not do much for the efficient delivery of the Government's work. In mid-1989 he went off to command his own battalion, stationed in Catterick, taking over just after it had completed its tercentenary celebrations. The Green Howards recruited largely in the old North Riding of Yorkshire, and Richard Dannatt is very much a regimental soldier, arguing that the regimental system is one of the Army's great strengths, and that 'we tinker with it at our peril': in 2004 and 2005, he says, 'we just got away with it'.

Something old, something new. The tough-minded General Sir Nigel Bagnall, CGS from 1985 to 1989, initiated a major shift in the Army's thinking. The central principle was that of 'mission command', based on orders that told a subordinate what he was expected to achieve rather than precisely how he was meant to go about his task. The Green Howards were part of the new 24th Airmobile Brigade, and learned new skills in rapid manœuvre by air. There were never enough helicopters, and although 'there was always the promise of greater investment in helicopters to come', the 'principle of tactical flexibility by movement through the air' was never properly funded, something that 'was to bite us hard a decade later'. Richard Dannatt went to the Staff College to run the Higher Command and Staff Course, another Bagnall initiative, though he spent much of his time revising the Army's doctrine in the era of the 'New World Order', and devising the campaign plan used by General Sir Michael Rose, sent out as the UN commander in Bosnia Herzegovina.

Command of 4th Armoured Brigade in Germany followed, although it was typical of the way the world had changed that Dannatt spent part of his time in this post commanding a UN sector in the Balkans, experiencing at first hand the difficulty of gaining confidence from a population that doubted continuing support: 'How can we put our trust in you, if you will be gone in a year's time?' Although the philosophy of 'mission command', conceived in a wholly different set of circumstances, worked well, and the troops remained committed to getting the job done in frustrating and often uncomfortable circumstances, there was a debit side, for much of the Army's kit was 'designed for longer, more static wars in different environments, with procurement processes modelled for the Cold War'; and although a great deal was expected of the soldiers on the ground, they were poorly repaid in terms of welfare provision.

Richard Dannatt's next job was as Director of the Defence Programme Staff in the Ministry of Defence at the time of the Strategic Defence Review that followed Labour's victory in the 1997 general election. The process saw the development of expeditionary armed forces, home-based but ready for overseas deployment: this necessitated calculations on the scale of particular operations and the requirement to sustain several at any one time. It was determined that the Army needed six deployable brigades, with two divisional headquarters – 1st Armoured Division in Germany and 3rd Mechanized Division at home – to oversee the training and administration of the brigades, and to command major operations as required. But the whole system made sense only if it was fully funded, and Dannatt argues that 'Gordon Brown's malign intervention' ensured that the Treasury failed to pay for the Government's own defence policy, thus leaving the process 'fatally flawed . . . from the outset'.

It was a relief to depart for Salisbury Plain on promotion to major general to command 3rd Division; but once again the Balkans threw their long shadow, and Dannatt's headquarters departed to command the British forces that moved into Kosovo in 1999. Back on Salisbury Plain he was much preoccupied with training his division on the Canadian prairie, a process severely impeded by a shortage of helicopters. He left 3rd Division early to serve as deputy commander of NATO's Stabilization Force in the Balkans, and then returned to the UK to serve as Assistant Chief of the General Staff, arguably the most influential major general's post in the Army. Dannatt digresses from his account of his time as

ACGS to chart the rise and fall of the Army's planned Future Rapid Effects System, a medium-weight vehicle 'light enough to get there quickly, but capable enough to do the business until heavier follow up forces arrived'. Ultimately the in-service date for FRES slipped further and further away, effectively killing the project, and leaving Dannatt reflecting that 'the whole . . . episode sums up what is worst about MOD decision-making in an environment in which resources are scarce and vested interests loom large, and in the absence of clear political and business leadership'.

In the wake of 9/11 it became evident that the United States intended to invade Iraq. In the absence of clear political direction, the British chiefs of staff planned on a minimum involvement, both on the grounds of cost and because there seemed to be 'limited national popular appetite for an attack on Iraq'. Although Dannatt testifies to his respect for the intelligence services, he admits that he found the intelligence on Iraq's weapons of mass destruction 'thin' and 'most uncompelling'. As he periodically stood in for CGS at chiefs of staff meetings, he knew that the chiefs were not seeing the 'killer intelligence . . . if it actually existed at all'. He condemns as naive the assumption that Iraq would take confident steps into the future once Saddam Hussein had been removed, and admits that the Army faced 'a severe – even impossible – challenge' to get ready for the war.

By the time the coalition invaded Iraq, Richard Dannatt had departed for Germany to command NATO's Allied Rapid Reaction Corps as a lieutenant general. For a time it looked as if the ARRC might be sent to Iraq, and no sooner had this been ruled out than deployment to Afghanistan was mooted, although it did not actually take place until he had handed over command. Preparatory discussions, however, led him to wonder if the West was prepared to find 'the resolve, resources and determination to see this through', an issue that remains wholly fundamental at the time of writing. In March 2005 Dannatt moved to Wilton as Commander in Chief, Land Command, becoming responsible for the whole of the deployable Army. The CGS at the time, General Sir Mike Jackson, had resolved to grasp the nettle of reorganizing the infantry, and one consequence of a shift to large regiments of several battalions each was that the Green Howards – 'after 318 years of loyal service to the Crown' – became 2nd Battalion, the Yorkshire Regiment (Green Howards). It is evident that Dannatt had reservations about the process, although he emphasizes that 'the future is in front and the past behind'.

Richard Dannatt concluded his last annual conference as Commander in Chief, before stepping up to succeed Mike Jackson, by telling his audience of generals and brigadiers that he had only joined the Army for three years in the first place, and had enjoyed thirty-six more years of service than he had expected, so they must not be surprised if there came a time when he felt compelled to fall on his sword. I was there when he said it. It struck me at the time that this was strong stuff, and it soon became clear that he was prepared to take risks 'to argue my case internally within Whitehall, but also to articulate it more publicly so that it would be heard by all the people I needed to reach'. This approach was controversial. There were those who argued that the Army was best defended by remaining firmly within the limits of what passed for political propriety, and who maintained that his policy of vigorous public engagement actually worked to the Army's disadvantage in Whitehall. Dannatt emphasizes that he had no choice in the matter, for he took the responsibility of putting the Army's case personally, despite the political desire 'not to have a public fuss in defence' and the MOD's knack of keeping the three single-service chiefs 'in some kind of unholy, unspoken balance'. No sooner was he in office than he warned the Secretary of State for Defence that the army was 'running hot', and that he had doubts about 'the utility and safety of some of the patrol vehicles we were using in Iraq and Afghanistan, and the availability of helicopters'. His most significant interview appeared in the *Daily Mail* – chosen because 'it spoke to middle England, the constituency with which I wanted to engage' within two months of taking over – and set the tone for much of what followed.

Richard Dannatt's conclusions on his time as CGS are uncomfortable. He argues that 'much of our planned investment in defence was at the very least of question-able relevance to the challenges we faced now and will face in the future'. He goes on to observe that, despite the potential costs of military intervention, political leaders are unlikely to 'pass by on the other side' when crises emerge. They need, however, to provide a rationale for the use of force that is compelling to both Parliament and public, and it is easy to see how damaging this lack of clear strategic narrative has proved as far as Afghanistan is concerned. A country facing the most severe economic crisis for seventy years will need to make wise investments in defence, and as things stand part of this investment is directed into areas that 'we would probably never use'. Dannatt is convinced that success in Afghanistan, while 'not discretionary', will be hard to achieve, in part because the balance of investment is 'too heavily weighted towards the future and too lightly towards the present'.

Defence needs to be sustained on a campaign footing, and the struggle against 'hybrid' adversaries – state, non-state and proxy forces – is likely to focus on competition for the loyalty and support of the people. Dannatt paraphrases General Sir Rupert Smith's comments on 'war among the people' to argue that 'war among the people is the context, and war about the people is the object'. Across defence we need more relevant capabilities – and within the Army we need cultural change so as to produce 'systemic and systematic support for the unconventional capabilities the Army requires in order to succeed in the kind of operations in which we are currently engaged and to which we are likely to remain committed for many years to come'.

Many of Richard Dannatt's views will be hotly debated, not least because they reflect, entirely unsurprisingly, an Army perspective. But even his most vocal opponents can scarcely deny the fundamental truth of his assertion that the real strength of our armed forces are its people – servicemen and women and their families. He argues that soldiers expect a fair deal, and believes that 'integrity establishes the moral baseline of leadership'. The privilege of leadership is earned by serving others, and in a society corroded by selfishness this great truth helps define an Army that lives by its values:

it has not so much a right, but a duty, to be different.

Dannatt has been decorated for his physical courage, though he skates lightly over it here. But moral courage is often much harder to exercise, for it takes real determination to break ranks, to challenge accepted views, to be an unsettling guest in a world of compromise and, by implication, to criticize old and valued comrades. During his time as professional head of the Army Richard Dannatt showed courage in confronting the challenges it faced, and if he sticks his neck out in the pages that follow it is surely no more than to abide by the principle that characterized his career – leading from the front.

Richard Holmes

Acknowledgements

This book would not have been written had it not been for the inspiration, encouragement and support of my family, in particular my children Tom, Bertie, Olly and Richenda. Pippa and I were sceptical about whether or not I should write a book about my military career, but the children were adamant that I should. Their insistent view was that so much had happened since 9/11 in particular that, as someone who had been closely involved with many of the key issues in defence in the decade that followed, I had a duty to record my account of those years and to offer my perspective on events. Having acceded to their point of view, I came to appreciate that my views on recent events were fully understandable only when seen in the context of my full career and early life – and so this book became also a personal autobiography and a record of my wider views on military matters past, present and future.

So I would like to record my sincere thanks to all my

family – Pippa, my wife, who has followed the drum through thick and thin, brought up our children almost single-handed and saved me from myself more times than I care to recall; Tom, Bertie, Olly and Richenda, my children, who have come on the journey with me; Lucinda and Emma, my two daughters-in-law, who are both a great joy to our family; and the next generation, my two grandsons Arthur and Freddie, into whose hands the future will fall. Without the love and support of all my family, nothing that I have attempted would have been possible.

I would also like to place on record my thanks for the professional and personal support given to me, and to Pippa where appropriate, by those officers and non-commissioned officers who have worked closely with me. Senior officers are supported by military assistants and aides de camp, of which I have had a splendid and talented team. I would like to thank my military assistants from 2001 to 2009, Lieutenant Colonels David Cullen, Andrew Hughes, Chris Ryder, John Patterson, Felix Gedney, Ian Gibb, Edward Chamberlain, Harry Holt, Alistair Aitken and Simon Gilderson, and Majors Ben Cattemole and Ben Wilde, for their wise professional counsel and good humour. I would also like to acknowledge my succession of aides de camp from 1999 to 2009, Captains Toby Greville, Zac Stenning, Philip Searle, Justin Hunt-Davies, Nick Thom, Ollie Pile, Rupert Thomas, James Rob, Toby Glover and James Ashworth. Having re-learnt how to manage my own affairs over the last year, I am hugely grateful for the way that they all ran my diary, fixed everything and tolerated my periodic moments of grumpiness or changes of mind – saints one and all! I am also most grateful to those who have driven me, made sure I appeared in the right uniform or helped me look after our official guests: these include Colour Sergeant Steve Crighton MBE, Colour Sergeant Paul Simpson MBE, Sergeant Mac McClennan, Sergeant Bernie Allsopp and Corporal Mal Franks.

Although I take full responsibility for every word and photograph in this book – and any mistakes or errors are entirely mine – I would wish to thank very warmly all those who have assisted in its publication. In particular I wish to thank my agent, Charlie Viney, not only for his huge help in getting this project off the ground, but for his persistence through the months when I was adamant that I was not going to write a book. His perseverance paid off to the benefit of all. I would like to thank my publisher, Bill Scott-Kerr of Transworld, for putting together a thoroughly professional and pragmatic team who have let me plough my own furrow with only gentle pulls on the reins, in particular Simon Thorogood, editorial director; Gillian Somerscales, copy-editor; Sheila Lee, picture editor; Patsy Irwin, who master-minded the publicity for the book; Helen Edwards, who secured the serialization; and Zoe Willis, who oversaw the audio version.

Having already accepted full responsibility for the final product, I would nevertheless wish to record my gratitude to those who read and commented on the text: Martin Bell, Tom and Lucinda Dannatt, Charles and Tricia Marnham, John Powell, and John and Fee Sharples. I would also like to thank Nick Gurr and Andrew Jackson for securing safe passage of the text through the Ministry of Defence, ensuring that the

Official Secrets Act had not been breached inadvertently, and Lloyd Clark and Rob Lyman for assisting me in the production of some of the text from my notes, and for their research and encouragement. I am also grateful to Patrick Sanders and Anna Crowther for their detailed research in the latter part of the book. Finally, I would like to thank Professor Richard Holmes for his very generous Foreword. I hesitated to ask this most accomplished and busy of men to undertake this task, but after many years of professional and personal acquaintance I could think of no one better. I fear that he has over-sold what is to come.

Keswick, Norfolk
July 2010

Introduction
Without
Fear or Favour

My small party had arrived at Camp Bastion airfield in the early hours of 14 July 2009. The camp was shrouded in darkness but still busy, a breeze muffling the background growl and whine of helicopters, as we joined two hundred soldiers waiting in double file to begin the farewell ceremony for our eight recently fallen comrades, killed in the bloodiest few days of the British Army's latest operations in Afghanistan. It was a sad moment in the short history of our current involvement in this war-torn country. As I took my place close to the open tail-ramp of the huge C-17 transport aircraft, the sergeant major called us quickly to attention. We saluted as the eight caskets were borne past, each draped in the Union Flag, each carried by six young soldiers from 2nd Battalion, the Rifles – comrades-in-arms to the last.

Standing opposite me were the battalion commanders to seven of the dead men: 2 Rifles' Lieutenant Colonel Rob Thompson and 4 Rifles' Lieutenant Colonel Rupert

Jones, whose father, Lieutenant Colonel 'H' Jones VC, had laid down his life at Goose Green in the Falklands some twenty-seven years earlier. Their men looked sad, but these officers remained resolute, though their fixed expressions spoke volumes. I was humbled by their strength in such trying circumstances and proud of them all. The coffins were taken into the hold and set down reverently for their long journey home. The chaplains uttered prayers of committal and the plaintive notes of the Last Post drifted across the apron. The pall bearers left the aircraft, the ramp was raised and the floodlights were dimmed. We fell out, talking quietly but without much to say. All too soon the sun would be up on another day in Helmand Province.

The sombre gathering at Bastion reinforced my belief that we had been asking a great deal of our troops recently. It was less than two years since 2 and 4 Rifles had been the last battalions to defend Basra Palace in southern Iraq, battling Iranian-backed militias to facilitate a handover to Iraqi authorities. Despite the controversy surrounding our intervention in Iraq, Basra had been transformed since the handover had taken place, so much so that in March 2009 I had been able to walk along the popular waterfront of the Shatt al-Arab waterway wearing neither helmet nor body armour. I talked to locals over cups of green tea and learned about their aspirations for fresh water, an unbroken electricity supply, new jobs, sensing their eagerness for freedom of expression and a better standard of living now that both Saddam Hussein and the militias were gone. Their basic needs convinced me that with the requisite resources, a strong will and positive intent, Britain retained the ability to enhance the lives of millions. Yet in Iraq our minimally resourced military effort had nearly led to humiliation; now it was Afghanistan that was testing the British commitment to countering global, Islamist-inspired terrorism. Camp Bastion's poignant farewell to our brothers-in-arms had done nothing to shake my conviction that Britain's history, ambition and global stature all required us to take a major role in the country if we were to achieve the success that our growing sacrifice demanded. The latest eight fatalities had taken the number of British troops killed in Afghanistan since October 2001 to 184 – a figure surpassing those who had died in Iraq, and a grim milestone. Only days before I had been at RAF Lyneham when the bodies of Lieutenant Colonel Rupert Thorneloe (the most senior British officer to be killed in action since 'H' Jones) and Trooper Josh Hammond – the eighteen-year-old soldier who died beside him – were returned home. Following the cortège to the town of Wootton Bassett I had stood among the Wiltshire people who conveyed the nation's respects and sadness. We were losing some of our very best.

The dignity of the simple, moving ceremony at Camp Bastion contrasted starkly with the furore caused by journalists reporting on this, my last visit to Afghanistan as Chief of the General Staff. Initial stories had centred on an apparent helicopter shortage but quickly moved on to my own, wider concerns about inadequate manpower and resources. It was erroneously reported that these issues were a stick with which I intended to beat the Government. Before I had even returned home, some narrow-minded politicians had sought to offset the political embarrassment by tabling personal questions about me, focusing on the cost of my entertaining, use of helicopters and cars, accommodation and house staff. Their purpose was to discredit me, which I took as tacit acknowledgement that in the face of the undeniable evidence they had lost the argument over resources for Afghanistan and were now looking for revenge. It was a shabby, petty way to conduct business. As Army chief, I was simply seeking to ensure that my people had the right tools with which to do their hugely demanding and dangerous jobs. Yet the sniping did not cease until my retirement from the Army on 28 August 2009 – even though the publication of my modest expenses had merely revealed my detractors' rather sad intentions. It was an episode which contributed to my decision not only to tell the story of my life as a soldier but also to discuss recent military developments and provide an assessment of the British Army, while looking at likely future operations. Thorny issues abound but they need to be grappled with – none more than the linked questions of whether there is a need to enlarge Britain's land forces and whether our national spending on defence should be related more closely to the challenges of the real world, which today are increasingly among the people and on land.

A formal Defence Review has been required for several years, but the political appetite for one has been lacking, even though the defence environment has become infinitely more complex and demanding over the last decade. The review should be comprehensive and robust, built round a realistic view of Britain's future world role and relationships. It needs to indicate the likely character and nature of future conflict, for only then will it be possible to make a judgement about Britain's defence requirements in the twenty-first century and the equipment needs to achieve the capabilities necessary to meet those requirements. Ensuring the nation's security is the responsibility of politicians, defence professionals and the military top brass; but the task ultimately falls to those in uniform at the sharp end, and depends on their being willing to live in unpleasant conditions, take critical decisions under intense pressure, overcome fear and exhaustion, and see a close comrade killed or badly wounded while continuing to soldier. The ability of these remarkable people to do their jobs is critically underpinned by the support they receive from the population generally and, in particular, from their loved ones, who form an integral part of the Army family. Having served many times in Northern Ireland, been on lengthy operations in the Balkans and enjoyed a series of stimulating yet challenging appointments, I have experienced the great joys of soldiering but also known something of its hardships. After moving house twenty-three times in thirty-three years of married life and watching a son in the Army complete tours in Iraq and Afghanistan, I am acutely aware of the stress and strain that being a soldier places on a family.

A career in the armed forces makes more demands on the life of an individual and his family than most, and when I originally entered the Army I had not intended to be a soldier for long. Yet, even though I eventually stood down as Chief of the General Staff forty years to the day from taking the Queen's Shilling, I have never regretted my decision to join up. I can recall many trying episodes over the decades, but positive memories abound – and they are dominated by those times when I enjoyed the unique comradeship which only comes from having shared an extraordinary experience. Being a soldier is a vocation, and the Army is more like a family organized for the needs of its people and the achievement of its goals than just another employer. We are not perfect (far from it), but the Army demands that our troops aspire to 'Be the Best', are proud of our high standards and continually adapt as the conflicts to which we have to respond themselves evolve in character. In our contemporary society individualism prevails, traditional values are regularly ignored and authority is often seen as something to be challenged. The Army has to be different. Our terms of service are unique, for our liability is unlimited and some risks cannot be mitigated by legislation. We live by core values – selfless commitment, loyalty, integrity, courage, discipline and, perhaps most importantly, respect for others – and so give ourselves purpose, structure and a moral baseline. We do not just serve ourselves; we serve the nation.

All British Army officers start out at the Royal Military Academy, Sandhurst, where the motto is 'Serve to Lead'. Our nation needs those who are prepared to serve for the greater good and those who are prepared to lead – without fear or favour – in the service of Queen and country. This need has been constant throughout its history, and I see no reason for it to change. In what follows I will seek to explain why.

1

We All Start Somewhere

At least one well-known story starts with three men in a boat. This one – far less glorious – starts with four officer cadets halfway through their Sandhurst training, knowing next to nothing about boats but attempting to race to Paris by water. We had left Big Ben at noon on 29 August 1970, vying for position with two other boats and crews, all hoping to be the first to touch the Eiffel Tower. Our crew consisted of Gordon Allen, David Budge, Anthony Barne and myself. The boat was a 10-foot-long aluminium river assault craft, onto the back of which had been bolted a Johnson 40-horsepower outboard engine. Had we been so minded we could have water-skied behind it, but we hadn't thought of that. We set out with hope far outweighing experience. Just below Tower Bridge we spotted a pub by the river at Wapping and, ignoring the race for a while, we stopped for a beer. Suitably refreshed, we powered our way contentedly to Gravesend, happily thinking that this was the life. We then turned a bend in the river, and were nearly swamped. Huge waves rolling in from the North Sea surged towards us, breaking over our shallow bows and quickly filling the boat. Steering in something of a panic towards the bank, all the while wallowing like a floundering whale, we managed to reach safety and, breathing sighs of relief, beached the craft.

We had assumed that it would be up to the job. But in our naivety we had not considered the savage sea. With some consternation we reflected that we were still on the River Thames and yet waves had very nearly sunk us! In our youthful imaginings we had thought that we would merrily skip across the Channel in our little warship, racing our way to Paris and glory. A moment of reflection was called for. This was supposedly an 'Adventurous Training' expedition, and we suddenly realized it was going to be a trifle more adventurous than we had anticipated. A genius among us then suggested that if we stretched our Army-issue groundsheets across the angular bow, forced them up in the middle using a piece of driftwood that we had picked up off a mud bank, and held the whole thing in place with our double-hooked elastic bungees, we would have an elegant solution to our wave-swamping problem. Encouraged by this bout of inventiveness we duly constructed our spray baffle, an innovation which – extraordinarily in retrospect – survived all the way to Paris.

Battling across the Channel in a Force 5 wind against 8- to 10-foot waves, a journey punctuated by periodic surges of fear, was an experience I will never forget. We were lucky to get across, in an exercise which I am certain the sheer volume of traffic in the English Channel, to say nothing of the need in this age for all the right permits and licences, would now prohibit. Reaching the relatively calm network of the French canal and river system did little to remove the danger to our flimsy craft, however, with huge tunnel-filling barges bearing down on us in pitch darkness in complete contempt, threatening to squash us like metallic plasticene in any one of the thirty-five enormous locks through which we had to navigate.

Admiral Lord Nelson would have turned in his grave at our efforts – but we were soldiers, not sailors. Or perhaps he would have given our foolhardy determination something of a cheer as five days later, against all the odds, and rather surprised ourselves at our survival, we reached Paris, touched the Eiffel Tower first and celebrated with the same Watney's Pale Ale that had kept fear at bay in the Channel. Of our rivals, one boat had sprung so many rivets on the crossing that it sank in Calais harbour, while the other limped into Paris looking more like a mobile swimming pool than a boat. After all that, it was something of a relief to be digging a trench on Salisbury Plain on our next Sandhurst exercise.

I had never intended to be a soldier. At school, my initial ambition had been to go to Cambridge, read law and become a barrister. That plan was, however, quickly put to the test. I was delighted to be called to interview at Emmanuel College, Cambridge, and not altogether surprised when my interviewer asked if I did any reading about the law – a question a helpful friend had warned me to expect.

'Yes, Sir, I read the law reports in *The Times*,' I replied, feeling quite pleased with myself.

'And what cases recently have caught your attention?'

This question seemed a little below the belt, but thinking quickly I replied as confidently as I could: 'I have found the Bodies on the Moor Trial to be absolutely fascinating.'

Very pleased that I had even been able to name a trial, I rather hoped that the conversation would now change tack. Not so. 'And what about that trial did you find so interesting?'

By this stage I knew I was in trouble, as I was no real student of the law, and anyone with a casual interest in current affairs was aware of the existence of that particular trial. Nevertheless, I persisted: 'I was amazed that the criminals, Brady and Hindley, had got away with it for so long.'

There was a long silence. The game was up. The professor looked at me somewhat quizzically over his half-rimmed glasses, paused, and then observed – quite politely in the circumstances – 'I think, Mr Dannatt, that you might be better suited to joining the police force than reading law at this college.' I knew then that Cambridge was not for me. So did he.

It came as something of a surprise to my parents when, a couple of months later, I announced that I had decided to join the Army. Furthermore, as I was under eighteen, would my father kindly sign the necessary papers which I had in my pocket? They had come to take me out for a Sunday from school. I dropped my bombshell over coffee after lunch at the Royal Albion Hotel, Broadstairs. My choice of the Army as a career was something between a surprise and a shock for my parents, who were of the Second World War generation, for whom military service had been an unpleasant necessity. My father, a qualified architect by the time the Second World War broke out, had volunteered for a commission in the Royal Engineers and spent just over four years serving in India and the Far East, while my mother had spent most of the war in the East End of London as a Women's Voluntary Service officer. My parents did not see each other from 1941 to 1945. Back in London, my mother and her parents at one period spent thirteen weeks consecutively sleeping in the cellar of their house during the height of the Blitz, the house next door being totally destroyed one night. Her father had seen earlier service, also as a Royal Engineers officer, spending most of the First World War in France, and had been mentioned in despatches. But in the 1960s – unless one came from a military family, which we did not – volunteering to join the Army in peacetime, after the previous generations' experiences of the two world wars, seemed anathema to them.

But I had made up my mind that it was the challenge of a practical outdoor life that I sought, not an academic route to an office-based profession, and so it was to Sandhurst, not Cambridge or any other university, that I was determined to go. My parents, hearing that I had set my heart on a military career, quietly acquiesced. I passed the Regular Commissions Board, the gateway to a commission in the Army, and was given a date on which I was to present myself at the Royal Military Academy, Sandhurst. Before reporting to Sandhurst, I had to go through the technicality of actually being sworn into the Army. I did this on 28 August 1969, having spent that morning watching the Essex cricket team play Leicester at the county ground in Chelmsford.

As the players went in for the lunch interval, I caught the bus to the local Army recruiting office. I signed the necessary papers, swore the oath of allegiance, pocketed a day's pay – the 'Queen's Shilling' – and caught the return bus to the cricket ground. I was back in my seat by the time the players came out for the afternoon session, and I spent the rest of the day wondering whether I had done the right thing.

But there were eighteen years of early life before Sandhurst. The things that are most relevant about those years are the people and the events that had an influence upon me. There were several, and I will record them here.

We all start somewhere; I was born on 23 December 1950 in what became my first home, a house called Broomfield Wyck overlooking the village green in Broomfield, just outside Chelmsford in what was then still rural Essex. The far distant origins of my family are now lost to time, but there are well-documented records going back 250 years placing us in Essex, centred on the village of Great Waltham, about 5 miles from Chelmsford. Indeed, several generations of my forebears are buried in the graveyard of St Lawrence, Great Waltham. My mother was relieved that I had appeared, albeit two weeks late, before Christmas. My father was able to register my birth at the same time as he registered his mother's death: she died the day before I was born. Before life came into focus on my own account, we – my parents, my elder sister Juliet, and I – moved closer to Chelmsford, where my father was in architectural practice with my grandfather.

I knew my grandfather as an elderly and fairly distant

man, whom I visited from time to time, held in great respect but never really knew well personally. He always came to lunch with us on a Friday, an occasion which demanded much scurrying around by everyone. Paradoxically, I felt that I knew much more about, and was much more strongly influenced by, his father, my great-grandfather, even though he died in 1914. William Dannatt left a memoir entitled *The Faith of a Farmer*, which was published after his death in 1917, and reading this book as a youngster had a significant impact on my own life in a number of ways. The historical facts, tracing our family back to William's great-grandfather, apparently a displaced Huguenot from France who had originally settled in Leicestershire, were of only passing interest to me; it was what my great-grandfather wrote of himself that I found fascinating.

My great-grandfather had always determined to be a farmer, despite his own father's dismissing it for offering 'nothing but a bread and cheese living'. 'Never mind,' the young William had insisted in 1869, 'I want to be a farmer.' He spent the next ten years of his life learning his chosen profession. Then came a year during which it rained so hard and so heavily that the harvest – or what remained of it – could not be collected until November. This year, 1879, turned out to be one that changed the course of English farming; and the disastrous, water-logged decade between 1879 and 1889 was my great-grandfather's opportunity. The unprecedented rainfall of these years totally saturated the farmland on which so many people had previously made their living, rendering it unusable. The only possibility of continuing to make any success out of farming lay in introducing a new system of drainage, a subject to which my great-grandfather had given much thought. An ardent diarist, William Dannatt set out his approach to his profession in an earlier book, published in 1914, which he called *Practical Hints from the Notebook of an Old Farmer*. When he was setting out on his chosen career, farms lay empty on every side, abandoned to the water as worthless. He secured a large acreage and put his new drainage system to work.

This is not the place to record the story of William Dannatt's achievements, but as a young man I found the principles upon which he operated both instructive and inspiring. First, he gave the fullest personal consideration not only to his men, but to his horses – the technology of his day. He did not believe in the delegation of responsibility. Tasks could be delegated, he argued, but not responsibility. 'A farmer ought to be up in time to meet his men in the morning, and if his heart and soul, to use an old expression, be in his business he will do so.' Second, he was very single-minded: 'A man's mind, much less his body, cannot very well be in two places at the same time, so that, when he is engaged in another place, a chance is often lost that can never be regained.' But he was not at all hidebound in his ways, arguing that 'an important thing in farming is to get out of the old rut'. He was always looking out for or inventing new methods of farming. He elaborated a convention of the time which said 'Never use manual labour if it can be done by horses' by adding: 'Do not use horses if the steam-engine is cheaper. Do not use the steam-engine if the motor or some other power can be found to do it cheaper.' The farmer's business was 'to produce the fruits of the earth at the least possible cost'. Looking after your men, remaining focused on the job in hand and being prepared to embrace change seemed to me a wise formula to follow.

Perhaps it was working so closely with nature that also gave my great-grandfather an affinity with religion, for he was a no-nonsense, practical Christian. Two mottoes governed all of William Dannatt's farming. The first was: 'Do your best, and leave the rest; but in the middle of it, ask God to bless.' And then he added a second: 'Do the next thing.' If there was something else that crossed your mind to do, do it, and do it there and then. He felt that if the maximum energy was put into any endeavour then success, while not guaranteed, was more likely to come about than not. In a quaint way that I came to recognize, he summed up his philosophy thus: 'A man cannot create anything himself; things are created for him to tend, foster, and to care for, and great is his responsibility towards man and beast, especially towards the former.'

The memoir my great-grandfather left ran to over a quarter of a million words, but he never finished it. He died comparatively young at the height of his farming success, on 6 November 1914. His last months, in which he was confined to his bed, produced some of his most sensitive writing about the countryside he loved, tempered by his frustration that the world around him was descending into war. 'What enhances the pleasure this year is the beautiful weather for the harvest. No anxiety as to the crops being spoilt by rain; to wake up early, before daybreak, and find morning after morning the same picture of a fine day.' In his last days, as war clouds were gathering over Europe, he wrote passionately: 'The main thing is to feel that the wars we engage in are in the right, and promote righteousness and justice in the world. If we are engaged in any war which does not promote and further these objects, we had better be the conquered ones.' That last comment was a bold statement, but a correct one. Doing the right thing was more important than politics or nationalism. His Christianity suffused his entire view of life. Almost the last words in his diary seemed to place his whole life in its full context and justify the title of his book: 'Oh that men would think more of the next world and less of this, to escape the snares of this, to seek first the kingdom of God, to have faith in Christ, to live in Him!'

This old Victorian and Edwardian left a powerful legacy. Notwithstanding his lofty ideals, he was a practical man and his memoirs also included a full account of his love of cricket, hunting, shooting and his pipe. His accounts of stag-hunting in Essex in his youth surely challenge the current perception of Essex, now thought of as just a London-fringe county. I would dearly love to have met that man.

For me, as for my great-grandfather, cricket has been a lifelong passion. My earliest attempts at playing were made in the garden with my maternal grandfather, another person whose influence on me was very considerable. Frank Chilvers had spent his working life in railways, taking early retirement from the old London and North East Railway Company when the entire railway system was nationalized in 1947. Prior to that, from his office in Liverpool Street, he had overseen all railway operations between London and York and throughout the east of England. He had done this for the full duration of the Second World War – a particularly challenging task in the days of the Blitz when German bombs were constantly smashing both track and trains – and as a younger man he had run ammunition trains up to the front in France during the First World War: so he understood as well as anyone the difficulties of being a railwayman at war. To a small boy he was a fount of fascinating stories. He had, moreover, two other great attractions in my eyes. He loved cricket; and, having retired, he had plenty of time to spend with me. In the summer we would play our own test matches in the garden and spend days watching Essex compete in the county championship; in the winter we would play endless games of table tennis and tinker with my ever-expanding model railway. A cigarette smoker since his days in the trenches, he would puff smoke at the model engines to add to the fun. He was also one of the most amusing men I have ever met, with a seemingly endless supply of jokes and boundless sense of humour. In fact, he was a man of extraordinary talents. His Christian faith ran deep, and he served as a part-time Baptist minister, something of a tradition in his family. His storytelling was one facet of his way with words; another was his ability to preach a thoroughly sensible and comprehensible sermon. If I have any ability to speak in public it has undoubtedly come down from my grandfather and on through my mother, whose own professional qualifications were in elocution and voice production. Like her father, she was much in demand as a speaker, besides chairing a variety of organizations. In his later years, my grandfather lived with us, albeit in a separate part of our house, and always had lunch with us. The railwayman in him continued to come out in his obsession with time. If lunch were not ready at 1 p.m. precisely we would be in trouble. A tactic to deflect his ire was developed: when I was at home, if lunch was running late I would go through to his sitting room and detain him happily with a gin and tonic. This practice worked to everyone's advantage.

Of course, not just my grandfather but my whole immediate family loomed large in my early life. My father was very committed to his architectural practice, which he ran from offices in the centre of Chelmsford. His diary was always full, his time inevitably being taken up not only with meeting clients, developing plans and overseeing projects, but also with the process of running a business and managing his staff. Sometimes business was good, at other times one could sense that things were a little tight. My father's father was still the senior partner in the practice, remaining so until he died in his nineties, and my father stayed faithful to their original partnership agreement of splitting profits down the middle. Financially, this was not brilliant for my father, whose needs increased as his father's decreased, but I never heard him complain. However, once my parents had decided that Juliet and I would go away to boarding school, there were big bills to be paid – which is one of the reasons why, when she was able to, my mother returned to work on a part-time basis, lecturing in voice production at the London Bible College. The College took many generations of aspiring clergymen through the basics of working out what they wanted to say, and my mother helped them in actually saying it.

Despite my parents' busyness, we were very close as a family, and family holidays were an important part of the annual calendar. We usually went away somewhere for a week in the Easter holidays, and always for two or three weeks in the summer. My father was a great believer in getting to know Great Britain rather than going abroad, so I have happy memories of holidays in North Wales, Devon and Cornwall, the Isle of Wight, Scotland, the Lake District, and Frinton and Southwold on the east coast. Only once did we go abroad as a family, to Switzerland. Over Christmas we always stayed at home, our cousins coming to us on the evening of Boxing Day every year for supper and games.

A great stalwart of our family was Emily Church, known to all of us as Mimmie. She had come to work for my mother's parents aged sixteen, just before my mother was born, and never left. She went through every stage from nanny to housekeeper to companion, and died in her seventies as a close member of our family. To me, she was like an extra grandmother. If something needed doing, Mimmie would do it, and if someone else was given the task she would seem to be offended. She was quite wonderful – if there was a worked example of self-less commitment, it was Mimmie – and we all loved her dearly.

Juliet was my only sibling and, as she was both a girl and nearly four years older than me, our lives developed on separate tracks. She went away to boarding school, Wadhurst College in Sussex, when she was eleven and subsequently went to a teacher training college before embarking on a teaching career, which she much enjoyed. She married Graham Fenner, a friend of mine whom I introduced to her and who became headmaster of Northbourne Park prep school in Kent; but sadly, Juliet developed breast cancer and, after a brave battle with that wretched illness that has taken away so many who are close to me, she died. She is buried in Betteshanger Churchyard near Northbourne Park. We all felt her loss very deeply; my father, indeed, never recovered from it. More happily for the future, Juliet left two wonderful children, Louise and James, who have both made a great success of their lives in different ways. Somewhat selfishly, I would love to have had a brother or sister around in recent years to have played a part in keeping my feet on the ground. But it was not to be.

It is not just people who are an influence on one's early years; places, too, make their mark, and in particular, schools. I attended three. The first was at St Anne's in Chelmsford, where I stayed until I was almost nine. Those years left me two legacies. One was the beginning of a love of history, taught there by a wonderful woman known to us as Miss Flower, and the other was the beginning of a profound dislike of my first Christian name, Francis. Disaster with this name struck early. One occasion which is seared into my memory was a school-friend's birthday party, where I discovered, on arrival, that I was the only boy. The mother of the little girl whose birthday it was had decided to ask all the girls in the class, and as a 'Francis' I was on the guest list. The finer detail of the spelling of that name had eluded the mother. Henceforth, for me that name was living on borrowed time! I eventually switched to my second name, Richard, when I was fifteen, following a request over the public address system at an event I was attending for

'Miss Francis Dannatt to go to Reception'. That was it.

Juliet was already away at boarding school when, just after my ninth birthday, I left St Anne's and went to Felsted Junior School as a boarder. This was the preparatory school to the main school and was about 10 miles from home. My father had acted as the school's architect for a while and my great-grandfather had sold it some land for use as playing fields, as well as the very pretty Bury Farm House, which the school had converted into an arts and crafts centre; so I felt from the beginning that in a small way I belonged there. Five very happy years passed. Among a number of good friends I made there, one stood out. Ewing Grimshaw and I, having squabbled terribly at first, quickly developed a close friendship that lasted beyond school and into the Army: we were in the same Company at Sandhurst and went to the Staff College together. Unlike me, Ewing came from a very distinguished military family. His father had commanded a battalion of the 1st Punjab Regiment during the battle of Kohima and had been awarded a Distinguished Service Order in the field in Burma by no less a figure than General Bill Slim himself. Years later we became godfathers to each other's children. It was a tragedy for his beautiful wife, Rachel, and his three young children when he died of cancer in 1996 – eight years after I had lost my sister to the same terrible illness. I found the loss of such a close friend very hard. I am left with wonderfully happy memories of many years of friendship, from prep school days playing conkers and marbles together to Sandhurst and the Staff College; and the knowledge that Ewing's eldest son, and my godson, Nick, is a tremendous credit to his late father. We all have some gaps in our lives that can never be filled. Among mine are those left by Juliet and Ewing.

Felsted also meant that I could now play cricket properly, and it was confirmed as my favourite game. Some little boys want to be engine drivers; my schoolboy ambition was to play cricket for Essex. In the Easter holidays in those days Essex County Cricket Club ran coaching for its junior members, of which I was one. We used to meet at the county ground in Chelmsford and practise in the nets if it was fine or in the pavilion if it was wet, which it often was at Easter. At the time the pavilion was completely unaltered since my father had changed in it when playing hockey on the same ground for Chelmsford Hockey Club. When he came to pick me up he was always amused that nothing had altered there since the 1930s. But my abiding memory was being taught how to play a proper forward defensive stroke by the England and Essex star player Trevor Bailey – known in the game as 'The Boil' for the solid batting style that made him very hard to dislodge. To eager students of the game like me, he passed on the virtues of a straight bat and getting your nose over the ball. I filed these nuggets of gold away as I returned to school in 1963 for my fourth summer term of cricket.

Early in that term I was delighted to find that I had been selected for the First Eleven, and as a newcomer to the team I was more than happy to bat at number nine. In our first match, against the Under Fourteen Eleven from the main school, our batting collapsed and I found myself at the crease sooner than I expected with a lot of time to play out to give us a chance of a draw. The skills I had so appositely acquired during the Easter holidays were put to the test. As I blocked every ball with my Trevor Bailey forward defensive stroke, the clock ran down, our team survived and the match was drawn. Everyone seemed quite pleased with me; I had saved the game. In the second match of the season I was moved up the batting order and went in at number seven. This time, however, what we needed was some quick runs to ensure a win before time ran out. Unfortunately I had not mastered the art of developing my forward defensive stroke into one that could apply power and score runs. I duly did what I knew best and blocked every ball again. Once more the game was drawn, but I was no longer so popular. I soon found my natural home in the Second Eleven, where from the age of twelve I accepted my lot in cricket as a solid player, quite prepared to open the batting, take the shine off the new ball with my forward defensive shot and let others score the runs. At prep school, public school, Sandhurst and Staff College alike I was very happy to fill this role, and invariably captained the sides in which I played. Later on, in regimental cricket, I decided that as the commanding officer I was probably more use to the team not as a player but as the umpire!

In fact, my finest moment in cricket was not on the pitch but off it, during the Headingley test match against Australia in summer 2009 when the BBC *Test Match Special* team asked me to do the tea interval interview. Sitting in the commentary box chatting with Jonathan Agnew and Phil Tufnell on live radio was a most amusing experience. Yes, the Trevor Bailey story came out, but so too did a discussion about whether we would ever see test cricket played in Pakistan again. I very much hope so, but whether we do or don't is intimately linked to our military success in Afghanistan, and against Islamist militants more generally in Pakistan. Of course, the world is bigger than cricket, bigger than any sport: but sport is an important part of the fabric of life and should not be at the mercy of politics, religion or violence, or any combination of the three.

Schools and cricket grounds aside, another place that had an influence on me was Great Wood Camp, run by a nationwide Christian youth enterprise called the Scripture Union. Set in a woodland clearing halfway up a short valley in the Quantock Hills not far from the village of Over Stowey, Great Wood was idyllic from a young boy's perspective. I first went when I was eleven and continued throughout my teenage years. We lived in log cabins on the edge of the clearing, beside a small stream that just cried out to be dammed up and then dammed up again, releasing water to the inconvenience of others. Days were ordered and very full. We were up early, starting with 'flag break' when the Union Flag was unfurled with all of us standing around in a horseshoe in our cabin groups. Lord Baden-Powell would have felt much at home. Throughout the day sport, trekking and adventure games in the forest completely exhausted us; the evenings often finished around a huge camp fire as the sun disappeared behind the hills. It was early to bed as there was no electricity and only one hurricane lamp per cabin. The highlight of every ten-day camp was the two- or three-night expedition across Exmoor. In our cabin groups of eight we were given routes to follow by map and compass, pitching our small tents beside streams in the heart of R. D. Blackmore's Lorna Doone country. Our routes were always planned to finish in the village of Lynmouth, where a cream tea was the reward that had kept us going, not minding the overfull packs on our backs or our sodden feet. The camp was run by volunteers and led by another of those marvellous clerics who had a significant influence on me, the Reverend John Inchley. To us boys, he was both very old in years and young at heart. He led his team of camp officers in such a way that the outdoor experience was both huge fun and a natural link to the more meaningful things in life. An interwoven appreciation of traditional Christian and British values, set against the backdrop of adventure, friends and forests, had a lasting effect on me following the successive summer visits to Great Wood.

Idyllic camps in the Quantocks were, however, only brief interludes in the workaday year. My parents decided that when I was thirteen I should not go on from Felsted Junior School to the senior school, but should have a change of scenery and move instead to St Lawrence College in Kent. One of my close friends, David Ross, whose father, the Reverend Derek Ross, had been our much respected prep-school headmaster and was himself an Old Lawrentian, went with me – or, more accurately, I went with him. In contrast to the Essex farming village setting of Felsted, St Lawrence was on the edge of the Kentish port town of Ramsgate on the Isle of Thanet. Apart from the fact that my new school was about a four-hour drive from home, I was very happy with the decision. David and I were in Tower House whose housemaster, the Reverend Martin Martin-Harvey, was a wonderful man and a patient mentor to us boys. We respected him enormously. He was an Oxford hockey blue and had been decorated with a Distinguished Service Cross for his service as a Royal Navy chaplain in the war. As a bachelor he had endless time for all of us, but we never took advantage of his gentle manner. We wanted our house to be the best because of our respect and affection for him.

That said, we were not saints. In the mid-1960s public schools were pretty unreformed. Everyone knew their place in the hierarchy. The prefects ruled the house, the fags at the bottom of the pile did all the dirty jobs, and everyone in between was so grateful that they were no longer fags and could not wait to become prefects. During the day we were under the authority of the teaching staff, but our lives revolved around the house; and although 'Martin' was our father-figure, it was the pupil head of house who was the one to really watch out for! In those days, boys could still beat boys with a cane. If someone had transgressed such that the agreed sanction was a number of strokes of the cane then, with the housemaster's permission, this punishment was duly administered. This periodic and rather unnerving ritual always took place in the evening after the junior dormitory lights were out. We would hear the procession of prefects clumping their way from the senior end of the house, past the junior dormitories and into the Junior Common Room. The next sound was the table-tennis table being moved across the wooden floor to give the head of house more elbow room. Then another senior prefect would come into the dormitory of the offender and announce in a chilling voice: 'Smith, the head of house wishes to see you in the Common Room now. Put your trousers on.'

The hapless chap would duly dress, debate whether to put a book in his pants but decide against, and then report to the head of house in the Common Room.

'You know why you are here, Smith. Bend over.'

We would then hear a running of feet as the head of house built up a head of steam and then a swish of the cane. 'One,' we would count. More running feet, another swish: 'Two.' And again: 'Three,' 'Four,' 'Five' – and, on occasion, 'Six.' There would be muttering in the dormitory: 'He's given him Six – that's outrageous, it wasn't worth that many!'

The victim would return to the dormitory where, after the prefects had trooped back to their end of the house, the examination followed. Down came the trousers for all to inspect where the blows had landed. If they were square on the buttocks it was considered acceptable, but if any were high on the back or low on the legs there would always be more muttering: 'If he can't do it properly, Martin shouldn't let him do it at all' was the usual refrain. But for fags, muttering was about as far any protest was going to go. In general, we accepted the law of that part of the jungle. That is, all except one remarkable boy, Hugh Anderson.

Hugh was a highly intelligent individual with very strong views. He was the antithesis of the rebel public schoolboy in the 1960s film *if...* – not a schoolboy anarchist but a genuine reformer. He felt there was a better way. He campaigned against the archaic system of privileges and against the use of the cane in particular. But he went far beyond that, encouraging the school to be much more outward-looking. He instigated a social services scheme in the local neighbourhood and soon had over half the school visiting elderly people, providing entertainment in the Over-Sixties Club and other associations for pensioners and ex-servicemen around Ramsgate, and doing other voluntary work. He was held in high regard both as an intellectual and as someone who cared deeply about people; and he had cast-iron credibility among his peers because he was also a sportsman and captain of cricket. Hugh and I shared many interests. Leaving a year before me, he went straight to Cambridge, where he became President of the Cambridge Union Society in the first term of his second year – an unprecedented achievement.

Hugh certainly left his mark on St Lawrence College. The beating of boys by boys ended, the privilege system was radically overhauled, and the social services scheme (which he handed over to me) expanded to take in other schools in the area. By 1970 Hugh was running a political campaign, 'Students for Labour Victory', in the lead-up to the forthcoming general election. He was a genuine socialist in the original sense of the word. He had a deep Christian faith and felt that it was far better to do things for the benefit of others than merely to talk. Tragically, like too many of my close friends, he was diagnosed with cancer and died in his second year at Cambridge, while still running 'Students for Labour Victory' from his hospital bed. The impact of his short life was evidenced by the attendance at his memorial service in London, where the congregation included both Harold Wilson and James Callaghan. For myself, Hugh's commitment to doing what he felt to be right left a deep impression. His was an example I consciously decided to follow.

But where should I follow it? It was during my last year at school, after that abortive interview at Emmanuel, that my focus switched from the bar to the Army. The aspiration to be a barrister had been fuelled in part by a love of debating. Indeed, Hugh Anderson and I had both been in the team that won the *Observer* Inter-Schools Debating Competition for St Lawrence in 1968. However, I had also become an enthusiastic member of the Combined Cadet Force at school. Such enthusiasm was frowned on by most of my peers. Worse still, I even joined the corps early to play a bugle in the corps band. Even though I ever only mastered three of the five required notes, I enjoyed marching with the band, periodically blowing such sounds as I thought might be useful. I progressed from the band into the engineer part of the Army section and, by my last year, with my sights set on Sandhurst, had become the senior under-officer of the whole tri-service contingent. The school corps had given me only a glimpse of the Army, but I had seen enough to convince me that this was the initial career direction I wanted to take.

Although St Lawrence had only a modest tradition of boys going into the armed forces, one whom I knew slightly, John Sharples, had gone to Sandhurst on leaving two years ahead of me. I got in touch with John and he very kindly gave me a full tour of the Academy and some useful tips about the interview process. Visiting Sandhurst made me even more determined that that was where I wanted to go. I felt it was a purposeful and hon-ourable career to choose. Ewing Grimshaw, who had remained at Felsted, preceded me to Sandhurst by one term and gave me some very helpful advice about how to approach the selection process at the Regular Commissions Board, where all potential officers were tested over three days. One bit of advice in particular stayed with me. He told me that on the individual assault course there was a window-frame obstacle, and there were two ways to get through it: either place two boards, one on either side, and crawl up and over, or dive through. He said that even if you did not have time to complete the whole assault course, the staff would always say there was just time for the window frame. And he said: Whatever common sense tells you about crawling up boards, just dive. On the day, I dived and was very grateful to Ewing as I landed in a crumpled heap on the far side. After the disappointment of Cambridge I was delighted to be accepted by the Army and given a place at Sandhurst for that September.

One by-product of getting a place at Sandhurst was that it gave a great boost to my standing with the father of a girl I rather had my eye on at school. Although St Lawrence was a boys' school, a small number of girls from nearby St Stephen's College joined us for some subjects in the sixth form, and I was studying History and English with Caroline. Her father, a former Indian Army officer who had transferred to the Royal Artillery when the British left India in 1947, thought that as I was going to Sandhurst I must be a reliable sort of chap, and on Saturday evenings he would lend me his car so that Caroline and I could go out. I don't think he knew that I had only passed my driving test at the fourth attempt and I cannot now remember how these motoring adventures were squared off at school, but Caroline and I had enormous fun that summer careering around East Kent in her father's somewhat aged Ford Cortina. I only kept in distant touch with Caroline over the years, but was very sad to learn that she, too, among my friends, had died of cancer too early in life.

My visit to the Regular Commissions Board at Westbury in Wiltshire had another outcome of some significance for the future. After the many tests, interviews, exercises and other assessments, my final interview was with an extraordinarily tall and imposing brigadier. We had one of those life-changing conversations.

'What part of the Army are you thinking of joining, Number 35?' (Everyone at Westbury is called by a number, not a name.)

'Well, Sir,' I replied, 'I thought that I might like to join the Royal Armoured Corps,' basing my response solely on the enthusiasm expressed by my school acquaintance John Sharples for the 3rd Dragoon Guards – a main battle tank regiment – which he was about to join.

'Ever thought about the infantry, Number 35?'

This was an interesting and somewhat challenging question, as I had not thought about it, nor did I think creeping around the jungle, which was what the infantry seemed to do in those days, was entirely up my street.

'No, Sir,' I said, completely honestly.

'Would you like to find out a bit about the infantry?'

I thought that I had better show that I was broad-minded, so I said that I thought that would be very interesting.

'Well, I see you live quite close to Colchester, where my old regiment, the Green Howards, are based. Would you like me to fix a visit there so you can see what the infantry gets up to?'

I thanked Brigadier John Scott profusely for his kind invitation, and soon thereafter a letter duly arrived from the second-in-command of the 1st Battalion, the Green Howards, offering me some dates for a visit. I accepted, took a few days off school, and found myself attached to A Company, 1st Battalion, the Green Howards, commanded by a certain Major P. A. Inge. For those who know the Army or defence well the significance of that name needs no explanation, but for others I should record that Major Peter Inge went on to become Chief of the General Staff and then Chief of the Defence Staff, and is now a highly respected member of the House of Lords and a Privy Counsellor. He was, and is, a remarkable man, of whom more later. Staying with his company was a fascinating and hugely enjoyable experience, so when another letter arrived a couple of weeks after my visit saying that if I would like to join the Green Howards they thought they could find me a place, I was delighted. And that was the decision made. Thereafter, in answer to the question 'What part of the Army are you going to join, boy?' the answer came proudly: 'The Green Howards.'

So the future was settled. From St Lawrence I would go to Sandhurst and become an Army officer. Probably from the perspective of my parents' bank balance it would have been better if I had left school at that point. But I stayed on and took another couple of A levels, without any great enthusiasm, and embarrassed myself with the results. If I am honest, I probably spent far too much time that summer running the corps and the social service scheme, debating, captaining the Second Eleven at cricket and driving Major Nelson's Ford Cortina around East Kent.

But hindsight is a wonderful thing. When the exam results came out, my parents were very forgiving.

And so it was that on Sunday, 11 September 1969 I dragged my suitcase up the steps of the Grand Entrance of Old College at the Royal Military Academy Sandhurst to start my military career. Standards of personal behaviour and appearance were, and are, very high at Sandhurst, so perched on top of my head was a newly acquired brown trilby hat, as required by the instructions for new officer cadets. The whole business was a completely novel experience. While I began the induction process my parents, who had driven me to Camberley, were escorted to the gymnasium for tea. There they were met by one of the staff on parent-greeting duty, Captain Zach Freeth. He was, and is, another remarkable man of strong and practical Christian faith, an athlete who had skied for Great Britain, winning the gold medal in the Commonwealth Games. His background, and that of his wife, Clare, is in Zimbabwe, at that time Rhodesia under the Ian Smith breakaway government, and the story of their extended family's experiences is one of the most harrowing to have come out of the country in recent times. One hopes and prays that Zimbabwe's nightmare will end before that beautiful country is completely ruined. But at the moment of handing me over to the Army, meeting Zach Freeth was a major reassurance to two still rather sceptical parents; and thereafter he and Clare took a close interest in my progress through the Academy. All these years later, I still see Zach Freeth in the Swiss ski resort of Verbier, where he serves as a part-time chaplain to the British community there. We meet in the English chapel and on the ski slopes where my youngest son, Olly, has worked as an instructor and ski school manager for the last five years.

Inevitably, it wasn't long before the perspective of us brand new officer cadets was reduced to the state of the shine on the toecaps of one's drill boots or the crease of one's trousers. Many a free-thinking young man has entered Sandhurst's hallowed portals intent on taking the whole experience in his stride, only to find that that the well-honed process of removing airs and graces born of school or home was more thorough and more effective than any youngster could ever imagine. Yet it was all to a purpose: to build up a new professional self-confidence and a dependence on the team around you. Very quickly the group identity of the platoon began to form: to this day I could tell anyone the strengths and weaknesses of all twenty-two members of mine. At the start, we were a classic Sandhurst mixed bag of new entrants into Dettingen Company, one of the nine companies that then made up the Academy. We completely spanned the social spectrum, with fairly equal representation from the private and state-funded school sectors. We had members from England, Scotland, Wales and Northern Ireland, and two from overseas: one from Jamaica, the other from Jordan. By the end of two years there was not much we did not know about each other. I shared a room with a very robust Scotsman from Edinburgh, John Fairley. His twin brother, Neil, had also started at Sandhurst at the same time, but was in another company, although we were later to be together at university. John Fairley was a complete life-saver to me in my first term. Much store is placed initially at Sandhurst on one's ability to master foot drill, turn oneself out smartly and be punctual under enormous pressure of time. John, by virtue of his previous experience in his school's Combined Cadet Force, knew how to polish boots properly, a skill I had not acquired at St Lawrence. Being able to polish boots to the standard required was a real bonus in the early days, as was mastering the knack of how to halt. In my first letter from Sandhurst to my parents, I expressed my admiration for John Fairley and his much-needed help. 'I am sharing a room with a Scot from Edinburgh – a nice guy who fortunately is very keen and good so he is a great guy to have around to give me a hand with things that are not so easy, like halting. Sounds silly to say that halting is difficult, but well, it is!!' Just stopping walking is one thing; to do it the Army way, quite another.

If halting was difficult, standing still without smiling was another posture I found difficult to acquire. Early on, during a room inspection by our cadet sergeant, my security drawer, in which like all the other officer cadets I was required to keep my rifle magazine and breech block, was found to be unlocked. (Unlikely as it seems now in these very security-conscious times, in those days we kept our rifles in our rooms secured by what amounted to not much more than a bicycle chain.) I was duly marched in front of the senior under-officer and charged with the offence of 'insecure drawers'. Unfortunately the gravity of the charge momentarily passed me by, the thought of other kinds of 'insecure drawers' crossed my mind, and I could not resist a smile. This did not help, and I found myself doing a large number of extra drill parades ruminating on when, and when not, to see the funny side of life.

I had entered Intake 47, which was one of two batches of officer cadets taken into Sandhurst in 1969. Our course was for two years, and in the days when only a small proportion of the national sixth form went to the limited number of universities that then existed, Sandhurst was our university. We worked hard and we played hard. We grew up. Rather like school, out of hours the Academy was run by the senior cadets, while during the working day our instruction was given by the permanent staff of officers, warrant officers and senior non-commissioned officers. Indeed, someone around that time quipped that Sandhurst was rather like 'a minor public school where the Combined Cadet Force had got out of hand'! Fair or not fair, the system whereby the senior cadets in each company ran things meant that as your two years progressed you became increasingly used to taking responsibility and acting responsibly.

The course itself was a mixture of military training and academic work. We tolerated the academic stuff and loved the practical soldiering. We had fun too. Our formal blue uniforms served as dress for major parades, for dining in the evenings and for the June Ball, the high-light of the cadet social calendar. For military training we were issued with green combat kit: my intake was the first to be allowed the luxury of a sleeping bag, rather than two blankets, for sleeping in the field on exercises.

Those two years passed quickly but were a valuable foundation to our military careers. Perhaps the most important thing we began to understand was leadership, as the key responsibility of an officer. Maybe it seems obvious that this would be so at an institution like Sandhurst, dedicated to turning out leaders, but in the hectic round of a packed training programme the finer points of what the Academy was, and is, all about could have been lost. In our discussions about leadership, we agreed that some leaders are born, but most are made, and that personal leadership can be developed by studying the principles of leadership, looking at leaders that you admire and modelling yourself on them. We debated, extensively, what qualities a good leader should exhibit. One list that caught our attention was drawn up by Field Marshal Lord Harding, a former Chief of the General Staff. He said that good leaders needed five essential qualities: absolute fitness, complete integrity, enduring courage, daring initiative and undaunted willpower. Interestingly, he stressed the adjectives as much as the nouns. To these five key qualities he added three others to be developed, namely knowledge, judgement and team spirit. From my subsequent experience I would endorse all these observations, and in recent years I have argued that these stipulations are as applicable in the political and business worlds as much as the military – especially the requirement for integrity.

Forty years ago we were also impressed by the new functional approach to leadership development put forward by Professor John Adair, a former member of the Sandhurst staff who had moved on to working for the Industrial Society. Using a classic Venn diagram of three interlocking circles to illustrate his point, he argued that a good leader needed to weigh up the contrasting but complementary needs of achieving the task in hand and looking after the overall requirements of the whole team, while simultaneously being mindful of the strengths and weaknesses of all the individuals involved.

This thoroughly sensible approach, which is now accepted wisdom, struck certain chords with us.

However, in our hearts we knew that for all the lists and theoretical approaches, there would be no substitute for experience, and we knew that the experiences upon which our leadership skills would need to be built lay ahead of us. The Sandhurst motto, 'Serve to Lead', was inscribed on our cap badges as officer cadets, but I do not think any of us really knew what it meant in practical terms until years later – the idea of a servant leader, while really important, is difficult to grasp as a teenager, which is all that we were then. Our focus, quite simply, was just on getting commissioned into our chosen regiments and dealing with whatever life threw at us. We were still young, much younger than officer cadets are today.

In my final term as an officer cadet I was the senior under-officer of the company, somewhat akin to being head of house at school, and among my duties was to command the company on parade. Here I came up against my old problem connected with halting, which had caused me so much trouble in my first term. On Academy parades, having led the company around Old College Square, Dettingen Company would form from column into line, facing me and marking time, waiting for me to give the order 'Halt!' This had to be done as the left knee came up past the right knee – or was it the other way around? I always struggled with this. I also knew that moral courage was a really important attribute of an officer. On one Saturday morning Academy parade towards the end of our final term, I was faced with the usual dilemma of when to order 'Halt!' and once again got it wrong. The company stuttered to a standstill rather than halting crisply. For our long-suffering Scots Guards company sergeant major, Mr Stephenson, this was too much, and a stream of corrective invective came my way from the rear of the company. I felt that to unloose such a torrent at the senior under-officer, who was in command of all the other cadets, was not acceptable, and heard myself shouting back: 'Don't you speak to me like that on parade, Mr Stephenson!' It was certainly the morally courageous reply to have made, but not the wisest. Very quickly after the parade our company commander, Major John Hemsley, was faced with the unusual situation of the company sergeant major marching the senior under-officer in front of him. Exercising the judgement of Solomon, Major Hemsley pointed out that once commissioned I could claim with justice that it would not be right to be shouted at by the company sergeant major, but that for another month I was still a cadet and needed to remember that. I apologized profusely to Mr Stephenson, and thankfully the incident was closed. The toughest of men, but also one of the most generous, Mr Stephenson sent me a Christmas card in December 2009 thanking me for what I had done for the Army in my time as Chief of the General Staff. A lot of water had gone under a lot of bridges since we had shouted at each other on Old College Square in July 1971!

The Sovereign's Parade marks the culmination of every main course at Sandhurst, and on 30 July 1971, when Intake 47 had finished its training, Her Majesty the Queen was represented on the saluting dais by His Majesty King Olav V of Norway. For fellow cadet Charles Thom and me this was particularly special as we were both being commissioned into the Green Howards, of which King Olav was the colonel-in-chief, an honorary position he had inherited from his father, whose great-aunt, Queen Alexandra, had given her name to the regiment. The climax of the Parade is the moment when those to be commissioned march up the steps of Old College and through the Grand Entrance, memories of being apprehensive cadets two years before lost in the pride of being about to take the Queen's Commission and to lead soldiers. None of us knew, of course, what the future would hold; but we were eager to find out.

2

Muddling Through

Belfast harbour and the city beyond looked bleak and forbidding as I gazed across from the top deck of the Liverpool–Belfast ferry, coming into dock on the morning of 15 August 1971. I was in charge of a draft of forty reinforcements – six recently commissioned officers and thirty-four young private soldiers straight out of basic training – destined for the Green Howards and the Duke of Wellington's Regiment. I was only in charge of the party because a surname towards the beginning of the alphabet had given me an Army number that made me very slightly senior to the other five brand new subalterns. On reflection years later, I was surprised the divisional depot had not sent a corporal or sergeant with our party to keep an eye on the young soldiers. In the event we all survived both the severe swell in the sea and the beer in the bar, but I could not wait to disembark and find out what was really going on. The television, radio and newspapers had covered little other than

Northern Ireland that August, as the tensions between the Roman Catholic Nationalist minority population and the Protestant Loyalist majority had increased. The climax had been reached early on the morning of 9 August, when detention without trial – internment – of those suspected of involvement in the Irish Republican Army (IRA) had been ordered. Widespread rioting had broken out immediately in all the Roman Catholic areas of Belfast and Londonderry. I was acutely aware that on 9 August one member of my new battalion – Private Malcolm Hatton – had been shot dead, and just the night before our party had left the depot in York to set out for Belfast, another Green Howard soldier, Private John Robinson, had also been fatally shot during rioting. Ironically, he was the first Roman Catholic British soldier to be killed in the Province at the hands of the IRA in its new campaign. Sadly, he would not be the last.

We were whisked off the ferry ahead of the other passengers and met by a heavily armed escort, the Duke of Wellington's party going their own way and the Green Howards heading to North Belfast. Our escort was under command of Second Lieutenant Graeme Cooper who, having been commissioned from Sandhurst six months earlier, now had the air of a seasoned veteran. His confidence impressed me hugely, but was strangely daunting at the same time. Could I match this so quickly? In my naivety, as we sped from the docks through the early morning Belfast city traffic I expected our canvas-sided 4-ton truck to be shot at at any moment. With some relief we reached Flax Street Mill, just off the Crumlin Road in the Ardoyne district of North Belfast. This was battalion headquarters of 1st Battalion, the Green Howards, and the base for both B and C Companies. I had reached my new home.

The next few hours were a jumble of events, leaving unforgettable memories. I was posted to B Company and would take over No. 7 Platoon. I was introduced to my new company commander, Major Richard Rockett. I was shocked to see a man who looked old enough to be my grandfather; I did not know that he had always had grey, almost white, hair or that at this point, after a spell of non-stop violence, he was utterly exhausted. He had just lived through the toughest month of his life – constant shooting and rioting, soldiers killed and wounded, almost no sleep. It was a miracle that this most caring and gentle of men was coherent and on his feet at all, let alone welcoming me most politely to the company. I grew to respect him hugely.

Richard introduced me to the company sergeant major, Bill Laws. Immediately, all the fear engendered in me by Bob Stephenson at Sandhurst swept back. For those who do not know the Army system well, officer cadets at Sandhurst call sergeant majors 'Sir', and sergeant majors also call officer cadets 'Sir', the difference being that the officer cadets mean it, and the sergeant majors do not. Now I was commissioned I did not need to call my new company sergeant major 'Sir' at all, but I found Bill Laws so scary that I invariably did so, at least for my first few weeks. Years later he became a good friend, but early impressions go deep. Next I met Clive Mantell, whose platoon I was to take over. He greeted me: 'I've got three hours to hand the platoon over to you before I am off to battalion headquarters to take over as operations officer because he was shot last night.'

Things were going from bad to worse. 'I've just got time to take you out onto the ground to see the area and then we will have a few minutes to go through the platoon book before I have to go.' Things were moving rather fast.

It is worth recording that whereas today, and indeed since the mid-1970s, the Army has always done extensive pre-deployment training before going on operations, in 1971 our commitment to Northern Ireland seemed very much a 'come as you are party' and general military common sense was deemed sufficient to see you through. But between leaving Sandhurst on 30 July and joining the battalion on 15 August I had been on leave, certainly not studying the situation in Northern Ireland, other than observing what was covered in the newspapers. Suddenly, very suddenly, life had become serious.

Clive wanted to take me out on a familiarization patrol straight away, which required some rapid administration. I needed a rifle, some ammunition and a flak jacket. I was put into the hands of my new platoon sergeant, Denis Hurst, who, like the rest of the platoon, did not really want to see Clive Mantell leave them after two years as their boss, especially so early in an operational deployment. I was, therefore, passed fairly quickly on to one of the section commanders. Corporal Albert Austin seemed happy enough to take me under his wing, finding me a rifle, ammunition and flak jacket, and a helmet and bed space to boot. It was fortunate that I had arrived off the ferry dressed in my combat uniform so that I at least had some appropriate clothes in which to go on patrol, because I was told that the rest of my luggage had been 'lost'. In fact, and unbeknown to me, it was suspended on a rope hanging over Flax Street itself. Later, I discovered that by regimental tradition every newly joined officer has some prank played to his disadvantage on arrival. By that stage, the whole day seemed like a bad joke, but to be honest I was already too tired to notice.

Suitably equipped, I joined Clive and a patrol down in the yard ready to go out and be shown around our company's area of responsibility. Before we set off Clive gave me a quick thumbnail sketch of the situation. The Ardoyne district of Belfast was a hard-line Roman Catholic, Nationalist and Republican area. It was very much on the front line of the conflict between the Republican community, who wanted to see Northern Ireland leave the United Kingdom and become part of a unified – and predominantly Roman Catholic – Irish Republic of thirty-two counties, and the Loyalist community, who steadfastly insisted that the six pre-dominantly Protestant counties of Northern Ireland should remain a largely self-governing Province that was at the same time an integral part of the United Kingdom. Our task was not only to try to keep the peace between the Republican and Loyalist communities, but also to counter the growing insurgency from the Provisional IRA, which wished to take Northern Ireland out of the United Kingdom by force of arms. PIRA had strong support in the Ardoyne area, reinforced by the arrest of so many of their people the previous week. With that potted history lesson absorbed, we set off.

Flax Street Mill, our base, was one of the biggest clothing factories in Belfast, but in the face of the Troubles had largely ceased production, offering instead considerable accommodation for the Army. We left the main gates, turned right into Flax Street itself and 'went firm' – Army parlance for stopping to take up a fire position – at the junction of Flax Street and Butler Street. 'Look over your shoulder,' Clive said. 'They have painted the wall white, so that when we come through at night our silhouettes show up better. Don't stop here in darkness.' We moved on, turning left into Butler Street, and paused again. 'There's a really good field of fire here right up the street – always best to leave a half section here to cover you as you go on further.' I was beginning to think that this was not what the newspapers had led me to expect. This was not just rioting and civil disorder: it was war. 'And this is the Brompton Gap. It's the only passage between these old streets and the new estate to the north: make sure you dominate it, otherwise gunmen get a free ride through.' We moved through the Gap into the new estate. 'Well, this burnt-out road is Farringdon Gardens. It used to be Protestant but they were forced out and rather than leave their houses to the Catholics, they burned them. Actually, I think one of our people started it. A chap came running out of his house about three weeks ago saying he'd had enough and was leaving. He said he had turned the gas on, did anyone have a light? One of our chaps gave him a cigarette lighter, then whoosh!'

Clive turned around to head back to the Mill. We patrolled down Jamaica Street, across the waste ground between Etna Drive and Jamaica Street, and back into Flax Street. Once back in the base we unloaded our rifles and I breathed a sigh of relief. It was August and I felt very hot in this unfamiliar flak jacket – and in a most unfamiliar environment. Clive just had time to tell me that Sergeant Denis Hurst was a very experienced platoon sergeant, Corporal Ted Hulse commanded No. 1 Section and Corporal Albert Austin No. 2 Section, and No. 3 Section was under the temporary command of Lance Corporal Taylor pending the return of Corporal John O'Brien from a recruit instructor's job at the depot in York. In total the platoon was twenty-seven strong. They were experienced soldiers, not many youngsters, and – well now, he had to be off.

Six hours after leaving the ferry, I felt the whole future of Belfast lay in my hands. But Richard Rockett calmed me down a little: 'Let Sergeant Hurst command the platoon for the next six days while you go around our three-day company cycle of patrols, standby and guards twice, and then it's all yours!' Reunited with my luggage by that evening, I went to bed with my head spinning. Just before I dropped off, Corporal Austin knocked on my door to give me my identity discs – my dog tags – just in case I was shot. I suppose I slept that night; I really cannot remember.

The next three and a half months passed in a flash. It was an unusually hot autumn in more ways than one, but a very, very special time. I learned afterwards that the platoon had said to themselves, on learning of Clive Mantell's departure, that they would give the new officer three weeks. At the end of that time, if they approved of me then I was in, but if I did not come up to scratch they would contrive to dump me – and I have no doubt they could have. In the event, I was very fortunate. As it happened, after three weeks the platoon was not in good shape: we were down to only nineteen – one had been shot, six had been blown up, and Lance Corporal Taylor had lost all his front teeth to an incoming milk bottle in a riot. However, 7 Platoon seemed to decide that I was all right and, as things turned out, I was to be their boss for the next eighteen months. We were to have a lot of adventures together.

I had joined the platoon at the end of the first month of a four-month tour in Northern Ireland. In 1971, this was the standard length of tour by any Army unit in the Province, it being judged, quite correctly in my view, that the pace and intensity of events were such that a unit could not endure longer. Internment had undoubtedly stirred up the hornets' nest, because although some PIRA leaders were arrested, most had got wind of what was going to happen and had fled elsewhere, leaving low-level suspects and many innocent people to be rounded up and deposited in Long Kesh Camp, soon to be renamed Her Majesty's Prison Maze. Notwithstanding the criticism of the initial internment process, the arrests continued. Many were the nights one would go out with half the platoon at three or four o'clock in the morning, quietly surround a house, kick the front door in and grab some suspect from his bed, deposit him in the back of an armoured vehicle and be back in bed oneself within half an hour. If the intelligence against the target was good, then there is no doubt that the campaign would have been advanced, but if it was faulty – and it undoubtedly often was – our actions probably resulted in another dis-affected family joining PIRA. Getting this balance right is the constant challenge in a counter-insurgency, as we were to discover again in Iraq and Afghanistan. In Belfast, on one occasion as we went in the front door the suspect, hearing us, leaped out of the bedroom window on the first floor and sprinted down the street – stark naked. We let him go, helpless with laughter. This was not what I had learned at Sandhurst.

In fact, the whole experience of those first weeks and months for me seemed at the time to bear very little relationship to what we had learned at Sandhurst. Yes, there were principles that could be applied; but at the age of twenty you do not think in terms of principles, just surviving the here and now. I learned many tactical lessons quickly. At Sandhurst we had been taught to disperse rioters by forming the platoon into a square box formation and standing in a menacing way in front of the crowd, even beating our batons against our shields to encourage dispersal. In our tactical doctrine there was thoughtful provision not only for a soldier to be designated as a scribe to record events, and for space within the platoon formation to accommodate the presence of a magistrate to read the Riot Act, but also for two men to unfurl a banner which said 'Disperse or we Fire' – helpfully written in English on the front, and in Arabic on the back. This might have been appropriate in the Middle East in times past, but was most definitely not in Belfast in 1971. One night, exactly three weeks after I had joined, my platoon was ordered to disperse a crowd of Catholics on the Crumlin Road, just down the hill from Holy Trinity Church, who were threatening the Protestants on the other side of the Peace Line. In two one-ton Humber lightly armoured patrol vehicles – nicknamed 'pigs' – and a larger Saracen armoured personnel carrier we crashed out of Flax Mill, turned left into Flax Street and right onto the Crumlin Road, stopping just short of where the crowd was threatening the Peace Line by the Chief Street barrier. We paused. I thought, decided, and then ordered the men to de-bus. Sergeant Hurst formed the platoon into something approaching a classic box a hundred yards short of the crowd. There was no scribe, magistrate or banner, but the square box was good. I thought again, and ordered the two 'pigs' to go in front of the platoon as some form of protection before we began our advance, which was intended to push the people back into their area and away from confrontation on the Peace Line.

My little army moved forward: two sections up, my radio operator and I between them so I could see what was going on, with Sergeant Hurst and the reserve section to the rear with the Saracen – all good Sandhurst stuff. As we advanced the people dropped back, until, just short of the Crumlin Road/Butler Street junction, I saw what the others behind the two 'pigs' could not see: the tell-tale signature of incoming home-made grenades. They look the same as when someone throws a burning cigarette out of a car window. I shouted 'Grenade!', but in the confusion no one heard, and the left-hand 'pig' rolled over both grenades. There were two loud explosions. The vehicle jerked up in the air and stopped. Corporal Austin's section stopped too, nearly all of them down with shrapnel wounds. The crowd turned and ran. I left Sergeant Hurst to deal with the casualties, helped by the other forward section, and leaped into the Saracen with the reserve section. We raced up the hill after the crowd. Reaching the Crumlin Road/Butler Street junction, we were immediately engaged with high-velocity rifle fire. The bullets seemed to whack around everywhere. I thought they were coming through the side of the vehicle until I realized I was sitting by the back door, which was open, and they were hitting the door and ricocheting. Albert Austin had somehow caught up with us, determined to avenge his decimated section, and had taken up a fire position under the Saracen where, from behind one of the huge wheels, he was returning fire down Butler Street.

By this time Sergeant Hurst could spare the other section, so I ordered them to drive past us up the Crumlin Road and try to get behind the gunmen who were firing at us. They were doing well to achieve this until disaster struck again, on this occasion self-inflicted. One of my soldiers in that section was shot in the foot – or, more to the point, shot himself in the foot. Oh dear! Asked afterwards: 'How did that happen?' the soldier concerned (whose nickname, rather appropriately, was 'Dozy') replied: 'Well, Sir, I often rest my rifle muzzle on my boot, and fiddle with the trigger!' Soldiers – and I love them – come in all shapes and sizes! So that night, 7 Platoon, B Company, 1st Battalion, the Green Howards was reduced from twenty-seven soldiers to nineteen. But my excitement was not over. At the height of proceedings I was vaguely aware of a presence over my shoulder, but was too busy to take much notice. The next morning – the situation on the ground having calmed down – my commanding officer sent for me. There followed one of only three conversations I had with the legendary Lieutenant Colonel Ronnie Eccles.

'Do you know who was behind you last night?' he asked.

'No, Colonel.'

'Well, it was the brigade commander, Brigadier Frank

Kitson, who had come to see how things were going on the front line.' I knew the name. 'Well, he decided you were doing all right, so he went away.'

I was so relieved. I had only ever read about this person – Brigadier Kitson – as a guru in counter-insurgency, experienced from the Mau Mau campaign in Kenya and others elsewhere. If he felt I was doing all right, it must be OK. Despite our much reduced state, 7 Platoon thought the same, and decided to endorse me as the new boss.

Our cycle of duties followed a regular pattern. When 5 Platoon was on guard duty, 6 Platoon was on patrol and my platoon (7) would be on standby, to react to the unexpected. After two days we would rotate responsibilities. So life went by on a six-, rather than a seven-day cycle. Incident followed incident, shooting followed shooting, and rioting was a daily occurrence throughout August and September. As a platoon commander I was likely to be out on the ground four nights in every six, the other two being spent on watch keeper responsibilities in the company operations room manning the radios and telephones, from midnight to six the next morning. On the patrol or standby nights, I would apply my camouflage paint to my face with increasing diligence, on the basis that it was the only thing I could do for myself before going out on the ground that might increase my chances of staying alive. Frankly, if you did not get shot at one night, then the probability was that you would on the next. The pressure was relentless but it was also exhilarating. Adrenalin and a great team spirit kept us going. However, the effect of taking casualties and inflicting them on the terrorists maintained a grim focus on reality. And I continued to learn lessons. On one occasion, when the platoon had taken a short break in the Ardoyne bus depot during an extended patrol, shots were fired at one of the sentry posts. I grabbed some soldiers to go out and see if we could find the gunmen. Waiting for me as I came back in through the gate was Sergeant Hurst, who proceeded to hit me hard on the chest. 'That will teach you to risk my soldiers' lives, going out without a radio,' he chided. Sergeants are not supposed to hit their platoon commanders, but the tactical point was well made, and remembered.

The remainder of that first tour flashed by, the days merging into one another. Lance Corporal Peter Harrington was shot dead by a sniper as he was protecting an ammunition technical officer defusing a bomb just yards from our Flax Street base; Private George Crozier was killed by a single shot to the head while manning the sentry post on the roof of the Mill itself; and Private Peter Sharpe was killed on the junction of Chatham Street and Kerrera Street while protecting children of one community going to school through the area of the other, an utterly tragic waste of life. Not long before that, two plain-clothes policemen, sitting in an unmarked car, had been watching the Peace Line in the same area by the Ardoyne shops when two gunmen drove up, sprayed the vehicle with automatic fire and sped off. My patrol arrived there minutes later, but there was little we could do. One of the policemen was already dead behind the steering wheel, and the other, younger, man died as we were doing what we could for him, while waiting for an ambulance to arrive. All these casualties caused growing comment, leading someone to say to me: 'The trouble with Northern Ireland is that there is an awful lot of religion here but not much Christianity.' I found that difficult to come to terms with, but it had to be thought about – very hard.

Out on patrol one night shortly after our fifth soldier had been killed, I stopped for a moment quite close to one of the Republican clubs. They were always noisy places and the music usually good, invariably with people singing evocative songs as the beer flowed. Ardoyne was an urban community similar to that of so many British towns and cities, and the people were very close to each other. To me it was extraordinary to be patrolling down streets that looked just like Coronation Street, taking cover behind red post boxes or telephone kiosks and, when necessary, shooting out street lights to prevent gunmen spotting our movements. But that night the singing of the traditional IRA song 'We're off to Dublin in the green, in the green . . .' from within the League Club turned to 'Five Green Howards sitting on a wall'. Well, that clear rejoicing in our casualty list to date was completely unacceptable from my point of view. We threw open the club door, the patrol rushed in, I leaped onto a table and gave the assembled company fifteen seconds of my view of things. Surprise did not last much longer. As I jumped down from the table, we disappeared back through the door just as a hail of beer cans and glasses came crashing around our ears. We felt we had made our point.

Not long after this episode, we learned from intelligence that two of the leading individuals on the wanted list were likely to be in one of the three main Republican clubs on a particular afternoon. A battalion operation was mounted to close down the whole area and raid all three. The club 7 Platoon targeted was largely empty, but 6 Platoon hit the jackpot in the League Club: both key gunmen were there. One gave up without a fight, but the other needed quite some persuasion; however, by the time we left we had taken two of the top PIRA 'players' off the pitch. Extraordinarily, just after the battalion had returned to Germany both men managed to escape from the top security Crumlin Road Prison. Our commanding officer sent the prison governor a suitably unappreciative telegram.

So we left Belfast, reflecting sadly on the five of our friends who had been killed, the twenty seriously wounded and the other seventy-five injured in some way. But the Provisional IRA had been dealt a serious blow too, with many killed, wounded or captured; perhaps as many as fifty in total. An anonymous Ardoyne civilian wrote to the commanding officer soon afterwards:

Thank you to all the Green Howards for the protection and help you have given us here, often under extreme difficulty and in great danger. I cannot speak too highly of your friendliness and cheerfulness; as to your behaviour and discipline, you all amaze me when I think what you have had to put up with from day to day and the lies that have been told about some of the incidents in which you have been involved.

On that positive, but rather atypical note, the battalion left Belfast at the very end of November 1971 to return to Elizabeth Barracks, Minden, West Germany. For most it was a very welcome homecoming, but for me, having joined the others in Belfast, it was a bit of a shock suddenly to find myself in a barracks that I did not know any better than the surface of the moon. I had to start all over again. But we were all delighted with the news that the commanding officer had been awarded the Distinguished Service Order and the regimental sergeant major an MBE for gallantry. A lieutenant in my company was given a Military Cross, three corporals were decorated with the Military Medal, and two others were mentioned in despatches. It had been a tough four months for the battalion, and an extraordinary introduction to real soldiering for me.

We all took a well-earned three weeks' leave over Christmas and returned to work in a very cold German winter. The contrast between the operational tempo in Belfast and the steady life within the British Army of the Rhine was considerable. Yes, of course, we were all part of the same Army; but there were two scripts. In Germany we were part of the NATO Alliance, tasked to train to deter the forces of the Warsaw Pact from attacking Western Europe. The received wisdom at the time was that, given their superior numbers in men, armoured vehicles and materiel, the Warsaw Pact would have a relatively easy run to the Channel ports, but some time before that NATO would 'go nuclear' and that would be game over, or not. In any event, our job at platoon and company level was to train to fight a mobile defensive battle, preserve as much of our fighting power as possible, and wait for nuclear release. Not surprisingly, against that scenario, we did not take our training as seriously as we should have done. As infantry-men, however, we knew that Northern Ireland was just around the corner again, and this kept us focused.

No sooner had I found my feet within the battalion in Germany than I returned to England to attend, somewhat belatedly, the Platoon Commanders Battle Course at the School of Infantry in Warminster, just on the edge of Salisbury Plain. This course was the professional follow-on from our initial training at Sandhurst for young infantry officers. My problem – one I shared with a number of others on the course – was that we had already been on operations, had fired our rifles in anger and had dealt with the dead and dying. Many of our instructors had not had this opportunity. So there were always going to be problems. It was largely a case of biting your lip and getting on with the training, but one memory sticks very closely in my mind. We had just finished a particular field exercise when one of my fellow students – who must remain nameless – was hauled out from among us and put in front of the commandant of the School of Infantry, none other than the fearsome Brigadier Frank Kitson, who had by then been posted from Belfast to the School. My friend was given the most almighty rocket for producing the biggest display of girl-guidery ever seen at the School of Infantry. The nameless warrior, who was not one of the strongest on the course, returned to our mess that evening suitably chastened. The next morning, however, he was summoned once again to see the commandant, to be told that in the Operational Awards List for Service in Northern Ireland published that morning he had been awarded the Military Cross. Staff and students alike were at a loss to know where to put themselves. For my part, I crossed swords with my instructor once too often, leaving the course with a very average report.

Rejoining the battalion in Germany I was just in time to go with B Company to Canada as part of only the second British battlegroup ever to train in armoured warfare on the prairies of Alberta, western Canada. The nearest town had the quaint name of Medicine Hat. Our base was at Suffield – hence the title of the organization, the British Army Training Unit Suffield, or BATUS, which has become part of Army folklore over the last three or four decades. But it was not just where we trained that was important; what we were training for had equal significance. While part of the Army, at any one time, was gaining invaluable experience of counter-insurgency operations in Northern Ireland, another part was developing a deep understanding of the skills required to conduct conventional manœuvre operations against a more traditional enemy, the Soviet Union and the Warsaw Pact. To those who thought about these things, the principles behind the two types of operations were more similar than different. At the time it was felt that Germany was where the bulk of the field Army lived and Canada was where we trained, but Northern Ireland was where it all really mattered. Nevertheless, the net effect of all this was to produce an Army that was increasingly competent and confident in its own abilities: principles of command and control were increasingly understood, as was the integration of all the various elements of the Army, so that the infantry, the armour, the artillery and air support all worked to the same plan and within the same tactical doctrine. Indeed, it has often been said that if the Cold War was won anywhere, from a British Army perspective it was won at BATUS; and if the basis of success in Iraq in 1991 and 2003 and the stabilization operations that followed was laid anywhere, then it was at BATUS, where successive generations of officers and soldiers have learnt the basic principles and skills of the battlefield. Moreover, BATUS has the great quality of size: the training ground is nearly half the size of Wales, so there is plenty of space there to conduct realistic live firing and field exercises in a relatively unconstrained way.

Our focus on armoured warfare was short-lived, however, because on getting back to Germany we discovered that we had been warned to return to Belfast. The situation in the Province had deteriorated sharply after the highly controversial shooting of thirteen civilians in Londonderry on 30 January 1972 – what became known as 'Bloody Sunday'. In the aftermath of these events, the IRA had established de facto 'no-go' areas behind barricades in the hard-line Catholic areas of Belfast and Londonderry, excluding the police and the Army and attempting to portray itself as a kind of protective authority within these areas. Quite clearly this state of affairs could not be allowed to continue, and so that summer the Army conducted Operation 'Motorman', designed to end these 'no-go' areas with a major show of strength and coordinated barricade clearance. While the operation, which began at 4 a.m. on 31 July 1972, was a significant tactical success, it had demanded a surge in the number of troops deployed in the Province up to around 24,000. This had the effect of pulling other units, like my battalion, forward in the operational cycle; so we were now scheduled to return in October, just eleven months after our previous tour. By this time, however, the Army had got its training act together and we spent the late summer and autumn doing exercises specifically related to Northern Ireland, using special ranges and mock-up houses and streets. As the campaign matured over the next three decades these training facilities became very sophisticated, but in 1972 we were impressed with even the embryonic beginnings.

All too soon the training period was over, and the advance party of commanders and intelligence staff deployed back to Belfast in early October. This time we were in the south-west of the city with my company, now under the command of Major Leslie James, occupying the partly burnt-out Woodburn Hotel on the Stewartstown Road. Here, between Catholic Andersonstown and Protestant Suffolk, life at first seemed quite quiet compared to the previous year, even potentially dull. However, it was not long before violence erupted.

At the time there was considerable population shift within Belfast, with former mixed areas becoming exclusively either Protestant or Catholic as fear drove people to seek safety in numbers within their own communities. Only a couple of weeks into our tour a large Catholic crowd poured down Lenadoon Avenue, threatening Protestant families in Horn Drive. Before we had time to get on the scene a number of houses were burning and the frightened occupants were leaving in panic. My platoon endeavoured to calm things down, but it quickly became clear that if we left that night and went back to our base in the Woodburn Hotel then more families were going to leave. One of the Protestant community leaders, the Reverend Robert Bradford, minister of the Suffolk Methodist Church, was adamant we had to stay on the ground to protect his people. Responding to this, Leslie James ordered my platoon to occupy a couple of the empty houses on the junction of Lenadoon Avenue and Horn Drive and establish a permanent presence between the two communities. And that set the pattern for the next four months. The Catholic community up the hill, many living several families to a house, put huge pressure on us to let them live in some of the fifty or so empty houses down the hill; but housing policy stated that Suffolk was a Protestant estate and the Northern Ireland Housing Executive either could not or would not allocate them to Catholics. Thus we had empty houses that Protestants were allowed to live in but would not occupy through fear, and Catholic families who were desperate for accommodation but were not allowed to move into them.

Keeping the peace between these two communities became something of an art form – but nobody was satisfied. We decided on a number of confidence-building measures. A barbed-wire fence was placed across the waste ground between the two communities, and both were allowed to form vigilante groups to watch each other. Frankly, in my view, this helped us do our job, provided they came to us if they were suspicious of something rather than taking action themselves. I felt we had to try to take the vigilante groups 'under command', or at least exert some moral authority over them. This policy nearly backfired one evening. The name Lenadoon had a somewhat Western ring to it, so the platoon gave me a star badge and started to call me the

Sheriff. This was not helped by the fact that I often carried my privately owned Smith and Wesson .38 revolver in an outside holster. I shudder now with embarrassment at the thought, but we were young then and the revolver was the product of the previous tour when most of us platoon commanders had decided that just being equipped with a rifle was insufficient. Its long barrel meant close-quarter work was difficult, as I had discovered crawling down the aisle of the Old Park Cinema after we had been fired at from the roof. As I stuck my nose around every row of seats, expecting to be shot at any moment, my rifle seemed pretty useless. But in a rifle company then there were only three 9mm Browning pistols, and they were definitely not to be issued to platoon commanders. So I had bought my .38 revolver from a gunsmith in Chelmsford while I was on leave after the Ardoyne tour; Bob Purse, by then commanding 5 Platoon, had bought a Smith and Wesson .357 magnum; Wiff Burrage, commanding 6 Platoon, already had a Walther PPK pistol. Thus equipped with badge and revolver, one evening I watched with my patrol from the shadows as the Catholic vigilantes formed up for their nightly muster parade. When they were assembled, and much to their surprise, I stepped forward out of the darkness into their ranks and began to inspect them. This exercise in moral authority was going all right until I noticed coming down Lenadoon Avenue the double Land Rover patrol of the new commanding officer, Lieutenant Colonel Raymond Ashforth, and his escort. I was in trouble. Vigilantes were a local arrangement and officially frowned upon. I was short of honourable options. I marched smartly across to where the CO's patrol had stopped, horrified to see not just the colonel but with him the adjutant, Captain Stuart Adlington, and the regimental sergeant major, Mr Latham MBE. I halted as crisply as my revolver in its holster allowed, saluted and reported: 'Catholic vigilantes on parade and ready for your inspection, Colonel.' If looks could kill, the glare from the RSM would have finished me there and then. Colonel Raymond looked at me, looked at the vigilantes over my shoulder and pragmatically told his driver to drive on. The adjutant was not so charitable the next morning, nor was the RSM.

For the remainder of that four-month tour, with our presence in the middle, there was no further trouble between the two communities, and once things had settled down Leslie James rotated my platoon with Wiff Burrage's 6 Platoon every two weeks. Somewhat selfishly, I learned a huge number of lessons in low-level diplomacy and politics – discovering that much can be achieved in these conflict situations by talking, negotiating, giving a bit, grumbling a bit, but always staying in control. I also learned another lesson, which really shaped things for me later on. At the height of our problems between the two communities, I was told that the General Officer Commanding Northern Ireland, Lieutenant General Sir Harry Tuzo, was coming to visit my platoon area. This was my chance to seek guidance from the senior general in the Province on how to resolve our 'who lives where' conundrum. General Harry arrived and I briefed him on our situation as I walked him around the area. My soldiers and the general's body-guards were looking in all directions. 'So that's the problem, General,' I said. 'What do you suggest we do?'

General Harry looked at me for a moment, then put his arm on my shoulder and said: 'Well, Richard, we've got broad shoulders in the British Army – just muddle through!'

'Right, Sir, muddle through, of course!' I replied.

Years later, and long after he had retired, I told General Harry that story and he was horrified, much in the same way as I am now about the star and the revolver. The lesson I learned from that conversation was that pragmatism is fine up to a point, but there must always be a plan. There must be a better way than 'muddling through'. Later, I discovered that the way starts with deciding what you need to achieve, then working out how to do it, in order to be able to explain to those on the ground how to make sense of their low-level tactical activity. It is all about balancing ways, means and ends. Back in 1972, from my worm's-eye view, we were just making it up as we went along. However, I was only a second lieutenant and, if muddling through was the plan, then muddle through we would.

By early 1973, the pendulum of problems for the Government had swung in a different direction and it was the Protestant community that was beginning to flex its political muscles. Sensing an opportunity, the Ulster Workers' Council placed considerable demands on both the Stormont and Westminster governments. A standoff developed and a day of protest and a general strike was called for 7 February 1973. The military's response was to make contingency plans to contain violence, not in the Catholic north or west of the city, but in Protestant East Belfast. At that particular moment, the Belfast reserve battalion, 1st Battalion, the Parachute Regiment, was on leave, so other units were required to produce a reserve force. One constituent part of this ad hoc force was Support Company, 1st Battalion, the Green Howards, of which Major Neil McIntosh was the company commander. My platoon was to form part of that company for the day. My own feeling – picked up from those wiser than me – was that the Protestants would huff and puff and not much else. We did not expect to deploy anywhere exciting that day, and indeed we took the chance of all being together to have our photograph taken. I was pleased to have the opportunity, because we had had quite a change of personalities in the last year: Sergeant Tony Outhwaite had replaced Denis Hurst as platoon sergeant, and Corporal Dave Howell, a big battalion heavyweight boxer, had become one of my section commanders. The faithful Albert Austin still commanded No. 2 Section.

Despite my predictions of inactivity, by about noon the local radio stations were beginning to report very large crowds gathering in East Belfast. Early in the afternoon I was ordered to take my platoon to join the rest of Support Company at their base in Andersonstown itself. I should note here that in any infantry battalion most of the older soldiers with specialist mortar, anti-tank and machine-gun skills serve as part of Support Company, so we were given a fairly frosty reception by them as we, a mere rifle platoon, reported for duty. However, we did not have much time to be rude to each other before word came from brigade headquarters that we were required in East Belfast as fast as possible. Major McIntosh disappeared very quickly to find out what was going on, while the main body of Support Company under Company Sergeant Major Moore – apparently not renowned in the battalion for his map reading – took the rest of us across Belfast from west to east, successfully.

We arrived at the Short Strand Bus Depot just after 2 p.m., to be met by a highly energized Neil McIntosh. 'Orders,' he said confidently, and I opened my notebook. 'Situation,' he said (always the first part of an Orders sequence). Then 'Confused,' he said, and I wrote in my notebook, 'Confused', wondering afterwards what on earth was the point of writing that? Then Kinty, as we all knew Major McIntosh, said: 'Look, no one knows what on earth is going on. The Prods [Protestants] are up in arms and want to make a point, we need to keep it under control as best we can. 35 Engineer Regiment look after this area normally, but have said now that the infantry is here, it's over to us.' No sooner had Kinty finished this introduction to what lay ahead than we heard the crack of high-velocity rifle fire outside. 'Ah, it's getting serious,' Kinty observed. 'Richard, I want you to take your platoon by whatever route you can find to the junction of the Newtownards Road and Albert Bridge Road, and stop yobbos forming up there.' I was given a radio on the 35 Engineer Regiment communications net, and already had a map of East Belfast. I returned to the platoon and briefed the section commanders as best I could – finishing up, in essence, 'Follow me, and I will tell you what to do when we get there.' As we set off for our destination, I in a lightly armoured Land Rover, the rest of the platoon in three armoured 'pigs', I was very conscious that all along our route were very angry people: stones were being hurled and shots fired. But frankly, the biggest fear of a platoon commander, born of many bitter experiences at Sandhurst, was of getting lost, so my chief preoccupation was finding the road junction that Kinty wanted me to dominate. The fact someone had fired a full magazine of bullets into the side of my vehicle, and had then been shot and killed by one of my soldiers, completely passed me by until much later. It was to be a very testing day.

We reached the junction of Newtownards Road and Albert Bridge Road and I deployed the three sections to cover the three-way intersection. Immediately we came under uncomfortably accurate rifle fire from back down the Newtownards Road. Normally, I would have known the ground well enough to be able to outflank such a situation, but none of us had ever been there before. I had the only map, and I wasn't too keen on reading it with bullets whizzing around. This was no time to be subtle, and doing nothing was not an option. We had to attack to regain the initiative.

'Corporal Austin, you take the right, I will take the left – half section fire and movement, and we will sort this lot out.'

The eight of us, four each side of the street, set off back down the Newtownards Road with crack and thump ringing in our ears. To professional infantrymen like us, differentiating between crack and thump is important. The 'crack' overhead tells you that a high-velocity bullet has passed by quite close; if you can attune your ear to listen for 'thump', that will tell you where the firer is and how far away he is. The problem in a built-up area is echo, so our 'cracks' that day were very real, but our 'thumps' were rather confusing.

Nevertheless, we needed to get some fire down so, glimpsing a gunman, I put three rounds down the street to give the others the idea that we could only close with the enemy if we combined fire and movement; if we didn't, the whole platoon would be pinned to the junction. Alternating firing at targets as we saw them, Corporal Austin's half section and mine advanced back down the Newtownards Road from doorway to doorway, lamp-post to lamp-post. I was aware of a lot of firing, but as the commander I was more focused on what we were trying to do than on my own personal circumstances. Afterwards the others told me that bullets were whipping around me in alarming fashion. Perhaps it was as well that my attention was otherwise engaged. At one stage Corporal Austin zig-zagged across the street and shared the doorway I was taking cover in, dropping to his knees and loosing off two rounds from behind mine. It went quiet and down the street I saw a couple of people come out holding what looked like white flags.

'They want to surrender,' I said.

'Steady on, Sir,' replied the wise corporal, holding me back from stepping out into the street to round these people up, just as another burst of fire came from behind the white flags.

'Enough is enough,' I thought, remembering the radio on the Engineers' net that I was carrying. 'Hello, Zero, this is Foxtrot 35, request armoured backup.' I thought it was time to get back to the rest of the platoon as I could hear plenty of firing going on elsewhere. I remembered Sergeant Hurst's lesson from the year before: with the only radio in my possession, the others were vulnerable if they took a casualty. An armoured vehicle manned by the Royal Engineers appeared and we all piled in, one of my younger soldiers smelling quite awful, having involuntarily soiled himself. Years later I recalled this incident when I was told that the Wehrmacht in the Second World War had an expression that 'fear was brown'.

As we rejoined the rest of the platoon, Corporal Dave Howell came across to report to me what had been going on while I had been away with Albert Austin's section. We were standing by the back of my Land Rover while Private 'Tapper' Hall, my driver that day, was kneeling down in a fire position protecting our front. Suddenly a hail of bullets clattered down the little side street from behind us. Dave Howell went flat on his back with a bullet in his chest, and Tapper Hall slumped forward with one in his back. I sprinted for cover while Corporal Austin poured fire back whence it had come. At that point in the day the tables had turned against us. We dragged the two injured men into cover. Tapper was still conscious initially, but faded away from us before the ambulance arrived. Dave Howell was, however, extraordinarily and quite illogically, very lucky. He had been hit by a .303 bullet in the chest, with sufficient power to knock this heavyweight boxer flat onto his back. Once in cover, we opened his flak jacket and his combat jacket to find that the bullet head had just pierced his skin with a tiny trickle of blood flowing, and that was all. I am not a ballistics expert, but even to a layman that was a quite remarkable outcome. Having accepted that he was not about to die, he zipped his jacket up again and carried on commanding his section. Whether he slept or not that night, history and my memory do not recall.

After the frenetic pace of the afternoon – the mortars and the anti-tank platoons had fought equally hard battles, and Sergeant George Clarke was later decorated for gallantry – things quietened down. Our company quartermaster sergeant came to find us with an ammunition resupply and, even more welcome, with fish and chips. Some of the local people began to venture back onto the streets. 'What on earth happened today, then?' I asked one.

'Well,' he said, 'we are really fed up with the Government, and you people are the nearest expression of them that we can make a point to.'

Thanks, I thought, aware that Tapper Hall was fighting for his life in hospital. If I have found politics and the military hard to separate over the years, perhaps some might understand that the crossover goes back a long way.

Very sadly, having fought for life for several days, Tapper Hall died in Middlesbrough General Hospital, quite close to his home, three weeks later. Our tour having finished by the time of his funeral, many of the platoon and I followed his coffin to his grave, recognizing him, as did all those who knew him, as one of those wonderfully dependable private soldiers on which the British Army is built. Some months later I was awarded the Military Cross for our actions that day – an honour I was happy to share with my platoon, and in Tapper Hall's memory.

It was during the Andersonstown tour that a friend in the regiment, John Powell, who had just returned after three years away at Durham University, suggested to me that I should reconsider my earlier decision not to go to university at all. I was not sure at first: three years away from the practical excitement of soldiering seemed a long time to me. But John persisted, telling me to write to Sam Stoker, the registrar of his old college at Durham, Hatfield, and see what he thought. This time, if I was to go to university, it was History, not Law, that I would study. At the same time I applied to the Army for permission to do what was then called an 'in-service degree', which entailed three years studying for a degree at a civilian university. The Army agreed, and after a series of interesting interviews at Durham revolving around Latin O Level, which I had failed eight years before, it was agreed that I be offered a place to read Economic History which, unlike History itself, had no Latin language requirement.

I was sad to leave the battalion. My old platoon gave me a tankard with all the kings and queens of England and their dates engraved on it, which they thought would allow me to combine business with pleasure, and I headed off to Durham. I had decided that, although I was four years out of school, I wanted to seem like a normal fresher at university. This lasted about two minutes. I parked my car, walked in through the gates of Hatfield College and was met by a third-year student who politely said, 'Hello, my name is Bill Enderby. You are not a normal first year, are you?' I suppose my shoes were too shiny and my hairline had already receded too far to allow me to get away with it. Bill showed me to my room and helped me with my stuff. Shortly afterwards, my room-mate arrived. I was to share a room with PC 649 of the Bedfordshire and Luton Constabulary, Ian

Bridge. Sam Stoker had thought that it would be good for both of us – and he was right: Ian and I became firm friends. We introduced ourselves and I suggested a cup of tea. Ever the resourceful soldier, I said that I had a kettle in my trunk, which I opened. Ian's eyes came out like organ stops as he spotted my .38 Smith and Wesson revolver and Bob Purse's .357 magnum on top of everything else. 'Hey, steady on, you won't be needing those here,' he said. I agreed he had a point, and then we had a cup of tea.

Limits on space and the reader's patience preclude an extensive recital of three years of student exploits at Durham, but there were certain life-changing highlights. On my third night at Durham, not very impressed by the Freshers' Week parties at the Student Union, Ian and I decided to go to the Durham Union Society's Freshers' Debate in the Great Hall of Durham Castle. As a college-based university like Oxford and Cambridge, Durham was very proud of its Union Society, run on very much the same lines as its counterparts in the two 'other places'. The motion to be debated at the Durham Union that night was about the value of politicians to our society. There was an impressive line-up of speakers reflecting all colours of the political rainbow. As a somewhat cynical pair of public servants, Ian and I thought we would go and see if this was more up our street. I do not remember much of the fine argument by the eminent speakers, but I do remember looking very frequently to my left, where I saw a very pretty girl in a green skirt and long black leather boots, perched up on a windowsill so that she could see what was going on. That girl stuck very firmly in my mind. It was several months before I got a

My great-grandfather, William Dannatt (on horseback and right), overseeing haymaking on one of his farms at Great Waltham, Essex.

Left: My maternal grandfather, Frank Chilvers, with whom I played and watched endless games of cricket.

Right: Aged two, with my six-year-old sister Juliet. Juliet very sadly died of cancer in 1988.

Below left: Shrimping on Swanage beach in Dorset with Mimmie, who was part of our family for nearly sixty years.

Below right: On the beach at Frinton-on-Sea in Essex, with my mother, my father and Juliet.

Above: Andrews House at Felsted Junior School in June 1962. Ewing Grimshaw, my close friend through school, Sandhurst and Staff College, is in the back row on the extreme right. I am second from the left on the front row.

Below left: In the Tower House cricket eleven at St Lawrence College with Hugh Anderson (front) – whose example of how to get things changed in a conservative public school was inspirational. I am behind him on the right.

Below right: With Anthony Parker, James Johnson and Christopher Wallis as The Gents in 1965. We played rather indifferent folk music.

Above: Commanding the guard of honour at the annual inspection of the St Lawrence College Combined Cadet Force in June 1969.

Below: Commanding Dettingen Company on the Sovereign's Parade at Sandhurst in July 1971. On the far left is Company Sergeant Major Bob Stephenson, whom I so exasperated by my deficiencies in giving the order 'Halt!'.

Left: A rather eager platoon commander being kept in order by Sergeant Denis Hurst and Corporal Ted Hulse as we monitored a crowd from behind an armoured vehicle on Flax Street, North Belfast, August 1971.

Below left: Presenting the friendly side of the Army.

Below right: Corporal Albert Austin, not believing a word of what he is being told!

Bottom: Abandoned Protestant houses, burnt by their former occupants: New Ardoyne, August 1971.

Above: Corporal Albert Austin's No. 2 Section of 7 Platoon on 7 February 1973 at the Woodburn Hotel, West Belfast, hours before they were involved in that day's mayhem in East Belfast.

Below: With Major Roger Chapman in Gough Barracks, Armagh City, in June 1975. By this time I was at Durham University, but back with 1 Green Howards for the summer vacation.

Left: Richmond Lodge, better known as the 'Honeymoon Cottage', in Montgomery Barracks, Berlin – our first home. Between 1977 and 2009 we moved twenty-three times.

Above: In command of a guard of honour on the Glienecke Bridge, Berlin, as the body of a Second World War Russian soldier is handed over. The white line was the boundary between East and West.

Below: Leading C (King Olav's) Company on a Freedom Parade through Pickering, North Yorkshire, in April 1981. In front of me are the commanding officer, adjutant and RSM, to my left and just behind is Company Sergeant Major George Clarke, who won a Military Medal in East Belfast on 7 February 1973. Note the large crowd!

Left: On United Nations duty in Cyprus in July 1981 – not the most demanding operational tour carried out by the battalion in recent years! Begun in 1964, this UN mission to police a buffer zone between the Turkish and Greek Cypriots was still continuing in 2010.

Below: With Brigadier Nick Ansell (in front of me), welcoming Margaret Thatcher to Headquarters 20th Armoured Brigade on Soltau Training Area, West Germany, in June 1983. The PM's Press Secretary, Bernard Ingham, is getting out of the Puma helicopter.

Our wedding at St Peter Mancroft, Norwich, on 19 March 1977. In the guard of honour on the far right is the late Captain John Hamilton, killed on West Falkland in June 1982 while serving with 22 SAS. He was awarded a posthumous Military Cross.

mutual friend to introduce her to me. On investigation I had found out that Philippa Gurney was at St Mary's College, had been at Tudor Hall School and was reading English and Theology. It was a further three years on from then before she and I got married in the Church of St Peter Mancroft in Norwich. I was very glad that John Powell had suggested I apply to Durham.

If I had worried that three years at university would take me away from the Army for too long, my worrying was misplaced. I had only been at Durham a few months before I was summoned back to Belfast to attend Tapper Hall's inquest, which I knew would be a sad and sobering experience. I flew from Manchester Airport to Belfast, thoughtfully putting my .38 Smith and Wesson in my suitcase before I left. Tucked into my waist belt, it accompanied me while I gave evidence at the hearing and was back in my suitcase by the time I checked in for my flight back from Belfast's Aldergrove airport. I was still thinking about the events of 7 February the year before when I noticed for the first time that suitcases were being searched. When my turn came, I said quietly to the searcher that he might like to open my suitcase away from the general public, as he would find on the top of the contents a Smith and Wesson .38 revolver and six rounds of ammunition – and, by the way, 'Here are my Army ID card and my firearms certificate.' The searcher did as I suggested, not unreasonably calling over the Royal Ulster Constabulary sergeant who was supervising the search area. He looked at my paperwork and thanked me politely. I proceeded to the departure lounge. Some little while later, however, I noticed two young men in long raincoats going around the passengers clearly looking for someone. Like the POW escapee from Colditz, I pulled my newspaper higher over my nose. This, of course, was no deterrent.

'Excuse me, Sir; are you Lieutenant Dannatt of the Green Howards?'

I could not deny this.

'Would you come with us, Sir?'

I followed these two individuals from the Royal Military Police out of the departure lounge into a small room. A conversation ensued relating to my revolver, the law, Army regulations and what changes had been made to the latter during the last few months. Knowing that ignorance is no defence, I realized that I was in trouble. I found myself temporarily arrested, before signing over my revolver to the forensics department of the local police for testing and flying back to Durham somewhat chastened by all the events of the day.

Back in Durham I became increasingly involved in the Union Society, reliving my earlier love of debating and mindful of the achievements of my late friend Hugh Anderson at Cambridge. Hugh had been elected Secretary of the Cambridge Union in the third term of his first year, and President in the first term of his second year. I decided I would try to do the same at Durham. Standing for the only two elections I ever wish to be involved in, I was duly elected Secretary of the Durham Union for the Summer Term of my first year, and then President of the Union for the Michaelmas Term at the start of my second year. I hoped Hugh would have been pleased that I was following in his footsteps. A year later my former room-mate, Ian Bridge, was elected President at the start of our third year. I was delighted by that.

Durham may not have been surprised to see an Army officer like me dressed in white tie presiding over its debates, but a police constable in white tie and tails was something else. Ian was brilliant. But Ian, like so many of my friends, having had an astonishing career in the police, business, commerce and politics – and standing godfather to my eldest son, Tom – succumbed to the scourge of cancer in 2007. I was privileged to give the address at his funeral.

Back in summer 1974, as Secretary of the Durham Union, I could not resist the temptation to accept on behalf of Durham an invitation to a debate at the Historical Society of Trinity College, Dublin. The motion for debate was: 'This House believes that 1984 is but a decade away.' In 1974 this seemed like fun, and to an Army officer who should have gone nowhere near Dublin, it was an opportunity not to be missed. I said I would go. Taking care to leave behind my Army ID card and anything else that could associate me with the British Army, I flew to Dublin. We had a highly entertaining debate – I do not recall who won – followed by a very good party, after which I set out on foot for where I was staying, the Royal Hibernian Hotel, somewhere in central Dublin. After a little while I realized I was lost. It was about midnight. I thought to myself: 'Dannatt, you are a British Army officer who should not be in Dublin, and you are lost. You are in black tie and have had a couple of drinks, and you are now walking past the General Post Office in O'Connell Street where the 1916 Easter Rising started. You are in trouble!' I have never been so pleased in my life to see a hotel as I was when, a little while later, I found the Royal Hibernian. And my timing was good, because only a few months later the IRA blew it up.

Part of the arrangement by which officers like me could take three years away from the Army was that in both summer vacations we would return to our regiments. As it happened, in the summers of both 1974 and 1975 1st Battalion, the Green Howards was back in Northern Ireland. So in July 1974 I rejoined them in Gough Barracks, Armagh and the following year I spent my summer vacation in Crossmaglen, South Armagh. Neither attachment was to be without incident. In 1974 B Company, to which I returned as company operations officer, was under command of Major Roger Chapman and we ran a number of ambitious operations all aimed at killing or capturing the local IRA 'players'. There were several of these people, all of whom – though well known to our intelligence staff – shall remain nameless here for understandable reasons. On one occasion, apparently good intelligence came in that the Post Office in the village of Moy was to be robbed to raise funds for the IRA. A plan was devised to surround the Post Office, wait until the attack had been carried out, and then capture the perpetrators red-handed. A helicopter was to stand off above in order to chase any getaway car that might escape our cordons and roadblocks on the ground. I was to be the observer in the Sioux helicopter and direct the efforts of our ground units. A Sioux has a crew of only two, on this occasion me and the sergeant major pilot. We took off from Gough Barracks Square and climbed to hide above the clouds. It was a wonderfully clear day, so the clouds were fairly high. We went up and up, the village of Moy looking very small beneath us.

What happened next I am not quite sure, even to this day, though I know a lot more about helicopters now than I did then. In the event the pilot said we had a major problem and needed to get onto the ground as quickly as possible. I sensed a note of urgency in his voice. We dropped from many thousand feet like a stone. My ears were bursting. The helicopter sounded like a vacuum sweeper with a twig stuck in the drum. We approached the ground at 45 degrees at great speed and I thought that was it: 'Well, I have had a good life but it is going to end in an Armagh field.' I did not realize then that a helicopter can land like an aeroplane on its skids on grass, if it has to. We had to, and we did. I breathed a huge sigh of relief as the pilot jumped out with a hammer and hit something solid. All went quiet.

'Have you got a gun, Sir?' he enquired.

'No. Have you, Sergeant Major?'

'No, Sir.'

So there we were, stuck in a field in Armagh with a dead helicopter and no weapon. In mitigation, all I would offer is that, having set off from the security of Gough Barracks, we had expected to return there and so neither of us had thought to bring a gun – not very clever, in retrospect. Luckily, after some tinkering and a few judicious blows by the hammer, the Sioux was persuaded to come back to life and we limped home. Needless to say, the Post Office in Moy was not robbed that day, much to the discomfort of our intelligence staff. Perhaps the noise of our faulty helicopter had something to do with it.

The following summer was more difficult. South Armagh was the heart of Republican 'bandit country', and we were fighting for our lives. There was no question of trying to win the hearts and minds of these local people, as we might try to do in a classic counter-insurgency. They were Republican to the core, and that part of South Armagh was almost an anomaly within the United Kingdom, jutting right into Eire. Yet even that part of Northern Ireland was in name and law part of Her Majesty's domain, and we were determined that British authority would be upheld. The trouble was that statistically it was very likely that a given number of patrols would be caught either in a major multi-weapons ambush or by a sophisticated improvised explosive device (IED). To the cynics among us, the best way to avoid casualties was to sit in the base and watch television, but of course this would have relinquished both the ground and the initiative to the terrorists. We had to be out and about, showing the flag, clearing explosive devices and escorting the police in their routine duties. But there was nothing routine about South Armagh. Even to get to the bases at Crossmaglen, Forkill and Newtownhamilton everything and everyone had to move by helicopter. The battalion headquarters helipad at Bessbrook was for many years the busiest in the United Kingdom. I spent a large part of the summer of 1975, while my university chums were doing whatever students do during the long vacation, as the second-in-command of A Company, while the real incumbent of that post, Captain Charlie Alderson-Smith, was away doing his junior staff course. The company commander was Major Peter Willis, a highly competent tactician and a delightful man who had been one of my instructors at Sandhurst five years before. I felt privileged to be serving under him. He was a very keen cricketer, too, and I recall we took an afternoon away from Crossmaglen to play a key Army Cup fixture on the Army headquarters ground at Lisburn. I was standing at second slip, with Lieutenant Colonel Peter Inge, the Commanding Officer, standing at first slip; Peter Willis was bowling. At a critical moment the key batsman from the Worcestershire and Sherwood Foresters Regiment, sensing a win, nicked one. I dived to my right, catching the ball successfully in my outflung right hand. 'Welcome back to the regiment,' said Peter Inge, with Peter Willis beaming that he had got a vital wicket.

And it was cricket that Peter Willis and I discussed a few days later as we stood side by side, shaving, on what turned out to be the last morning of his life. For some days reports had been coming in of a suspicious milk churn near a road junction between Crossmaglen and Forkill. Aerial reconnaissance had confirmed our analysis that this was probably an IED which we needed to clear. Peter planned a deliberate operation. We would fly in a platoon of soldiers to occupy a series of positions on dominating high ground as an outer cordon around the area and then, when all was secure, we would fly in a specialist search and bomb disposal team to clear the device. After a couple of cancellations because either the specialists or the helicopters were not available, we launched the operation on 17 July. The platoon that was manning the outer cordon reported that all was secure, so Peter Willis and I flew in to a corner of a field, followed almost at once by the search and disposal experts. Peter briefed Sergeant Major Gus Garside, the ammunition technical officer, and Staff Sergeant Sam McCarter, the

Royal Engineer search adviser, on where the suspect device was. I chatted quietly with Corporal 'Magic Fingers' Brown, who was Sergeant Major Garside's assistant. I knew him well because, originally a Green Howard, he had been the B Company clerk during my first two tours in Northern Ireland. As the company clerk he could type – hence the nickname 'Magic Fingers' – and he had most kindly begun typing the very mediocre novel that I had been writing to try to stay awake during my 'doom watch' night duties in the company ops room on the Andersonstown tour of 1972–3. After the first chapter, I had spared him the rest. Shortly afterwards he had opted for a career change and embarked on his bomb disposal training: thus we came together again in this field in South Armagh.

Minutes later, Peter and I started to go forward with Garside, McCarter, Brown and Sergeant Evans, a forensics expert from the Royal Military Police. After a few yards moving cautiously towards a gap in the hedge by a signpost from which we knew we could point out to the others the exact location of the device up the road, Peter stopped me and gave me an air photograph from his pocket, telling me to study it ready for another operation in the same area that weekend which he wanted me to lead. So I stopped, while the others went on. Half a minute later, by which time they had gone only another 30 yards, there was a tremendous explosion. The ground shuddered and clouds of debris and dust filled the air – but through it all, I could see no one. I ran forward to where I had last seen them. Corporal Brown lay dead on the ground, the others were nowhere. Ever the optimist, I immediately thought 'thrown clear by the blast', but realized at once it was wishful thinking. My radio crackled and I heard David Husband, the commander of the cordon platoon, calling for a casualty evacuation helicopter. A Scout arrived very quickly and, leaping in, we flew low over the crossroads, but I could not see anyone. The risk of secondary devices stopped us looking on foot at that moment. Then a radio message came that a man had been seen acting suspiciously earlier and was being held just up the road. I ran round there to find Corporal Tony Warriner with a suspect at gunpoint. 'We saw him coming down the hill towards this car,' Warriner said, 'but the car has got a puncture and he was changing the tyre in something of a hurry, so we have detained him. He didn't realize he was inside our cordon.' Despite the protestations of some locals who had gathered, the man was arrested and taken away for questioning. Corporal Tony Warriner, later to be my company sergeant major and then my regimental sergeant major, had done exceedingly well. The suspect was charged, tried and convicted on four charges of murder – those of Peter Willis, Gus Garside, Sam McCarter and Calvert Brown – and sentenced to four terms of thirty years' imprisonment. I gave evidence against him in the Crumlin Road Court House the next year. The trial took up six of the eight weeks of my second to last term at Durham.

All these years on, I know that man well, and now – if not before – he knows me, although we have only spoken to each other once, and that was at Cortreasla Bridge on 17 July 1975 when I arrested him. I am sure he would say that he was only doing his job, and I would say that I was only doing mine. The difference was that I was upholding the law and he was breaking it. The issue, of course, is that if you want to change the law or the sovereignty of a piece of territory then the legitimate route is through the ballot box and not via the bomb or the gun. That is a principle worth dying for. Peter and the other three gave their lives that day for that principle. The bomber, who in this book will remain nameless, served fifteen years in prison of the thirty years of his sentence, released early under Northern Ireland's prisoner-friendly judicial system. To this day, four British Army families grieve for those they lost that sunny day in July 1975, and I know that the bomber still grieves for the loss of his father in an earlier campaign in the 1950s. I understand personal grief, but we must do better than an eye for an eye. Moreover, in a mature democracy like ours, there is no substitute for upholding the rule of law – the alternative is anarchy, which is quite unacceptable in the twentieth and twenty-first centuries.

So I need not have worried that three years at Durham would remove me from soldiering. The minor miracle was that I got a degree at all. As it turned out, Economic History was a rather more useful subject than straight History would have been. The inside pages of some of the better newspapers have made much more sense to me over the years as a result, and my studies yielded a significant contribution to my understanding of how to manage the increasingly large Army budgets for which I became responsible later on. Indeed, we might have got into an even worse mess than we did at the time of Tony Blair's Strategic Defence Review of 1997–8, when, as Director of the Defence Programme Staff, I was partly responsible for the distribution of the money, had I not read Economic History at Durham, notwithstanding my lack of Latin – and, perhaps more critically, my having passed Maths O Level at only the third attempt.

Still, despite the conflicting interests of Northern Ireland, the Durham Union Society and meeting my future wife, I graduated in June 1976 with a second-class (albeit a lower second-class) degree in Economic History. Attending the Congregation Ceremony in the splendour of Durham Cathedral, however, became a lower priority than joining Pippa's family holiday in Scotland, days before returning to my regiment full-time. Pippa's father was a wonderfully patient instructor in the finer art of salmon fishing, something which I had never tried before. Those very special few days on the west coast of Scotland passed too quickly. Then it was time to load up my car and head across Europe to the divided city of Berlin, where my battalion had been posted, swapping the divisions of Northern Ireland for those of the epicentre of the Cold War.

3

Second Chance

For Cold Warriors of the mid-1970s like me, as I rejoined my battalion after Durham, Berlin represented a fascinating island of the free world in the surrounding Communist sea. Just getting there was quite a challenge. In 1945 the four victorious Allied powers had divided not just Germany but its capital, Berlin, among themselves. With the continued presence of the Red Army in eastern Germany, access to Berlin was easy for the Russians; but as the wartime alliance turned into peacetime enmity between East and West, access for the three Western powers – Britain, France and the United States of America – to the city, deep behind the Iron Curtain, was an entirely different matter. There were three land and air corridors into each of the three Western sectors of Berlin, one by road, one by rail and one by air. The air corridor agreement made in 1945 was that aircraft would fly at 10,000 feet. This was fine in the Dakota age of the 1940s, but by the mid-1970s flying at

10,000 feet in a modern airliner was a most disagreeable, bumpy experience. The land routes had made no progress either. The autobahn from Helmstedt in West Germany through East Germany to the British sector of Berlin was an extraordinarily pot-holed and bumpy hundred kilometres of bad driving experience, while the daily British military train from Berlin-Charlottenburg station to Braunschweig in West Germany via Magdeburg in East Germany was a living testament to the Cold War. The train was sealed in Berlin or Braunschweig, after which no one was allowed on or off until it reached its destination. All the passengers were effectively under command of the military authorities on the train. On both land routes the Russians made a major point of checking every last detail of all Western Allied passengers. For the uninitiated, among whom were the young soldiers of my regiment and their families from North Yorkshire, just getting to Berlin was daunting.

Once there, however, life in the British garrison took on a recognizably traditional rhythm. The three infantry battalions took it in turns to carry out various public duties, the most historically significant of which was to stand guard at Spandau Prison, where the only surviving member of the Nazi hierarchy, Rudolf Hess, was incarcerated. He was the sole prisoner, and when he died in 1987 the complete prison was bulldozed. For two years between 1976 and 1978 we undertook our duties and trained as best we could to prevent the Warsaw Pact from thinking that Berlin would be a walkover. That summer, 1st Battalion, the Green Howards had moved from Chester in north-west England to Montgomery Barracks in the rural suburb of Kladow. The back fence of our barracks was itself the boundary between East and West Berlin. We were living, quite literally, on the front line. Those wonderful battalion cynics observed quite drily that the double tennis court in the centre of our camp would make an ideal prisoner-of-war cage in which the complete battalion could be locked up within minutes if we were ever surprised in our beds by Warsaw Pact forces, which we easily could have been. The rest of the Berlin Infantry Brigade, to which we belonged, had a rather more robust defensive plan, but for the Kladow battalion, living on the edge of the free world, notions of being able to assemble ourselves in the dead of night, drive out of camp, cross the Havel lake in small passenger and vehicle craft and adopt a defensive position within the Grunewald Forest in less than several hours was always somewhat fanciful in the view of most of us. So it was into this important but largely symbolic environment that I returned to regimental duty in August 1976 and to which I brought Pippa after we were married.

The wedding took place on Saturday, 19 March 1977, and I had hardly been home at all between our engagement in October the previous year and our wedding. Pippa is the eldest of four girls in the close-knit Gurney family of Norfolk, whose roots were in banking and farming, and among whose forebears was Elizabeth Fry, the Victorian prison reformer. Pippa's parents and her three sisters, Sonia, Anne-Louise and Belinda, had made me really welcome from the outset. On one occasion just after we had become engaged, I was staying with Pippa's family and was included in a large Norfolk drinks party. A well-meaning person took me on one side and said in cautionary tones: 'Look around; there are three hundred people here, and in a few months' time you will be related to most of them!' Far from being put off by the prospect, I felt privileged – and anyway, Philippa Gurney was the girl I really wanted to marry.

Perhaps it was wishful thinking on my part, but it seemed to me that my major responsibility to our wedding was to be there on the day. As it turned out, even this apparently simple task proved more complicated than I had anticipated. We had been on exercise for two weeks in West Germany just before I was to take two weeks' leave to be married. I drove from Sennelager, our training area in West Germany, back to Berlin, took over the house in which Pippa and I were to live, made things as civilized as I could and headed back to the Hook of Holland to catch the ferry. Up to that point I had hardly been to bed for a couple of days, so I planned that, having driven once again down the Berlin Corridor, I would stop for three hours and have a nap in a lay-by somewhere before driving the final six hours to the ferry. Unfortunately, the optimism of the plan exceeded my ability to stay awake, and I nodded off very shortly after exiting the Berlin Corridor at Helmstedt. As my car veered off the autobahn with me fast asleep at the wheel, it caught one of the warning posts: the shock of the impact woke me up, and I saw my headlights not shining onto an autobahn but illuminating a field. Mercifully, I had chosen to fall asleep at about the only point on the autobahn where the adjacent field was flat level with the road itself, and I had the presence of mind not to jerk the steering wheel back towards the autobahn but to glide into the field at 70 miles per hour. It had rained recently and the ground was wet. I tried to drive out of the field but my wheels spun and I was stuck.

Wedding timelines flashed through my mind. I had no option but to walk back up to the autobahn and ring for help, in my terrible German, on the emergency telephone. Eventually I was connected to the British Military Police post at Helmstedt, from which a patrol deployed to help me. The sergeant who came to my rescue had served under the Green Howards the year before in Northern Ireland, and so his only concern was to get me out of the field and on the road again. Even so, I had lost valuable time on my journey and arrived at the Hook of Holland just as my ferry was casting off for England. With a deep breath, I rang Pippa to say that I loved her very much and was much looking forward to getting married on Saturday – but was coming home a day late. This was not a great start, and I am not sure that my performance in turning up on time for domestic engagements has improved over the years.

However, I eventually got home to enjoy a most wonderful wedding. The service in St Peter Mancroft Church in the centre of Norwich was conducted by the vicar, the Reverend David Sharp, assisted by the Venerable Peter Mallet, the Chaplain General to the Army, who asked Pippa on her arrival at the church door: 'Are you sure you want to go through with this?' Fortunately Pippa said 'Yes' – and so we were married. There were six hundred family and friends in the church and Pippa was surrounded by a cloud of nine brides-maids and pages. My Sandhurst friend and fellow cross-Channel boating adventurer, David Budge, was my best man. It was Lent, but a dispensation was given about flowers in the church and it looked magnificent. As I was walking proudly down the aisle with Pippa on my arm, I caught Peter Inge's eye: he mouthed 'Smile', which I duly did, and have been doing ever since. The spring that year had been warm and dry, and the gardens of Pippa's home, Bracon Lodge, were looking wonderful with banks of daffodils up the drive. The reception passed far too quickly, and before we knew it we were on our way, driving initially to London and then – after what remained of my two weeks' leave – heading off to Berlin. For me it was back to work, but for Pippa it was a new life.

By the time we were married I was the adjutant of the battalion, in which capacity I was principal staff officer to the commanding officer and responsible for the day-to-day running of the battalion, including discipline. The adjutant and the regimental sergeant major are generally fairly unpopular people, charged with keeping everyone else up to the mark. At the time Pippa and I married, Lieutenant Colonel Peter Inge, who had originally recruited me into the regiment, was the CO; Warrant Officer Class 1 Ken Graham was the RSM. For Pippa, Army life was more than a slight shock. The CO's house was within the barracks itself, and at its front gate was a small bungalow known popularly as the 'Honeymoon Cottage' into which we moved. Enjoyable as it was to have some privacy, our house was some way away from where all the other officers lived, so getting to know the other families was the immediate challenge for Pippa. However, she started to work in the battalion kindergarten and quickly became acquainted with the Green Howard children and their wonderfully broad

Yorkshire accents. Unhelpfully, as adjutant I worked all hours conceivable and, when not doing that, I (equally unhelpfully) played cricket. Pippa has been brilliant about the amount of time that I have been away over the years, something for which I have been and shall be eternally grateful, but if I could rewind the clock I would arrange things differently. It is easy to get priorities out of kilter.

That said, Berlin was a great place to start married life. As one of the principal cities of Europe it was a superb place to live. Berlin was redolent with history, as it was with history in the making, and it was a city of great culture and great fun. There were three major opera houses, two in the East and one in the West – to all of which we could go, by virtue of being Allied soldiers – and we did: but wherever one went one could not get away from the haunting and uncomfortable images of *Cabaret* in the 1930s and the apocalyptic fulfilment of Wagner's prophetic *Götterdammerung* – the Twilight of the Gods – in 1945. Many of our friends and relations came to stay in Berlin, and we would invariably take them to an opera in the East, always a fascinating expedition. From our house to the opera and back was a round trip of 57 miles, including a border crossing at 'Checkpoint Charlie', where, provided I showed my British Army identity card, we were all allowed to pass into East Berlin. I would have made an earlier trip to the Staatsoper to buy tickets; but what we never knew until we arrived was who else would be in the audience. As Allied soldiers we had to wear uniform, and therefore we would be in mess kit with scarlet jacket and red-striped trousers; the rest of the audience could have been top

Party officials from the Government or the workers from Collective Farm 314. We were always sold tickets in the front couple of rows, so we could be kept an eye on. So it was not entirely like going to Covent Garden or Glyndebourne, but the productions were on a large scale, dramatic and engaging. Afterwards we would dine in a restaurant that was a relic of the 1930s, where we would eat well and pay little, courtesy of the exchange rate between the East and West German marks. The head waiter looked as if he had indeed been at his post since 1939.

For the soldiers of the battalion, Berlin was a welcome break from Northern Ireland – we had done six tours of duty in the Province between 1970 and 1976. As the rather boring public guard duties in Berlin only came around one month in three, there was plenty of time for sport, such military training as Berlin allowed and getting to know one of the principal capital cities of Europe, a metropolis at the heart of the superpower standoff which defined the Cold War. 'Showing the Flag' was an integral part of daily life for the British garrison, epitomized by the annual Allied Forces Day Parade when, along with our French and US allies, we showcased our military strength through the centre of the city to reassure the West Berlin population that we were there to protect them – and to impress and deter our Soviet former allies, although I was never quite sure that 4-ton trucks with pallets on the back trailing along behind the marching infantry and the rolling main battle tanks were that impressive. Additionally, for the British, there was the annual Queen's Birthday Parade. For keen watchers of the British military, such a parade conjures up images of the Household Division Trooping the Colour to perfection on Horse Guards Parade in London, but in Cold War Berlin the display of soldiery was rather more extravagant. On parade for Her Majesty's Silver Jubilee Birthday Parade in Berlin in June 1977 were 1st Battalion, the Welsh Guards, 1st Battalion, the Green Howards and 2nd Battalion, the Parachute Regiment, together with an assortment of tanks, other armoured vehicles and trucks. Our flight of Gazelle helicopters were also due to make an appearance. This spectacle was always staged on the Maifeld, a huge grass parade ground adjacent to the 1936 Olympic Stadium, a venue much favoured by Adolf Hitler.

On the day, the stands were packed with thousands of Berliners, French and American guests and our families. Unfortunately, the brigade commander had one of those nightmare moments that happen to the best of us and muddled up the sequence of his words of command. At the climax of the parade, when all three infantry battalions in extended line should have marched forward together – 'in review order' – prior to giving a final Royal Salute and firing our rifles in a *feu de joie*, the brigadier gave the wrong word of command. 'Help! What do I do now?' flashed through hundreds of soldiers' minds, including mine, in a split second. Sensing the problem, the regimental sergeant major of the Welsh Guards steadied his people, ordering 'Stand still'. The Welsh Guards heard this and indeed stood still. Half the Green Howards, in the centre of the parade, heard it and stood still too, but the Parachute Regiment and the other half of the Green Howards started to march forward. It was a shambles, and got worse because the brigadier had his back to his troops and was unaware of the chaos unfolding behind him. He gave more words of command, but by this time the director of music knew we were in trouble so the massed bands stopped playing. The brigadier thought he had not shouted loud enough, so gave the next orders again – at the top of his voice. Nothing happened and no one moved. It was very embarrassing. From the spectator stands the chief of staff took the initiative and marched out to the brigadier and had a word in his ear. The hapless brigadier spun around. The expression on his face said it all: 'They've mutinied!' We all felt terrible.

Eventually, with much shuffling and non-drill-book activity, order was restored and the parade was completed to some rather ironic applause from the crowd. As I marched off, I found myself next to a regimental friend, Captain John Westlake, who muttered under his breath, 'The worst thing is that it gives the French something to laugh at – at our expense!' The following year, Her Majesty came to her own Birthday Parade in Berlin. We all, including the brigadier, spent a very long time rehearsing.

The intervening year, however, took an unexpected turn of events from my point of view. Just eight months after Pippa and I were married, on the second Friday in November, the battalion held its annual Armistice Day service. Lieutenant Colonel Leslie James, my old company commander, was by then the commanding officer. He and RSM Ken Graham presided over the event. There was some surprise that the adjutant, who would normally ensure that everything went according to plan, was not there. Some time after the service, John Simmons, a close friend who had joined the regiment on the same day as me in 1971, discovered me semi-conscious on the floor of battalion headquarters. I was rushed to the British Military Hospital and, after twenty minutes' examination there, was put back in the ambulance and sped through Berlin, blue lights flashing, to the Neu Westend Clinic, the main teaching hospital in West Berlin. The paymaster rummaged through his records to see if I was a subscriber to the Army Widows Fund.

That afternoon and evening passed in a blur. Pippa was found and brought to the German hospital by our padre, Robin McDowall. She asked the doctor who was looking after me for a truthful prognosis, and he, trying to be helpful, replied: 'It's, how you say in England, fifty–fifty: we win some; we lose some.' I had had a major stroke, supposedly unheard of at the age of twenty-six. Unfortunately the brain scanner at the hospital was broken, so the doctors were using old-fashioned diagnosis. But, in any event, I was completely paralysed down my right-hand side and could hear myself talking utter rubbish in answer to questions being put to me. I knew the right answers, but other words came out. A day later I knew I was in deep trouble when Pippa, sitting beside my bed, was joined by my parents. As adjutant, I knew that only happened if things were dire. But, self-evidently, the worst did not come to the worst and I have been fortunate enough from a rather poor situation to have made a full recovery, although to this day I wear my shoes out unevenly and get more tired on the right-hand side.

Two years later, when I appeared in front of the medical board that would decide my future, the president of the board said: 'Well, you were extremely ill; but you have made a remarkable recovery. It's one of those million to one things that we cannot really explain. Put it behind you and crack on.' I have followed this good advice over the years, but in the early weeks after the event I found myself in a most unusual situation in Berlin, being a spectator on life, when normally I had been a frenetic player. The bigger issues in life began to come into focus in a way that they never had before. Not surprisingly, many close friends and members of my family wrote to me, but I had one letter that made far more impact on me than all the others. It was from a long-retired Coldstream Guards officer, Major Bill Batt, a well-known landowner, farmer and magistrate in Norfolk, whom Pippa and I both knew well. In his letter he asked me to look at two short passages in the Bible, and in doing so he reminded me of the commitment I had made earlier in my life to live as a Christian. It was a sudden shock to realize, looking death in the face, that in fact I had been living a pretty selfish and self-serving existence, often too far removed from the commitment that I had thought I had made previously.

The first verses to which Bill Batt pointed me were from Hebrews, chapter 12, verses 5–7: 'My son, do not regard lightly the discipline of the Lord, nor lose courage when you are punished by him. For the Lord disciplines him whom he loves, and chastises every son whom he receives.' Lying flat on my back in hospital gave me the opportunity to review my life, and to realize that despite my good intentions I had often failed to live up to the Christian standards I professed to believe in.

I now had a second chance. As I slowly recovered, I reflected upon several occasions in the past when, on the balance of probabilities, I could well have lost my life. But, typically of a young man, even when I had looked death in the eye I had just shrugged these things off. However, on 11 November 1977 I was not able to shrug anything off. I was paralysed, frightened and confronting the prospect – should I survive – of life never being the same again. But in his letter, Major Batt had also suggested that I should read verse 11 of the same chapter of Hebrews. I did so. 'For the moment all discipline seems painful rather than pleasant; later it yields the peaceful fruit of righteousness to those who have been trained by it.' From this I understood that, having committed myself to life as a Christian, a half-hearted commitment was not going to be enough. It was a question of whether or not I was going to live a life in which belief and faith really mattered.

As I recorded earlier, the day I had that stroke was 11 November – Armistice Day: the day when we remember the surrender of Germany that concluded the First World War. On reflection it occurred to me that the moment of surrender is two things – it is the end of the struggle and it is the beginning of peace. I found on Armistice Day 1977 that a far better way of living my life was not to go on struggling with my Creator, compromising and ignoring His challenges, but to recognize that there was a more purposeful and peaceable way of life to be found in accepting that I would do whatever He wanted in my life, and not necessarily what I wanted. That day, and its consequences, have had a vast impact on what I think and do. In a huge way it helped define who I then became, both as a person and as a soldier.

* * *

Having had two years 'off' in Berlin, there was a certain inevitability that the battalion would next be posted back to Northern Ireland. This time, however, we were all going, families included, for a two-year 'residential' tour. We were to be an additional resident infantry battalion in the Province, so we were not taking over from anyone but establishing a new role and a new barracks. It was an indication that the situation was beginning to improve as more battalions with their families were moving to the Province, with fewer on 'emergency' unaccompanied tours of duty. We were to live alongside the civil and military airfield at Aldergrove and our focus was to be on Belfast. The four operational companies would rotate between deployed duties in the city, standby duties as reinforcement for those on deployment, general military training and home leave. This would be the pattern for the next two years. There was therefore a degree of predictability about events which the families, in particular, appreciated.

Pippa and I were in fact only expecting to be in Aldergrove for about four months, until my appointment as adjutant came to an end; I was then to go to Sandhurst as an instructor. But before that there was the small matter of our first child. We arrived in Northern Ireland in early September 1978, the month before the birth was due. After some deliberation it was agreed that Pippa would have the baby in Craigavon hospital – a modern hospital, but nearly 40 miles away and in a largely Republican area. To my enduring shame, on the day Tom was born I thought Pippa was going for a routine pre-natal appointment and, as I had an 'important' meeting to attend, I let her drive herself to

Craigavon and admit herself to the maternity ward. So I was more than a little surprised to get a call telling me that if I wanted to be present when the baby was born I had better get a move on. Leslie James, the CO, very kindly lent me his staff car and I got to Craigavon not very long before Tom made his appearance on 25 October. I have never been able to apologize enough to Pippa for being such a rotten husband that morning. But we loved our brief time together in Northern Ireland and were made to feel very welcome by the local community. So it was with a certain amount of sadness that, just three months later, we packed up again and moved from Aldergrove to Sandhurst.

This, we thought, would most likely be my last job in the Army. Back at Durham, I had assured Pippa that I had never intended to make the Army a full career; now, having had an exciting seven years, and still not fully fit after my stroke, I wanted to review my career options. At Sandhurst I found myself working for Major Rupert Smith, himself recovering from being blown up in Crossmaglen some time earlier. Rupert, of course, went on to complete a very distinguished career commanding the British 1st Armoured Division in the First Gulf War, the United Nations Protection Force in Bosnia at the culmination of the civil war there, and the Army in Northern Ireland at a critical moment in the peace process, before finally becoming NATO Deputy Supreme Allied Commander Europe at the time of Kosovo. He was probably one of the brightest and best generals we never had as Chief of the General Staff or the Defence Staff. His book *The Utility of Force* is a classic for serious military students. Partly under Rupert's guidance and partly with the help of Eric Morris, one of the principal members of the academic staff at Sandhurst at the time, I sat the Staff College entrance exams during that first year back at the Academy.

However, in parallel, I had been applying for various appointments outside the Army, with varying degrees of success. I had decided to make my decision by Easter 1980. As we approached my self-imposed deadline I had two job offers on the table in which I was interested. Then, before Easter, the Staff College exam results came out unexpectedly early. Despite not yet being fully fit, I had passed what were highly competitive exams to win a place at the Staff College – which, I knew, was the springboard from which I could work to move up into the more demanding appointments in the Army. I was delighted, and this opportunity effectively made my career decision for me. Comparing one thing with another, I knew that the attractions of soldiering were greater than those of the other two options, namely working in a bank or learning to run a factory in the food industry.

So that was it – I would stay in the Army, at least for the foreseeable future, which I defined at the time to be another ten years. Pippa accepted my decision with good grace, and also the subsequent news that, rather than stay on at Sandhurst in Camberley for another two terms before going to the Army Staff College, which in those days was also in Camberley, I had agreed to go back to my battalion to command a rifle company for nine months. This meant promotion to acting major, and the prospect of getting back to leading soldiers. But it meant another move. As Pippa was by then expecting our second child, it was, I now realize, a case of Dannatt being pretty selfish again. There is an expression in the Army which describes wives as 'following the drum', and for Pippa to uproot again and come back to regimental duty with me was a classic case of following that drum. As soldiers we ask a tremendous amount of those we marry, and of our children, too, inviting them to live in pretty poor housing at times and expecting the children to move to new schools and find new friends every two years or less.

We moved from Camberley to Catterick in North Yorkshire just after Christmas 1980. I had discovered that the battalion was due to go to Cyprus for six months in May 1981 as part of the United Nations peacekeeping force on the island, but just as we were moving to Catterick I also heard that it would be taking over Frankland Prison as part of the Ministry of Defence's support to the Home Office during its dispute with the Prison Officers' Association. Timing was not brilliant for the Dannatt household. We arrived in Catterick on 4 January, the battalion took over Frankland Prison with my company running everything inside the walls on 8 January, and Bertie, our second son, was born on 12 January – the first boy born in the hospital that year. I had just begun the morning prison management meeting when I got a phone call to say that Pippa was in the military hospital in Catterick. The meeting was adjourned as I jumped into my Land Rover and headed south down the A1, arriving just in time to witness Bertie's arrival – and then, as paternity leave was not an option in those days, quickly returning to my prison just outside Durham. Pippa stayed in the hospital for several days, often as the only incumbent of her ward. It was not that surprising that eventually the military hospitals were all closed. Hospitals need patients, and the military population was declining.

Commanding C Company for those nine months was a tremendous experience. I was fortunate to have as my second-in-command Captain David Santa-Ollala, who had been awarded the Military Cross after our 1975 tour in South Armagh, and had previously had the rather unusual experience of commanding a company himself at a very early age. David had been a platoon commander in A Company when Peter Willis was killed, and was still in the company when disaster struck again. On the day the battalion returned from its next tour in Northern Ireland in 1976, Peter's successor, Major Mike O'Sullivan, Captain Charlie Alderson-Smith, the company second-in-command, and Second Lieutenant Timothy Campbell, another platoon commander, were all travelling home together by car when it hit a tree, tragically killing all three. Peter Inge, who was still the CO, decided that David Santa-Ollala, although very young, was the only officer left in the company whom the soldiers knew, and that therefore he should take command. David typically rose to this challenge superbly, as he did later when he commanded 1st Battalion, the Duke of Wellington's Regiment, adding to his Military Cross a Distinguished Service Order for his outstanding command of his soldiers in Bosnia. Also in C Company in 1981, my company sergeant major was George Clarke, who had been awarded the Military Medal in 1973 for his actions in the streets parallel to me on 7 February that year. It was a strong team that I was joining.

But we were not to fight any battles together in 1981. Our first task was to run everything inside Frankland

Prison. This was an interesting challenge in more ways than one. Frankland was a new prison, and had not yet been officially opened: indeed, there were no locks on the internal doors yet, so at every key point was a soldier with a padlock, key and chain. Moreover, the main gates of the prison had not been fitted with their electric motors, so every time they needed opening or closing four soldiers had to give them a hefty shove. We also learned to be scrupulously fair in our dealings with the prisoners. At meal times they all had to have exactly the same size portion of food, down almost to the same number of chips, or there would be trouble. However, I think our regime was both firm and fair, and the prisoners respected us for that. As it happened most of them were from the north-east, as were our Green Howard soldiers, so they had that much in common.

After we had been at Frankland for a month, the Home Office and the Prison Officers' Association settled their dispute and we learned that 'our' prison was to close, the inmates being distributed around the country so that the building work at Frankland could be completed. One of the deputy governors with whom we had been working we found to be a rather irritating individual. As he was in charge of the prisoner dispersal plan, we thought we would make a point. We gave one of our soldiers a false prison identity record and slipped him into one of the cells. There was then a major furore over how we came to have an extra prisoner who had nowhere to go – and, for a while and much to our amusement, a very red-faced deputy governor. When the joke had run its course, we quietly extracted our soldier/prisoner and expunged his prison record.

That month the battalion spent at Frankland underlined once again the versatility of the Army and what can be done with a trained body of men and a properly functioning command and control system. Over the years the battalion had managed floods, fires and now Frankland Prison; and we still had foot and mouth, and fuel strikes, to come. For now, with prison duty complete, it was not long before the battalion was due to go to Cyprus to become the British contingent of the United Nations force on the island. We did a certain amount of pre-tour training in Catterick, but the eccentricities of the UN Cyprus role were such that most was left until we had actually got to Cyprus and taken over.

Just after Easter, Pippa and the two boys packed up once again and this time headed for our own house in Norfolk – somewhere that has always been a lifeline for our family. When we were married we were very fortunate to have been given by Pippa's father a very pretty mill house on the family farm just south of Norwich. Not much had been spent on it for a while and it had been divided into three flats during the housing slump of the early 1960s, but it was the most wonderful start to married life. Over the years, as we gained vacant possession of all three flats, we turned it back into the family house it once was, and it has become our permanent family home. It has provided valuable stability for the family and a firm domestic base during our twenty-three moves before I eventually retired in 2009. I fully recognize that we have been very fortunate as a family. Our children may have had endless addresses elsewhere, but they have known this house as their real home, and I am eternally grateful to Jim, my late father-in-law, for giving it to us. His rationale was spot on, namely that his eldest daughter would find being an Army officer's wife a whole lot easier to manage knowing we had a permanent home somewhere – even if we seldom actually lived in it. He was absolutely right about the stability it gave to our family, but I would suggest with great respect that he was not right about his eldest daughter, who over the years has been brilliant at rising to the challenges thrown at her by Army life, the media and everything else. However, having somewhere to call home and somewhere the children could base themselves when they went to Beeston Hall, their Norfolk prep school, was also really important; about that he was completely right.

My father-in-law was a remarkable man, and thoughtfulness was always a key part of his character. He had been a soldier as a very young man in the Second World War, an experience which greatly influenced so many of that generation. In the more discretionary wars fought today by our small professional Army, it is important to remember that two generations in the early and middle part of the twentieth century found themselves caught up as citizen soldiers in two wars vital to the survival of our nation. It is easy now for our population to think that these days fighting is only done by those people foolhardy enough to volunteer to serve in the armed forces. But there have been times in our recent history when soldiering was everyone's business: my father-in-law's experience was typical of his generation, and well worth considering in the context of today's pressures on our young soldiers.

Commissioned into the Grenadier Guards, he had landed at Anzio as part of their 5th Battalion in 1944.

Within days he found himself as a second lieutenant commanding his company, the other officers having been killed or wounded, before being badly wounded himself, left for dead in the confusion of the battlefield and then taken prisoner. Back home, his mother, Pleasance Gurney, was hosting a Red Cross event at the family home, Bawdeswell Hall, when a telegram arrived to say that Jim was missing, presumed dead. She carried on with the afternoon's activities regardless, not mentioning the telegram until the event was over. Remarkably, it turned out some long weeks later that Jim had not been killed, despite his helmet having been retrieved with the most enormous dent in it. Just before his final engagement the platoon mortar had been called into action but in the soft ground the tube was digging in and the fire was too inaccurate. Jim had placed his helmet on the ground as a baseplate upon which the mortar could fire. This was a great tactic but his helmet suffered such a huge dent that it was then unwearable. Later it was assumed that anyone wearing that helmet could not have survived, so he was posted 'missing, presumed dead'. He spent the rest of the war recovering in Italian and German military hospitals before going into a series of prisoner-of-war camps, finally being part of an Allied contingent that was marched east until they were liberated. After all those events, on his return to London he appeared unannounced, exhausted and filthy on his Aunt Mildred Ruggles-Brise's doorstep in Cheyne Gardens, London, and asked very politely: 'Could I possibly just come in and have a bath?' Unbeknown to him, his father was staying overnight for the weekly Barclay's Bank directors' meeting. In these more comfortable days one can hardly imagine the intensity of that reunion between father and son – especially as two of Jim's elder brothers had died earlier in tragic circumstances.

Like most of his generation, Jim Gurney hardly ever spoke about his war experiences, although I suspect scarcely a day went past when he did not think about some aspect of them. Furthermore, I believe the intensity of that generation's experiences is only now being equalled by some of our young people who have fought in parts of Iraq and Afghanistan. Fortunately we now understand the mental and psychiatric implications of combat much better than we did then, and quite properly so. The legacy of a fierce physical battle can be a mental battle that may last for years – for some, sadly, for ever.

In 1981, however, our Cyprus tour was to be about peacekeeping in the aftermath of someone else's war, not getting involved in fighting ourselves. The battalion split itself into two halves. For the first three months, A Company under Clive Mantell and my C Company, both under the overall command of our CO, Lieutenant Colonel John Byrne, formed the British contingent of the UN force known as UNFICYP. We were responsible for monitoring the ceasefire line and buffer zone between the Greeks in the south and the Turks in the north from just west of Nicosia nearly to the Mediterranean Sea. Tensions on the island had been growing since independence from Britain in 1962, culminating in what we would now call a vicious bout of 'ethnic cleansing' which provided the excuse for the Turkish Army to make an intervention in 1974, securing about a third of the island for the Turkish Cypriot community. Thereafter the island was literally divided into two communities. To maintain the separation between the opposing armed forces, the United Nations deployed a force along the 1974 ceasefire line and patrolled a de-militarized buffer zone between the Greeks in the south and the Turks in the north. In places the buffer zone was several kilometres wide, but in the centre of the capital, Nicosia, it was just the width of a narrow street. From 1974 to our arrival in 1981 the situation had changed little, and it is still not resolved as I write in 2010.

The tasks of manning observation posts and patrolling the buffer zone on foot and in vehicles were fairly tedious for the soldiers, but given the potential for even the small-est incident to escalate rapidly, meticulous attention to detail and close supervision were absolutely essential. In some ways the scrupulous fairness we had had to observe in Frankland Prison earlier in the year was a good prepar-ation for keeping an eagle eye on the opposing armies in Cyprus who, given half a chance, would try to move a fire trench or weapon pit by a metre here or a metre there. When there was an incident, the means of resolution was always negotiation and not the use of force: indeed, our peacekeeping troops were known to be far less well armed than the opposing Greek and Turkish troops, so we did not even have the illusion of credible strength behind us to back up our diplomacy. Impartiality, closely linked to that scrupulous fairness, was crucial.

Despite this, one day I decided to be unfair. Within my company's area of responsibility was the small Greek village of Dhenia, whose inhabitants were desperate to build more houses to accommodate all their people. Policy, however, decreed no building in Dhenia for a variety of rather obscure reasons. There were strong echoes of the housing problems over which I had had to preside in

Belfast in 1972–3: this seemed to me like another case of having to 'muddle through', a policy for which I had long since lost enthusiasm. Having had the problem put to me several times by the local elders on my visits, and having repeatedly had the same 'No house building in Dhenia' response when I relayed it to the UN headquarters, I decided that a Nelsonian eye to local action was a risk worth taking. I tipped the wink to the village elders and, like locusts descending, the entire village community built six houses almost overnight. The Turks, from a distance, eventually spotted what had happened, but by then Greek Cypriots were living in reasonable houses. If ever the dispute between the two communities is resolved and those parcels of land are found to belong to displaced Turkish Cypriots, then those people will have gained modest houses on their land. I hope they will appreciate the investment in their absence. In the meantime – for nearly thirty years already – a lot of other human beings have had somewhere decent to live. Policy is important, but pragmatism has its place.

The commander of UNFICYP at the time, an Austrian major general, grumbled about me to my CO, a protest was lodged by the Turks in the UN in New York and John Byrne suggested that perhaps I should have consulted him – but at the end of the day people were living in houses who otherwise would have been living in tents. My 'punishment' was going back to the village at the invitation of the elders for a thank-you dinner – only to be invited to eat, among much else, sheep's eyes.

A and C Companies finished our three months' UN duty 'on the line' just outside Nicosia and, having swapped over with the other half of the battalion, headed for the

British Sovereign Base Area of Dhekelia. When Cyprus gained its independence, Britain had retained certain areas of the island for strategic reasons, and my C Company now went to become part of the British garrison in our Eastern Sovereign Base Area, centred on the port of Dhekelia. If the duties with the UN force were fairly undemanding, they were even less taxing in the British area. It has not always been the case, nor has it remained so. In recent years, with the Middle East conflict becoming more intense and with our bases in Cyprus having been used since 9/11 as vital staging posts and holding areas for reinforcements for Iraq and Afghanistan, British troops in Cyprus have very much earned their pay; but in 1981 life in Dhekelia and the other Sovereign Base Area, Episkopi, was pretty quiet, as it was on the RAF station at Akrotiri. And here, of course, is a real dilemma for defence planners. In 1981 Cyprus seemed like a sleepy hollow and perhaps could have been given up; but the future is always highly unpredictable, and with hindsight, by 2001 giving up the foothold of our bases in Cyprus in 1981 would have seemed like madness. As it is, while the Government of the Republic of Cyprus is willing to honour the agreements that enable us to retain the Sovereign Base Areas, then it is not only in our national but in our wider interests to do so. And it is this dilemma that we face time and again. How are medium- to long-term strategic advantages to be weighed against short-term financial savings? There is no easy answer, other than to put in place a process whereby re-evaluation of our national security and defence policies is done on a regular basis, and not just when political advantage or financial crisis dictates – a theme to which I will return in later chapters.

Back in 1981, I was not to stay long in Cyprus to enjoy those quieter times, as the Staff College beckoned. I handed C Company over to John Powell, my Durham inspiration and close friend, and returned to the UK. Pippa packed up in Norfolk and we headed back to Camberley, moving into a house about two hundred yards from the one we had left eleven months, three moves and one additional child earlier. I had had a brilliant year; I am not sure Pippa's experience was the same.

The Army Staff College at Camberley was, and for many is still, an historic institution of lasting significance. Throughout our nation's history, the formal study of war has not been taken seriously by everyone, and up to the middle of the nineteenth century there were those who persisted in the view that it was an occupation purely for those who had a somewhat unhealthy interest in the subject. In the tradition of the gifted amateur, it was held that a young man could be thought well enough prepared for a career as an efficient army office after a reasonably good civilian education topped off with a brief period at the Royal Military Academies at either Sandhurst or Woolwich. But by 1857 things had changed and this attitude was being challenged. The Crimean War had revealed huge inadequacies not only in our tactical thinking, but in our logistic and, especially, medical thinking and practice. The Army and the nation knew it had to do better. A purpose-designed Staff College was built between 1859 and 1863 and the intellectual foundations were laid for an Army that took a more serious interest in its professional development. That said, even after the Second World War there were still some regiments whose officers thought that it was neither necessary nor really appropriate to spend time away from soldiers to study war formally. But by the early 1980s, when I entered the Staff College, it was fully acknowledged that if you wanted your career to progress, then it was vital to study for, and attend, the Staff College.

The Army Command and Staff Course lasted a year and was focused on the needs of the middle-ranking commander and staff officer, typically the brigade major or chief of staff of an armoured brigade based in Germany as part of the British Army of the Rhine. Armoured warfare against Warsaw Pact troops on the plains of northern Germany was the overall context that conditioned our tactical thinking at the Staff College at this time. It was considered imperative that 'staff duties', as the Army calls its formal written and oral communication processes, be carried out to the highest standards, and they were rigorously taught at Camberley – the red correcting pen of the directing staff on our written exercises was a source of much sleeplessness. But while great attention was given to the detail of the written and spoken word to be communicated to subordinates, even more time and effort were devoted to the study of military history, current affairs and the development of contemporary approaches to tactics and war-fighting. The Staff College, at that time, was very much the crucible in which the past and present were reduced to guiding principles, and our thoughts were assembled for the future. Attendance on that course was both a privilege and a key mid-career moment to think about the profession of arms in some detail. Fighting today's battles better is essential, reverting to preparing for yesterday's war is a potential disaster, but anticipating successfully the challenges of tomorrow's conflicts is the real game-changer. Camberley gave us the chance to do that. I loved that year.

On the practical level, in the 1980s the Cold War dominated our planning, with its cocktail of conventional fighting under the shade of the nuclear umbrella. But, as has so often been the case in the history of the British Army, it is the small wars in faraway places that shaped our thinking. Despite the enormous threat to Western Europe from the Warsaw Pact in the middle years of the twentieth century, the British Army's practical experience was gained in operations in Northern Ireland, in the Dhofar War in Oman in the 1970s and in various counter-terrorist incidents that fell principally to the Special Air Service, all on the back of the campaigns conducted during our withdrawal from empire and east of Suez in the 1950s and 1960s. Thus the Staff Course that I joined in 1982 was set to study the theoretical problems of conducting large-scale warfare against the Warsaw Pact in Western Europe – the most *demanding* situation we might face – but was largely taught by instructors who had won their spurs in counter-insurgency and peacekeeping situations – the situations we were most *likely* to face. The mix was a good one; but the Falklands conflict of 1982 challenged all that.

It was in the middle of the morning on Friday, 2 April 1982 that someone came into our syndicate discussion room at the Staff College with the electrifying news that the Argentinians had invaded the Falkland Islands. Despite the previous media coverage of Argentinian traders establishing themselves on South Georgia, the issue had not really been taken seriously in the country and had certainly not captured our attention at Camberley. We were in our first term on tactics, and far too preoccupied considering the problems created by the Warsaw Pact. 'The Falklands – where are they?' Someone was sent to the library to get an atlas, while someone else in all seriousness offered the view that they were just off the coast of Scotland. But quite quickly we realized that the Argentinian intervention posed a huge diplomatic and military challenge to the United Kingdom. While others hesitated, Margaret Thatcher decided that this affront to British sovereignty must be rebuffed forthwith. Within days a naval task force was assembled, commissioned and put to sea. Seventy-four days and 255 British lives later the islands were restored to British rule – an incredible feat of arms, and one conducted over eight thousand miles from home.

The Falklands conflict transformed our studies at Camberley. No longer was violence conceived of as the occasional outcome of a counter-terrorist or counter-insurgency situation; it could still be orchestrated by design on a large scale to achieve national aims. Furthermore, the diplomatic and political issues behind the campaign were so clear-cut, and so universally supported, that there was never a shadow of doubt in the fighting man's mind, be he sailor, marine, soldier or airman, that he was doing any-thing other than risking his life in the national interest, and with the support of the nation 110 per cent behind him. This is an absolutely critical element in the abiding covenant between the nation and the fighting man or woman. The thinking goes: 'The cause is right, so I will hazard my life for it and the nation.' The alternative, which my great-grandfather had agonized over in 1914, is unthinkable, and we came very close to the unthinkable in 2003 over Iraq.

Along with almost all my colleagues, I was very frustrated to be at the Staff College in 1982, thereby missing out on the professional experiences that others were gaining in the Falklands. No one in their right minds who has experienced the result of the application of violence to an essentially political problem will rush into combat; but, as professionals, we know that combat is the other crucible that refines the development of soldiering skills. This was very much felt by my fellow students in the Royal Marines and the Parachute Regiment, whose units did much of the fighting. But given that we could not be there, the Staff College was the perfect grandstand from which to view the conflict. Not only were we kept fully informed of events as they took place, but in the second half of the year all the main participants came to Camberley to give presentations on what they had done and to be questioned by us. The contrasting styles of the various commanders themselves gave us an object lesson in leadership. Most were modest about what they had done, but we saw some big egos on parade too, as well as some ducking and weaving over responsibility for one or two things.

Perhaps one of the most lasting and important legacies of the Falklands conflict, aside from the repossession of the Falkland Islands by the British, was the impression that achievement made on policy-makers in the Kremlin. Our actions in the South Atlantic sent a very clear message that a liberal Western democracy was not a soft touch and that when its core values and interests were challenged it would fight, and fight hard, for what it believed in. As the Cold War reached its climax later in the decade, our national response over the Falklands under Margaret Thatcher's robust leadership was undoubtedly noted in Moscow.

Those 255 British lives lost in the Falklands campaign made a bigger contribution to a safer future for us all than was realized at the time.

I guess the other big lesson that came out of the Falklands is that if something is worth having, or doing, then it must be resourced properly. Until 1982 it was assumed that thirty-five Royal Marines eight thousand miles from home made up a sufficient garrison to protect British sovereignty. A strategic miscalculation cost us those 255 British lives, and thereafter it has cost us billions of pounds paying for the airfield from which modern fast jets fly to secure the skies and for the large tri-service garrison that has been in place since 1982 to hold the ground, the sea and the seabed. Little or nothing in life is cheap, so decision-making on policy priorities is critical and the appropriate consequential funding therefore becomes non-negotiable. If you want to do it, you have to be prepared to pay for it – muddling through on the goodwill of our servicemen and women is immoral. Governments, please note.

The defining moment in any student's year at the Staff College is 'Black Bag' Day. This is the day when everyone discovers what appointment they are to go to after Camberley. Exactly why it is called that is a mystery, especially as the process is completely opposite to that of names and jobs being pulled out of a black bag at random. Evaluation of performance permeates everything that is done at the Staff College: detailed reports are written regularly throughout the year, and the Commandant and directing staff take immense pains, along with the Military Secretary's appointments staff, to ensure that the right student goes to the right job. All students know the pecking order of appointments, and so from that everyone can work out how they and everyone else have done on the course. On 'Black Bag' Day there is a brown envelope in everyone's mail box at the same time. Tension is high: some ambitions are met and some personal realities begin to be confronted. I opened my envelope hoping to find I was to go to the Ministry of Defence, with the comparative stability that might have brought for Pippa and the boys. But no: my posting was to be the chief of staff of 20th Armoured Brigade in Detmold, Germany.

Not for the last time in my military career, I wondered how I was going to tell Pippa the news. For me it was professionally exciting, but for her I knew it was what she least wanted to hear, because we already knew that two years later we would be rejoining my regiment, also in Germany. So my message to the family had to be that we were now going to Germany for four years. I knew this would not be popular. But my old schoolfriend and fellow student on the Staff Course, Ewing Grimshaw, came to my rescue. No sooner had I told Pippa my posting than, as if by chance, Ewing appeared with a bottle of champagne, declaring that the job I was going to was top notch – and he was right. We duly let our house in Norfolk and began to think about returning to Germany.

4

Outflanking the Enemy

It was a late September night in 1984, and fully dark, as the last of the brand new Challenger tanks of the Royal Hussars crawled into their positions. Just issued to the British Army, and now serving alongside the veteran Chieftain tanks of the 4th/7th Dragoon Guards, they halted overlooking the Pattensen Bowl, a low-lying plain surrounded by small hills in northern Germany. The enemy was not expected before first light. Both regiments were under command of 20th Armoured Brigade, of which I had been the chief of staff for a year, and Brigadier Garry Barnett, a former outstanding commanding officer of the Black Watch, was the brigade commander.

We were all taking part in 1st British Corps' periodic Exercise 'Lionheart' – but this one was different. Previous NATO thinking had been that a conventional attack by the Warsaw Pact's Group of Soviet Forces Germany would be so sudden and so powerful that the best Allied forces in the Central Region could do was to delay them for long enough to allow the politicians breathing space to negotiate some form of settlement. In the absence of an agreement, as Warsaw Pact forces flooded through the Fulda Gap in the American area to the south, and towards the Channel ports in the north, NATO would be left with little alternative than to begin the disastrous climb up the nuclear response ladder. How far and how fast that ladder was climbed was the stuff of academic debate and endless speculation. In any event, it was generally accepted that once foot had been set on the first rung – the first nuclear release in Europe – we were in unknown territory. Rational people knew there had to be a better way.

By the mid-1980s much had changed. In 1979 Margaret Thatcher had become the British Prime Minister, showing Churchillian qualities in leading the nation to the recapture of the Falkland Islands in June 1982. Ronald Reagan had become President of the United States in 1981 and as leader of the Western world had declared on 3 March 1983 that 'Communism is another sad, bizarre chapter in human history whose last pages even now are being written.' A few days later he went further and called the Soviet Union 'an evil empire'. The previous cosy policy of 'detente' with the Soviet Union was reversed, Western governments increased their spending on conventional defence and NATO's military thinking began to become more imaginative. Serious consideration was given to options other than immediate nuclear release and inevitable escalation up the nuclear ladder. The United States Army, having pulled itself out of its post-Vietnam malaise, had not only reorganized and re-equipped itself but had proposed to NATO a new military doctrine called Air–Land Battle, in which Allied air forces would strike attacking Soviet forces deep in Warsaw Pact territory, while NATO land forces would deal decisively with the first waves of attacking forces. In this way, both the first and subsequent waves of a Soviet assault would be confronted and reduced simultaneously. Meanwhile the German generals Hans-Henning von Sandrat and Helge Hansen, together with the British general Nigel Bagnall, had begun to instil into their European partners the thinking that if NATO land forces worked closely together, concentrated their resources and used new operational thinking in conjunction with our air forces, it was possible that the Warsaw Pact could even be defeated conventionally, without recourse to nuclear release. Whether this was ever a practical reality or not was, of course, never put to the test; but it served to instil a palpable new confidence, based on a return to an offensive spirit, within NATO armies.

As far as British forces were concerned the principal architect of this turnaround in thinking was General Sir Nigel Bagnall, initially as Commander 1st British Corps and then as Commander in Chief Northern Army Group, which included large numbers of Belgian, Dutch and German troops. He was a hugely respected leader whose influence was profound, not just on the British Army but across NATO. Many of us were in no doubt that, had push ever come to shove in that decade, he would have been the Montgomery or the Slim of his generation. Indeed, the ideas Bagnall proposed had strong roots in military history. Although subsequently defined in the rather clunky phrase 'manœuvre warfare', they emphasized that the enemy was to be attacked where he was weakest, and that the aim was as much to persuade him that he had been defeated as it was to demonstrate the physical reality of this in the destruction of his forces. Similar ideas had been at the heart, for instance, of one of the British Army's most successful campaigns, that against the Japanese by General Bill Slim's famous 14th Army in India and Burma in 1944 and 1945. But this had been a long time ago. A new man was needed to resurrect these concepts for a new age; and Bagnall's contribution to the development of the British Army in the 1980s and 1990s by so doing was immense. General Bagnall also held a rather special place in the hearts of the Green Howards, having won two Military Crosses with the regiment in Malaya before transferring to the cavalry.

As 20th Armoured Brigade assembled in the woods on the hills overlooking the Pattensen Bowl on that warm September night, we all knew we were part of this fresh thinking. To be frank, we did not all understand what the bigger issues were, but on the ground there was a real buzz of change and confidence. The plan at Corps and Army Group level was to allow Warsaw Pact forces to penetrate our defensive lines while we held prominent features (known as 'hard shoulders') from where we could launch surprise, armoured counter-attacks, co-ordinated closely with firepower from our artillery and from the air. The Pattensen Bowl was to be one such area of controlled penetration; the hills surrounding were to be the hard shoulders from which we would launch our attack. An enemy on the move is always vulnerable, so our intention was to manœuvre quickly to his flank and to launch our armoured strength into his side while he was driving west at best speed. In this way, we expected to halt his advance through a combination of surprise and our coordinated air and land firepower. To prove the undoubted success of this new thinking, 20th Armoured Brigade was to carry out just such a major counter-stroke against the 'enemy' on this key exercise. The heads of many Allied armies were visiting and we had rehearsed this aspect of the apparently 'free play' exercise many times over the previous months. However, come the day, things did not work according to plan.

Units from the Dutch Corps, playing 'enemy', decided not to follow the script. Expecting the Dutch 'enemy' columns to roll into the Pattensen Bowl the next morning, thereby presenting us with the perfect target array for our counter-attack, we were assembled to attack them from the south, and into their left flank. To start with all was fine – the Dutch forward units advanced on the expected axis to the north of Pattensen. However, during the night I began to get reports that the 'enemy' had swung south and was in danger of bumping into our hard shoulder rather than just motoring on into the Pattensen Bowl where we would attack them in the open ground at first light. I radioed my concerns to our divisional headquarters. All was in order, I was assured. Stay calm. As the night wore on, further reports seemed to reinforce my fears that the Dutch were doing their own thing; and, for all the reassurance coming out of our divisional headquarters, my worst fears were realized. Rather than pressing on at best speed through the open ground of the Pattensen plain, the Dutch 'enemy' probed its flanks and found the British armour in its ambush positions waiting to pounce the next morning. A series of running battles developed, with dismounted Dutch infantry causing havoc among the British tanks as they moved through the woods and onto the high ground. Next I heard that Brigadier Barnett had been captured in his forward tactical headquarters and that the 'enemy' were closing in on the village where I and the brigade's main headquarters were located. Hearing firing in the village, I ordered my command vehicle to break out of the headquarters so that in the event of disaster we could still exercise some form of command over the brigade. We roared down the street, as only the tolerant West Germans in those days would have allowed, and headed for a wooded ridgeline. Grinding to a halt, I jumped out to see where we were. 'Hello, Sir,' came a familiar North Yorkshire voice. 'I thought you were doing some fancy job on the staff. What are you doing here, then?' My flight from the battle had taken me into the adjacent brigade's area of responsibility and I had arrived on the mortar fire support position of 1st Battalion, the Green Howards – my own regiment. The embarrassment was complete.

The post-mortem following that exercise lasted some time. Still, despite the confusion on the ground, it was deemed to have validated important aspects of the new concept of NATO operations. More positively, the need to be able to move capable and well-equipped armoured formations around the battlefield not only reinvigorated our approach to training but underlined the need for good, modern equipment. In the positive spirit taken towards defence budgets in the mid-1980s, plans were accelerated to bring into service high-quality tanks, infantry fighting vehicles, self-propelled artillery and attack helicopters. In the event, these armoured vehicle programmes came to fruition years later, not to fight the Warsaw Pact on the plains of northern Europe as we had envisaged, but against a quite different enemy in the deserts of Kuwait in 1991 and Iraq in 2003, with the attack helicopters just making it into service for Afghanistan from 2006 onwards. Such is the lead time for military equipment.

While these new battlefield concepts were being worked out, Pippa and I had set up home in Hobart Barracks, Detmold, and Tom and Bertie had settled into a local Army-run kindergarten. Detmold was a small, delightful German town within which the British community was made to feel very welcome. For all of us it was a very happy posting. As a real bonus, our third son, Oliver, was born in the British Military Hospital at Rinteln in May 1984. As ever, Pippa ran the family pretty much single-handed. And, as anticipated, after two years in Detmold I finished my appointment on the staff of 20th Armoured Brigade and returned to regimental duty with the Green Howards. I was to take command of B Company, the rifle company I had originally joined in 1971. The battalion was stationed about two hours away from Detmold, in the large British garrison city of Osnabrück. So the family moved again.

From the moment I returned to the battalion, the focus was back on the familiar streets of Northern Ireland. A six-month tour of West Belfast was planned for mid-1985, and preparations for the tour dominated our lives. I reflected at the time that containing insurgency was a long-term affair. I had not expected when I first went to Northern Ireland in 1971 that I would be going back to those same streets fourteen years later. It was not easy to motivate myself for the return. I had served in the Province every year of the 1970s bar 1977, and when we left Belfast in 1979 I secretly hoped never to go back; but that was not to be. I had to dig deep into my reserves of professionalism for this latest tour, and Pippa had to dig deep into hers of domestic stoicism, looking after three little boys far from home on her own.

Frankly, 1985 was a fairly bleak year. The mood was not lifted by the fact that, at the end of the year, having returned from Belfast and before going on leave, we found that our very keen brigade commander was determined to include our battalion on his major exercise of the year. For a number of long-suffering regimental families, this was nearly the straw that broke the proverbial camel's back. For me, the ultimate irony of this rather unwelcome exercise came on its final morning. My company in its armoured vehicles was making a rapid cross-country move when we came under heavy fire from a wooded hill to our right. Using a previously rehearsed drill, the company wheeled right and immediately began to assault the enemy on the hill. Eventually my company sergeant major Tony Warriner and I, skirmishing together as a dismounted pair of riflemen, reached the summit of the hill, absolutely exhausted, only to be greeted by the defending Gordon Highlander company commander, Andrew Durcan, whom I had relieved in Belfast just six months before. 'Had a good leave?' he asked. I was lost for words.

Those six months in Belfast were very different from

the seven tours of duty that the battalion had previously conducted. The level of violence across the Province was much reduced, and the Royal Ulster Constabulary was firmly in the lead as far as security was concerned; indeed, many of our routine patrol duties hinged on escorting the police on their normal duties of serving summonses and investigating minor crimes. But Belfast in 1985 was still far from normal. B Company was initially based in McCrory Park, a hutted camp just off the Whiterock Road in West Belfast. As part of a process of 'normalization' we were due to pull out of McCrory during our tour, but, as always seems to happen in these situations, the other side sought to portray our move as a defeat for the security forces rather than a sign of progress in the campaign. McCrory Park was surrounded by terraced housing of the Coronation Street type and, although we had closed-circuit television cameras on high masts watching all around the camp, the inevitable happened. A truck drove up a side street and, from under the canvas covering its back, a set of homemade mortar tubes were uncovered and several rounds fired into the base. All this happened in less than a minute. There was considerable damage, but mercifully no casualties. One soldier was talking to his girlfriend on the welfare telephone when the rounds came crashing in. He dived to the floor, leaving the handset dangling and one rather worried young girl in Middlesbrough wondering what on earth those extremely loud explosions were.

Indeed, heavy mortar attacks had become a favourite tactic of the IRA. Shortly after the company had moved out of McCrory Park and up the hill to Fort Whiterock, we were attacked again. Once more several rounds found their way into the camp. This time we were eating in our small officers' mess when, hearing the tell-tale boom of the mortars firing, I suggested we might like to get under the table, which we had done by the time the rounds landed. Again, although there was some damage, there were no casualties. But the dynamics of the campaign had changed. The IRA no longer enjoyed the universal support of the Nationalist community and a war-weariness was beginning to set in. It was to take another twenty-two years of involvement by the Army finally to bring our operations in Northern Ireland to an end, but in 1985 one began to sense the beginning of hope. There was a palpable feeling abroad that we were at last seeing the beginning of the end of IRA terrorism in Northern Ireland.

During that hectic year of 1985 I had begun to think that a way of simultaneously providing some stability for the family and some academic development for me was to apply to read for a Master of Philosophy degree, as the Army allowed a small number of officers to do each year. I was delighted when I was accepted on to the programme and began to think about going to Queens' College, Cambridge, with the family living quite close by at home in Norfolk. But in the middle of the following year things changed yet again, as they were apt to do. I had just returned from another month away, this time with my company on an exchange with the Italian army, when I was told that I was the Army's nomination for the appoint-ment of Military Assistant to the Minister of State for the Armed Forces in the MOD in London. Indeed, I was required in London the next week to be interviewed by the Minister, along with another two candidates, one each from the Royal Navy and the Royal Air Force.

This was a rather exciting prospect, with exposure to the political side of our business for the first time in my career. Furthermore, it was a lieutenant colonel's appointment and I was still a major. At the time the Minister was John Stanley, the Conservative Member for Tonbridge and Malling. He had a fearsome reputation as a highly focused politician who drove his officials hard. By the time he interviewed me he had been in post for just over three years, and knew his ministerial brief well. I had just come back from a fairly undemanding month with an Italian infantry battalion in the sunny south of that country, and so had to pedal quite hard at the interview on any issue beyond the wisdom of letting British soldiers drink wine with their pasta for lunch. Somewhat to my surprise, and with mixed emotions at missing out on Cambridge for the second time in my life, I was offered the job. There could be only one answer – so Pippa, the three boys and I packed up in Osnabrück somewhat earlier than expected and headed back to England after three and a half years in Germany. We gladly re-established the family at home in Norfolk, where we were to remain for the next very happy three years, while I was a weekly 'boarder' in London.

Those three years proved to be the first of a sequence of appointments within the MOD over the next twenty years. I found working for John Stanley, then Ian Stewart and finally Archie Hamilton absolutely fascinating. The relationship between politicians and the senior military is crucial, and must be built on mutual trust and understanding. But the cards are stacked against its working out. The military know their business and are confident, used to weighing up a situation quickly and taking decisions. Admirals, generals and air marshals often have thirty years or more of experience behind them – both in the field and on the staff. The politicians with whom they deal as defence ministers – increasingly so as the Second World War and National Service generations die out – have no personal experience of the military, or have known it only very briefly as young officers who moved on into civilian careers very quickly. It is an inherently unequal relationship that requires great maturity on both sides to make it work. In those early years I saw high-handed attitudes on both sides lead to disastrous outcomes. As with everything difficult in life, dialogue, which includes listening and talking by both parties, needs to be practised faithfully. No one has a monopoly on wisdom. The soldier does not have a natural under-standing of the politics, and the politician does not understand that special ethos that makes the Army, Navy or Air Force work. It was a brilliant idea of John Stanley to ask for a Military Assistant to try to bridge that gap. The initial appointee had come from the RAF; I was the first from the Army.

Had I used my experience of the next three years in writing scripts for *Yes, Minister*, only a few of those scripts would have been used, the rest dismissed as implausible. Fact is far funnier than fiction – but the humour is only fully appreciated if you know the context well, which I guess is the scriptwriters' problem. Would they have made a programme about the minister who, stuck in the lift, demanded that his private secretary push his paperwork under the door so he could carry on with it? Or about the minister who heard that there was a bomb on a plane in Iceland, so sent sniffer dogs to help, only then to have the hapless hounds confined to quarantine for the next six months? Or about the minister who misheard what the head of state of a country he was visiting had said and in consequence nearly caused diplomatic relations to be broken off? I think the answer would be 'No' every time, but witnessing these things, and many more, was a fascinating and illuminating experience for a young officer at the political–military interface. If some thought I was naive later on in my career, they must also conclude that I had been spectacularly unobservant in my earlier years. On the contrary, those three years were a brilliant education.

The job of Military Assistant took the incumbent into the Chamber of the House of Commons. As you look towards the Speaker, with the Government on the left, there is a theatre-type box beyond the front benches where departmental officials sit, waiting to support their ministers if required. If a point crops up in questions or debate to which the minister does not know the answer, then he slips a note to his parliamentary private secretary sitting behind him, who sidles along the second bench towards the Officials' Box and asks the question. If the officials know the answer then the minister is lucky; if not, one slips out to a telephone just behind the Speaker's chair and frantically rings the relevant branch of the ministry in question, hoping that the official who should know the answer is not that moment 'away from his desk'. Being part of this process afforded a fascinating insight into the way our democratic and governmental process worked. On one occasion I was heading for the Officials' Box, in uniform, to deliver a message during a debate in which my minister was performing, only to be told by the policeman on duty behind the Speaker's chair that Army officers in uniform had not been allowed into the Chamber since Oliver Cromwell's time. I took his word for it and went elsewhere, leaving the Minister to fend for himself. I don't think he was best pleased, but the Government did not fall that day.

Inevitably the cycle of life in a minister's office was pretty relentless, not helped by the changeover of personalities. Even though my first year in post was John Stanley's fourth, over the next three years I worked with three ministers, three private secretaries and seven assistant private secretaries. Such turnover, of politicians and civil servants alike, cannot be good for the efficient delivery of Government work. That said, I came and went a little myself. Early on I had the opportunity to attend the second annual conference of what was then called 'The British–American Project for the Successor Generation'. This extended weekend in Philadelphia brought together twenty-four young Americans and the same number of similarly aged Britons to debate the issues of the moment. The thinking behind the programme was to try to fill the gap in the 'special' relationship between the United Kingdom and the United States, strong in the 1940s and 1950s but perhaps less so in the 1980s. We were invited to participate on the basis that the sponsors thought we might have something to contribute to British–American relations in future years. It was a fascinating few days. My fellow participants on the British side included Charles Moore, Chris Smith, Peter Mandelson and Julia Neuberger. At the time I felt that I contributed little, but my ears were wide open. I remain convinced that it is very much in the United Kingdom's strategic interests to maintain a close relationship with the United States. That conference in Philadelphia was a seminal event, as far as I was concerned.

Getting around the armed forces stationed abroad was an important part of the Minister's responsibilities, so during that appointment I quickly adapted to the way that Government ministers travelled in those days (and perhaps wish they still did). To be practical, British Airways first class ensures a degree of privacy that allows work to continue uninterrupted – even if one of my ministers always ate all his peanuts, and mine, during the safety briefing – and a level of facilities appropriate to the job: to arrive, for example, from an overnight flight from London to Kathmandu, via New Delhi, at 5 a.m. and go straight into live television coverage without a shave in a civilized washroom might have lowered the esteem in which others hold us. Arrivals did not, however, always go according to plan. On one occasion I could have murdered our defence attaché in one of the Gulf states. We had agreed a very low-key reception for the Minister, as we had been aboard one of HM ships for the previous twenty-four hours, going through the Straits of Hormuz at the height of the war between Iran and Iraq. The Minister was in a blue boiler suit and I was in Army combat kit. As our naval helicopter approached Abu Dhabi airport, I was horrified to see an enormous red carpet, long lines of ceremonial troops and a band. The Minister looked at me quizzically as we landed. I shrugged apologetically and mouthed 'Just go for it'. We were treated to the spectacle of our ambassador in an immaculate grey suit complete with a panama hat meeting this boilerman of a minister. I could not wait to get at the defence attaché around the back. I only occasionally get cross, but because these events are rare I can recall my temper on this occasion as if it were yesterday.

During my time in the Minister's office Pippa was expecting our fourth child. The hospital had already indicated that number four was to be another boy. That was fine with us as we had said between ourselves we would only have four children if we were happy to have four boys, which indeed we were. One evening, as I was working late in London, Pippa rang to say I might like to come home quickly. I think I broke the land speed record from the Ministry of Defence to Norfolk to get back in time to take Pippa to the Norfolk and Norwich Hospital for 'William's' arrival. A baby was duly delivered – but 'William' turned out be a daughter, not a son: enter Richenda Juliet Rose into our lives. I knew Pippa had always hoped for a daughter, so Richenda's arrival was a real joy, even if her three brothers were less amused. They had been looking for a fourth boy to balance up the teams for garden football nicely. Tom was away at prep school when his headmaster, John Elder, broke the news of his sister's arrival to him: John recalled that 'Tom took it like a man'. And over the years the boys have come to accept that their sister is marginally more use in family football than the dustbin that was initially placed in the goal in lieu of the fourth boy.

One of the last substantive pieces of work that I saw through the Minister's office was the final draft of *The British Military Doctrine*, a document inspired by General Bagnall, written at his direction by Colonel Tim

Granville-Chapman and sent to Archie Hamilton's office for ministerial approval. The document was seminal. It set out for the first time in very many years the Army's approach to the conduct of operations, encapsulating the new thinking that Sir Nigel Bagnall had been developing and applying as the Cold War reached its climax at the end of the 1980s. Transforming an Army's thinking is never an easy task. However, Nigel Bagnall's inspired leadership was complemented by this formal statement of our new doctrine and, of equal importance, by the institution of a Higher Command and Staff Course at the Army Staff College. This course was designed to imbue the brightest and best of the up-and-coming senior commanders with a full understanding of our new approach to business, which would then cascade down through the Army over time. The HCSC has been highly successful, developing into a fully joint course with the Royal Navy and the Royal Air Force. For me, however, as my time in the Minister's office in Whitehall ended, I dropped from the rarefied air of the strategic level in the MOD to the entirely practical business of commanding an infantry battalion.

It has long been said that the high point of anyone's military career is command of their own regiment. It was therefore a real privilege for me, eighteen years after I had been commissioned into 1st Battalion the Green Howards, to take command in July 1989. I took over from John Powell, who had led the battalion very wisely through a difficult two-year residential tour in Londonderry and then masterminded the regiment's tercentenary celebrations in our new garrison, Catterick.

For Green Howards, who are almost all recruited from the old North Riding of Yorkshire, Catterick was very much a home posting and exactly the right place to celebrate our three centuries of unbroken service to the Crown since being raised in 1688. It was a very special regimental occasion when our Colonel-in-Chief, His Majesty Olav V, King of Norway, presented new colours to the battalion. John was very much the right person to be in charge during those festivities and I was more than happy to take over when they were complete.

The parades and parties over, we applied ourselves to retraining to become an airmobile battalion. We were part of the very new 24th Airmobile Brigade and under the command of Brigadier George Kennedy. The brigade owed its existence to the new thinking of the time: our rationale was to exploit the speed of the helicopter over the ground and develop tactics that would get us inside the decision–action cycle of an enemy. A new command style – called Mission Command – was being adopted by the Army: this involves a commander stating in general terms what he wants his unit to achieve, delegating the detailed tasks to his subordinates and supervising only lightly, preferring to let others use their initiative where appropriate. Self-evidently, the commander of a force that can analyse, take decisions and move its units more quickly than an opposing force will be the one who can manoeuvre into a position of advantage and wrong-foot an enemy. We were now to do this in 24th Airmobile Brigade, enabled by the helicopters of the Royal Air Force and Army Air Corps, in the same way that we had been developing ground manoeuvre tactics when I had been the Chief of Staff of

20th Armoured Brigade five years before. All this was the practical outcome of Nigel Bagnall's initiatives. For the battalion it meant learning a lot of new skills, but in a professional Army such as ours the challenge of something new always gets people to raise their game. Over the next two and a half years of my command we were to exercise frequently in the United Kingdom and Germany, becoming pretty slick at moving the whole battalion, and our essential equipment and ammunition, up to a hundred miles by helicopter in just a couple of hours or so.

Inevitably we were constrained by the number of Chinook, Puma and Lynx helicopters that could be made available. Of course there were never enough, but there was always the promise of greater investment in helicopters to come. One programme that we thought in the early 1990s was just around the corner was the EH-101 medium helicopter. Eventually known as the Merlin, it finally came into service in the Iraq campaign of 2003–9. The absence of ground vehicles meant that everything we needed we had to carry, which produced a battalion that was strong and fit; and when helicopters were not available, the infantryman's boot took over. Frustratingly, this same lack of helicopters was to snag us in real operations in Afghanistan a decade or so later. The principle of tactical flexibility by movement through the air – not just to move large bodies of men, but to enable key commanders and specialists to get where they were needed – was widely accepted, but the concept never attracted sufficient funding, and this was to bite us hard a decade later.

I was very fortunate when I took over the battalion to

have a very capable set of subordinates with whom to work. George Robey, as second-in-command, was a master of detail and very steady, while my three rifle company commanders, Nigel Hall, Nick Houghton and Andrew Farquhar, were all future regular battalion commanding officers themselves. Eventually Nigel retired as a brigadier and Andrew as a major general; and Nick in 2009 became a full general and Vice Chief of the Defence Staff. My old company sergeant major, Tony Warriner, was my regimental sergeant major. The battalion and I were very well served by this strong team. We needed them – and more: for, as well as getting to grips with a new operational role, we all knew that we had to make sure that we were fully manned. Whatever happened, things were not going to be the same. There was strength in numbers.

The early 1990s were days of considerable paradox for defence communities, not just in this country but else-where too. There was much delight, and surprise, that the old dynamics in Europe had changed. No one had expected the Berlin Wall to crumble in the way that it did. I recall being at a dinner party in Germany in the very late 1980s when a senior German general said that it 'was in the heart of every German that one day we will be reunited'; but, he said, shaking his head, 'it will not be in my lifetime'. How quickly and how suddenly he was proved wrong. No one could really have predicted the speed at which the Soviet Union and the Warsaw Pact collapsed. But it happened, and a New World Order was proclaimed. Francis Fukuyama announced the end of history. Optimism was high. Defence accountants, their eyes on savings, had their calculators out as the concrete hit the dirt in Berlin. And despite the first Gulf War of 1990–1 – a strategic miscalculation by Saddam Hussein of ultimately terminal proportions – the end of the Cold War presented the opportunity for all Western governments to take a large peace dividend from their defence budgets. Our country was no exception. The military hospitals were closed and the Army overall was to be reduced by a third, shrinking from four deployable fighting divisions to two. Under a process known as 'Options for Change', it was obvious that the pain of cuts would be felt right across the Army and that the number of infantry battalions was going to be cut. I was determined that 1st Battalion, the Green Howards would not be one of those lost. The trick was to make sure we were too strong to be cut.

The formal head of the regiment, the colonel of the regiment, was by then General Sir Peter Inge, Commander in Chief British Army of the Rhine and shortly to become Chief of the General Staff. However, we could not just leave him to fight our corner in high places. We needed to give him the strong card of a very well-recruited battalion to play when the time came. So for a while I focused the whole battalion on recruiting. We ran radio and newspaper advertisement campaigns linked to a hotline back to the battalion, a call on which triggered a visit from one of our own recruiting teams. Soldiers who recruited their mates were given extra leave and we formed a very strong link with Middlesbrough Football Club. Then as now, Middlesbrough FC was teetering between the first and second tiers of English football, so I think they were as glad of our support as we were of theirs. My aim was to raise our profile right in the heart of our traditional recruiting area where, in the recession of the early 1990s, unemployment was very high. Our regimental band and corps of drums appeared on the pitch at Ayresome Park regularly, two Green Howard corporals were in charge of the ball boys at every home match – which gave them the chance to patrol the touchline in distinctive regimental track suits – and there was the Boro' Bugler. One of our buglers, dressed in his scarlet full dress uniform, sounded the charge as the Middlesbrough team came onto the pitch and at key moments in the game before corners or free kicks. Some visiting managers apparently objected, so the Boro' Bugler was eventually retired, but not before he had become a local celebrity and the subject of much television and radio coverage. Tom, Bertie, Olly and I had many enjoyable afternoons in the Directors' Box watching Middlesbrough play at the old Ayresome Park ground. The net effect of all this recruiting effort was that by the time the decisions under 'Options for Change' were announced we were over a hundred soldiers over strength.

Quite properly, a battalion that was over strength was always going to be given more work to do. I was asked to supply thirty soldiers to reinforce the King's Regiment in Northern Ireland and was happy to do so, but was less happy when I was ordered to send another ninety to reinforce 3rd Battalion, the Royal Anglian Regiment back in Londonderry. Chancing my arm a little, I refused to send ninety soldiers but offered to send a fully formed rifle company instead, complete with its own officers, sergeants and corporals. There was some tooth-sucking at Headquarters Infantry before my offer was accepted.

This then meant that, under the byzantine budgeting arrangements of the MOD, the authorized establishment of 3 Royal Anglians was reduced by a company and the establishment of 1 Green Howards was increased by a company. I knew I would lose some Royal Anglian friends, but it was a case of survival of the fittest. As it happened we supplied three additional companies to the Royal Anglians for six months each over an eighteen-month period. Coincidentally, during this period the complete battalion also deployed for a reinforcement tour to Northern Ireland, thickening up the existing troops in South Armagh during a major border operation.

Despite all this operational activity and our manning strength, it was still not a foregone conclusion that we would survive the 'Options for Change' cull. To some people's eyes the organization of the infantry had been messy for some time, with an assortment of large regiments like the Royal Anglians and the Light Infantry, which boasted three battalions each, and small regiments like the Green Howards with only one. Would it not be better to even things out? So it was that in 1991 the prospect emerged of the Green Howards, the Duke of Wellington's and the Prince of Wales's Own, all of which recruited from Yorkshire, being amalgamated into a Yorkshire Regiment of two or three battalions. At the time there was little logic behind such a move, but it was a popular idea among those with tidy minds. So real was the threat that on the day of the 'Options' announcement I said to Pippa at breakfast that I thought that by the evening I might well be commanding 2nd Battalion, the Yorkshire Regiment. Local interest in our fate was considerable after our high-profile recruiting activities, and so I decided to allow the media into camp to hear the announcement as I made it to the battalion.

During the morning I received a letter from the Ministry of Defence to say that the battalion would be retained, subject to the final statement of the Secretary of State for Defence in the House of Commons that afternoon at 3 p.m. From my time in the Ministry, I knew nothing was finally decided until it was announced in Parliament; so I kept what I knew from the letter to myself until the afternoon. Then, with the battalion formed up in the gymnasium in a hollow square – soldiers on two sides, journalists on the third – I listened to the Secretary of State on the radio in my office. When I heard him list my battalion among those to be retained, I headed for the gym and gave the battalion the good news, to a tremendous cheer and a rather unmilitary shower of berets thrown into the air. Sadly, and inevitably, 3rd Royal Anglians, whom we were reinforcing in Londonderry, were to be disbanded, together with the other two infantry battalions with us in 24th Airmobile Brigade – the Glosters and the Duke of Edinburgh's – who were to be amalgamated with each other. We kept our celebrating quietly to ourselves. In the end, the logic of numbers had prevailed and Peter Inge never had to play his hand; indeed, I am told that when the infantry in Yorkshire was discussed by the Army Board, others pointed out the sense of leaving things as they were. This decision held until the middle of the next decade when the situation changed again, but more of that later.

Although the survival of the regiment was for many the highlight of 1991, training and operations remained the highest priority. I took the battalion to Kenya for six weeks at the beginning of the year. Nigel Hall, by then second-in-command, observed that the switch from the snow and ice of Catterick in January to over 40 degrees Celsius in northern Kenya within twenty-four hours was quite a test to the system. Our exercise culminated in a major live firing battalion attack at Archers Post near the Somali border. After that I judged we were ready for whatever might be required of us. In the early weeks of the first Gulf crisis in summer 1990, when a defensive operation to stop the Iraqis driving further beyond Kuwait looked a possibility, consideration had been given to deploying an airmobile battalion like mine with its large number of anti-tank weapons, but when the situation stabilized the requirement changed. The operation to throw the Iraqis out of Kuwait that was launched in early 1991 was always going to need armoured and mechanized units and not light airmobile battalions, so the first Gulf War concluded without us – to the relief of our families, but to the professional frustration of some. In the event, the only part of the battalion that took part in the first Gulf War was the band, as medical orderlies. And so, for the rest of us, it was Northern Ireland again – this time reinforcing the Coldstream Guards on the South Armagh border for a month.

The year, and my tour in command, finished in Germany on a major NATO exercise to validate both the airmobile concept and that of a fully multinational division of troops working together. This experimental multinational airmobile division was under the command of Major General Mike Rose, under whom the battalion had previously worked in Northern Ireland.

There was no doubt in our minds at the time that in the future the armies of NATO must learn to work together more closely and at low level, but that exercise in 1991 tested the aspiration severely. On one occasion I tried to call for fire from a Belgian artillery unit, but by the time the fire orders had been translated and retranslated the enemy had departed the target area minutes before. Airmobility brings a range of training issues, and multi-nationality does the same: trying to address both at the same time was a very brave call in my view. Nevertheless NATO persisted with its plans and a Multinational Division with major contingents from Belgium, Germany, the Netherlands and the United Kingdom came together for about ten years. British participation eventually became a casualty of the Strategic Defence Review of 1997–8.

In my last few months in command of the battalion, I knew that I owed it to Pippa and my earlier career decision to re-examine whether, after this tour, I would stay in the Army or go elsewhere. After all, ten years previously I had decided to stay 'for the foreseeable future', which I had envisaged to be about ten years. Those years were now up. I went down to London to see Ian Willis, a friend who was a recruitment specialist. We talked in his office for a couple of hours, but I left none the wiser about what I should or could do. I walked down Birdcage Walk and turned left into St James's Park, where I bumped into a friend from Norfolk, David Prior.

'What are you doing here?' he asked. 'I thought you were commanding your regiment up north.'

I explained what was on my mind.

His reply was decisive. 'The recession that is just kicking in will be so deep and difficult that if you have a job that you even half enjoy, just stick with it.'

I raised my eyes and said, 'Thank you.' I had had the answer I was looking for.

So, after I had handed the battalion over to Nick Houghton, and said goodbye to Lance Corporal Simpson, my driver, and Lance Corporal Crighton, my orderly (although both were to return to work for me later), I departed to the Staff College, on promotion to colonel, and it was back to Camberley for the family. Initially, I was to be a student on the Higher Command and Staff Course; thereafter I was to take over the running of the course for the next two years. These turned out to be excellent years for us all. I had been away from the family for long periods of my time in command; now the predictability of life at the Staff College gave us all some stability. Tom, Bertie and Olly were all away at school, but the army quarter we lived in within the grounds of Sandhurst was a brilliant place for their holidays, more than one window falling victim to a cricket ball. Richenda went to a local nursery, then junior school, and some weekends we all went to Norfolk. For me, these two years at the Staff College provided an invaluable chance to really think things through from a professional point of view.

As it happened, no sooner had I started the Higher Command and Staff Course as a student than I became aware of a developing view that current Army doctrine, set out only a few years before but in the context of the Cold War, should perhaps be revised now that the Cold War was definitely over. I became aware of a further view that the person who was thought to be best placed to do this was the colonel running the Higher Command and Staff Course – in other words, me.

I paid considerable attention to the course and began to think about the challenge of revising our doctrine. It seemed to me that the new thinking that had so invigorated the Army in the last few years of the Cold War was still valid. Previously we had seen things solely in the context of the Soviet threat; but the principles of applying our strength to an enemy's weakness and of outmanoeuvring him in time, space and thought all seemed to me to remain valid. Such thinking had underpinned Field Marshal Slim's campaign in Burma in the early 1940s and Field Marshal Templer's counter-insurgency campaign in Malaya in the 1950s. The challenge now was how to apply these enduring principles in the context of a so-called New World Order where peace seemed destined to prevail, Francis Fukuyama had pronounced the end of history and Sam Huntington had not yet begun to worry about a clash of civilizations. But for all my reservations about the project, my premonition turned out to be right: I was duly tasked to revise our doctrine.

The task was not a solitary one: I had recruited a very bright lieutenant colonel in the Royal Tank Regiment, Stephen White, to work with me. The first challenge was to determine exactly what it was we were trying to do. On the one hand, there were senior people in the Army saying that the world was now so radically different that we must come up with a completely new doctrine; on the other, there were those, with whom I instinctively sympathized, who said that we had just set out the enduring tenets of our doctrine in *The British Military Doctrine*, published in 1989, so the requirement now was to draw on those truths and apply them to the new strategic circumstances in which we now found ourselves. Eventually this latter view prevailed and I managed to get endorsement for a mandate to produce a document that provided the conceptual link between the existing British Military Doctrine, which set out the enduring British understanding of the nature of conflict, and the tactical level of thinking which would describe how the doctrine should be put into practice.

In essence this endorsement recognized the key point about military thinking – which I have frequently argued has equal applicability in other spheres: namely, that we need to divide our thinking into three levels, the strategic, the operational and the tactical. It is at the strategic level where the big thoughts are thought, where the broad ideas are conceived, and it is at the tactical level where the rubber hits the road and bullets fly. However, it is the level in between that is so critical, for this is where ideas are turned into practicalities, where a plan is produced that transforms concepts into a series of steps that take you from thought to action. This is the operational level of war. It is the level where the general really earns his pay, because it is here that a plan is formulated that turns grand ideas into activities that can actually be delivered and measured; into success achieved by forces on the ground. This is what Stephen White and I set out to do in what eventually came to be called, in the catchy way of the military, *Army Doctrine Publication, Volume One: Operations* or *ADP Operations*. This is neither the time nor the place to go into the detail of what we wrote, but suffice it to say that I think we provided a handrail that was useful to a generation of commanders trying to make sense of things prior to 9/11. To summarize briefly, restating in simple terms what had been set out in *The British Military Doctrine*, we said that commanders should endeavour to *find* their enemy, in order to understand his strengths, capabilities and intentions, then to *fix* that enemy, in order to deny him freedom of movement, and then to *strike* in order to defeat him – defeat meaning not necessarily destroying him, but denying him the chance to achieve his aims. All this assumes that warfare is essentially a clash of wills, that when you believe you have been beaten, then you probably have been.

But in the mid-1990s a practical challenge to this analysis was already looming: namely, how to deal with the situation that was developing rapidly in the Balkans. Here was a war in which we were not participants, but in which we were becoming increasingly engaged as referees, as peacekeepers where there was no peace to keep. In the arresting image of my friend Charles Dobbie, who wrote the Army's attempt to produce a companion doctrine called 'Wider Peacekeeping', it is like a game in which the referee has not only to try to keep the two sides playing according to the rules, but also to do so when the spectators get up out of the stands and come down on to the pitch and join in. I think we now recognize that the Balkans in the 1990s constituted a peculiar set of circumstances that needed a bespoke rather than a generic response from us. Certainly subsequent conflicts in Iraq and Afghanistan, though very difficult, have exhibited more of the classic characteristics of first conventional war-fighting and then counter-insurgency. But the underlying doctrinal point is that whatever the specific nature of the problem, the enduring requirement is to identify the problem, set objectives to be achieved and then devise a campaign plan from which meaningful tactical activity can flow. All this is far better than the aimless 'muddling through' of my early Belfast days. Sadly, such 'muddling through' was again to characterize the early post-intervention years in Iraq from 2003; and although our campaign in Afghanistan was better planned, it had an atmosphere of 'muddling through' because it was under-resourced. I will return to those discussions in later chapters.

While all this theoretical activity was going on at the Staff College, the news media were awash with horrifying stories of the war in the Balkans. The cohesion that Tito had brought to the disparate parts of what had become the successful state of Yugoslavia had fractured after his death in 1980. A decade later, in the aftermath of the end of the Cold War, Serb and Croat ethnic and national agendas transcended Tito's vision of a multi-ethnic Yugoslavia, and the state disintegrated into civil war. The fighting appeared confusing, the situation out of control; at the centre of the storm was Bosnia Herzegovina, whose ethnic fault-lines had first been exposed in late 1991. International attempts to mediate between the warring parties since the first deployment of Lieutenant Colonel Bob Stewart's 1st Battalion, the Cheshire Regiment in September 1992 appeared half-hearted and weak-willed. It was clear that the world struggled to comprehend what was happening inside the former Yugoslavia as the old political structures died and ancient hatreds reasserted themselves, let alone what to do about it. There was certainly no appetite in Washington, London or Paris, despite loud calls from some quarters, for the United Nations to force an end to the fighting, in particular by authorizing NATO to use air power to break the Bosnian Serb siege of Sarajevo. The images on the television screen were a stark contrast to the beautiful, leafy surroundings of the Army's Staff College on the vast Sandhurst estate.

I was part way through running the Higher Command and Staff Course for the second time when one morning in early January 1994 the telephone rang. On the other end came a voice I knew well. Major General Michael Rose had left Camberley, where he had been an incisive and energetic Commandant of the Staff College, the previous April. He was now a lieutenant general and Deputy Joint Commander of the UK contribution to the UN mission in the former Yugoslavia, based at Wilton, near Salisbury. He came straight to the point.

'Richard, I am off to Sarajevo as the next commander of the UN force in Bosnia Herzegovina. I am less than happy that we understand exactly what we are trying to achieve, or how we are to get there. What I need is a campaign plan. You teach campaign planning at the Staff College; can you draft one for me for Bosnia?'

I agreed immediately. Here was a rare opportunity to translate theory into practice, and, on behalf of the Staff College, I leaped at the chance. General Mike was just about to fly to New York to meet the UN team. When he returned two days later, flying back into Heathrow on Concorde, he slipped down to Camberley to brief me. He had, in the meantime, assembled his thoughts, and over breakfast we discussed the shape of the plan. He gave me

172

his direction and then left to make his final preparations for his departure for Sarajevo. I got down to work, together with a small group of colleagues. The days that followed were a flurry of activity. We talked to the Foreign Office, the Ministry of Defence and the Joint Headquarters at Wilton, which oversaw the British military commitment to the former Yugoslavia, known as Operation Grapple, as we crafted a plan that conformed to the Army's developing doctrine with respect to campaigning, war-fighting and peacekeeping.

Two weeks later, the ink still drying on a draft plan safely tucked in my briefcase, I made the stomach-churning descent into the chaos of Sarajevo airport in the back of a C-130 Hercules aircraft stacked to the brim with food parcels. It was impossible to ignore the sights and sounds of human tragedy gripping the city as I stepped out onto the tarmac for the first time, a borrowed blue-covered helmet on my head, my breath snatched away by a bitter wind sweeping off the snow-covered mountains. The shattered, bomb-scarred buildings, the dull thump of shell-fire and the crackle of small-arms fire in the distance made an immediate impression, as did the few members I could see of the scurrying, fearful population. During daylight hours the only people to come out of their cellars were the desperate, scavenging for food and firewood. A dull grey haze of woodsmoke lay motionless over the shattered city. The Bosnian Serb siege was at its height and civilian morale, understandably, was low. I was not to know that I was to spend a significant part of my next few years in this extraordinary country.

General Mike was his usual forthright self, and we got down to business. The campaign plan we had drafted to flesh out his overall intent sought as an end-state 'peace, security and creating the conditions for economic renewal for all the peoples of Bosnia Herzegovina'. He saw what we called 'the centre of gravity' as the will of the people either to sue for peace or to want to continue to fight. So it was all about the attitudes of the people. Clarity of thought about the origins and context of the fighting was vitally important, as without it we could not find our way to a clear understanding of how this end-state could be achieved. The principal dilemma facing the UN lay in managing the tension between the belligerents' determination to fight, where motives and emotions were based deeply on issues of history, sovereignty and religion, and the UN's concerns to stabilize international relations, provide humanitarian welfare and salve its collective conscience, while being unable (because the UN itself was not a combatant) to resolve anything by force. The only way to stop the fighting was to persuade people, on all sides, to stop fighting of their own volition. It was a hugely demanding task, and the world's media was full of naysayers who suggested that it was impossible, and that only the use of force itself could resolve the problem. They may have had a point; but at the time this wasn't the UN's mandate. We had to get down to the task of containing the conflict within Bosnia Herzegovina, ameliorating the desperate humanitarian consequences of the conflict, attempting to create by our own diplomatic initiatives the conditions for a lasting peace agreement, and assisting the diverse people of the country to rebuild their shattered lives and economy.

It was a tall order, but General Mike struck me as the ideal man to attempt to confront the intractable. We suggested a number of options to him, only one of which was really desirable. The first was to recommend 'Withdrawal', which in the face of the international outrage over the continuing siege of Sarajevo was inconceivable. The second was to maintain the 'Status Quo' in the hope that exhaustion would force an end to the war in its own time and of its own accord. We had to regard the first option as a potential contingency, while the second option was clearly only a recipe for further failure as the present UN operation was merely trying to address the symptoms of the conflict, rather than addressing its causes. The third option, 'Peace Enforcement', while theoretically attractive, had already been ruled out by the UN mandate, and in any case no country had the political will to commit its own troops to the slaughter to enforce an artificial peace. In the circumstances the most appropriate course was to adopt our fourth, essentially pragmatic, option, which we described as 'Towards Peace'. This option entailed the channelling of all activities and energies to improving the efficiency of the humanitarian operation while at the same time actively seeking or even compelling the cooperation of the belligerent parties. It was essentially a bottom-up approach, focused on the wish of the people themselves for peace, and it was behind this unequivocal aim that General Rose threw the entirety of his enormous physical and intellectual energies. As I sat talking with him over the table in his cramped office in Sarajevo's Residency building I was struck by the capability of this remarkable man and was reassured by the certainty that the show was in good hands. His predecessor as head of the UN force, Lieutenant General Francis Briquemont of Belgium, had resigned suddenly at the end of the previous year, frustrated at the conflicting and often irreconcilable demands placed on his mission. Mike Rose, late of the Coldstream Guards and 22 SAS, had stepped immediately into the breach. I was to be proved right in my assessment of him, for it was largely by his single-minded pursuit of peace that all parties entwined in the Balkan imbroglio began the long and difficult process by which, at Dayton at the end of the following year, a viable peace was secured. However, his bottom-up peace process had to be matched by a top-down realization from the leaderships of the respective warring factions that they had achieved all they could from violence, and this took another year to come about: it was not until mid-1995 that the Serbs, in particular, were exhausted, and a peace agreement on almost any terms began to look attractive.

But all this fell away from me as I left the ravages of war behind, the C-130 climbing steeply over the snow-washed mountains that thrust high into the clouds at the end of the long valley in which Sarajevo nestles, and returned for a time to the intellectual challenges posed by my charges at Camberley. I now knew that the wars in the Balkans strained our understanding of the application of force. We were used to preparing for a serious conflict with a major power, and we had a good second-string understanding of both classic peacekeeping and counter-insurgency. The Balkans were something else: the many ethnic tensions released by the fall of Tito spawned an array of vicious nationalisms, of which we had very little understanding to begin with. We had to work out how to deliver aid to starving people within the context of their civil war. The character and nature of future conflict were undeniably shifting again; the question was whether Bosnia was a template for the future or an anachronism to be managed away. In the event, I feel, it had elements of both. The complexity of Bosnia was a clear signpost to the general character of future conflict, but the particular circumstances of the Balkans cautioned us against trying to develop a generic tactical doctrine too closely influenced by the particular characteristics of the Balkans. 'Wider Peacekeeping' tried to do this, and had a very short shelf-life. The trick in trying to shape future doctrine, training and equipment requirements is to distil from the confusion of current events those experiences and lessons that have generic application and apply them to a considered analysis of what the future might require. The alternative is to slip back into the comfortable, but dangerous, territory of preparing superbly for the last war, which will inevitably be the wrong war. However, I had not finished with the Balkans; indeed, as an Army, our involvement there was to last in some shape or form until 2009.

5

To End a War

What I didn't know when making my first, fleeting visit to Sarajevo in February 1994 was that I would become much more intimately involved in the Balkans the following year. With two extremely professionally satisfying years at Camberley drawing to a close I received the news of my appointment, on promotion to brigadier, to command one of the British Army's three remaining armoured brigades. The 4th Armoured Brigade, known as the 'Black Rats' after its brigade emblem of a black Jerboa rat, which dated back to the battlefields of North Africa in the Second World War, was based in the fascinating town of Osnabrück, nestling gracefully in a bowl on the northern side of the Teutoburger Wald. At the time the British garrison in Osnabrück was the largest outside Aldershot, and the commander of the brigade had responsibility for managing not only the troops in Osnabrück but also those in Münster, 30 miles to the south-west. The 4th Armoured

Brigade was a core element of the newly constructed 1st (UK) Armoured Division, itself a product of the 1990 'Options for Change' Defence Review, designed to secure a peace dividend from the end of the Cold War.

I was elated. Command is a great privilege and, I always thought, quite the best thing about serving in the Army. The division, comprising three armoured brigades – 4th, 7th and 20th – was designed to be able to fit into a multinational NATO or coalition corps, building on our experience of doing precisely this in the first Gulf War. Its sister formation was the 3rd (UK) Division, a mechanized division based in the United Kingdom with its headquarters at Bulford on the edge of Salisbury Plain. Each armoured brigade in Germany was described as 'square', in that it had four major units: two infantry battalions equipped with Warrior fighting vehicles and two armoured regiments equipped with the superb Challenger 2 tank. Ironically, even though these three brigades in Germany were among the most powerful that the British Army had ever organized on a permanent basis, command of one felt somewhat unreal in the post-Cold War environment, the threat from the Soviet Union and the Warsaw Pact having evaporated.

But the real world has its own way of focusing the military mind. Bosnia would not go away. Once the United Nations, and later the United Kingdom, had become involved in the Bosnian imbroglio there appeared no quick or easy exit for the British Army. As a country we had, somewhat belatedly, set our hand to the plough, and were committed to making the best of the UNPROFOR mission, however reluctant our political masters were at the time (though this was to change after

1997) to expend scarce blood and treasure on foreign military adventures. UNPROFOR, the United Nations Protection Force, had a difficult but narrow mission to alleviate the humanitarian effects of the Balkan war, but no mandate to address or get involved in the causes or the course of that war. Common decency, intensified by media pressure, had demanded that 'something be done' to end this brutal conflict in Europe in the last decade of the twentieth century, so it was right that we saw the commitment through and that we did so to the best of our ability, despite the obstacles that littered the way and the inevitable individual tragedies that always accompany such tasks. Those of us who take the Queen's Shilling know that soldiering is an inherently risky business, and the use of force is never casualty-free. I also knew that the Army would do the best it could, largely because of the dogged determination of the British soldier to make the best of every situation, no matter how grim.

It came, therefore, as little surprise to learn in late 1994 that my brigade headquarters was ordered to prepare to deploy again on Operation 'Grapple', the name we gave to Balkan deployments, in October 1995, assuming that the war would still be going on then and that we would still be required. If so, it would be just over three years since Bob Stewart's Cheshires had first deployed to the Lasva Valley to witness the fratricidal horror of the civil war between the Bosnian Muslims and the Bosnian Croats in 1992, a bitter bloodletting that ended with the Washington Agreement in March 1994. I was to deploy only with my headquarters. I would leave all the units of my own brigade behind in Germany and, once in Bosnia, take under command units deployed from right across the Army, effectively forming a 'second' 4th Armoured Brigade. As it turned out this was a rather odd experience: six units in Bosnia considered themselves to be part of 4th Armoured Brigade, while in Germany another six units knew they were part of 4th Armoured Brigade. I commanded both 'brigades' and for six months flip-flopped between the two, though spending the vast majority of my time in Bosnia.

Our training in Germany as a headquarters had not been without incident: during our final exercise one of my key staff officers had taken his own life. I was particularly glad that Pippa was on hand to deal with the consequences of this tragic event. Soon afterwards, on 26 October 1995, I arrived to take command of UNPROFOR's Sector South West, shaking Andrew Pringle's hand at Split airport as he caught the plane home at the end of his tour before making my way by road up into central Bosnia to the Sector HQ at Gornji Vakuf. I also 'inherited' Andrew's interpreter, Sanja, who proved invaluable over the next six months, as she had to many of my predecessors. Early on in the tour I asked Sanja how she thought of her own nationality in the complex environment of Bosnia. 'Yugoslav,' she replied straight away. 'My father is a Serb, my mother a Croat and I grew up in the Muslim part of Sarajevo.' I reflected on that answer often during the next few weeks, concluding that perhaps if Tito's Yugoslavia had lasted another generation or two then, just possibly, the ethnic and religious fractures that occurred there in the 1990s might never have happened. Maybe Yugoslavia could have held together as a state; but it had not, and now the country was mired in a bloody, vicious civil war in which we were all caught up.

The 5 October ceasefire brokered by Lieutenant General Sir Rupert Smith, Michael Rose's successor as commander of the UNPROFOR mission, had brought to an end an eventful summer in which many of the Bosnian Serb Army (VRS) gains of the previous two years had been dramatically swept aside. The predominantly Muslim Army of Bosnia Herzegovina (the ARBiH, which I will refer to as the Bosniac army), together with the Croats of the HV (Croatian Regular Army) and HVO (Bosnian Croat Army), who after their violent differences earlier in the war had joined together in the Croat–Bosnian 'Federation of Bosnia Herzegovina', had made substantial territorial gains in September at the expense of the Serbs, who had been punished for non-compliance with UN demands by targeted NATO air strikes and powerful artillery bombardments. These Federation operations had been conducted with careful precision, and had been so overwhelmingly successful that I suspected, from my experience of teaching at Camberley, that professionals – rather than the brave but (I suspected) moderately trained Croat and Bosnian 'armies' – had been at work. Were the NATO bombing and artillery strikes around Sarajevo, Banja Luka and Doboj somehow part of the same, well-orchestrated plan? Had the UN and even NATO been manipulated? If so, by whom? I could not help feeling that the Pentagon probably had the answer. Over the six months I was in Bosnia I spent quite some time talking to the commanders on all three sides, and these conversations confirmed me in my view that expert campaign planning had been brought in to align the situation on the ground with the outcome that international negotiators felt they could deliver.

In any case and by whatever means, the strategic Bosnian landscape had changed dramatically. For the first time in the war the Bosniac and Croat forces were holding the upper hand, boasting possession of about 50 per cent of the country, having reduced the Bosnian Serb proportion by about a third from its original 75 per cent. The parties were separated by a so-called Confrontation Line and, unsurprisingly, the Federation of Bosniacs and Croats had their tails up. It was in this situation, with the country exhausted by four long years of bitter war and the Bosnian Serbs forced to heed the international community by dint of artillery and air strikes in the late summer, that the warring parties agreed to sit around the table at Dayton, Ohio, in an attempt to negotiate a lasting peace.

The peace talks began in Dayton on 1 November 1995. Most observers realized that it was probably the last and best hope for peace in the country. The Americans by now were energetically committed to the process. It was not unreasonably cynical of me to think at the time that Bill Clinton wanted a significant foreign affairs success in his pre-election year, but whatever the motivation I was happy with the outcome: it was undoubtedly US pressure, clout and commitment that were to prove decisive in ending Europe's first war since 1945. The prospect of peace made an immediate impact on the UNPROFOR mission, breeding a new mood of positivism about what strong leadership, together with the threat and judicious use of military force, could achieve. The well-intentioned fence-sitting of the past had made a mockery of the UN, at least in the minds of many of those who had to enforce its decisions on the ground, which in the nervous, hand-wringing, non-interventionist Europe of the time had meant merely providing humanitarian aid. If a peace were agreed, NATO's job would be not merely to monitor a ceasefire – UNPROFOR had demonstrated this to be an imperfect approach – but rather to enforce compliance with the Dayton agreement. It was not before time, I thought. We were determined to enforce the deal with all the authority at our disposal, building on the powerful demonstrations of NATO military strength that had been made against the recalcitrant Bosnian Serbs during the summer. Closing the gate after the horse had bolted it may well have been, but we had learned a considerable amount about peacemaking and peace enforcement by this stage, were sick of hearing the repeated protestations of those prepared to slaughter innocents in the name of their particular cause or on behalf of their co-religionists or in pursuit of some specific ethnic agenda, and believed that we now had the right mandate to bring this sorry, senseless and bloody chapter in Europe's modern history to a decisive end.

My UNPROFOR responsibilities in Sector South West stretched from Tomislavgrad in the far south (bordering Croatia) to Zepče (on the front line with territory held by the Bosnian Serbs) in the far north: a distance, as the crow flies, of some 112 kilometres. The sector included a diverse but impressive international contingent. In addition to my single British infantry battalion (1st Battalion, the Royal Regiment of Fusiliers,

BOSNIA AND HERZEGOVINA 1995–1996

Vojvodina

CROATIA

Coralici
Bihac
Prijedor
Ljubija
Bosanska
Gradiška
Brčko
Sanski
Most
Banja Luka
Doboj
Republika Srpska
Kulen
Vakuf
Klujč
Krupa
Kotor Varoš
Maglaj
Tuzla
Bosanski
Petrovac
'The
Anvil'
Mrkonjić Grad
Skender Vakuf
Zepče
SERBIA
Majdan
Jajce
Zenica
Šipovo
Bugojno
Vitez
Glamoč
Srebrenica
BOSNIA AND HERZEGOVINA
Kupres
Gornji
Vakuf
SARAJEVO
*Federation of Bosnia
and Herzegovina*
Mt Igman
Pale
Livno
Gorazde
Split
Tomislavgrad
Jablanica
Mostar
*Republika
Srpska*
Ploče
MONTENEGRO
Dubrovnik
A d r i a t i c

S e a

Federation of Bosnia
and Herzegovina

Republika Srpska

- - - - - Inter-entity boundary line

0   100

kilometres

commanded by Lieutenant Colonel Trevor Minter) equipped with the ageing Cold War Saxon 'battle taxi', I had a reinforced New Zealand infantry company at Santici near Vitez, a Malaysian battalion at Jablanica, a Spanish battalion at Medugorje, 25 kilometres south of Mostar, and a Turkish battalion in the far north at Zenica. I was also Commander British Forces (COMBRITFOR), which gave me oversight responsibilities for British units in other sectors. In particular this included 2nd Battalion, the Light Infantry, commanded by Lieutenant Colonel Ben Barry and equipped with the very capable Warrior infantry fighting vehicle. Initially, they were detached from me as part of the international reserve force. However, by the time of my arrival things were changing, and the sector's territorial responsibilities had been grossly enlarged by the effect of the Federation's summer offensives. I now found myself responsible for an area twice the size it had been before, including territory that stretched high into the north-western area of Bihac, an area of some 250,000 square miles that had been a UN enclave or 'Safe Area' for much of the war. Unfortunately, the prospect of peace was seen by the exhausted UN as an opportunity to reduce its costs, and wholesale and sometimes unilateral reductions in troop levels were being made across the country. Several foreign battalions, such as the Bangladeshi battalion in Bihac, were being sent home and not replaced, and others, including the Malaysians and Spaniards, were being reduced.

I was immediately concerned about how I would manage to maintain control in Bihac after the Bangladeshis had left. Within days of arriving, accompanied by Major James Everard, my Military Assistant, and a small party which included my interpreter Sanja and a group of highly trained Joint Commission Observers, I decided to visit the Bangladeshi battalion to map out the future. We planned to fly, but in the Balkans the winter comes quickly, and atrocious weather grounded the helicopters. By the end of the week, only my second in the country, Gornji Vakuf was blanketed in a foot of snow. Instead, I drove by Land Rover through drifting snow on rutted roads across what had recently been Serb-held territory to the town of Mrkonjić Grad. There I rendezvoused with a Royal Navy Sea King helicopter, which had flown up from Split and had thus been able to skirt around the worst of the weather. The drive showed starkly the awful intensity of the recent fighting and the destructiveness of modern war. Whole hamlets lay in ruins. We drove in thoughtful silence through village after village, all of which were deserted and partially destroyed by the fighting. The evidence of battle was everywhere: empty ammunition boxes, wrecked vehicles and ruined homes. Later, looking down from the Sea King as we clattered our way on the 45-minute flight to Bihac, across territory recently 'liberated' from the Serbs, we saw the same sad story. It would take a very long time for the physical scars of the war to be removed. The less tangible ones, I considered, would take a little longer.

I was immediately impressed with the smart Bangladeshi battalion I met in Bihac. They had stood firm against every sort of provocation in the fourteen long months when the pocket had been surrounded on all sides by the Bosnian Serbs, and deserved warm congratulations for all they had achieved. They were a fine, disciplined and well-led body – in some ways more British in their turnout, uniforms and traditions than the modern British Army! But now they were due to return home within days, and it was not clear how I would monitor their part of the Confrontation Line without them. There were few enough troops to do this across the entirety of Bosnia anyway, and with national UNPROFOR contingents being wound down there seemed no option but for me to do the job from within my own sector resources. So, sitting round a table in the Bangladeshis' immaculate though spartan camp, we hammered out a plan. Lieutenant Colonel Trevor Minter had already agreed to my suggestion to get a small parcel of troops into Bihac to replace the Bangladeshis as a stopgap, before a slightly larger force could be deployed. I promised that the Fusiliers would arrive before the end of the week.

We then climbed back into the Sea King for the return flight. Quickly gaining height, we turned due south for the journey back to Gornji Vakuf. It was here, at 5,000 feet, that I was unexpectedly introduced to what I subsequently learned was one of the routine hazards of military flying in Bosnia Herzegovina. At cruising altitude to the west of Banja Luka we were suddenly 'locked on' by the search and attack radar of a Soviet-era surface-to-air missile belonging to the Serbs, the sudden noise caused by the automatic firing of defensive chaff violently shaking not only the helicopter, but all of us aboard. We took aggressive, evasive action, the helicopter dropping like a stone from 5,000 feet to tree-top level, breaking the lock-on and staying at low level until we were well clear of the danger. The sooner I got a liaison officer over the Confrontation Line to the Serb side to stop this provocative nonsense, I thought, the better. There was no need for such an uncomfortable and, if I am honest, somewhat unnerving, flight. As I said to the Royal Navy pilot, if I had wanted to be shot down in an aeroplane I would have joined the RAF.

As a postscript to the Bangladeshi deployment, on the battalion's last day in Bosnia, when most of their troops were waiting for their flight home from the Croat capital, Zagreb, about two hundred armed men attacked their former camp just outside Bihac. The Bangladeshi camp guard was overwhelmed; nine armoured vehicles, many valuable stores and supplies of fuel were taken before the hapless Bangladeshis were allowed to join their comrades in Zagreb for the journey home. I was told about this at once and flew straight up to Bihac to confront General Atif Dudakovic, the local Bosniac commander. He denied any knowledge of the attack, claiming it was carried out by renegades improperly wearing Bosnian Army uniform. I would have none of it, telling him that it was a perfectly executed military operation that he had planned and overseen. He was previously on record as saying: 'I will let the Bangladeshis go home, but without their equipment!' We shouted at each other, chin to chin, for about twenty minutes before I stormed off. The vehicles and stores were never returned. Five years later, when Dudakovic was Federation Army Commander and I was Deputy NATO Commander, we met again, and my first question to him was: 'Where are my vehicles that you stole?' He did not have a convincing answer.

Back in late 1995, while I was rushing around taking

stock of my vast area of responsibility, planning was also beginning for the transition from UNPROFOR to NATO's IFOR (Implementation Force) in the expectation that the Dayton talks would produce a positive outcome. The idea was that within four days of the peace plan being signed the UN would withdraw and NATO would take over. Lieutenant General Sir Michael Walker, Commander of the Allied Rapid Reaction Corps (COMARRC), would deploy to Sarajevo, a US division would take responsibility for the north-east of the country, the French would take control of the centre and the British would retain control of the south-west and west. I had little sight of the higher-level planning at this stage, being left to get on with the immediate challenges of monitoring the ceasefire on the ground. I was grateful enough for this. However, it soon became clear that the UK's Bulford-based 3rd Division, commanded by Major General Mike Jackson, would be in the lead, with my brigade as the sole British combat element. I very shortly afterwards received a call from Mike telling me that I might also get a Dutch battlegroup under command.

Meanwhile I completed a rapid transit of my new responsibilities, most of it by helicopter because of the distances involved. I had quickly come to the conclusion that to maintain a close knowledge of what was happening across this huge area and to exercise effectively the personal leadership required to influence events, I needed to travel, and to do so extensively, which again meant by helicopter. Communications were poor, and dialogue with members of the various parties in any case needed to be achieved face-to-face, and often repeatedly, to have any real value. Trust is a very personal dynamic. In a matter of days I quickly covered most of the sector, meeting Federation, Bosniac, Bosnian Croat and Bosnian Serb military commanders and politicians. By now snow lay thick on the ground across the entire region. On Mount Igman, overlooking Sarajevo, where the British armoured infantry of 2nd Light Infantry and our artillery and engineers played a key role in the Multinational Brigade, I was struck by the grins and banter of the British infantrymen, sappers and gunners living in primitive trenches and dugouts reminiscent of the First World War. I observed that there is no limit to the inventiveness of the British soldier, or his humour in the most adverse of circumstances. The soldiers had created very comfortable living conditions for themselves among the snow and the mud, using anything they could lay their hands on and a little imagination.

Bosnia was very much a media war, with the violence projected into countless sitting rooms around the globe almost as soon as it happened on the ground. Within days of my arrival, Martin Bell of the BBC made himself known to me, and thereafter was often thrusting – politely – his microphone under my nose. I found him refreshingly frank and straightforward. He was a man entirely without flannel, genuinely 'straight' and concerned that the international community use the vast resources at its fingertips to effect positive change on the ground. He had seen too little of this so far in the war, fine words all too often masking a pragmatic cynicism about what could – or should – be done. I noticed, however, that several interviews never got an airing: there seemed to be a degree of 'combat fatigue' with the subject of Bosnia among the British media after the summer's frenetic activity, coming on top of three previous years of war. I was to discover that the necessary though unspectacular detail of our mission was far less important to the editors back home than the prospect of some bloodshed. That always got people excited. Without an air strike or two, or a Serb tank to be brewed up, there was no news to report. If we, the military, are to succeed in these difficult missions, the media have got to be prepared to carry some 'boring' stories to record the progress that we are making. At the end of the day, our purpose is to bring peace and a better life for people less fortunate than ourselves, and the media have a role to play in this, whether editors or proprietors like it or not.

More locally, I realized that one of my chief tasks was to get to know the Federation members of the Joint Commission Policy Committee (JCPC), the bipartite process designed to manage the peace between Croats and Muslims following their earlier fratricidal war. I soon came to the conclusion, however, that a wider peace treaty would quickly make the JCPC redundant, and a more important task was to create effective relationships with all the key decision-makers and influential figures in all three of the factions. I began to do so, but meanwhile I also had to run the process set up to manage the three-week-old ceasefire between the Federation and the Bosnian Serbs. Both tasks necessitated a frenetic programme of visits during my first few weeks as I drove and flew over, it seemed, every inch of the sector.

At Zenica I met Monique Toufflé, the extraordinary Frenchwoman who was head of the UNHCR organization in my sector. Her major problem, she told me, was

As CO 1 Green Howards, informing the battalion (and the local media) in July 1991 that we were to be neither amalgamated nor disbanded under the 'Options for Change' programme at the end of the Cold War.

Left: A rather grubby CO sitting on top of his trench during one of the major airmobile exercises in Germany in September 1991.

Below: Holding a planning conference with my key staff in Headquarters 4th Armoured Brigade on exercise in May 1994. I am not quite sure someone got the point!

Left: On arrival in Bosnia in October 1995 I visited all my units in Sector South West of UNPROFOR. Kiwi Company of the New Zealand contingent greeted me with a traditional haka. The man with the big stick above his head was the company sergeant major!

Above: I also visited all the opposing military commanders, on this occasion calling on General Atif Dudakovic, the commander of the Bosniac 5th Corps in Bihac.

Right: Also under my command were a Spanish battalion who had struggled manfully to make sense of the fighting between Bosniacs, Croats and Serbs around the city of Mostar from 1992 to 1995.

Below left: Sanja Stanojevic had acted as the commander's interpreter for four British brigadiers. Here she assists me at a press conference in Split as we explain the plans for the implementation of the Dayton peace agreement.

Below right: Reassuring the local population that NATO would bring an effective and lasting peace to Bosnia was a major task. Here I am doing a phone-in on Radio Big in Banja Luka.

Left: Field Marshal Sir Peter Inge, the then Chief of the Defence Staff and Colonel of the Green Howards, visits my headquarters in Šipovo, Bosnia, in February 1996.

Right: I try unsuccessfully to persuade the Serb civilian inhabitants of Mrkonjić Grad not all to return to their devastated town immediately after the Croats handed it back under the terms of the peace agreement.

Below: Discussing with General Talic, Commander 1st Krajina Corps of the Bosnian Serb Army, the plan for the re-entry of Bosnian Serb forces into the 'Anvil' in April 1996. Captain Popovitch is translating.

Left: I cannot resist trying to operate a Royal Engineers' JCB digging a relief road around Šipovo.

Below: Richenda putting up a 'Welcome Home Daddy' banner on the front door of Talavera House, Osnabrück, in May 1996 to mark my return from Bosnia. Thank you, Chenny!

Below: The IRA mortars my brigade headquarters in Osnabrück in June 1996. Ironically, the only damage was to the Roman Catholic chapel in camp.

Bottom: I say farewell to the King's Royal Hussars in Münster at the end of my time commanding 4th Armoured Brigade by driving one of their Challenger tanks over a parked car. I am still waiting for the bill!

Above: As Commander British Forces, and as Colonel of the Green Howards, I wish Major Simon Fovargue all the very best as he prepares to lead A Company, 1 Green Howards into Kosovo as part of the Irish Guards battlegroup in June 1999.

Left: At a planning conference in Headquarters 3rd (UK) Division before the NATO operation in Kosovo, I am not at all convinced, once again, that someone has got the point.

Below: Lieutenant General Sir Mike Jackson, the commander of the NATO KFOR, asked me to get the British media off his back. Here I give an interview to Kate Adie in Pristina.

Above: On the day of entry into Kosovo, I brief the MOD's morning conference from Pristina, having flown over, and a bit beyond, the front line of NATO forces as they advance into Kosovo.

Above: The massacre of nearly eight thousand Muslim men and boys by the Bosnian Serb Army in and around Srebrenica in July 1995 resulted in General Radovan Krstic, Commander of the Bosnian Serb Drina Corps, standing trial at the International Criminal Tribunal for the Former Yugoslavia in The Hague. Here I give evidence as an expert witness.

Above: In 2000 I find myself back in Bosnia as Deputy Commander (Operations) of the NATO Stabilization Force, SFOR. Here I fail to keep the attention of the Secretary of State for Defence, Geoff Hoon, on a visit to Headquarters SFOR in Sarajevo.

Below: The 'Mostar Bank Job'. This painting shows soldiers raiding the head office of the Herzcegovacka Banka in Mostar. This was a night not to miss!

Left: My family – as seen through the eyes of the six-year-old Richenda – including Tess, the Labrador; Muffin, the King Charles spaniel; and Jimmy, the goldfish!

Right: Pippa, the boys and I visit Ayresome Park in November 1989 to watch Middlesbrough play Wimbledon at the start of our recruiting campaign. Eighteen months later the battalion was a hundred soldiers over strength.

Below: Family holidays in Cornwall have been a traditional feature in the annual calendar. We squeezed in a week in July 1995 just before I went to Bosnia.

the threat posed by the Muslim *mujahedin*, foreign Islamist fighters who had flocked to Bosnia to fight on the side of their co-religionists against the Serbs. A by-product of the CIA-backed campaign to rid Afghanistan of the Soviets in the 1980s, on the whole they were a dangerous and ill-disciplined lot, answerable only to themselves. Of course, I did not know then that we were to meet them again in the guise of the Taliban on their home soil of Afghanistan from 2001. But in 1995, even the Muslim soldiers of the Bosniac army seemed fearful of them. At the time, my understanding of the difference between 'Islamic' and 'Islamist' was very immature. Only later did I appreciate the negative and distorting slant that the Islamists put on one of the world's great religions for their own political ends. At the time in Bosnia, the *mujahedin* seemed to all of us to be just one more, if a rather nasty, dimension to the kaleidoscope of warring parties in the country.

With heavy snowfalls severely restricting air travel, I drove to Medjugorje, south of Mostar, to meet Slobodan Bosic, the Bosnian Croat minister for relations with UNPROFOR. The scenery, with the famous Neretva River running between deep granite gorges, was stunning. After a useful if rather formal meeting lasting little more than an hour we adjourned for another Balkan speciality, a very long lunch, which lasted four times as long as the original meeting. Perhaps the two were, I mused, actually part of the same continuum. I also visited the Multinational Brigade in the divided city of Mostar, which the Bosnian Serb Army had besieged in 1992, and which subsequently had experienced Muslim/Croat bloodletting. I had expected to pick up a useful feel for progress within the Federation, but to my mind the future looked disappointingly bleak: there appeared too much self-interest on both sides and too little progress on nation-building. I observed to my diary that night, perhaps a little obviously, that without a real Federation in which both Croats and Muslims pulled together, Bosnia Herzegovina had no future. I would have to deal with this issue again in 2001, but that's a later story.

My thoughts on how best to carry out the mission given to me by Lieutenant General Rupert Smith had been developing during these first days in theatre. At a snow-delayed meeting at Gornji Vakuf on 6 November I was able to lay out my plan to my unit commanders. Looking around the table, I was forcefully struck by the truly multinational nature of the UN mission. They were from several different nations: Britain, Canada, Turkey, Spain, Malaysia, Ghana, Afghanistan, Russia and New Zealand. The mission I had been given was to facilitate the completion of the Federation structure that had been in the making for the previous eighteen months, enhance the delivery of humanitarian aid and develop a wider peace between the Federation and the Bosnian Serbs. Using as my template the doctrine I had set out in *ADP Operations*, I defined my intent to focus on three complementary lines of activity. Deep (or long-term) activities focused specifically on those efforts directed at the centre of gravity – the will of the people to make peace or to continue to fight – such as public information, civil affairs tasks aimed specifically at changing attitudes, increasing understanding and creating the conditions for economic recovery. Close (or short-term) activities focused primarily on making the current ceasefire, and any future peace plan, work, through such things as monitoring the ceasefire line, bringing the warring factions together and assisting the process of building the Federation. Finally, rear activities would protect our own people. Specifically, these included completing preparations for winter operations, with work on route maintenance and constant attention to the twin hazards of mines and bad weather conditions. The main effort for the time being was on close activities, for if the ceasefire broke down all the rest would be pretty meaningless.

By this stage the peace talks in Dayton had been under way for a week, but we had no real feel for the progress, if any, that was being made. Despite this, planning for the arrival of IFOR by NATO's Allied Rapid Reaction Force (ARRC) staff was gaining considerable momentum. I had already developed strong views about the utility of force in the newly emerging situation in Bosnia Herzegovina, informed perhaps by my involvement in the campaign planning process for Mike Rose the previous year. I was convinced that if a NATO force deployed, most of its effort needed to be on civil reconstruction rather than on grand military manœuvres, although a show of force at the outset would probably be essential in order to demonstrate NATO's determination to enforce any peace deal that had been made. What this country really needed, I thought, was strong political, social and economic help. It had needed robust military intervention two or three years ago, and had not got it. The irony seemed to me that just as peace was breaking out the international community turned up for war, whereas when war was breaking out the international community turned up for peacekeeping – well, if the truth be told, it was not even that, just the protection of humanitarian aid. And what a noble but flawed gesture that turned out to be, despite many individual acts of physical and moral courage on the ground.

In pursuit of NATO's plans Brigadier Freddie Viggers, the Commander Royal Artillery of 3 (UK) Division, arrived on Saturday 11 November to head up the reconnaissance for the expectedly imminent deployment of the ARRC. Freddie gave me the latest news from Dayton, suggesting that given the apparently slow pace of negotiations the best guess for the timing of the IFOR deployment would be not much before late January 1996. The plan was that HQ 3 (UK) Division would deploy, but that my headquarters would be the only brigade HQ, and that my brigade would consist of the existing British combat units currently in theatre with UNPROFOR. This meant that Lieutenant Colonel Trevor Minter's quite excellent 1st Battalion, the Royal Regiment of Fusiliers, would be joined by Ben Barry's Light Infantry battalion, together with the gunners of Lieutenant Colonel Chris Nichol's 26 Regiment Royal Artillery and the sappers of Lieutenant Colonel Peter Wall's 32 Armoured Engineer Regiment. We would keep Major Bertie Polley's reconnaissance squadron of the Light Dragoons – adding a little cavalry 'dash and panache', as he would say – and gain a squadron of Lieutenant Colonel Nigel Beer's Queen's Royal Hussars, whose Challenger tanks would give the muscle we previously had lacked. I was delighted. All these units were well-trained, experienced and superbly led. It was expected that other, yet-to-be-specified, multinational contributions would be added to the division in due course.

Somewhat uncertainly I now found myself, the new boy on the block with only two weeks of Bosnia under my belt, guiding Freddie's team on its reconnaissance. We went by road – the best way to get a feel for the lie of the land, its smells and the immense logistical challenges facing the IFOR deployment, for given the appalling state of the roads and the heavy snow, it would require huge effort to maintain such a heavily mechanized force. So it was that on Monday, 13 November we left the cool sunshine of the Dalmatian coast by helicopter for snow-covered Gornji Vakuf, where we switched to Land Rovers and headed north to Bugojno. Here we crossed the old Federation–Serb front line, now eerily quiet, and made our way through territory recently captured by the Croats, up the Vrbas Valley through Dornji Vakuf and Jajce. The trip of about 300 bumpy kilometres took us to Kupres, Livno, Glamoč, Mrkonjić Grad and Šipovo, before returning to Kupres and thence back to base. For most of the journey we drove through village after ruined village, burnt, desolate and deserted testimony to the appalling waste of war. Our Bosnian Croat Army guide said it was all done by the Serbs as they withdrew in the face of the Croat–Federation offensive. However, there was much evidence of a very hasty civilian and military withdrawal, so I could not help feeling that at least some of the devastation had been wrought in revenge by Croats as they advanced deep into the Serb heartlands during their successful summer offensive.

A few days later, in order to meet the Bosnian Serb commanders, we made a similar journey by road across

the Confrontation Line to Banja Luka, the capital of
Serb-held north-western Bosnia. Driving again from
Gornji Vakuf to Vitez, we met up with the Spanish UN
Chief of Mission, Antonio Pedieure, before making our
way around the massive Vlasic mountain feature which
dominated that part of the country – held throughout the
war by the Serbs, but in Bosniac hands since March 1995
– on our way to Banja Luka. After several delays and
Bosnian Croat Army checkpoints, we reached the
Confrontation Line and crossed very carefully through to
the Serb side. Serb engineers cleared the minefield for us
and we set off for Banja Luka as the light failed. Serb
soldiers were everywhere. It was not hard to notice that
they were older than the Croat and Bosniac troops and
very scruffy. They looked to be a tired and a very nearly
defeated army. We stayed the night in the Hotel Bosna in
Banja Luka – a somewhat surreal experience, as the Serbs
had not seen international soldiers on their territory
before. The following day, after meetings with the
Bosnian Serb Army, we retraced our steps by road,
managing the same afternoon to fly into Bihac to meet
the commander of the Bosniac 5th Corps, the charis-
matic General Atif Dudakovic, with whom I had already
had my shouting match over 'his' treatment of my
Bangladeshis. As Bihac had now officially come under
my command, it was a very useful meeting. I noted in my
diary: 'Dudakovic is a tough man who has clearly had a
very good war. He was pleased with himself, but reasonable to talk to.' He told me that his personal ambition
was, one day, to become a NATO officer. In the event he
did not achieve that ambition before he retired, but
Bosnia is now within NATO's Partnership for Peace

programme and might, one day, join NATO. That was Dudakovic's dream.

Soon after this trip, General Sir John Wilsey, the overall British Joint Commander, based in the United Kingdom at Army headquarters in Wilton, rang to warn me that a decision in Dayton was now expected over the weekend, and that NATO could deploy before Christmas. The negotiations had been touch and go, but all of a sudden the logjam had broken: the peace agreement was initialled in Dayton on Tuesday, 21 November and formally signed in Paris on 14 December. An initialling ceremony was televised at 9 p.m. local time. We watched it on the flickering screens with a mixture of emotions. It was not hard to feel a sense of occasion as four years of seemingly interminable misery were brought to a formal end; but it was clear from the speeches that the Dayton Accords were full of compromise, the event passing off with resignation, even exhaustion, rather than euphoria. From what I had seen already I was certain that this would be an attitude shared by people in Bosnia. Indeed, there was very little celebratory firing on the front lines and both Sanja, my interpreter, and Ludo, our Bosnian Croat liaison officer, seemed very subdued. In essence, Bosnia Herzegovina was to be one state, but divided into two semi-autonomous entities: one entity to be the Federation of Bosniacs and Croats created after their civil war was settled in 1994, the other entity to be Republika Srpska, the Bosnian Serb area. The Accords laid down a very demanding timetable for getting the respective armies out of the field, handing certain pieces of territory from one side to the other and meeting a range of other military, humanitarian and political conditions.

These events, of course, had immediate implications for IFOR, UNPROFOR and my brigade. Expecting an announcement, Major General Mike Jackson had been with me in Gornji Vakuf for the past several days, and we immediately got down to agreeing a suitable date by which the transfer of authority could take place from UNPROFOR to IFOR, in other words from the UN to NATO. In the midst of this we heard reports that the Bosnian Croats, in advance of their withdrawal from areas that the Accords said they had to hand over to the Serbs around Mrkonjić Grad and Šipovo, had already begun burning and looting houses and factories there, activities about which I protested vigorously. Days later I was able to take Kate Adie of the BBC on a journey through the area we called the 'Anvil' (the large area of territory to be returned to the Serbs by the Croats) and the BBC subsequently carried the story of the Croat 'scorched earth' activities on the mid-evening news. I was pleased about this. If the treaty was to be worth the paper it was written upon, then all sides had to follow it, in letter and spirit, from the outset.

As the details of the peace plan trickled through, we got down to some rapid and detailed planning to ensure that we would be in a position to enforce the peace that had been agreed. In outline, all former warring factions had to withdraw from territory they had occupied and which had been allocated to either the Republika Srpska or the Federation. On D-Day – the implementation day of the Dayton agreement – IFOR troops would move into all the territory held by the warring factions and take responsibility for what was now known as the ceasefire line, identifying minefields and ensuring compliance. Thereafter the timetable dictated the withdrawal of all former warring faction troops from a 'zone of separation' behind the ceasefire line on both sides by D+30, 19 January 2006 (which was also the deadline for the release of all prisoners of war). Then, by D+45 the indigenous populations could return to their original homes, protected by IFOR. We had very robust rules of engagement to enforce these activities, and I was determined to use them if I had to. It was important that all of the local former warring faction commanders realized that this was not another UN operation, where the rules allowed troops to open fire only in self-defence. By D+90 the armies of the factions could return to provide military security for their respective populations, but for thirty days only: by D+120, they were to demobilize and return to barracks. The greatest challenge at the beginning, I thought, was going to be enforcing the 2-kilometre 'zone of separation' between the former warring factions with the severely limited resources available to me, all the way across a front that stretched for over 180 kilometres. The best hope of success seemed to lie in their simply getting on with it, almost regardless of us. In the event I need not have worried: war-weariness in many parts was overwhelming, and compliance proved to be remarkably high.

My contacts with the Bosnian Croats paid off, and we found no difficulty in securing a number of sites for my brigade to occupy in the Anvil, including a location for my brigade HQ in a burnt-out hotel, from which I would exercise command and control. We also secured factories, one in Šipovo and two in Mrkonjić Grad, for my British units. Over the following days these sites were repaired to the point of basic habitation, although they never reached the point at which they could be described as 'comfortable'. We occupied our new brigade HQ in Šipovo on Friday, 15 December. Everything had been looted and vandalized, down to the last plugs in the sinks – a practice well known to the British soldier. Colonel Juric, the local Bosnian Croat commander, told me that the last Muslims were about to leave; all the Croats had already gone. He asked me whether we could take over the Bocac Dam and electricity plant, which produced power for Banja Luka. Given that Banja Luka was in Serb hands, I took this request from a Croat as a good sign for the future; moreover, I applauded the logic of his argument that it would at least prevent the dam being sabotaged by other withdrawing Croats before the Serbs reoccupied the Anvil three months later. So I agreed, feeling that there was some hope for the country!

On the same day I held my formal orders of our operations around D-Day, attended by all the commanding officers and their staff from across the brigade, including Nigel Beer of the Queen's Own Hussars, over from Catterick in advance of the arrival of his Challenger 2 tanks by sea, and Lieutenant Colonel Theo Damen from the Netherlands. Our plans, called Operation 'Resolute Rat', envisaged a high-profile demonstrative deployment by the Light Infantry, Fusiliers and Light Dragoons into all three former warring faction areas on D-Day (soon to be confirmed as Wednesday, 20 December). In the following weeks we would be reinforced by the arrival of the Challenger 2 battle tanks of the Queen's Own Hussars, the remainder of Lieutenant Colonel Peter Wall's 32 Armoured Engineer Regiment and Theo Damen's 42 (Netherlands) Mechanized Infantry Battle Group. I was confident that the heavy firepower we could deploy would be more than sufficient to achieve our military tasks. The civil reconstruction challenges, however, were another matter entirely.

I continued to scuttle around ensuring that all the factions knew my plans for D-Day and understood what was required of them. I felt that knowledge of our plans would dispel their uncertainty about our intentions and begin the process of building up confidence. Long journeys by Land Rover and endless hours in the helicopter (at one stage, in atrocious weather, I nearly persuaded myself never to step into a helicopter ever again) took me to Banja Luka to meet the Bosnian Serb generals, Talic of their 1st Krajina Corps and Tomalic of their 2nd Krajina Corps; the Bosnian Croat Brigadiers Dragicevic of their Vitez Command and Glasnovic of their Tomislavgrad Command; Bosniac Generals Dudakovic of their 5th Corps in Bihac and Alagic of their 7th Corps in Travnik. When D-Day arrived, on 20 December 1995, it was almost an anti-climax given the amount of preparatory work that we had managed to achieve, but perhaps that was the point: all the preliminary work had been worth the effort. Trevor Minter's Fusiliers secured a crossing point over the ceasefire line south of Banja Luka called 'Black Dog', Bertie Polley's squadron of Light Dragoons moved 5 kilometres into Serb territory in their Scimitar light tanks, and Ben Barry's Light Infantry prepared to move from Vitez to Sanski Most the following day to take control of a crossing point we called 'White Fang' (named, like 'Black Dog', after one of our camp dogs: what is it about British soldiers and dogs?). On D+1 I drove to Sanski Most to catch up with Ben Barry, and at White Fang I met two old men, probably Serbs, who lived very close by. They asked if our arrival meant the end of the fighting. I said it did, and the older man's eyes filled with excitement and hope. It was one of the most moving things I had ever seen – tears from an old man whose life is behind him, but who hopes for a better future for those who are to follow. Since then I have seen it several times: the delight that brings tears to the eyes when the chance of peace and better times is offered.

By the end of D+1 there had been almost complete compliance. The Light Infantry were firm in the north around Sanski Most, with the White Fang crossing under control. The Fusiliers were well deployed, if rather stretched, in the centre and the south and had the Black Dog crossing under control, while the Light Dragoons were on the Serb side carrying out very useful patrols along the ceasefire line and towards Banja Luka.

So far, so good! The main effort was now to develop our liaison with all the former warring factions and begin detailed patrolling of the ceasefire line area to enforce the zone of separation. The first Joint Military Commission, an arrangement instituted by the Dayton agreement, to oversee compliance with the peace accords, took place on my birthday, Saturday, 23 December, chaired by Mike Jackson. At the meeting itself, each of the five corps commanders was compliant to the point of friendliness; however, not everything went as planned. The very next day a promised prisoner exchange between the Croats and the Serbs failed. The Croats had apparently decided unilaterally to release a group of Serb prisoners as a goodwill gesture for Christmas. But in fact it was a cynical ploy. On arrival at Black Dog they decided not to release their prisoners because the Serbs had apparently cried off from their side of the exchange. What I had failed to appreciate was that the Croat (Catholic) calendar had Christmas on 25 December but the Serb (Orthodox) calendar had it some two weeks later. Although I reminded the Croats that the initiative had been theirs and that it was supposed to be a unilateral gesture of goodwill, they refused to release their prisoners and took them away. I became fairly angry, a reaction which, with a BBC crew present, was widely broadcast on Christmas Eve and seen, among many others, by my family at home. My youngest son, Olly, sensing my mood, was heard to comment: 'I feel rather sorry for that Croat Colonel. Dad has got one of those really grumpy looks on his face!' Still, all the parties would have to release all their prisoners by D+30 in any case, so I thought the Croats' gesture rather futile.

This episode aside, progress was better than I could ever have hoped. By Boxing Day all five corps in the divisional area had agreed unanimously to advance their moves back to their new lines in the zone of separation by D+25 (14 January), some five days earlier than Dayton had decreed. The next step following this was to be the Areas of Transfer operation, under which parcels of land would have to be transferred from one side to the other by D+45 (3 February).

We remained under the media spotlight for much of this time, although Sarajevo tended to attract most of the attention. On Tuesday, 9 January Martin Bell dropped into my HQ in Šipovo for a chat about how things were going. The operation, though successful so far in many respects, had opened up the opportunity for so-called 'mission creep', a charge often levelled at soldiers by others. This expansion of operations beyond the initial brief is often thought to be an insidious distraction, focusing minds and resources away from the point of main effort. Martin and I discussed the vexed issue of burning houses in Šipovo and Mrkonjić Grad, as I had already done with General Jackson, and we had a sharp divergence of views. Martin believed that to get involved with the law and order aspects of policing behaviour ran the risk of the very kind of 'mission creep' which he saw as a problem characteristic of the UN. However, I argued that unless IFOR acted robustly we ran the risk of seeming impotent in the way the UN had. If this happened we would face not 'mission creep' but 'mission collapse'. I accepted that my logic worked only if there were some civilian authorities to exercise the law and order function, but I was as keen as possible to demonstrate that the IFOR commitment was not designed merely to provide physical or military security: we had also to help, where we could, in the effort to enable people to start rebuilding their lives. We were not military tourists, which had been the charge levelled against UNPROFOR, but active participants in a process to get life started again amid the rubble and chaos of war. We could help. Identifying minefields, opening routes for traffic, removing road-blocks, coordinating governmental and non-governmental agencies, providing information and generally providing impetus and 'push': all this was work for which we were ideally suited.

We were helped by the onset of some unseasonably warm weather. After the fierce snowstorms of the previous month, we were now bathed in sunshine and temperatures that remained above freezing, with no wind or rain. This eased the arrival of the Challenger 2 tanks of the Queen's Own Hussars, which deployed into the Anvil on 13 January, having been brought up from Split on the back of transporters. Getting these beasts up-country was a huge logistical task, but they were very impressive and gained us a lot more military credibility. I was pleased that we had made the effort. When they were deployed alongside the Warrior platoons of the Light Infantry and the Saxons of the Fusiliers I could not imagine any military non-compliance by the former warring factions (outside of sheer incompetence, which was a possibility) when the final withdrawal from the zone of separation began on 14 January. I was proved right. Compliance was described by the troops on the ground to be 100 per cent.

Our next big test was to manage the return of Bosnian Serb refugees back to their homes. On 13 January I travelled to Banja Luka to meet the mayors and senior officials of Mrkonjić Grad and Šipovo, exiled since they had fled three months before at the conclusion of the summer offensives. It was sadly pathetic. They asked me about their houses, factories, roads, shops, bridges and churches. I had to tell them that all were extensively damaged and many totally destroyed. As I spoke, I could see their eyes filling. Despite this they were very keen to return as soon as possible, and I told them that we would do all that we could to help them. The following day, back in Šipovo, the stark human terror of ethnically based civil war was brought home to me. Father Adolph, the Catholic priest of the hamlet of Majdan, a small Croat community of three hundred souls located just inside the future Serb area, came to see me. He wanted reassurance that his people would be safe under the new Bosnian Serb administration as all his people were terrified of being slaughtered when the Serbs returned. I agreed to attend Mass the following Sunday and to speak to the people after the service, to try to persuade them to stay and not flee the area.

In fact, I visited Majdan earlier than I had expected. On the Friday before my planned Sunday visit I received a message that the people were terrified, and were all preparing to leave. I immediately drove into the village, but could not find anyone. It looked as if I was too late. The place was deserted. It turned out that the people were crowded into the school, having a debate about what they should do. Understandably, they did not want to be the next victims of what the world had come to call ethnic cleansing. I went into the schoolroom. All eyes turned in my direction as I entered and, from a standing start, I gave them a fifteen-minute oration (through Sanja) on why they should try to stay and not run away. I promised IFOR protection, and as I left the school a platoon of Fusiliers and a Challenger tank came rolling into the village, a very visible demonstration of that protection fixed up by Major Philip Macey, the local Fusiliers company commander, earlier in the day. I assured them I would return on Sunday to speak to them again at Mass.

Two days later, on Sunday, 21 January, accompanied by Martin Bell and Christopher Bellamy of the

Independent, I joined the villagers of Majdan at a well-attended Mass. Martin gave me one of his remote microphones so he could broadcast what I said. It was very, very cold in the unheated church, and I shivered fairly uncontrollably throughout the service. When I came to speak I chose to base my arguments on the authority of the peace agreement, a copy of which I took with me. I stressed that the decision to stay or to leave was theirs alone, not mine or IFOR's, but that their decision must be based on the facts. First, the war was over, a peace agreement had been signed, and Majdan had been allocated within the territory of Republika Srpska. Second, Dayton specifically set out the human rights of all individuals, and the international community would ensure they were upheld. I stressed that my authority came from the peace agreement, nothing else, and urged them to trust it too. Looking to the future, I asked them to find it in their hearts to try to begin to trust the Serbs. As we were in their church, taking my own Bible out of my pocket I put the thought to them that they should first trust God, and then trust the peace agreement; and that they should trust us, as the NATO IFOR, to do all we could to protect them. Trust, I said, was what was required.

The people were polite, but quiet. Sadly, they had made up their minds to go. I was unable to overcome the fear that these people had of living under the Serbs. Given the years – centuries even – of mutual antipathy between these ethnic groups, I should not have been too surprised at the outcome; but I was disappointed that, despite the power of the international community, the Croat people of Majdan could not trust us to protect them. Nevertheless, I was determined that we would not merely sit back and supervise the ethnic cleansing that the extremists had begun, and that IFOR would do everything in its power to try to break the cycle of fear and violence that would otherwise plague this country long into the future.

The following day I met up with the Serb mayors of Mrkonjić Grad and Šipovo and escorted them around their devastated towns. They appeared phlegmatic rather than angry, shocked at how much destruction had been caused but determined to return with their people and to start to rebuild their lives again. From them we learned that large numbers of people were planning to return from exile on 3 February (D+45). We had to be prepared for this. Interestingly enough, the 'mission creep' debate I had had with Martin Bell was raising its head regularly in our discussions within IFOR. Part of the problem was that those who designed the multi-agency strategy at a political level within the international community had little idea of how it would actually work on the ground. I suspected, too, that decisions were made in New York and elsewhere to placate the specialist international agencies and authorities, without sufficient thought always being given to whether the wherewithal existed to deploy, in sufficient strength and at the required pace, to deliver services and help when they were needed. It was certainly clear to me that many regarded IFOR merely as a military instrument, and had not considered what we might be able to do to help the resettlement of refugees, other than providing the physical framework of security. The truth was that IFOR was ideally placed to assist in a number of areas, at least initially, where specialist agencies were simply not available. For instance, the Red Cross was instructed to manage prisoner releases, but had neither the capacity nor the local contacts to make this happen in the timescales dictated by Dayton. We had both. Likewise, IFOR was expressly forbidden to get involved with the management and recording of war crimes and mass graves: this was the exclusive remit of the International War Crimes Tribunal at The Hague. Unsurprisingly, the Tribunal had no presence on the ground. We had. Again, IFOR was expressly forbidden to become involved in the provision of law and order, as this was the sole responsibility of civilian police. Unfortunately, we had yet to see a single international policeman, or any sign of credible civil authorities to lead the reconstruction effort. In all these areas IFOR, I believed, was perfectly suited to bringing immediate aid to the civil power. Yet we were not being asked to contribute, and in some cases we were being expressly prevented from contributing because to do so would cross into someone else's jurisdiction. It was above all very frustrating; for I was convinced, as were my subordinate commanders, that IFOR possessed an enormous reservoir of resources and goodwill from which it could help at least some parts of the initial civilian relief effort in the time that would inevitably lapse before all the complex civil structures of normality could be rebuilt. I was determined that this was an issue to which I would return if and when I had more influence on higher-level decision-making.

My dilemma, as I saw it, was that if we did not take a broad view of the IFOR mission on the ground, among the people, where help was most urgently required, our authority would wane in the eyes of those who most needed help. The other obstacle to our efforts was the stated time limitation on IFOR's deployment of just twelve months. As many of the local people said to me, 'How can we put our trust in you, if you will be gone in a year's time?' It was a very fair point, but had still not been taken on board by the US leadership by late 2009, when President Obama announced a short-term uplift of US troops to Afghanistan, but only for about eighteen months. Decisions about troop numbers must be driven by conditions on the ground, not timelines – always a challenge for liberal democratic governments facing the tyranny of the ballot box every four or five years.

By late January the bad weather had returned, and we were faced with appalling driving conditions. We were already suffering from a spate of road traffic accidents across the brigade area, though fortunately there had been no serious casualties yet. Danger continued to lurk in the threat from anti-tank mines, countless thousands of which littered the country, many unrecorded. We had had several narrow escapes earlier in the tour, and though the major routes had by now been cleared, there were still many hundreds of minor tracks, few of which had been reconnoitred, let alone cleared. We had to exercise extreme care. Then, on the evening of Saturday, 27 January, I heard the worst news possible: one of our vehicles had struck a mine. Information came rushing in. A Scimitar armoured car from C Squadron, Light Dragoons, which had recently joined my brigade, had hit a mine about 24 kilometres north-east of Glamoč, had been blown up and had caught fire. No one got out of the vehicle. All three men – Lieutenant Richard Madden and

Troopers Andrew Ovington and John Kelly – were subsequently reported dead. I had hoped that we might be fortunate to get through the whole tour without a fatality, but it was not to be.

The following day I visited the squadron in Glamoč. They were very subdued, several tearful and some in shock. Padre Peter Hills of the Fusiliers had spent the night with them and had taken a short service that morning, which apparently helped many of the soldiers deal with their grief. I stayed for a couple of hours, chatting with Major John Ogden, the squadron leader, and members of the squadron. After the success of the first five weeks, the death of the three men was a massive blow. It was, of course, a desperate tragedy for the families; it was also a very salutary reminder to all of us of the mine threat and of our (and my) responsibilities as commanders.

With only days to go before the return of the refugees into the Anvil – we expected anything up to 40,000 or 50,000 Serbs to return any time after D+46 – the inter-agency situation seemed to be getting better, if a little too slowly for my liking. We had set up 'Task Force Anvil', with joint chairmanship shared between IFOR and the UNHCR. I had offered this arrangement in order to mitigate the problems we had identified with the co-ordination of military and civil affairs. Civilians seemed quite happy to be protected by the military but were not at all keen to be organized by us. I accept we tend to be rather bossy and in something of a hurry, but we have a very strong interest in getting the job done and going home. Our second meeting was held in Šipovo on 30 January, when for the first time we had full representation from all the necessary civilian agencies: the head of UNHCR in Banja Luka, Vladimir Tchirko; Inspector Phil Coffey from the new International Police Task Force; and Jereown Senneff, our United Nations Civil Affairs officer. Good progress was made and functional responsibilities for security, utilities, infrastructure, and humanitarian and information issues were agreed. Although we were officially in support of UNHCR it was clear that we were providing the necessary leadership impetus, but they were providing the experience and network of contacts with the aid agencies. I was pleased; this was what we were here for. With goodwill from all concerned, it could work. The former warring factions were no longer fighting; now it was up to IFOR to help them convert their swords into ploughshares.

One of the key needs was to slow down the speed of the Serb population's return, otherwise the fragile infrastructure we had put in place would be overwhelmed. So later on in the day I did quite a long programme for TV Srpska, giving a full brief on the situation and trying to persuade people not to return in a hurry, but to send the heads of families first, just to have a preliminary look. Time would tell how successful this attempt at an overt information policy was. The other item of interest was the discovery by ABC TV of a mass grave quite near Šipovo. Our line of response was quite clear: we would conduct a brief verification by our own military police and then report all the details to the International War Crimes Tribunal at The Hague. I was expressly forbidden to do more than that.

My attempt at information dissemination got me into

some unusual situations. One of these was a number of two-hour radio chat shows on 'Radio Big' in Banja Luka. I selected all the music (really contemporary stuff like Frank Sinatra, Simon & Garfunkel and Bill Hailey!) and we talked about the peace agreement in a phone-in programme. As planned, it gave me the chance to talk to Serb listeners about what was happening, especially to those who were intending to return to their homes in Mrkonjić Grad and Šipovo. I took a series of calls from listeners who had questions about human rights and freedom of movement. I think it paid off: between us, Sanya and I managed to get our points across.

Then, on Friday, 2 February, the day before D+45 when the Croats were due to evacuate their seized territories preparatory to a Serb civilian return, I called on Colonel Totic, the remaining Croat commander in Mrkonjić Grad. Trevor Minter and Philip Macey were with me. It proved to be a rather historic meeting. Totic briefed us on the plans for the Croat withdrawal from the Anvil and on progress to date; we raised a couple of outstanding issues. Then he simply got up, told us the office was now ours – including the telephone and four bottles of wine for whoever came next – put his hat on, saluted, shook our hands and walked out. The Croat withdrawal from Mrkonjić Grad was complete. It was done with dignity and good order, and I much respected Totic for it. He was as good as his word. On Saturday we wandered through the town in glorious sunshine. Mrkonjić Grad was totally deserted. It felt quite peculiar and seemingly suspended in time. It was more like a film set than a real town. Houses, shops, offices, the hotel and church – all were empty, in a town severely damaged but big enough for twenty thousand people. It was a very extraordinary feeling for us all. The only live thing I discovered was a chicken, alive and well in the wrecked hospital.

Then – bedlam. On the Sunday that followed, accompanied by a thick, enveloping mist, the eerie emptiness was replaced by hundreds of Serb cars and buses and thousands of returning people. The deluge we had been waiting for, the first fruits of peace, had begun. I was ecstatic, but at the same time nervous that we would be overwhelmed. We had arranged a press conference in the square in Mrkonjić Grad for 11 a.m. to explain our plans for the arrival of the civil population. The square was packed: among the many TV crews and reporters present were several Serbs, here to test the veracity of the peace deal that some in Republika Srpska believed would not deliver on its promise to return people to their homes. Then people went their various ways. I watched people go into their houses for the first time. The disbelief and shock were plainly evident – hands raised in horror at the scale of the damage, much of it wanton vandalism. The mayor commented to me that they might be able to repair the houses quite quickly, but the repair to themselves would take much longer.

His comments made me think. The fact that we had begun to implement a long-awaited peace accord was cause for celebration, but the international community needed to remember that the end-state was a long way off. That point would have been reached only when justice had been achieved. In IFOR we would do our part to escort the armies of the factions back to barracks, and to some degree assist in the 'normalization' of civil affairs, but I worried lest we were unwittingly allowing ourselves to sleepwalk into a moral vacuum that ignored the issue of war crimes and individual culpability. Justice could so easily become the major casualty of the desire to end the war. For those of us on the ground there was the real prospect of IFOR being vilified for not assisting with the search for war criminals and the securing of evidence – on the ostensible grounds that we did not have the manpower – and the whole mission suffering because of the straitjacket into which we were being forced. On reflection, I think that the international community did not realize how strong its position was in late 1995 and early 1996, and that it should have demanded more from the former warring factions and been bolder in its ambitions. There is a lesson here for the future.

A related danger was the possibility that the perpetrators of atrocities across Bosnia Herzegovina would think that the peace agreement meant that they could escape without sanction. During one of my regular meetings with the Serb general Bosko Kelecevic, he suggested almost in passing, following the recent high-profile arrest of another Serb general in Sarajevo, that he was sure no more of the Serb military would be arrested, as they had been only following orders. I had to point out that even soldiers must evaluate the orders they receive against their own moral judgement, as the Nuremberg trials after the Second World War had concluded. He looked a little crestfallen at my response. On that very same day, and to our great frustration, Radovan Karadzic was seen in Banja Luka, but our orders were not to arrest him, unless he fell conveniently into our hands – which was very unlikely, as he travelled around with about a platoon-sized group of bodyguards. It would be over a decade before he was eventually taken into international custody. Peace is one thing, but peace with justice is quite another, and much more important. As it turned out, later on my eldest son Tom's wife, Lucinda, was to work as an international criminal lawyer for the International Criminal Court in The Hague and then in Sarajevo – work I followed with great interest and approval.

Amid all this activity and reflection, we received a lightning visit from the MOD's Operational Audit Team, led by Brigadier Andrew Ridgeway, to assess what we were achieving with all the money the taxpayer in the UK was spending on our deployment. It provided a useful opportunity for me to think about the strengths and weaknesses of our deployment. On the credit side of the balance sheet I told Andrew that our military doctrine, adapted to what I called 'manœuvre peacekeeping', was working well. This entailed getting inside the factions' decision–action cycle and outmanœuvring them in thought, time and space, all within the overarching philosophy of Mission Command – the business of setting clear missions and then delegating responsibility to subordinates, who could act as they felt fit, so long as it was within their commander's intent. Morale among the troops was high, as were their commitment to the mission and their willingness to get the job done despite the personal privations and irritations which they had to suffer. I observed that maintaining this attitude was made easier by the fact that we boasted well-trained troops, who had been prepared for the operation.

On the debit side I noted that, as I had observed to Mike Jackson, we were not yet an expeditionary minded and equipped Army, despite the Falklands and the Gulf. Much of the kit we had was designed for longer, more static wars in different environments, with procurement processes modelled for the Cold War. We had very poor provision for what I described as 'camp stores', such as adequate tents, generators, heaters and portable ablution units, which were not available quickly, where and when they were needed. This was probably inevitable, but I was concerned that we should get it right next time. Such assets would allow us to move rapidly from one base to another, a characteristic of this operation: one platoon commander I spoke to was in his eighteenth platoon location. What he needed was not the infrastructure of a permanent camp but the essential components to create a temporary patrol base anywhere. Likewise, we suffered from an overly bureaucratic and centralized financial regime, which prevented my units from buying locally where they could and spending money on necessary local infrastructure projects which, in turn, would secure local support for the mission. Finally, we expected much of our soldiers on the ground, but repaid them very poorly with what I described as 'welfare' provision. When we expected our troops to make heavy sacrifices through unaccompanied operational tours abroad, we needed to work harder to provide things such as international calling facilities, so they could call home to friends and family. These were entirely lacking in Bosnia in early 1996. Other national contingents had them: why didn't we? We owed it to our long-suffering troops to get it right next time. If I was thought to be something of a nuisance on this issue in 2006, it was simply down to my experiences a decade before.

My fears about the pressure of too many refugees in the Anvil were highlighted when on Saturday, 10 February the unprotected UNHCR warehouse in Mrkonjić Grad was rushed by a mob of hungry people – there were no commercial food supplies at the time – who had got to hear that there were supplies available. To meet the crisis the UNHCR immediately agreed to release one hundred tons of food and we said we would oversee its distribution. On Sunday, 11 February they released a further 60 tons of emergency food aid, and by the next day we estimated that we had fed about eight thousand returned refugees, almost all of whom had previously had no food. The original plan made by UNHCR and the civil authorities was for about five hundred 'family enablers' to return early to start getting the town infrastructure sorted out. Clearly there was no possibility of exercising much control over the people, especially in the prevailing deep snow and cold temperatures. There was therefore no alternative to UNHCR releasing food for us to distribute, which we did in Šipovo, Mrkonjić Grad, Gorni Ribnik and Baraci. This would stave off the problem for a few days, but it couldn't continue indefinitely. I was pleased to note that by the next Thursday some street traders had appeared and that the feeding system through the locally organized Committee of Refugees seemed to be working. Two weeks later, by Friday, 23 February (D+65), the numbers living in the Anvil had risen to some 14,750, and all of them appeared to have something to eat, even if it was only the basic US military MRE food packs. (My soldiers, no great supporters of these bland, high-calorie 'Meals Ready to Eat', quickly dubbed their MREs 'Meals Rejected by Ethiopians'.)

One of the tasks we had taken on with gusto was the provision of an International Information Post in both of our principal towns, Šipovo and Mrkonjić Grad, to act as the focal point for all civilians asking about food supplies, minefield fears, medical questions and so on. My own medical unit also ran a primitive clinic in Šipovo which treated some 180 patients in the first two weeks, and we slowly expanded this work to the outlying areas, especially Gorni Ribnik and the Kluječ municipality. In addition to the basic medical cover we were able to provide, we helped a Danish charity which had located itself in Mrkonjić Grad. Plans for the longer term seemed entirely dependent on the availability of cash, but so far no governments or charities appeared much inclined to dig into their pockets. Meanwhile, of course, we, as IFOR, sat in all the factories, preventing worthwhile economic activity restarting – although it's only fair to say that, realistically, the civil authorities and population were not in a position to begin factory production for many months, certainly not until substantial inward investment funded new machines.

On Saturday, 24 February my hopes for Bosnia Herzegovina's long-term health were raised a degree or two by a meeting with the former Muslim population of Mrkonjić Grad. They were keen to return, and to live among their Serb neighbours again as they had done for generations. I was not sanguine that they would be able to go back safely, but was pleasantly surprised by the welcome they received. Arriving in creaking, decrepit old buses, they first visited their houses, as they had asked to be allowed to do, and then headed off to the centre of town. At once they began to meet long-lost friends on the

Serb side, embracing each other with much kissing and hugging. Given all the supposed and real animosity the war had created, this reaction seemed quite extra-ordinary. We then all drove on to the IFOR HQ for a planned meeting with the Serb town authorities, which was extremely cordial, and plans were discussed for a permanent return.

Having seen the successful return of civilians to the Anvil, we now prepared for the phase, beginning on D+90, that would entail the return of the Bosnian Serb Army to replace us as the guarantors of security, as a way of reassuring the local Serb population, for a maximum of thirty days before they finally returned to barracks. To help oversee this process I had been allocated, to my great pleasure, a battlegroup of the Malaysians who had served us so well in UNPROFOR. They were very keen to take on this new role and I admired their doggedness and enthusiasm. The only difficulty was the weather: several inches of fresh snow had just fallen, and the camp they were developing at Glamoč was very exposed. I felt for them.

Our constant complaining about the prohibition on our assisting adequately, or even minimally, with civil infrastructure tasks seemed at long last to have been heard in London. General Mike had sent back some stiff calls to the UK and an MOD fact-finding team who visited my HQ on 8 March let slip the news that the Foreign Office and Overseas Development Agency were likely to grant £13 million for reconstruction. To say I was pleased was an understatement; and the prospect of being able to do something other than to stand guard in their Challenger tanks and Warrior fighting vehicles, when they saw innumerable opportunities for getting involved with helping the returning refugees, was a huge relief to the troops on the ground. At about the same time NATO also announced that IFOR would take a broader view of its mission, in view of the slow deployment of some of the civil organizations and agencies. For us, this would mean that the so-called 'mission creep' could become official and our broader civil activities would be legitimized. Then, on 20 March (D+90), the day on which the Bosnian Serb Army was allowed back into the Anvil, I met a wonderful character by the name of Gilbert Greenall, who was working for the Overseas Development Agency. To my very great surprise and delight he had brought with him a bag of real money. At long last!

Such a challenge was right up Gilbert's street. A qualified doctor and light aircraft pilot, he had spent a short time in the Household Cavalry and was now splitting his time between farming and working overseas for the Government. He gave provisional agreement for the immediate funding of various projects for Šipovo, including a JCB and two tipper trucks for bulk rubbish/debris collection, £50,000 for water supply repairs and up to £200,000 for the renewal of the road through the town and on to Jezzero. All three were exactly the kind of high-profile projects that would show local people that we really were doing something to help them. When I told my unit commanding officers they were equally surprised – we had grown too cynical, I suppose, to believe that something might actually be done – and delighted to be proven wrong.

Sadly, this enlightened view of the use of money in

support of military operations was not to become a lasting policy. Clare Short's new Department of International Development, created after the 1997 general election, was to claw back all such funding in support of longer-term policies focused on the elimination of world poverty – highly laudable, but of no use in supporting British troops in Kosovo, Iraq and Afghanistan. If the three key elements of a successful counter-insurgency policy are muscle, message and money, then I would suggest that, as a nation, we do muscle all right and we can get the message right on occasions; but invariably we fail to realize that money spent wisely and immediately can be highly effective as a weapon when targeted with tactical precision, for-strategic effect.

My plan for the D+90 operation was to conduct quite a large and high-profile deployment to monitor the Serb troops' movement back into the Anvil area. To get maximum advantage out of it, and to enhance the deterrent effect, I also planned to do a full rehearsal on the day before, which would be a good training opportunity for all concerned, especially the Malaysian contingent, for whom it was to be their first NATO operation. When I met with the representatives of the six corps-sized formations of the former warring factions on Saturday, 9 March for one of our regular Military Commissions, I proposed, and all parties unanimously agreed, that in the same way that we coordinated the initial D+30 movement into the zone of separation, they would all move their troops out of the field and into barracks on a coordinated basis from D+115 onwards. They all signed up to the mechanics of the plan, with no dissension. It was,

I observed at the time, almost too good to be true: the plan was working exactly as it had been agreed at Dayton. In true Bosnian fashion we cemented our agreement with a good lunch. Bosniacs, Croats and Serbs tucked in together, chatting and laughing with each other. Looking on, as an outsider, it was clear to me that everyone was relieved that the long, crazy war was finally nearing an end.

But not everyone behaved so. The following Sunday, Sky TV released an interview with Radovan Karadzic in which he taunted NATO for its inability to arrest him, and indeed asserted that it would be stupid of us to try. I looked on with interest, knowing that he would not be able to run for ever, but having no idea that he would elude capture for so long.[*] I had been given orders that if he did come into the Banja Luka area he should be detained. Such an arrest would undoubtedly have been another major bump on the path to peace, but I thought that it would certainly be very worthwhile. Privately, though, I believed that arresting General Ratko Mladic was quite another matter. The Bosnian Serb Army was very loyal to him and an arrest at that time could have had a very violent backlash, one that was not worth the risk given the sensitive process in which we were then immersed. Like Karadzic, this monster could not run for ever. One day justice would apprehend him.

On the afternoon of D+89 – Tuesday, 19 March – I deployed Brigade HQ into the field, near Mrkonjić Grad,

---

[*]Karadzic was arrested by the Serb authorities in 2008 after thirteen years on the run and extradited for trial to the International War Crimes Tribunal in The Hague.

in preparation to monitor the Bosnian Serb Army's re-entry into the Anvil. I chose deliberately to make it a brigade operation, with a full rehearsal on D+90, the Serbs having recently advised us that they would be moving back on D+92. Not only was I taking no chances with the prospect of either non-compliance or wilful disobedience, but I was determined to have on hand all the power of a British armoured brigade to nip any dissent in the bud. After all, this is what we were there for. It would also be a very useful signal to the watching civilians – and the factions' militaries – that we were no tinpot army, but meant business.

The first day of spring – Thursday, 21 March 1996 – dawned as a crisp, cold and clear morning. At 8.09 a.m. the first Bosnian Serb column approached the Black Dog checkpoint and proceeded on its journey towards its former barracks of Kula Camp. Their four published columns became six, probably as a result of breakdowns and poor convoy discipline, and were closely monitored by our air and ground forces. From the air, fast jets of 5 Allied Tactical Air Force, flying from Italy, passed low over their columns and pairs of armed Lynx aircraft kept a close eye upon them. On the ground we were able to count their vehicles and personnel – some 194 vehicles and 470 soldiers by the end of the day. They tried to move three different types of weapon into the Anvil that they had not notified to us, but we spotted all three and ordered their withdrawal. The Sarajevo press contingent had been lured into the Anvil, perhaps attracted by the promise of a diversion from routine Sarajevo news, and I gave them a briefing and took questions in mid-afternoon. I think they all went on their way well satisfied and having enjoyed their day in the sun: for those fed on a diet of gloomy Sarajevo pessimism, a dose of good news from our sector was probably a welcome relief. There was more to Bosnia than Sarajevo, and despite the headlines our experience was that most people in the country were fed up with war and wanted peace, almost at any price.

Three days later I authorized the closure of the Black Dog checkpoint, its purpose fulfilled. Within days, and with little prompting, the Croats and Muslims in the Vrbas and Lasva valleys agreed to remove their own checkpoints on the roads. Many small steps had been taken across the country to implement the immediate requirements of Dayton: viewed together, they amounted to a considerable success for all, not least for the various faction leaders who were determined to comply with IFOR's instructions. It is often the case that belligerents cannot make peace in and of themselves, or of their own volition. Perhaps it becomes too difficult to forget the bloodshed, and fighting continues only to prevent the loss of what has already been sacrificed. In Sector South West in Bosnia Herzegovina in 1996, my experience was that all parties – Bosniac, Croat and Serb – almost fell over themselves to comply with instructions to stop fighting, to separate and to demilitarize. I even thought that they enjoyed IFOR's unequivocal and power-backed instructions: the international community had finally cut its teeth, and the people respected us for it as a refreshing change from the impossible equivocation of the UNPROFOR era. It may have had something to do with their Communist heritage, but it probably also had something to do with their war-weariness, and in most reasoning people a sense that the racist extremists who had started and subsequently fuelled the war with their ranting and hatred had led the country deep into four years of previously unimagined darkness. Peace now offered the flickering of a new dawn, and all I saw about me were people eager to bathe in its warmth and to enjoy its light.

There remained much to do. The process in which we had all taken part still had a long way to run, perhaps over years. But it was a start, and we were proud of the role we had played in creating a framework for a new life for this extraordinary, though recently benighted country. Refugees were flooding back into the Anvil, and a huge task of reconstruction was required that would not be complete for many years. The exhumation and reburying of the dead from the previous year's summer offensive would keep emotions raw for a long while to come, while the full and complete release of prisoners from Republika Srpska was still awaited.

The last task we faced was demilitarization and the return of troops to their barracks by D+120. This went well in the event, with 97 per cent compliance, the 3 per cent non-compliance being down to incompetence. The only expression of discontent we heard was from the Croats unhappy that they had not been designated a barracks area at Kulen Vakuf in the north-west of the division's area. I was nearing the end of my time in command and preparing to hand over to Brian Plummer's 1st Mechanized Brigade from Bulford, and had arranged to meet the Croat commander, Brigadier Glasnovic, in Tomislavgrad to say my farewells. Mike Jackson asked me in passing to tell Glasnovic that the

Croat request to IFOR to keep troops in Kulen Vakuf could not, indeed would not, be complied with. I agreed.

Having arrived in Tomislavgrad by helicopter I found that Glasnovic was not available as he was, I was told, involved in an important meeting. I told his chief of staff, Colonel Marin, rather forcefully that I must see Glasnovic and a few moments later, slightly flustered, he appeared. I passed on the message that Croat forces were to leave Kulen Vakuf by midnight on Thursday, 18 April and he accepted immediately. I was amazed. Glasnovic then asked me to join him and the others for lunch. I accepted and accompanied him across the road to the Hotel Tomislavgrad. On entering the dining room I was staggered to see all the most senior Muslim and Croat officers in the Federation tucking into a very affable lunch. All the corps commanders were there, as were the two Army commanders, Delic and Budimir, and their defence ministers. We had been worrying about the future of the Federation, but here in one room I found all the senior military and civilian players enjoying a meal without any hint of IFOR or another third party. Perhaps, I thought reflectively as I took my seat and gratefully accepted the proffered glass of slivovitz – it had been a long six months – there was hope for the Federation, and Bosnia, after all.

For the international community I felt that the lessons to be learned were starker. Where military intervention is required, it must be strong, robust and timely. Where a fractured state needs help, the international assistance needs to be broadly based and to cover not just the military lines of operation, but governance, the rule of law, justice, human rights and economic support. Media reporting needs to discipline itself not just to report fighting, atrocities and bloodshed, but to give coverage to where progress is being made. Perhaps of greatest importance is the restatement that strategic objectives set out by governments must be linked to tactical activity on the ground by soldiers and aid workers through a properly worked out operational-level plan – a campaign plan – drawn up by the appropriately trained and empowered theatre commander, be he ambassador or general. Strategic success is delivered by the soldiers on the ground, but is enabled by a properly thought through and resourced operational-level campaign plan. There are no short cuts. Sadly, Iraq was to prove this point yet again.

6

Under New Management

The Bosnia tour complete, medal parades held and some leave taken, I had a few weeks remaining in Germany before handing 4th Armoured Brigade over to Brigadier David Richards – the first of four occasions when I was to pass my job to this outstanding officer. But that tour had a sting in the tail, with an Irish flavour. On my last Friday afternoon in Osnabrück, I returned home early as our daughter, Richenda, was due to have a leaving party for her schoolfriends in the garden. I had not been home long when I heard a familiar 'boom, boom' ringing across the city. 'Sounds like someone is being mortared,' I thought, not at first realizing that we were no longer in Bosnia. And then I thought: 'That sort of thing didn't happen in Bosnia; that's more like the IRA. Well, if it is, someone will ring me.'

I was right. A couple of minutes later James Everard was on the telephone. 'Brigadier, you are not going to believe this, but Brigade Headquarters has just come under mortar fire.'

I think he was rather disappointed when I said that I had already worked that one out, but that I would come back into camp to see what the damage was. Then, thinking out loud, I said to James: 'Look, if the IRA is being really clever, they know that I will come into camp, and if I was them I would put a close-quarter shooter near my house to catch the Brigadier as he reacts.' James agreed, and I asked him to send a Military Police patrol to escort me.

A few minutes later a couple of German civil police cars arrived outside Talavera House and instructed me to drive between them in my own car as we set out across the city. Unfortunately, they had interpreted their mission to be to get me to Quebec Barracks as quickly as possible. My desire was only to get there safely. We drove in a three-car convoy at about 80 mph straight through the centre of Osnabrück, through every red traffic light, until, in a complete muck sweat, we arrived at brigade headquarters – to find that, yes, the camp had been mortared but also, mercifully, that no one was injured. A lorry had been driven to the back gate and a number of improvised mortars fired. Some had made it over the fence, others had not, and the attackers had cleared off on a motorcycle. When the dust settled, we discovered that the principal damage done was to the Roman Catholic chapel – a bizarre irony of Bosnian proportions. That said, later that evening our formal farewell party was to be held in a large marquee about 100 yards beyond where the mortars had landed. It could all have had a very different outcome.

* * *

Days later, and not for the first or last time, I swapped my combat suit and the adrenalin of a command appointment for a grey suit and the serious business of a staff job in the Ministry of Defence in Whitehall. I had become the Director of the Defence Programme Staff, a post to which I felt I was particularly unsuited. 'Programmes' in the Ministry of Defence are about money. If something is 'in' the programme, it means that it will be funded and will usually happen. As the brigadier in charge of that part of the MOD, I found that I had quite a degree of influence over what was 'in' the programme. I also had influence over what was 'in' the programme and then taken 'out' as a savings measure, as well as influence over what was previously 'out', but then found its way back 'in' if someone argued their case strongly enough. It was an annual game that all could play, but my small staff of eight officers from all three services, along with my Civil Service colleague, Trevor Woolley, and his equally small civilian staff, were in something of a refereeing role. In the annual scramble for resources, many people of all shapes and sizes beat the well-worn path to my door pleading their case for either retention or inclusion in the programme. One senior Royal Marine officer, who shall remain nameless – but with whom I had previously attended the Higher Command and Staff Course – came to see me and very politely offered me personal physical violence if I were ever minded to cut the money from the Royal Marines protected mobility programme. I took the hint; the funds for this very important project stayed in place, and years later, in 2006–7, the Royal Marines' Vikings were the protected vehicles of choice in

Afghanistan. Later still, as the threat changed, their protection was found to be inadequate, but that was another issue.

Another tactic widely employed in the annual planning round to defend one's corner was to put up a savings measure that everyone knew would be too controversial to be taken. This was known in the trade as a 'Royal Yacht' – essentially, an unthinkable saving. The term, and the tactic, unfortunately met its demise when the Royal Navy actually did offer the Royal Yacht *Britannia* as a savings measure and, to save £60 million, Michael Portillo, the then Secretary of State for Defence, took it. There is no longer a Royal Yacht. Not surprisingly, as pressure on spending has increased in recent years, all three services have become much more wary about offering 'untakeable' savings as they run an increasing risk of being 'taken'. The short-lived furore in October 2009 over a £20 million saving from the Territorial Army budget shows how taut the string had become.

After I had been in post a year, during which my family had settled happily back into life in Norfolk and I was once again a weekly boarder in London, the general election of 1997 returned Tony Blair as Prime Minister. The dynamics within the Ministry of Defence changed. George Robertson became Defence Secretary, with John Reid at his right hand as armed forces minister. These two were charged with overseeing a fundamental Defence Review. Since the end of the Cold War much had already changed in defence: big cuts had been made under the 'Options for Change' programme and further reductions had been made under the 'Defence Costs

Study', but nevertheless a wholesale policy review was more than necessary. What became known as the Strategic Defence Review was quite properly guided by the ministers and chiefs of staff from their vantage point on the sixth floor of the Ministry of Defence, while the detailed work flowed down to the various staff branches. In the policy shop a very capable civil servant, Jon Day, played a leading role in the whole review, while Trevor Woolley and I as the money men felt obliged to try to keep the policy aspirations affordable. Not surprisingly, the three single-service planners were never very far from our shoulders.

The strategic and economic environment of 1997–8 provided a helpful context to the Strategic Defence Review. The unpopularity of John Major's Conservative Government at the time of the election was in sharp contrast to the health of the national economy, which provided Tony Blair with an opportunity to create a very usable set of armed forces with the potential to employ them beneficially in the national interest. In 1997 the aberration that was the first Gulf War, as some saw it, was well behind us. Likewise, the conundrum of trying to keep a peace in Bosnia when there wasn't one to keep was also past its worst, leaving a moment of comparative strategic equilibrium. The review did not need to be hurried. Choices could be made. In particular, there was a conscious development towards expeditionary armed forces that could increasingly be home-based but ready for deployment overseas. No credible threat to the external security of the United Kingdom was considered probable for at least ten years, so the approach that became known by the informal mantra of 'go first, go fast, go home' began to gain support, as did the notion of the United Kingdom's armed forces being 'a force for good'. It was considered that preparing to deploy quickly, and then doing what needed to be done swiftly and efficiently, was conducive to the likelihood of then being able to return home quickly, perhaps after only a matter of weeks or months, before re-setting the compass for the next adventure. And, of course, in the early days after the Strategic Defence Review that is exactly what happened – in Sierra Leone, East Timor, Macedonia and initially around Kabul at the start of the Afghan intervention.

To enable us to do this, future operations were characterized in wonderfully simple language as small, medium or large. In Army terms, 'small' meant a battalion-size operation of up to a thousand men and women under a lieutenant colonel, 'medium' a brigade of around five thousand under a brigadier and 'large' a division of some tens of thousands under a major general. Appropriate higher command, control and logistic supply would be provided as necessary. It was planned that none of the units deploying would do so for more than six months and that there would be a two-year gap between deployments. The mathematics of this were quite simple. For every unit deploying for six months there would be four more in the pipeline, either recovering, training or preparing to deploy; so a total of five were required for every deployment – the so-called Rule of Five.

The other major factor was how many of these operations we should plan to do at the same time. For the Army the big decision was that we should be able to deploy permanently one brigade group on a 'medium' size peacekeeping-type mission like Bosnia, thus requiring five such brigade groups to man the cycle – the worked manifestation of the Rule of Five. But in the spirit of 'go first, go fast, go home' we also needed another brigade at high readiness to conduct a 'medium'-scale war-fighting intervention somewhere else, for a maximum of six months. Thus a sixth ground manœuvre brigade was required so that we could run two simultaneous 'medium'-scale operations: one war-fighting for six months, the other on indefinite peacekeeping duties elsewhere. However, to cover all the options, including a 'large' operation like another Gulf War, we would need to put at least three of these brigades together as a division, trained and equipped for a war lasting six months. Finding the manpower necessary for this would also mean calling heavily on the part-time Territorial Army, which was to be reorganized to complement the Regular Army where necessary.

To complete the picture there was also the possibility that we might have to carry out at very short notice a 'small' operation, for example evacuating British citizens from a trouble spot somewhere in the world. In terms of land forces this type of task fell principally to the Royal Marines' 3 Commando Brigade and the Army's 16 Air Assault Brigade.

So at the end of the Strategic Defence Review the Army emerged with the core requirement of being able to conduct two simultaneous 'medium'-scale operations, requiring a total of six brigades of combat troops, which we would divide into two divisions for training and administration – the 1st Armoured Division in Germany and the 3rd Mechanized Division at home. Either of these two divisional headquarters would be capable of commanding a major operation. The theory made sense. It now remained to be seen whether the theory was to be fully funded and how it all stood up in reality.

There was another major factor that bore heavily on calculations with regard to the Army – Northern Ireland. In 1997 the Good Friday Agreement and the resultant peace process was in its infancy and still very fragile. This necessitated the continued commitment of six infantry battalions to the Province on semi-permanent two-year tours of duty, the troops living with their families in protected garrisons. Another six battalions were on short, intense, six-month tours of duty, living and operating mainly in Belfast, Londonderry and South Armagh. And on the mainland in the rest of the United Kingdom there was another standby battalion. All this translated into a total of thirty-seven infantry battalions of foot soldiers required to furnish the Northern Ireland roster. So our ability to do things around the world would also be constrained by the available manpower, as well as by money and the unforeseen.

Although military business is often most easily described in Army terms, the results of the Strategic Defence Review for the Royal Navy and the Royal Air Force were also represented in the language of large, medium and small. For those services the implications were translated into the numbers of fast jets available for operations and the composition of naval task groups, but the principles were the same as for the Army. For all three services, there were two other factors that had a bearing on costs. One was the readiness of units; the other was the degree of cost-efficiency that could be achieved by centralizing certain functions.

The higher the degree of readiness at which any unit was kept had a direct bearing on the amount of training it required and the money needed to pay for it. I chaired the Readiness Working Group, and after tortuous and byzantine discussions had to accept that there was no one solution that would fit all three services. The Army and the Royal Navy's cycles meant that units and ships could rotate between high, medium and low readiness categories with the consequent differentials in the cost of their training at any one time, but the Royal Air Force fast jet community seemed to be different. Like many, I struggled to understand this and was quite awkward about it. Sensing a problem, the Chief of the Air Staff thought that the solution for this Army brigadier, who was in danger of upsetting the RAF's applecart, should get a taste of what front-line flying really involved.

I was invited to visit RAF Leuchars in Scotland to spend some time with a Tornado fighter squadron. I duly toured the base, met lots of pilots and ground crew, was togged up in all the flying gear and did a sortie out over the North Sea. I think that part of the Chief of the Air Staff's 'cunning plan' was to teach me a lesson, so a sick bag was conveniently provided in the cockpit. However, when soon into the flight I told the pilot that their plan was about to work and that I was struggling to get my oxygen mask off, with all the rather nasty implications that entailed for the ground crew, the pilot returned the aircraft to a calmer equilibrium. My stomach having returned to its proper position, I then rather enjoyed flying through the sound barrier – though I guess someone on the ground in St Andrews heard a very loud bang! I went away from RAF Leuchars impressed by the professionalism of our fast jet operators but none the wiser as to why we still needed so many fast jets in the post Cold War era. Of course, flying a hi-tech aircraft is very demanding – as I discovered later when I began to fly helicopters – but I began to realize that the real cost of fast jets lay not in the number of aircraft we owned, but in the number of pilots and their standard of training. If everyone has to be fully trained pretty much the whole time, there is of necessity a tremendous amount of flying training to be done and therefore a very big bill to pay. This intense flying activity, combined with the sharp rise in the costs of the aerospace sector due to the technological sophistication of modern aircraft, seemed to me to promise an exponential rise in costs. So my conclusion in 1997 was that we had to be very, very careful in taking decisions about the numbers of fast jets we needed to own, and fly. If money was not a problem, then all bets were off, but I doubted that we would ever find ourselves in this enviable situation.

A number of other things happened quite late in the review, all in the name of cost-efficiency. One late decision produced a coming together of all three services' logistic and supply organizations into the Defence Logistic Organization; another put the majority of all the three services' helicopters under the Joint Helicopter Command. The rationale behind both decisions was sound, although in practice both highlighted the tensions between effectiveness in the 'battle space' – where the Navy, Army and Air Force add their real value on operations – and in the 'business space' – where the accountants calculate cost-efficiency. Some things defy the harsh reality of the slide rule or pocket calculator. There are, as Oscar Wilde noted, those who know the cost of everything but the value of nothing. The creation of the Joint Helicopter Command ultimately resulted in a situation where none of the three services actually 'owned' responsibility for helicopters, with the further result that in 2004 the Defence Management Board felt comfortable in taking £1.4 billion from the helicopter programme. The three services thought that they had higher priorities at the time, but the fatal result was a much reduced helicopter procurement and maintenance programme which was to have a significant effect in Afghanistan in the summer of 2009 and beyond. Of course, had more money been available at the time, the saving would never have been taken from the helicopter programme, but defence was under a very tight cash squeeze then.

The final decision to emerge from the Defence Review, which popped up at almost the last moment, was that to procure two new aircraft carriers for the Royal Navy. The purpose was to provide air cover over deployed land forces. Of course, as an Army person I was delighted by this, but somewhat puzzled by the lack of debate as to whether such air cover was best provided by aircraft launched from carriers at sea or otherwise launched from friendly land air bases with range extended by air-to-air refuelling where necessary. But the aircraft-carrier decision was brilliant news in public terms and very clever in political terms. By announcing that the two vessels would come into service in 2012 and 2014, the New Labour Government could take all the credit for a very visionary statement of national resolve and intent without the near- to medium-term worries about funding the project. Cynically, one wondered whether the hard-nosed calculation was that by the time real money had to be allocated to this expensive programme, the political and economic cycle would have turned, passing to an incoming Conservative Government the difficult decision whether to confirm the aircraft-carrier programme against the financial odds, or to cancel or modify it. In any event, the announcement of the decision created great headlines at the time, but the implications for the rest of defence, and perhaps other parts of the Royal Navy, would be felt later. As I write in 2010 the new Coalition Government has indeed got to address the air-craft-carrier issue. There is no doubt these ships are highly desirable; but the jury is out on whether they are both essential and affordable.

So the 1997–8 Strategic Defence Review was hailed as a great success. It was led by policy imperatives, which was good. It set a logical baseline for the future commit-ment of our armed forces, which was also good. Indeed, it stated that the United Kingdom intended to use its armed forces to act on the world stage as a 'force for good', which was highly laudable. But did all that really answer every part of the question? The harsh reality was that the SDR could achieve all it set out to do only if it was fully funded. To do what this policy-led review aspired to would cost £X billion, but in the event some-thing less than £X billion was provided, a discrepancy exacerbated by a tough year-on-year savings target laid on the Ministry of Defence by the Treasury very late in the whole process, and then further exacerbated by a series of operations embarked on by Tony Blair that broke the planning assumptions made in the review. History will pass judgement on these foreign adventures in due course, but in my view Gordon Brown's malign intervention, when Chancellor, on the SDR by refusing to fund what his own Government had agreed, fatally flawed the entire process from the outset. The seeds were thereby sown for some of the impossible operational pressures to come. Why didn't Tony Blair resolve this problem, particularly when it put at risk his own aspirations for an 'ethical' foreign policy – as Robin Cook described it – that entailed the prospect of significant military operations abroad? I was forced to the conclusion that he lacked the moral courage to impose his will on his own Chancellor. I was also somewhat bemused a few years later to have a conversation with Gordon Brown when he was Prime Minister about a book he was writing. Entitled *Wartime Courage*, it described 'the courage, sacrifice and eventual triumph' of the World War generations. Brown wrote that he hoped that he had described a 'precious store of moral capital that following generations, inspired by it, can draw on in another age'. I am still not sure whether he ever realized that by denying the proper funding of his own Government's declared policy, he was condemning more young men and women to the same sacrifices he railed against in a previous generation. This sad episode led me to the conclusion that if war is too important to be left to generals, then the funding of war is too important to be left to politicians.

It was with something of a sigh of relief that after three years I left the introspection of the Ministry of Defence and the intensity of the Whitehall Village on promotion to major general and appointment to the command of 3rd (UK) Mechanized Division, headquartered at Bulford Camp on the edge of Salisbury Plain. This meant another family upheaval. Pippa and I moved to Clive House, Tidworth; the three boys were already at either university or boarding school, and now Richenda, our youngest, started at Leaden Hall School in The Close in Salisbury. For children of highly mobile service families there really is no alternative to boarding school to produce the continuity of education that children need. Some think that the allowance given towards the cost of school fees is just an officers' perk; so it is perhaps worth recording that my Green Howard driver, Sergeant Paul Simpson, also chose to send one of his daughters to Leaden Hall School. We often shared school runs at the weekend. The allowance is entirely practical, taken up by soldiers of widely differing ranks and situations who share the same educational aspirations for their children, to make sure they get a fair start in life.

The 3rd (UK) Division had been significantly affected by the Strategic Defence Review whose deliberations I had just left. A division is one of the Army's largest groupings of units, numbering many thousands of men and women. In simple terms it is the largest of our tactical units and trains to fight battles, engagements and major operations within an overall campaign plan drawn up at a higher level. The challenge of such a command was very exciting. That said, there were pressing organizational changes to be made as a result of the review. A very sensible decision had been taken by General Sir Mike Jackson, at that time Commander in Chief, Land

Command, that the Army's two fighting divisions, 1st Armoured Division in Germany and my division, should have their administrative responsibilities reduced to the minimum so that they could focus solely on training and operational preparation. This meant that in the United Kingdom I would hand over all non-operational responsibilities to the major generals in command of the non-deployable 2nd, 4th and 5th Divisions in Edinburgh, Aldershot and Shrewsbury respectively, who would become solely responsible for all administrative, legal and Territorial Army tasks, leaving me free to prepare 3rd Division for operations. At the same time, to re-organize the division fully I had to oversee the amalgamation of 5th Airborne Brigade and 24th Airmobile Brigade to form the new 16th Air Assault Brigade, which would become part of the new Joint Helicopter Command, and also to set up our third ground manœuvre brigade, 12th Mechanized Brigade. The basic premise of the review had been that both operational divisions would have three deployable brigades, each of which would move through a readiness cycle, always ensuring that there were adequate numbers of troops to sustain the ongoing peacekeeping operation while sufficient were held for a short, sharp war-fighting intervention. All change causes friction and attracts cost, but we were well on the way to doing what had to be done when the world's eyes returned once more to the Balkans.

To many Balkan-watchers, Kosovo was a problem that would need to be resolved sooner rather than later. Although a very small entity, no larger than Northern Ireland in terms of population and territory, it sits at the crossroads in the Balkans in terms of both ethnic mix and the development of rival economies. Spiritually, the defeat of the Orthodox Christian Serbs at the Battle of Kosovo Polje in 1389 had led to five hundred years of domination by the Muslim Ottoman Empire. This situation had only been reversed in the chaos of the twentieth century, with the Serbs reasserting their dominance over the Croat and Muslim populations on the back of Tito's imposition of his own form of Communism. But with the demise of Tito the latent animosity of the parties within Yugoslavia re-emerged, leading first to the war in Croatia and then to that in Bosnia, with both of which I was all too well acquainted. Sensing the complete failure of his desire for a greater Serbia, Slobodan Milosevic decided to build on his Serb nationalist triumph in Kosovo in 1989 by forcing the Muslim Albanian population of Kosovo onto the back foot. Although in 1999 90 per cent of the Kosovan population was Albanian and Muslim, the administration was firmly in the hands of the minority Serb population, who were committed not only to the preservation of access to the Orthodox Christian sites in Kosovo but also to Serb political, cultural and economic dominance. It was therefore no great surprise that in the late 1990s the Kosovo Liberation Army began to gain recruits, competence and resolve.

For the United Kingdom, weary after years of difficult engagement in Bosnia (though recently buoyed up by the success of the rapid intervention in Sierra Leone), the prospect of becoming a key player in a new initiative in Kosovo was less than appealing. But Tony Blair, exercising his newly invigorated military muscle, led the charge in confronting Slobodan Milosevic, first by threatening and then by attempting to coerce him into changing his policy towards Kosovo. In the face of stubborn intransigence from Belgrade, the commencement of the bombing campaign in spring 1999 was something of an inevitability. However, the expectation of achieving acquiescence within a few days by this means was soon to be dashed. The Serbs were more resolute than expected, and the prospect of a ground intervention to force the issue began to gain currency, at least in UK military circles. The British-led Headquarters Allied Rapid Reaction Corps (HQ ARRC), led by Mike Jackson, had deployed in early 1999 to become the backbone of any negotiated settlement of the Kosovo issue. Such an agreement was bound to involve a degree of power-sharing between the Serbs and the Albanian Muslims, an outcome that seemed even further away following recent episodes of ethnic cleansing and the improper use of force by the Serb security forces. When the early days of the NATO bombing campaign appeared to yield no immediate prospect of success, military planning began to turn to the possible need for a ground operation. With the United States remaining on the sidelines at this stage, the lead within NATO was going to fall to the United Kingdom.

So it was that my headquarters began planning in earnest for a land intervention into Kosovo. The operation would, of course, be under command of Mike Jackson's ARRC, temporarily headquartered in Skopje, Macedonia, in the hope that military force would be needed only to police a negotiated settlement, not to fight for it. But in my headquarters we were thinking seriously about what would happen if the tough diplomacy, accompanied by heavy NATO air attacks, failed. There were three primary approaches into Kosovo for a ground force. The most direct and central approach would necessitate forcing a route across several bridges, in addition to passing through two mountain tunnels, any or all of which could have been easily denied by withdrawing Serb forces. The second – eastern – approach was feasible only if we were to advance initially into Serbia itself, thereby risking opposition from the Serb Army, forced quite properly to defend its sovereign soil. The third – western – approach required passage through mountainous terrain in Albania, probably a severe and even impossible challenge to the armour-heavy NATO force. My planners and I paused to try to work out the least bad option.

Curiously, even as a consensus began to build both in the United States and within NATO that a ground intervention might actually prove to be the best way of overcoming the growing impasse, Slobodan Milosevic indicated that he was ready to talk, and withdraw from Kosovo. Exactly why he changed his mind went with him to the grave when he died during his later trial for war crimes and genocide in The Hague, but the pressure of the bombing, his indictment as a war criminal and the growing support for a ground campaign all played their part. Our focus turned immediately to the terms and practicalities of the Serb withdrawal. Mike Jackson found himself leading a very delicate international negotiation of great significance. This he achieved brilliantly, resulting in a clear timetable for the Serb forces to exit Kosovo.

I assumed that this would prove to be the end of any

potential involvement by my headquarters, but London took a different view. Although Mike Jackson would command the NATO peace enforcement operation, the MOD decided that, given the very large numbers of British troops involved (4th Armoured Brigade, 5th Airborne Brigade and 1st Signal Brigade), there was a need for a senior national headquarters to look after British interests. That was to be Headquarters 3rd (UK) Division. So, somewhat in a hurry, we packed our bags. The decision to deploy was taken on a Thursday: we were to fly on Saturday.

Experience from Bosnia told me I would need some form of decent vehicle to move easily around the difficult Balkan terrain, and a Land Rover Discovery was the answer. I did not have one. Following the Strategic Defence Review, 'Smart Procurement' had become the guiding principle to solve equipment issues, so I decided to procure a Discovery smartly. The 'system' could not produce one overnight, so a local Land Rover dealer was very pleased to let me have a dark green demonstrator model, taxed and ready to go within hours. A cheque was duly issued; the vehicle was delivered to my headquarters in Bulford, loaded and emplaned at RAF Lyneham the same evening. When I arrived in Skopje the following morning, it, together with Sergeant Paul Simpson, my driver, and Sergeant Chris Brice, my close protection team leader, were on the airfield to meet me. The vehicle did sterling service throughout our tour, and I would have been really stuck without it. But, as I was to discover, there is 'smart procurement' and 'Smart Procurement'. Months later the 'system' fought back. The problem was not that I had acquired the Discovery in a very 'smart' way, but that we had omitted to claim a refund on the unused portion of the road tax disc that had come with the demonstrator model. The £24,000 to buy the vehicle was not an issue, but the £90 not refunded on the tax disc was. On my arrival back in the UK, I was greeted by a very stiff letter drafted by the Command Secretary and signed by the Commander in Chief, Land Command, General Sir Michael Walker. Let no one say that the Ministry of Defence wastes money!

By the time NATO was ready to move into Kosovo, 4th Armoured Brigade had been joined by 5th Airborne Brigade and we, the British, were supplying by far the largest part of the intervention force. Our job was to police the Serb Army's withdrawal from Kosovo and provide the basis for a fair society which respected the rights of all the citizens of Kosovo. It was therefore with particular concern that we heard on Friday, 11 June, the day before our planned move into Kosovo, that a Russian armoured column was making its way from Bosnia to Kosovo. Soon afterwards we heard that six Iluyshin transport aircraft were even then en route to Pristina airport. The Russians were clearly minded to pre-empt the NATO operation so carefully negotiated by Mike Jackson, and thus to cause maximum political embarrassment. Mike rang me to warn of what appeared to be happening. I jumped into my Discovery to drive to his headquarters in the Gazela Shoe Factory just outside the Macedonian capital, Skopje. On the way I radioed Hamish Rollo, my chief of staff (a brilliant officer who subsequently reached the rank of major general before tragically dying from a heart problem in 2009 while still serving), to ask whether our small HQ would be capable of taking under command elements of 4th Armoured Brigade and 5th Airborne Brigade if we needed to mount a coordinated response to the Russian move. Unflappable as ever, Hamish asked for a couple of moments while he thought about it.

In the event we got into the well-documented standoff with the Russians at the airfield, to say nothing of the equally dramatic impasse between Mike Jackson and the NATO Supreme Commander, General Wes Clark. Clark was arguing that NATO forces should prevent the Russians from landing, regardless of the potential international consequences. My recollection of that extraordinary afternoon, as the last safe moment to launch the heliborne troops of 5th Airborne Brigade towards Pristina airport approached, was that of Mike Jackson beginning to brief Wes Clark over a video conference link on his plans for dealing with the Russians when they arrived. Whatever the outcome of the conference, London had told me, as COMBRITFOR, to be prepared to play the national red card if necessary, and to veto any use of British troops on a pre-emptive operation. So far as I was concerned, if Wes Clark ordered Mike Jackson to secure Pristina airport against the approaching Russian airborne troops or armour it was not going to be done with British troops. More to the point, if it was not going to be done with British troops it was not going to happen at all. However, halfway through Mike's explanation of the current situation the video conference link was lost. By the time it was restored, the go/no go time slot for the heliborne operation by the Paras and Gurkhas had passed and, on the first day at least, the issue had suddenly become academic. The troops waiting on the helicopter landing sites were stood down for the night, feeling a mixture of relief and disappointment. Whether the video conference link was lost by genuine accident or by some inspired plug-pulling I do not know, although undoubtedly the net effect was beneficial. In the event, after a further standoff between Jackson and Clark the next day – 'Sir, I'm not going to start World War Three for you' – the situation eased and the Russians at Pristina airport quickly became more of a logistical embarrassment to their own government than a strategic threat to NATO, who subsequently had to supply them with food and water.

In complete contrast to the high drama of the Russian episode, the actual move into Kosovo by the main body of the NATO force passed fairly easily. On the British axis of advance – the high-risk central approach, crossing a series of bridges and passing through two major tunnels – all went pretty much according to plan. However, Mike Jackson's understandable desire to urge the ground units of 4th Armoured Brigade to move more quickly led Brigadier Bill Rollo (a cousin of Hamish's) to retort that he could do so, provided helicopters would stop landing on the road ahead of his armour, in order to drop more ammunition to the airborne troops further ahead of him than they could possibly need. For my part, I had asked Mike Jackson how my national HQ could help and he had growled: 'Just keep the British media off my back.' During the previous few days we had set up a fairly comprehensive series of briefings and press conferences to feed the appetite of the media and to keep them away from him as the operational commander. On

12 June itself I had agreed to do a live link to the MOD morning brief in London and a series of live reports to the main television and radio channels. Having watched the armoured columns cross into Kosovo at first light, apparently outnumbered by a mass of television and radio trucks, I jumped into an RAF Puma helicopter to get a first-hand feel of the situation before I went on air. In my enthusiasm, we flew further into Kosovo than I intended and soon found ourselves far beyond the front line, overflying the Serb positions. Hurriedly deciding that discretion was the better part of valour, we made a swift U-turn that had us heading back to British lines. I then spotted what seemed to be someone's tactical headquarters and ordered the pilot to land, so as to get an update. Creating more dust than good manners permitted, I nevertheless found myself at the forward headquarters of 1st Battalion, the Parachute Regiment, the leading British battlegroup. The commanding officer, Lieutenant Colonel Paul Gibson, seemed a bit surprised but quite pleased to see me. Looking around, it was my turn to be surprised. I had dropped into what seemed like a Falklands reunion. In addition to the staff of 1 Para were Colonel John Crossland, late of 2 Para, who had fought at Goose Green and was now our defence attaché in Belgrade, together with Robert Fox of the *Daily Telegraph* and the London *Evening Standard*, another veteran of Goose Green. They had both clearly decided the best vantage point was with the forward troops. And, of course, they were right.

To the satisfaction of all, it quickly became clear that the Serbs intended to observe the timelines that had been agreed with Mike Jackson and the focus of the operation happily turned quite quickly from security to politics, a situation which has characterized the West's intervention in Kosovo from 1999 to the present day. The eventual decision to grant independence to Kosovo was always going to be a major blow to Serb pride, but after their excesses during the various Balkan wars they were in no position to do more than huff and puff. The long-term future of Kosovo remains unsettled: too small and poor to be properly independent, it is too Albanian and too Muslim to be a genuine part of Serbia. In so many interventions it is far easier, though not necessarily easy, to go into somewhere than to come out; and in Kosovo this remains the challenge for NATO and the European Union – and a number of European countries seem very keen to stress the importance of maintaining large contingents of troops in Kosovo rather than making them available for operations in Afghanistan. Britain left Kosovo, finally, in 2009; but by then my small national HQ had long departed, returning to Bulford, after a busy few Balkan months, in August 1999.

The duty of an army when not deployed on operations is to prepare and train for whatever the future holds. Again, as I had set out when writing the new doctrine at Camberley just a few years before, the trick is to analyse the experiences and lessons of the present and keep developing approaches to operations that are likely to bring success in the future. This thought dominated my remaining time in command of the 3rd Division. The reorganization following the Strategic Defence Review was completed when the new 12th Mechanized Brigade was established in Aldershot under the command of the very energetic Brigadier John Cooper. However, I was concerned about two aspects of our training. The first was that, since the end of the Cold War, we had had no practical opportunities to exercise our units on a large scale. Both Bosnia and Kosovo, notwithstanding the complexity of the internal ethnic issues, had required a large-scale military intervention to facilitate the eventual peace settlements. So it was critically important that we retained the capability to exercise on a large scale in order to be able to prepare for the complexities of high-intensity war-fighting. There is no substitute for getting hundreds of troops and vehicles out into the field, without which you can never properly practise dealing with the unexpected – the so-called 'fog' of war, as we call it. The second was that we were not giving sufficient thought to the advantages that helicopters could bring to the battlefield. The Army had a major procurement programme running that would bring the Apache attack helicopter into our hands quite soon and thereby provide a dramatic leap in our military capability, but I did not think we had thought enough about its future tactical potential.

Towards the end of our time in Kosovo, Hamish Rollo and I came up with a potential solution to both problems. We decided to propose a different way of using BATUS, the major British Army training area in Canada, to give the key elements of our ground manœuvre brigades – 1st, 12th and 19th – a proper run-out, for the first time since we had stopped exercising over open German countryside in the early 1990s. We planned a major exercise – Exercise 'Iron Anvil' – in 2001 as a 'trade' test for the new 12th Mechanized Brigade. It would involve parts of all four major units of the brigade exercising together, across open country, on the Alberta prairie. It would be expensive, but I thought well worth the cost. In the event the exercise took place as planned, but not until the year after I had handed over the division to my successor.

To prove the concept, and to generate some practical thinking about how the Army would use its new Apache attack helicopters on the future battlefield, we planned another ambitious exercise in Canada for 2000. This was called Exercise 'Iron Hawk'. (Every exercise in the 3rd Division, known as the Iron Division, has the word 'Iron' in its title.) I had previously persuaded Headquarters Land Command to let me form a wide-ranging 'Air Manœuvre Development Group', drawing on the expertise of the Army Air Corps, Royal Air Force, Royal Marines and various elements of the Army, in order to work out how we could best exploit the advantages of manœuvre in the air dimension, principally by helicopters, in coordination with traditional ground manœuvre units. Clearly there was something new here, and we needed to make the most of it, although we weren't really sure what we were going to get.

Exercise 'Iron Hawk' took 3rd Regiment, Army Air Corps to Canada with their old Lynx helicopters pretending to be Apaches, the Household Cavalry Regiment with their tracked armoured reconnaissance vehicles, and 1st Battalion, the Queen's Lancashire Regiment as an infantry force. The 2nd Royal Tank Regiment were to be the enemy. It was the biggest exercise the Army had ever run in Canada, indeed the largest it had organized anywhere since the end of the Cold War. I deployed part of my divisional headquarters to command the exercise, with the headquarters of 16 Air Assault Brigade under Brigadier Peter Wall and the headquarters of 1st Reconnaissance Brigade under Brigadier Martin Speller to command the exercising troops. My plan was fairly simple. The helicopters and armoured vehicles would operate closely with the infantry in an attempt to heighten the pace of battlefield operations and by so doing hopefully wrong-foot the enemy force. I told the exercise director, Colonel Hamish McDonald, that I did not want to know the enemy plan.

As the first part of the exercise unfolded, I suddenly realized that, having brought everyone out to Canada to exercise them, it was I who was now under the greatest pressure. Disappointingly, the first battle went rather badly, but we learned many lessons and became progressively more efficient – which is what training, after all, is all about. Importantly, the exercise confirmed our assumption that exploitation of the third dimension – the air – was a significant force multiplier to any ground operation. Repeating lessons we had learned from experimental airmobile brigades in the 1980s and 1990s, we recognized that we needed helicopters for all kinds of essential activity: for troop and equipment lift, for reconnaissance, for moving commanders and small parties around the battlefield, and for providing close air support to troops on the ground. It was abundantly clear to us all that the Army, the Royal Marines and the Royal Air Force all needed major investment in helicopters for attack, lift and command support tasks across the entirety of the future battlefield. I knew this from my peacekeeping experience in Bosnia and Kosovo; now I was convinced of the need in both peace enforcement and more conventional operations. Unfortunately, this was one area where we remained woefully under-resourced.

Perhaps because of my leadership of the Air Manœuvre Development Group, or perhaps from my time in command of my own battalion in the airmobile role, I was delighted to be rung up by Brigadier Richard Foulkes, Director of the Army Air Corps, to ask if I would consider following General Sir Michael Walker in the honorary appointment of Colonel Commandant of the Army Air Corps. As a committed enthusiast for what helicopters could bring to the battlefield, I was delighted and accepted at once. Such appointments, when one steps outside one's own part of the Army and into another, are always a great privilege, a little bit like joining another family, except that as colonel commandant one immediately becomes a tribal chief. In the case of the Army Air Corps I knew that they would need to teach me to fly helicopters in order to allow me to engage with both air and ground crew from a position of first-hand experience. This was an exciting prospect; but before I could get too closely involved the Balkans called again – twice.

General Sir Roger Wheeler, Chief of the General Staff, rang me to ask whether I would be prepared to go to the International Criminal Tribunal for the Former Yugoslavia in The Hague to give evidence, as an expert witness, in a trial relating to the Srebrenica massacre in 1995. I said that of course I would do this, and soon found myself making a series of visits to both Bosnia and the Netherlands to prepare my evidence. The accused was General Radovan Krstic, who, in July 1995, had been commanding the Drina Corps of the Bosnian Serb Army. It was alleged that his troops had carried out the massacre of nearly eight thousand Muslim men and boys around Srebrenica in the middle of July 1995. It was quite clear from the material I reviewed that the intent behind the massacre had come from the top and that Krstic's direct orders had been received from General Ratko Mladic himself. The issue before the court was the extent of Krstic's personal involvement. To prepare for the case I not only had extensive discussions with the prosecution team in The Hague but visited most of the execution and burial sites with a remarkable French gendarmerie officer, Jean René Ruez. He had spent years investigating the massacre and was very close to all the issues.

Although five years had passed, many of the murder sites, such as the House of Culture – in reality a cinema – in Pilica, had not been touched. Blood was splattered across all the walls. It was not difficult to imagine the terror that fell on those defenceless men and boys as they were machine-gunned and grenaded within the locked doors of the building. There were many such sites dotted around Srebrenica, Bratunac, Zvornik and Kozluk. The logistics of terror had included buses to move prisoners to their places of execution. Sometimes the bus drivers had been made to conduct the first killings in order to guarantee their silence. The horror was meticulously planned and efficiently executed. The organized ruthlessness of the almost industrial-scale genocide had extended to the exhumation and reburial of bodies that had been interred inefficiently the first time round. Among the evidence that ultimately convicted Krstic were fuel requisition orders approved by him, or his staff, to power the diggers that moved the bodies. The hasty exhumations and reburials compounded the forensic nightmare for the investigators. Mechanical diggers are no respecters of the grave.

As the trial developed, the weight of evidence against Radovan Krstic grew. At the start he presented himself as a simple, professional military officer, doing the best he could and always obediently following orders. Indeed, his career in the old Yugoslav National Army had begun at about the same time as mine in the British Army. But there the similarities stopped. His various defences were swept away in the face of the overwhelming evidence against him and he was convicted, sentenced to forty-two years' imprisonment on charges that included direct complicity in war crimes. During the trial it became very apparent that his principal failing had been a personal, moral one. His body language in the dock increasingly indicated that he knew that his principal mistake was in blindly accepting the order given to him directly by Ratko Mladic on 12 July 1995 to instruct his troops to conduct mass killings. Of course, the personal risk to him of adopting a morally correct line was considerable, but in his heart of hearts he knew that as a professional officer he had failed the greatest test. He had used obedience to orders as the excuse for his own complicity in the murder of helpless civilians. This profound personal failure condemned eight thousand men and boys to a ghastly death and thousands of Bosnian Muslim families to a life of unremitting grief. Jean René

Ruez, the French investigator, suffered a major breakdown.

It was not long after I had returned to the division following the Krstic case that the Chief was on the telephone again. This time General Wheeler was ringing to tell me my next appointment. I had hoped to go back to London, but I was wrong.

'I want you to go to Sarajevo for about a year as Deputy Commander for Operations of the NATO Stabilization Force [SFOR],' he said.

It is a great strength of the Army that you do what you are told.

'Right, Sir, delighted,' I replied – but, chancing my arm, added: 'But can I just delay by long enough to run my big exercise in Canada first?'

He agreed and I hung up. I swivelled my chair ninety degrees to the right and looked out of the window. 'How am I going to explain this one to Philippa?' I thought.

Well, another strength of the Army is that many of us are fortunate enough to have very understanding wives. Although Pippa was not very amused, as it meant leaving the 3rd Division early and removing Richenda from school in Salisbury, at least the consolation was that the family could head back home to Norfolk while I went back to Bosnia. A consolation for me was that I was allowed to take some of my own team with me. Lieutenant Colonel Chris Ryder from the 3rd Division agreed to come as my Military Assistant, as did Captain Zac Stenning, my aide de camp. Those faithful sergeants Paul Simpson, my driver, and Steve Crighton, my orderly, both said they were up for it too. We said our goodbyes to the division, fired our pistols on the range to pass our annual weapon proficiency tests and packed for Sarajevo. No sooner had news of the job become public than Sergeant Chris Brice of the Royal Military Police, my previous close protection team leader in Kosovo, rang up to say that he was coming too, to keep an eye on me.

It is probably a truism in life that going back somewhere is not a great experience, and I found returning to Bosnia four years on from my last long posting to be profoundly depressing. As we had first suspected, the Dayton peace agreement had provided for an excellent ceasefire and for subsequent military disengagement, but was flawed as a mechanism for securing a lasting peace. I am certain that in 1995 the international community failed to recognize just how strong a position it was in, with all three parties tired of war and desperate for peace. Perhaps, with hindsight, the Dayton agreement was insufficiently ambitious. On my return in late 2000, while the actual fighting had stopped and the armies had been largely disarmed, the friction between Republika Srpska and the Bosnian Federation was as sharp as ever. Indeed, I was saddened to find that severe tension also existed within the Federation between the Croats and the Muslims. Elections had just been held, but a new government was not immediately forthcoming. That said, this problem was not confined to Bosnia. The United States was struggling at the time over the ratification of George W. Bush as President, courtesy of Jeb Bush's Florida. I was amused to read the wry comments in the Sarajevo newspapers which frequently offered electoral assistance to the Americans!

Security was pretty good in the country, so I judged that my main task was to integrate the military elements of the three former warring factions into something approaching a small, affordable, national army. My right-hand man in this task was a very competent Dutch brigadier, Peter van Uhm. I got to know and like Peter immensely: this introduction later proved very beneficial, as he was to become Chief of the Netherlands Army when I was Chief of the General Staff, although he then leapfrogged me to become the Dutch Chief of Defence. Tragically, in his first week in that new appointment in 2008 his son was killed in Afghanistan. But in Bosnia in 2000 we had no inkling of this future grief. Peter and I spent much time meeting the heads of the Bosniac, Croat and Serb armies, both individually and collectively. In my first Joint Commission meeting with General Atif Dudakovic, the head of the Federation Army, I took great pleasure in immediately asking for the nine armoured vehicles that his troops had stolen from my UN Bangladeshis in 1995. As usual, this produced prevarication and denial, an attitude that set the tone for our subsequent dealings. Meanwhile on the Serb side my meetings struggled to get beyond rather unsubtle questioning about who was likely to be the next indicted for war crimes. Many of the former senior Serbs were already in The Hague, and nervousness among the remainder was high.

But the most pressing issues of my time in Bosnia revolved around money, and the balance of power between the Muslims and Croats in the Federation. The defining event was what we came to call the 'Mostar Bank Job'. It was an event worthy of Michael Caine. The background was pretty straightforward. As we saw things in 2000, the Washington agreement of 1994 that had ended the war between the Muslims and Croats was hardly worth the paper it was written on and represented something of a shotgun marriage, while the Dayton agreement of 1995 provided no real basis for a stable Bosnia in the long term. The elections in 2000 revealed the real tensions within the Bosniac–Croat Federation, itself one of the two parties to the Dayton agreement. If the Federation collapsed, so too would Dayton, negating all the progress made by the international community in the years since 1995. No one wanted to see that happen. But the electoral defeat of the hard-line Croat HDZ party and the forcing out of power of the Croat HDZ Tri-President Jelavic brought things to a head. The hard-liners saw their future to be in breaking the Federation, or at least in taking control of that part of Bosnia in which a majority of Croats lived. Linking these areas with Croatia would have been, for the future of an independent Bosnia, an absolute disaster. When we examined the problem we could not at first understand how the HDZ, having lost the election, could still appear to retain power. Indeed, their part of the Federation Army seemed on the brink of mutiny. On closer analysis it became clear to us that the HDZ zealots had considerable financial clout, buying the support of their soldiers and thus reinforcing their political power through the judicious use of their own money, much of which was generated by Mafia-style black market activity. Their informal 'treasury' was the Herzcegovacka Banka, and their system of distribution was through its branches. To break this malign power, which threatened the success of both the Federation and of Dayton, we had to 'do' the bank: no bank, no power. When contemplating what needed to be done I ruefully observed that 'doing' a bank was not in the Sandhurst handbook. We had to improvise.

The first part did not go well. The High Representative of the international community duly signed an order taking over the Herzcegovacka Banka, but this did not impress the Croat bank officials when it was presented to them mid-morning one sunny April day. Within minutes the international bank team were chased away by an angry crowd. An embarrassing hiatus threatened to develop, but I had created a plan for this sort of contingency. So it was that at precisely 2 a.m. on 18 April the 2nd Battalion, Princess of Wales's Regiment found itself surrounding the head office of the Herzcegovacka Banka in Mostar. With a French battalion securing the outer cordon, and helicopter gunships and fast jets patrolling the airspace above, Royal Engineers blasted a hole in the rear wall of the building. British soldiers then entered the bank and gained access to all five floors. Every portable computer, disc, file and paper record was carefully gathered up; the mainframe computers were dragged to the ground floor and extracted through the large hole in the back wall of the building, while the safes in the basement were blown in by three black-clad gentlemen who had flown in that evening for the purpose. Going down to the cellar to see how they were getting on, one of them looked up at me with a fistful of banknotes, remarking: 'Bit singed, these ones, Guv!' By 6 a.m. our work was done, and I returned the key of the front door to the very shaken night watchman, who had remained shivering on the doorstep under the gentle grasp of one of my soldiers, clearly wondering what he was going to tell his masters when they arrived in the morning.

To prove our integrity, I took him to the top floor to inspect the vending machine. We might have taken everything else, I told him, but we were not thieves, and their chocolate and soft drinks were intact. Although the front door of the building remained locked, the fact that there was a gaping hole at the rear of the building did not seem a point worth discussing at the time! Shortly after first light we were all back in the French barracks enjoying coffee and croissants, with five lorry-loads of useful evidence and cash in our possession.

The Bank Job ended the Croat bid to break the Federation, and kept the Dayton peace process in play. Days later, Paddy Ashdown arrived as High Representative amid high expectations, and within a week I had left Bosnia once again for London, and the joys of the Ministry of Defence.

7

9/11 and the End of the New World Order

One morning in early April 2001, razor in hand, I was staring at myself in the mirror above the washbasin in my room in Camp Butmir, the NATO headquarters in Sarajevo, when I heard the BBC *Today* programme make passing reference to the fact that, contrary to popular speculation, the next incumbent of the historic post of Black Rod, the official who runs the House of Lords, would not be a woman. Instead, the next Black Rod would be a serving general who would take early retirement to fill the appointment. For most, that news item was of only passing interest, but for one or two of my military colleagues and myself this snippet of information had personal significance, for it meant some unexpected, and short-notice, moves within the ranks of the generals. And so it was. Lieutenant General Sir Michael Willcocks retired from the Army to become the next Black Rod; Major General Kevin O'Donoghue replaced him, on promotion, as the United Kingdom's

Military Representative to NATO in Brussels; and a vacancy was created as Assistant Chief of the General Staff in London. It was not many days before my telephone in Sarajevo rang and I heard General Sir Michael Walker, the Chief of the General Staff, inviting me to return to the UK early and take over as his Assistant Chief. I was delighted by General Mike's phone call. I very much looked forward to working directly for him, and also tackling the enormous responsibilities that were part and parcel of the post. There was just time to do the Mostar Bank Job before packing my bags. As I left Sarajevo, the international bank officials were still counting the cash and the Croat bank officials were working out how to fill the large hole in the back wall of their bank through which we had extracted their mainframe computers.

Having handed over as NATO Deputy Commander in Bosnia to a good friend, Major General John Kiszely, I flew home in a small executive jet provided by the RAF. I took all my personal team with me on the flight: Captain Philip Searle, my ADC, and Sergeants Steve Crighton, my orderly, Paul Simpson, my driver, and Chris Brice, my close protection team leader. We landed at RAF Coltishall in Norfolk to let me get off and go home, while the others flew on to London and some well-deserved leave.

In theory we give ourselves fairly generous post-operational leave after a long spell away on tour, and I was due about a month off. However, reality and theory often part company, and on this occasion I reported to London less than a week after leaving Sarajevo. My induction into my new post as ACGS was to sit through an all-day meeting of the Executive Committee of the Army Board, known in the trade as ECAB. The committee was considering a series of discussion papers under the general title 'A Strategy for the Army', continuing the process of implementing the outcome of the Strategic Defence Review. To listen to the discussion was thought to be as good a way as any to learn the new job. Unlike my previous two appointments in the Ministry of Defence, when I had been working in the Central Staff and taking a view on issues across the whole defence field, this time I was very much in an Army appointment and charged with looking after the Army's interests, albeit still within the wider defence context.

Each of the three services has an Executive Committee which runs its domestic policy and management business. I was now a member of the Army's most senior committee and was to remain a member of ECAB, on and off, for the next seven years. As Assistant Chief of the General Staff I was very much the junior member although, somewhat perversely, its principal business manager. The Chief of the General Staff (then General Sir Michael Walker), as the professional head of the Army, chairs the Board and is personally responsible to the Secretary of State for Defence for the overall performance of the Army. The second most senior is the Commander in Chief (then General Sir Mike Jackson), who is responsible for the manning, training and operational readiness of the Field Army, including the Territorial Army. The Civil Service is represented on the Board by the Second Permanent Under Secretary (then Ian Andrews), who uniquely sits as a member of all three service boards. Whether this ever led to split loyalties I never knew, but it gave him a fascinating insight into how all three services' thinking was developing. When I joined the Board the post of Adjutant General, responsible for all personnel issues, was filled by Lieutenant General Sir Timothy Granville-Chapman, a deeply intellectual officer with a huge appetite for work. The rest of the Board was made up of two other major generals with historic titles: the Master General of the Ordnance (responsible for equipment procurement) and the Quartermaster General (responsible for supply and distribution). These posts were filled by Peter Gilchrist and David Judd respectively. The final member, reflecting the importance of the Province to the nation and our very lengthy deployment there, was the General Officer Commanding Northern Ireland, at the time another very fine officer, Lieutenant General Sir Alistair Irwin. In equivalent business terms, the Chief of the General Staff equated to the chairman of the board, the Commander in Chief to the chief operating officer and the Second Permanent Under Secretary as something between company secretary and finance director, with the other three as operating division directors responsible for procurement, supply and Northern Ireland matters. As the Assistant Chief, I found myself effectively the chief executive, charged with keeping the whole show on the road. ECAB met ten or eleven times a year and, as the chief executive, I realized that I was responsible for the orchestration of the agenda and for ensuring that sufficient energy was going into the implementation of our agreed plans.

Mike Walker's 'Strategy for the Army' was a very well-intentioned attempt to relate the demands of the day –

Bosnia, Kosovo, Northern Ireland and other lesser commitments – to the manpower and equipment that we had available, while keeping an eye on the needs of the future. Up to that point, the 'go first, go fast, go home' mantra had worked well. The big issue for discussion was whether this was the template for the future, or merely an option we should retain among others. In particular, there was debate about our capability to conduct conventional manœuvre warfare again, in the way that we had prepared to deploy in the Cold War and had actually deployed in the first Gulf War in 1990–1. As always in the Ministry of Defence, policy options are very closely related to spending programmes. For the Army, the emerging big issue was our medium-weight forces: they either did not exist or were provided by some pretty obsolete vehicles. We had come out of the last decade of the Cold War with some excellent heavyweight warfighting equipment programmes – the Challenger main battle tank, the Warrior infantry fighting vehicle, the AS-90 self-propelled artillery system – and with the prospect of the Apache attack helicopter just around the corner. Our light forces, based around the Parachute Regiment and other designated light infantry and air assault battalions, were moderately well equipped for rapid deployment, although certainly not well equipped for protracted fighting, if that was what was required. The main gap in our overall capability as an Army, therefore, was in the medium-weight area – the area where we provide forces light enough to be deployed to trouble spots by aircraft and fast shipping, but heavy enough to conduct serious combat operations on arrival, if necessary. We needed to identify a medium-weight programme of troops and equipment light enough to get there quickly, but capable enough to do the business until heavier follow-up forces arrived. The solution became known as the Future Rapid Effects System programme: FRES, in the inevitable military shorthand. It was to be at the heart of the Army's future equipment needs for ten to twenty years.

At risk of digressing in my own personal narrative, I must tell the whole story of FRES in a single thread, beginning in 2001 when I arrived as the new Assistant Chief and concluding in 2009 when I stood down as Chief of the General Staff. It is not a happy tale. In 2001, as Assistant Chief, responsible to my boss for the forward development of the Army, I quickly associated myself with the FRES programme, sensing that this was a key issue for the Army. I required various papers to be written laying out the detailed arguments. After some extended discussion, ECAB approved the FRES proposals and the requirement was passed to the equipment procurement department of the Central Staff in the MOD. In the uncertain strategic environment of the first decade of the third millennium it seemed highly logical for the Army to have a capable force that could be moved rapidly to pre-empt, deter or nip in the bud potential trouble. And if that requirement existed, then it was also logical to procure the necessary equipment to fill that capability gap as quickly as possible. Thus FRES was to be a short lead-time programme, probably provided by existing technology and from equipment that could be bought off the shelf. We aspired to bring these new items of equipment into service from 2007 or 2008.

The intention was to acquire a family of vehicles with a common chassis, adapted into a number of variants to meet the needs of the differing parts of the Army. Thus FRES would not only provide the required rapid deployment capability but would in doing so replace a range of ageing vehicles, some of which went back to the 1960s and 1970s. We were not aiming for a highly technical solution, merely something that could meet most of our needs in a timely fashion. Early discussions with the defence industry looked promising: we had a need, they saw a business opportunity. To provide the basis of funding for the project we agreed to cancel two existing programmes, one a reconnaissance vehicle called Tracer, the other a heavy armoured troop carrier called MRAV. Both of these programmes had their origins in the Cold War. The Tracer and MRAV production money was in the right years of the MOD budget – 2007 to 2009 – so by cancelling those programmes and diverting the money it looked as if we were well on track.

Interestingly, the United States Army identified much the same requirement at the same time, though they planned to go one major step further. Their requirement was for a completely new Future Combat System to replace all their armoured vehicles as soon after 2010 as possible. However, their interim solution, the Stryker programme, was very similar to our FRES programme. They were looking to buy something off the shelf and field it as quickly as possible, while they developed their Future Combat System. Our ambition was more modest; indeed, our Challengers, Warriors and AS-90s, with which we had emerged from the Cold War, would continue to suit our heavy war-fighting needs well into the

2020s and beyond. However, for both armies, Stryker and FRES respectively would fill the medium-weight capability gap quickly. Indeed, had we known in early 2001 how the decade just begun was going to turn out, we would have put even more energy into these programmes. But it was not to be.

The United States Army duly acquired six brigades – about equal to the size of the entire British Army – of Stryker vehicles, and they were highly successful in both Iraq and Afghanistan. I spent a day in 2008 in Baghdad with a Stryker battalion. It nearly broke my heart. They had almost exactly what we had said we needed. As I write in 2010, the British Army still has no FRES vehicles. Our acquisition programme got completely bogged down within the highly centralized bureaucracy of the Ministry of Defence. On the mischievous pretext that the Army did not know what it wanted, a firm of external analysts was brought in to examine our requirement. Despite the fact that ECAB had agreed in 2002 exactly what was needed, the thought that the Army's thinking needed further clarifying gained hold and sowed seeds of doubt in the minds of what was then called the Defence Management Board, later more simply the Defence Board. The external analysts were tasked by the Central Staff to refine our requirement. They took some two years to do so. This imposed the first real delay. Thus, the money we had freed up to spend in 2007–9 on production of the first vehicles could not be spent by the Army, and was therefore available to be diverted elsewhere in the defence equipment programme. Thus it ended up neatly filling in other potholes of unaffordability elsewhere in the defence budget. As a consequence we had to accept that the earliest date we could bring FRES into service would inevitably slip, and it did, back to 2012.

In January 2006, by which time I was Commander in Chief, ECAB was briefed that further delays meant that the likely date for bringing FRES into service was now between 2015 and 2018. To the members of the Board, by that time under the chairmanship of General Sir Mike Jackson, this was outrageous. The newly appointed Minister of State for Defence Procurement, Lord Drayson, was persuaded to come to Salisbury Plain to see for himself just what the Army did, and did not, have by way of fighting vehicles, heavy, medium or light. Having previously been totally consumed by fast jets and aircraft carriers, he admitted to me as we drove away from Salisbury Plain that he had not realized the Army had a problem. Progress at last, of a sort! To his initial credit, he shook matters up in London and a competition was held in 2007 between the three contending vehicles that could most closely meet our requirement. I was delighted that he had understood the urgency of the programme. The competition was to be concluded by the end of November 2007, with the expectation that development and production contracts could be placed soon after, reinstating the chance to bring the first vehicles into service in 2012. However, in early November Paul Drayson resigned from the Government, leaving FRES high and dry, without a ministerial champion and at the mercy of its critics. Worse was to follow. Paul Drayson's successor, Baroness Taylor, was very new to defence and took a further six months to make the decision, by which time the project's critics had begun to brief against the winning contender. The project had ground virtually to a halt.

While this inelegant process was limping along, the threats to our troops in Iraq and Afghanistan had intensified, necessitating the very rapid acquisition of a range of protected patrol and transport vehicles. Some even suggested that these constituted a fulfilment of the Army's FRES requirement, such was the woeful level of understanding of the overall concept. Again, worse was to come. In 2008 the Defence Board, disregarding the opportunity costs elsewhere in the equipment programme, decided to proceed with the two new aircraft carriers for the Royal Navy, and in 2009 compounded the problem by reluctantly agreeing to procure the full quota of Typhoon aircraft for the Royal Air Force. With the fourth major spending requirement, the replacement of our nuclear deterrent, not really a topic for debate, the only place to go to balance the books in 2009 was the Army's FRES programme. Concern over the development potential of the winning contender was the given reason, but affordability was the real driver. So, to save money immediately, FRES was first shunted out to 2015, and then to 2018 – which, to those who understood the dynamics of the project, actually meant nearer to 2022. The project was effectively dead, leaving the Army at the end of the decade no better off than at the beginning. Yes, we had some heavy war-fighting equipment of 1980s vintage, which, with the focus on Afghanistan, we are unlikely to need in the foreseeable future; and, as the decade ended, we had an eclectic mixture of assorted vehicles bought specifically for Iraq and Afghanistan but of doubtful use elsewhere –

assuming, that is, they survive the rigours of the Afghanistan terrain. All this raises the question of what the Army does for a modern, comprehensive, armoured fighting vehicle programme after Afghanistan. This is one of the most critical issues that needs to be addressed in the next Defence Review.

We had made a plan in 2001, but intrigue, financial mismanagement and other vested interests put paid to it. I will return to this sorry tale in a later chapter. To me, the whole FRES episode sums up what is worst about MOD decision-making in an environment in which resources are scarce and vested interests loom large, and in the absence of clear political and business leadership. We have to do better in future.

As so many people of my generation remark, in the same way that we all know where we were when President Kennedy was assassinated, so too we can all remember where we were when we first heard about the attacks of 11 September 2001. I was in Cyprus visiting British units. In the later afternoon, in a gap between engagements, I was on the Commander British Forces' privately owned yacht, barrelling in an uncontrolled way in a strong wind towards Egypt, when everyone's mobile phones starting going off. Air Vice Marshal Bill Rimmer immediately decided that our short excursion was over and we returned post haste to shore to find out what was happening. Watching the television news, we experienced exactly the same reactions as millions around the world – incredulity, and then the dawning realization that nothing was going to be quite the same again.

Back in the Ministry of Defence, as the dust settled

quite literally in New York, the response was to look again at the conclusions of the Strategic Defence Review of 1997-8 and re-evaluate it in the light of 9/11. This decision spawned what became known in the MOD as the New Chapter of the SDR. This piece of work had a mixed outcome for the Army. There was to be increased spending on Special Forces and on our counter-terrorist capability at home and abroad, and there was to be an expanded role for the Territorial Army in assisting the Fire and Rescue Services at home. Some on the Central Staff, however, saw in the New Chapter an opportunity to look again at the Army's structure, believing that the Army had done too well out of the original SDR. As I was leaving the MOD in late 2002, they concluded that the Army no longer needed six fully deployable ground manoeuvre brigades, and that five, together with a few independent infantry battalions, would be more than sufficient for future demands on the Army. How ridiculous – pathetic even – their arguments sounded a few years later when we found we needed not just five or six brigades, but a total of ten in order to meet the combined needs of Iraq and Afghanistan.

Out in the real world, far from the destructive vested interests in the MOD, a combination of the CIA, Special Forces and the United States Air Force expelled the Taliban from Afghanistan. Ever the good coalition partner, the United Kingdom put its hand up to lead the initial International Security Assistance Force (ISAF) which deployed to Kabul under my successor at 3rd Division, Major General John McColl. This first intervention was a notable success. John McColl had exactly the right temperament to handle the hastily empowered

Hamid Karzai, and British troops had exactly the right approach on the streets of Kabul. At that time there was no attempt, or even intention, to deploy outside the capital. A *loya jirga* (literally a 'grand assembly' in Pashto), drawing representatives from across Afghanistan, coincided with the end of this six-month deployment. Hamid Karzai was formally made the caretaker Prime Minister, and was decent enough to comment that John McColl was probably more popular in Kabul than he was. This deployment also seemed a further justification of the 'go first, go fast, go home' approach to our interventions abroad, as at the end of six months we handed our responsibilities over to the Turks. That said, we initially struggled to find a NATO member nation that would follow us, and I remarked somewhat presciently at the time that it felt as though we were in something of a relay race, running around the stadium with no one to take the baton.

However, in Washington another theme began to develop, echoed quietly in London: what next in this new 'global war on terror'? There was a very respectable argument that Afghanistan should remain the focus of international attention. After all, the West had abandoned the Afghans once in recent history – after the Russians had been expelled in 1989 – thereby allowing the civil war that followed to tear the country apart, and creating the conditions for the ungoverned space which Osama bin Laden exploited to establish his Al-Qaida network and training camps. But apart from continued efforts to find bin Laden and Mullah Omar, the West's attention was drifting away from Afghanistan again, this time towards Iraq. One has to wonder what might have been if Hamid Karzai had been properly supported from 2002 and the kind of effort that was made from 2006 had actually begun years earlier. The argument was that Afghanistan should always have been the main effort of the West, the Afghans should have been properly supported and thus the vacuum into which the Taliban returned prevented. But for the key decision-makers, especially in Washington, unfinished business remained in Iraq; and it was there that international eyes turned, to the detriment of the hapless Afghans and, eventually, of the armed forces of NATO.

Life in London during 2002 had something of a schizophrenic quality to it. On the one hand, and officially, Iraq did not pose a threat to the United Kingdom. While it was abundantly clear that the Americans wanted to achieve regime change in the country, it was no part of British policy at the time to become entangled in such an enormous and risk-laden venture. On the other hand, and at the level at which it could be officially denied, it was growing increasingly likely that the United States would once again lead a coalition into Iraq. It was also becoming clear to those on the inside of British Government decision-making that if this were to happen, it was extremely unlikely that we would not be part of it, if only because of the nature of the relationship between Tony Blair and George W. Bush. The human dynamics in this relationship were obvious. Tony Blair had been the first world leader to go to the States to show solidarity after 9/11, and that was good for the United Kingdom, and felt very good for Mr Blair. After all, the United States was among our oldest and most trusted allies. So it seems highly probable that when George W. Bush asked our Prime Minister in spring 2002: 'We are going into Iraq, are you with us?' there was only one answer Blair could give, regardless of the virtues or otherwise of the case for military intervention. History and the Chilcot Inquiry will be the judges of the wisdom of Tony Blair's acquiescence in one of the most devastating decisions in modern times.

From where I sat in the Ministry of Defence, a number of things were happening. Our senior liaison and exchange officer embedded within the United States Army was regularly calling me with updates on the United States' preparations, including the Americans' realization that they were one Army corps headquarters short in their planning and might be going to ask the UK for use of our corps headquarters from Germany. Such a headquarters would be capable of commanding one of the major axes of advance into Iraq. This possibility had a deeply personal aspect to it, as I was due to command that headquarters from January 2003. The headquarters in question was that of the Allied Rapid Reaction Corps, which, although staffed in the majority by British officers and enabled entirely by the British Army, was assigned to NATO and included officers from some seventeen other NATO nations. In theory it could be deployed on a national or coalition operation, although it never had been. Its previous two deployments, to Bosnia in 1995–6 and to Kosovo in 1999, had been carried out under the NATO flag. The thought now was that it might form part of the US-led coalition plan, perhaps commanding a northern axis of advance into Iraq from Turkey. Of course, officially, this was never discussed; but in some military circles in the United States it was a possible option. In the event, neither the Turkish option nor the use of the British-led headquarters materialized.

In London, there was a growing focus on the intelligence that underpinned the case for war. This has been well documented by the Butler Inquiry, but my abiding recollection of the intelligence to which I was privy is just how thin it was. The UK's case for war was based on the existence in Iraq of weapons of mass destruction, as regime change was, apparently, not an objective that the UK could support, at least officially. But I found the intelligence about weapons of mass destruction most uncompelling, and could only assume that the really key stuff was kept for the eyes of the most senior people. But who were they? I was seeing the intelligence as the Assistant Chief because periodically I stood in for Mike Walker at the chiefs of staff meetings. So if the chiefs were not seeing the killer intelligence, who was – if it actually existed at all? On reflection, I respect the integrity of the Defence Intelligence Service and our Secret Intelligence Service too much to point a finger in their directions, but the so-called 'dodgy dossier' and its free-style foreword, penned in or near Downing Street, are quite different matters, as the Chilcot Inquiry heard.

The other dynamic that was odd in London at the time was the mood around the chiefs of staff's conference table. In the absence of political direction, the chiefs were doing what the military always does, namely making sensible contingency plans in order that it would be able to react quickly when the politicians eventually decided what they wanted to do. Questions about the legality of the undertaking had not begun to be aired publicly, but there was a tacit assumption that any UK involvement would need to be kept to the minimum, both on grounds of cost and in recognition of the limited national popular appetite for an attack on Iraq. This translated into a variety of modest naval, air force and Special Forces packages, and a very marked reluctance to commit the Army. I found this rather hard to understand. Whatever else happened in Iraq, the requirement to stabilize the country following an intervention, either opposed or unopposed, was always going to be a manpower-intensive undertaking: it was ever thus. If the UK was to join the coalition and play any role beyond a token one, it was inevitable that the Army would have to be committed, and not just for the hopefully short war-fighting phase but for the stabilization phase too, which, from our past experience, we knew was likely to be much longer. I recall making that point at a chiefs' meeting: it was in no one's interest to let the US military think they could swiftly conduct the combat operations and then walk away from the subsequent nation-building, leaving it to others. It seemed logical to me that if the UK was to be effective as a coalition partner, we needed to be in at the beginning and see the thing through on the ground. Otherwise we should not get involved at all.

Of course, this all highlighted the very vexed question of planning for the 'morning after' in Iraq – which in the event was, as is now universally agreed, an abject failure. In London at the time there was a clear acceptance that such planning was needed. Our engagement on this subject was with the US State Department, led by Colin Powell who, we were led to believe, would be charged with leading post-conflict Iraq. In retrospect we were naive. Our calculations simply did not take into account the personalities and political motivations of both Don Rumsfeld, the United States Defense Secretary, and Dick Cheney, the Vice President. This was the neo-cons' great (though mercifully short-lived) strategic moment, and Colin Powell, great general that he once was, stood no chance as Secretary of State against the twin barrels presented by Rumsfeld and Cheney who, crucially, had the attentive ear of George W. Bush. Control of post-war Iraq was wrested from the State Department before the first shot was fired, on the basis that a lightning attack would remove Saddam Hussein, impose a pro-West regime very quickly and leave Iraq to make its own firm, confident steps on its journey into a bright new future. The retired United States general Jay Garner would be the midwife on the ground for this process, with the very honourable British general Tim Cross as his deputy. Would it have been so! Unfortunately, the naivety of that thinking in Washington was on a par with the alleged manipulation of the intelligence-handling back in London. On such premises, at the time, some thought that modern war could be fought. Iraq taught them, painfully, the utter foolishness of this notion.

Closer to home, the practical and pressing problem for the Army was equipment and supplies. The big logistic stockpiles of the Cold War, held 'just in case', had gone, and our strategy for a major operation was based now on the principle of 'just in time'. This strategy depended on having warning times that were long enough to allow us to place the proper contracts, fire up industry and move the newly provided supplies from the factory to the foxhole. If it proved impossible to make these important procurement decisions in a timely manner, the Army would always struggle to get ready. In the event, for fear of news of military preparations leaking out before the political process was complete, the Army was given a severe – even impossible – challenge to get to the start line in March 2003 in good order. We did not make it in every respect. However, by the time 1st (UK) Armoured Division rolled over its line of departure and into Iraq, I had left London for Germany, where I was a spectator on these events as the new Commander of the Allied Rapid Reaction Corps.

Between my appointments as Assistant Chief of the General Staff and Commander of the ARRC, I was allowed one of those privileged, and peculiar, moments in the life of the British Army. Our Army is based on a regimental structure which is one of its traditional strengths. All of us swear an oath of allegiance to our Sovereign and are commissioned (in the case of officers) or enlisted (in the case of soldiers) into our chosen corps and regiments. Those parts of the Army become family. You belong to this or that regiment, and every family has its figurehead. In my case I became a Green Howard, eventually commanded the 1st Battalion and later, as a brigadier and general, spent nine years as the colonel of the regiment, effectively the tribal chief. Some parts of the Army, however, do not naturally grow their own senior officers, but, quite properly, like to have a senior officer to represent their interests and be their figurehead chief. I was very privileged to spend six years as the Colonel Commandant – tribal chief – of the Royal Military Police, and made some very good friends among that remarkable bunch of people as they sought to demonstrate and enforce the highest standards of discipline and behaviour in the Army. The colonel commandant shares in the good times and the bad. The murder of six Royal Military Policemen in Al Amarah in 2003 was one of those moments, as was presenting their next of kin with the medals of their fallen sons and husbands in the Chapel of the Royal Military Police in Chichester some time afterwards. It is a huge privilege to be invited to join someone else's family.

But in October 2002 my other honorary appointment began to feel less honorary. I had been invited to follow Mike Walker as Colonel Commandant of the Army Air Corps. I had commanded my infantry battalion in the airmobile role so had become something of a professional passenger in helicopters. I had also formed the Air Manœuvre Development Group when I was commanding the 3rd Division to prepare our thinking for the introduction of our Apache attack helicopters. Now, though, I was being invited to actually join the Army Air Corps, in which, to be a credible mainstream officer, you have to be able to fly. I could not, so I was invited to learn.

So it came about that in the autumn of 2002 I spent six weeks at the School of Army Aviation at Middle Wallop as a student pilot. My instructor, Captain Keith Bryant, was a hugely experienced pilot and trainer but looked upon his newest charge with some misgivings. Early on, however, we agreed that he would teach me to fly and I would make the coffee. We got on brilliantly. I started to learn on a single-engine Squirrel helicopter, which I quickly discovered was easier said than done. Hovering is a great skill, but not one that comes naturally. With your left hand you control the power, while with your right hand you control the attitude of the aircraft. Simultaneously with your feet you try to balance what you are doing with your hands, taking into account the effect of the wind outside. At least, that is what I thought I was doing. On my ninth flying day the dreaded moment arrived as I touched down on the airfield and Keith told me he was getting out and that I was to do another circuit on my own. Oh help! Like all rookie pilots I talked to myself out loud during that short, nerve-laden flight. Up at 700 feet per minute, turn left over the church accelerating to 90 knots, turn left again levelling at 1,000 feet, then on the base leg, with Danebury Hill Fort on the right, do pre-landing checks and identify where you intend to land, turn left once more losing speed and height and then a final left turn to approach your chosen landing spot, glancing left and right to assess your real speed against identifiable landmarks on the ground as you push the aircraft forward and down until you are just a few feet above the ground, at which point the upward power of the engine downdraught fights the weight of the aircraft and it doesn't really want to land at all. At that moment you feel all is lost, but pride prevents you pulling away to go around again, so, holding your breath, you drop the power lever, the aircraft settles on the ground, movement of a life-threatening nature ceases, and you stop talking to yourself! I was very glad when Keith climbed back in, took control and said that was enough for the day.

Over the six weeks I was at Middle Wallop I flew fifty hours in seven aircraft types, including an Apache – out of which I climbed thinking that this was a young man's game, not something for a fifty (or so) year old. I was very proud to be presented with my Army pilot's wings. To those who think the combination of Dannatt and helicopters to be somewhat toxic, I would simply comment that until you have tried to fly one yourself you have no idea how difficult it is and you have no real appreciation of how air manœuvre can transform the battlefield. We sell ourselves short when we skimp on helicopters. It was for those professional reasons that I became very close to battlefield aviation and the Army Air Corps, and was honoured to be a member of their family. On suitable occasions, Pippa wears her Army Air Corps brooch with as much pride as she wears her Green Howard brooch – and on very special occasions she wears both.

Sporting my newly acquired helicopter pilot's wings, I began my two years as Commander of NATO's Allied Rapid Reaction Corps. This was a mixed experience. It was intensely rewarding to be part of an organization whose whole purpose was to train and prepare for operations at a high level in defence of the Atlantic Alliance, but intensely frustrating not to be invited to take part in those operations, particularly when one's own Army was engaged in two major wars in Iraq and Afghanistan. But soldiers, who have seen others bleed and die, are the last people to rush into fighting unnecessarily. The professional curiosity aroused by a new challenge must always be tempered by recognition of the harsh cost in human tragedy that war brings. That said, I kept my multinational staff very much in the picture during 2003 and 2004 as developments on the world stage unfolded. We had no idea when we might be required.

With many others we watched the early moves of the coalition attack into Iraq and shared the excitement of the entry into Baghdad and the toppling of Saddam's statue. But as 2003 gave way to 2004, and the pressure on British forces in the south and on the coalition more generally mounted, it came as no great surprise to me when David Richards, who had followed me as Assistant Chief of the General Staff, rang to say that the chiefs of staff that morning had considered six options for the reinforcement of Iraq, four of which had involved the deployment of Headquarters ARRC. There had been a request from the United States for the UK to consider taking over responsibility for all nine Shi'a Muslim provinces of central and southern Iraq so that the Americans could focus on the north and west of the country, and on Baghdad. If the Government were to agree to this request it would inevitably be a job for HQ ARRC: we had no other corps-level HQ in place that could deliver this requirement. We felt professionally well equipped to do this, but there were complications. As a NATO-assigned headquarters with seventeen nations contributing personnel, it was simply not possible for the UK Government, even as the sponsor, to decree that the whole headquarters would deploy. But as always, if and when the politicians decided, the military would be expected to move overnight. Ahead of any authorization I called a meeting of all seventeen senior national representatives to put the issue to them, leaving it to them in turn to put it to their ministries of defence and governments as they saw fit. My basic point was that the US-led coalition was now in Iraq for better or worse, but that it was absolutely not in anyone's interests to see the one world superpower fail. The United States needed support; my government was providing that, and I hoped their governments would do the same.

A period of reflection followed. My senior national representatives consulted their capitals and came back to me with their informal answers. Thirteen of the seventeen were on, if the request were to be put formally. At least that meant my excellent chief of staff and fellow Green Howard, Major General Nick Houghton, could start to put a sensible manning plan together for the headquarters, should we deploy. But then the real world began to play its part. The Whitsun early summer Bank Holiday followed, when Parliament went into recess, followed by the sixtieth anniversary of D-Day on 6 June 2004 and then the G8 'Sea Island' summit. During this period nothing much seemed to happen in Whitehall. When Government reconvened, I have it on good authority that Tony Blair chaired a Cabinet sub-committee to consider the US request and asked it: 'So, who is putting us under pressure to do this?' Quite reasonably, Cabinet colleagues in turn assured him that their US opposite numbers were doing nothing of the sort, perhaps forgetting that the original request from the USA had been couched in their usual polite and non-pressurizing way, asking us to help if we could. So that was settled. A polite refusal was sent to the United States, and in HQ ARRC we put away our Iraq maps, and began taking out the Afghan ones.

We did not have to wait long. Less than a month later, Tony Blair announced at the NATO summit in Prague that we, the UK, would take the lead in a major new NATO deployment to southern Afghanistan in mid-2006. Wow! Where did that come from? Of course, as always, we in the ARRC knew that it would be our job, and under my successor, David Richards, it was. But the strategic implications of that announcement begged many questions. The assumption had to be that if the UK was going to increase its force levels in Afghanistan in 2006, then we would be substantively out of Iraq by then. The SDR of 1997–8 had organized us for one major war, not two, so a new commitment to Afghanistan would have to replace that to Iraq, not be added to it. It was not just a matter of scarce manpower but of equipment. Interestingly, years later when I was Chief of the General Staff, I asked to see the minutes of the chiefs of staff's meetings to find out what discussions had taken place in April, May and June 2004 about the proposed 2006 Afghan deployment. Nothing seemed to have been recorded. I did not know what to make of that.

At the time of this posting in Germany a longstanding issue remained to be resolved. This was the fact that a major proportion of the British Army was still based in Germany. When I arrived in January 2003 for my sixth tour of duty in that country, I could not help wondering what we were still doing there, almost sixty years after the end of the Second World War and twenty years after the collapse of the Soviet bloc. Indeed, as I got back into my car after my introductory courtesy call on the Oberbürgermeisterin of Stadt Mönchengladbach, I reflected on her profuse thanks for the fact that the British were the fourth largest employer of civil labour in the town. It was perfectly natural that I asked myself, why? Why were twenty-two thousand British servicemen, and their families, still in Germany? There was no strategic reason, national or NATO, that necessitated the continuing basing of British forces in Germany. The simple reason was that there was nowhere for those servicemen to be based in the United Kingdom. I resolved to do what I could about this. Germany was an attractive posting, and many families enjoyed the extra allowances paid for living there; but this had to be offset against the relative difficulty for wives to get jobs or develop careers, and the considerable cost to the Ministry of Defence. By the time I had handed over as Chief of the General Staff in 2009 we had a plan to reduce our presence in Germany from twenty thousand to fifteen thousand troops, including the relocation of HQ ARRC from Germany to Gloucestershire. This will save us £1.25 billion over twenty-five years, and significantly enhance the benefit that the ARRC can bring to national military development and training. Many of the non-British officers working for me in the ARRC commented that they loved working with the Brits, but how much better it would be to do so in the United Kingdom. It was planned that from the summer of 2010 they would have the chance.

In January 2005 I handed over command of HQ ARRC to David Richards, allowing him to focus on preparing to take the headquarters to Afghanistan the following year. I had paid a preliminary planning visit to Afghanistan the previous autumn, and from it I had formed the very clear view that if we wanted to produce a stable government in that country then the most important task, even more important than that of restraining the Taliban, was endeavouring to convert the national economy from one predominantly based on the illegal cultivation and sale of the opium poppy to one based on legal cash crops. In my view there could be no good governance while a major proportion of the money flow was based on corrupt and illegal activity, and much of it flowed into the hands of our enemies. I was surprised that, four years after the NATO invasion of Afghanistan and the collapse of the Taliban regime, little seemed to have been achieved in this area. At a working dinner in November 2004, hosted by Ros Marsden, our ambassador in Kabul, and attended by many senior Afghans and members of the international community, we discussed these ideas keenly, concluding that only by taking a genuinely comprehensive approach to all the problems of Afghanistan would we then have the chance of producing a stable country. To deny Al-Qaida the space to re-establish itself would require more than just counter-terrorist activity focused on killing or capturing Osama bin Laden and Mullah Omar and more than just military action to constrain the Taliban. It would require a far wider strategy, commensurate with British counter-insurgency doctrine, to persuade the Afghan people to support Hamid Karzai and his fledgling government and to take a stake in their country's future. I came away from that visit wondering whether the West would be able to find the resolve, resources and determination to see this through. Our track record of walking away from Afghanistan when the going got tough did not augur well for the future. However, after 9/11 the security of Afghanistan and the security of the West, in particular the United Kingdom with its large Afghan and Pakistani populations, were very much bound together. For the

UK, and the British Army specifically, there was the not insubstantial matter of Iraq to be resolved first. It was on that theatre of operations that my attention was focused at the start of my next appointment.

The senior operational appointment in the British Army – something similar to the chief operating officer of a major business – is Commander in Chief, Land Command. Based in Wilton, near Salisbury, HQ Land Command is responsible for the entirety of the deployable army. I took over as Commander in Chief in March 2005 from General Sir Timothy Granville-Chapman, who was moving up to London to become the Vice Chief of the Defence Staff. Many of us had long been of the view that he was brilliantly suited to that demanding post, managing many of the most difficult strands of defence policy and business at the highest level. His intellect and logical analysis of issues complemented the more intuitive approach of the new Chief of the Defence Staff, Air Chief Marshal Sir Jock Stirrup. When I got to London myself the following year, I found that each provided an interesting foil to the other. But for now, as Commander in Chief, my responsibilities were for the training and preparation of the Field Army for operations and for maintaining the infrastructure of the Army as a whole. Of course, General Sir Mike Jackson, as Chief of the General Staff, had overall responsibility for the Army; but the Commander in Chief and the HQ Land Command staff effectively ran the Army on the Chief's behalf. Self-evidently, then, the two top men had to have a good working relationship and be in each other's minds, something I had noticed previously had not always been the case. I was determined that it should be so on our watch.

Among the difficult issues around this time with which Mike Jackson had to deal was the reorganization of the infantry. To a casual observer, the middle of a major operation such as Iraq might not seem the right moment to be reorganizing something as crucial to our fighting effectiveness as our infantry. But with the commitment to Northern Ireland scaling down and financial pressures mounting, the size and shape of the infantry inevitably became a policy issue – and quite a distracting one at that. Students of the British infantry will know that its organization has been a very long-running and emotive saga, with roots deep in history; now, under pressure from the financiers in the centre, Mike was determined to grasp the nettle firmly.

One of the main drivers for change was a decision taken on cost and efficiency grounds to stop the expensive practice of 're-roling' infantry battalions every few years. This involved training infantry battalions for a particular role (armoured infantry, mechanized infantry, light infantry, air assault, etc.) in which they would remain for a number of years before retraining them for another, substantially different task. The argument in support of the practice was that it maintained freshness and challenge for the infantry; the argument against was that it was very expensive – costing about a million pounds to convert a light infantry battalion to the armoured role, for instance – and meant that those battalions being retrained were unavailable for operations. Once ECAB had taken that decision, the related issue of the so-called 'Arms Plot', the programme by which battalions moved around every few years between the UK, Northern Ireland, Germany and Cyprus, had to be addressed. Those who understood the infantry knew well that its life in the future would be very different from that of the past: the trick was to make it better and, in part, to sell the idea successfully to those whose lives and professional careers it would affect most.

The determining driver for change, however, was the vastly improved situation in Northern Ireland. This led those who knew the cost of everything, but perhaps not the value, to conclude that the Army could do its business with four infantry battalions fewer. To many this seemed a bold suggestion, given our ongoing commitments in Iraq, Kosovo, Bosnia and Cyprus, but to my mind it was a depressing constant in the regular inter-service battles in Whitehall by people who did not appreciate the value of well-trained infantry, especially in the type of warfare with which we had been engaged since the end of the Cold War, and which, with an enhanced deployment to Afghanistan to come in 2006, looked set to continue for many years hence.

The implication of these decisions was that battalions would in effect become permanently based in one location and in one role, and that in future individuals, not whole battalions, would be moved around for career development, variety and choice. Issues of home ownership and working wives or husbands were also important factors. The result was that all the infantry would need to be in large regiments of several battalions each, with individuals owing their allegiance to the regiment and not just one battalion. For many this was a culture change of some significance, particularly in those parts of the Army where the 'tribal' influence was strongest – Scotland, Wales, the North-East and the North-West. It had a devastating impact on my own regiment, as it meant the end of the Green Howards, after 318 years of loyal service to the Crown, and their incorporation into the much larger Yorkshire Regiment. To be specific, 1st Battalion, the Green Howards (Alexandra, Princess of Wales's Yorkshire Regiment) became 2nd Battalion, the Yorkshire Regiment (Green Howards).

At the start of the infantry reorganization debate, as Commander of the ARRC, I was not a member of ECAB. Therefore I was not present when the decisions about the re-roling and arms plotting of the infantry were taken, but I flew across from Germany later that particular day to join ECAB members for a subsequent meeting of No. 1 Board, which decides senior officers' promotions and appointments, and of which I was a member. As I went into the meeting room at the Staff College in Camberley, I saw Lieutenant General Sir Alistair Irwin, the Adjutant General, with his head in his hands.

'What's up?' I asked, knowing Alistair pretty well.

'This is the worst day of my life,' he replied, going on to explain how the ECAB discussion and decisions had gone.

I felt for him. At the time he was the only born and bred infantryman on ECAB, and as a fellow infantryman I could understand his anguish. The logic of the situation was clear, but logic and emotion and history do not always go hand in glove. The real problem was 'selling' the outcome to those battalions whose identities would change for ever.

Alistair had previously written a very well-argued paper considering what was best about the British infantry. In particular, he had stressed what he described as the 'golden thread' that ran from the past through the present and into the future. It was an excellent paper, and argued against wholesale change. For Alistair, as an officer in the Black Watch, a regiment whose history and traditions were central to their ethos, this golden thread was vital; and the decisions taken by ECAB in the wider interests of the Army would strike at the heart of the Black Watch. Alistair's perspective reflected that of many in Scotland. Of course, on the day of the decisive meeting Alistair could have resigned in protest, but what would have been the point? The decisions would still have been taken in the Army's wider interests, and his resignation would not have changed the outcome. Instead he nobly continued, working to secure the best outcome for his regiment, Scotland and the Army.

In the event, a compromise was reached. All the former Scottish regiments became part of the new Royal Regiment of Scotland, but each battalion proudly retained the name of its former regiment, thus securing part of the crucial link with the past. So the 1st Battalion, the Black Watch became the Black Watch, 3rd Battalion the Royal Regiment of Scotland. What's in a name, some might ask? Much. The British infantry tradition had proved, in the minds of very many of us, to be of inestimable value in the motivation, morale and ethos of those who were training to fight, and perhaps die, in the service of their country. It was not to be treated lightly. Alistair did a great job in balancing the historic needs of his regiment against the future needs of the Army. Sadly, many in the Highlands did not see it that way, and Alistair has been given a very hard time by a number of his kinsmen well north of the border. I hope that time will be a healer and many in Scotland will realize that they owe Alistair Irwin not a litany of complaint but a substantial debt of gratitude.

That said, the history of the British Army invariably points to the strength of the Army being the strength of the regimental system. We tinker with it at our peril, and in 2004 and 2005 we just got away with it. Later, as Chief of the General Staff, it was up to me to own and implement those earlier decisions, and in the frenetic world of the Army in recent years I believe we have come through this reorganization intact. For some it has gone better than for others, but the future is in front and the past behind. We have always adapted and must continue to do so.

As Commander in Chief, however, I had to lift my eyes above the parapet of regimental issues and focus on the fact that I was directly responsible for some 65,000 members of the Regular Army, the Territorial Army of some 35,000, the Army Cadet Force of around 30,000 adults and youngsters, and some 20,000 civilians working in a variety of administrative, clerical and semi-skilled roles. I also was personally responsible for a budget of about £6 billion. And we were fighting two wars, one more than the SDR of 1997–8 had set us up for. But, nevertheless, I loved my eighteen months as Commander in Chief. It gave me the chance to get around the Army at home and overseas, to find out what soldiers and their families were thinking, to work out where the pressure points were and what should be done to relieve them. Pressures were not hard to see. Iraq, from mid-2005, turned from bad to worse, and we were committed to a major new deployment in Afghanistan from mid-2006. My staff and I could see a perfect storm forming: what was to be done?

Naturally I agonized over these issues as Commander in Chief, but I also had another perspective which influenced me, this time as a father. My middle son, Bertie, had been commissioned into Pippa's father's regiment, the Grenadier Guards, and had served two tours in Iraq (one with 2 Para, the other with his own battalion) and one in Afghanistan. So I was able to see things, not just from my official visits to Iraq and Afghanistan and around the Army, but from a very personal angle too. Bertie's insights were hugely useful. I was very struck by one episode in which he was involved during his first tour in Iraq in As Samarrah, the principal town in Al Muthanna Province, probably the quietest province in Iraq. On 21 January 2006 the pro-Sadr Shi'a militias, clearly frustrated by our continued presence, felt that they ought to make a show of strength to underline their position; Bertie's commanding officer, the CO of 2 Para, thought this should be countered by a coalition show of strength. Bertie was ordered to take his platoon of Paras into the hard-line sector of the town. The patrol was initially accompanied by two Iraqi policemen who, having sniffed the wind, made their excuses and departed. Not long after this, Bertie's patrol came under intense fire from all directions with small arms, machine guns and rocket-propelled grenades. Dismounted and in the open they had no alternative but to beat a hasty retreat to the town's police station from where they had deployed. I asked Bertie shortly afterwards what the experience had been like. He asked if I had seen the film *Black Hawk Down* and said no more. I felt that my own experiences as a platoon commander in Belfast paled in contrast to his.

As it happened, about two months later I visited 2 Para, who were still in As Samarrah. Bertie had left by this time to rejoin the Grenadier Guards before the start of their own deployment to Iraq, but I was taken on a 'battlefield tour' by his old Parachute Regiment platoon. They clearly had had a most ferocious encounter. In the fullness of time one member of the platoon was awarded a Military Cross and three others, including Bertie, were mentioned in despatches. Mercifully no British soldiers were killed or injured, although the same could not be said of the Shi'a militiamen, who suffered heavily. But Bertie's comment to me afterwards was most telling. 'Dad,' he said, 'it only happened because we were there. It's their country: our presence is only exacerbating the problem.' I noted the comment carefully.

As 2006 wore on, the pressure on the Army mounted. Casualties from off-route explosive devices in Iraq became a growing concern. At the same time our policy was to reduce our forces in order to hand over the four provinces under our control to the Iraqis, thereby reducing the pressure on us in preparation for the increased load we were now preparing to shoulder in Afghanistan. And all this was happening against a very difficult budgetary position set in London. Those of us in the Field Army could not see how the logic of at least a modest reordering of the defence budget towards those parts of our military that were doing the heavy lifting for the nation could be resisted. But by this stage in my career I had not come to expect Whitehall to respond logically, or even coherently, to the immediate challenges it placed on the Army. There seemed to be a frustrating pattern to the readiness of the political establishment to demand tasks of the Army which it was perversely unwilling to fund or adequately provide for in terms of equipment and resources. Decision-making, especially with regard to equipment – fast jets, aircraft carriers and so on – seemed incongruously to be related to a planet far removed from the immediate realities of our military commitments in Iraq and Afghanistan. The Army was being expected to achieve success on operations with a 'make and mend attitude' that ignored the seriousness of our mission. Without the proper equipment and adequate trained manpower in the short term, we risked long-term failure. It was hard, however, to persuade either politicians or Treasury civil servants of the dangers into which they were forcing us. Resourcing the armed forces in Afghanistan appropriately was not the same as some of the other spending priorities for Government: it was life and death for the young volunteers out on the ground. We could not let them down.

In my last month as Commander in Chief I held my second and last annual conference for my generals and brigadiers and set out for them very clearly what my priorities were to be as I moved from Headquarters Land Command to the Ministry of Defence later in the summer. The Army was under huge pressure and London needed to know this. The Army would not let the nation down, but the nation needed to support the Army, and quickly. It was in this light that Pippa and I made preparations for our move to London, and for my final posting in the Army.

8

'A Very Honest General'

Alanbrooke, Montgomery, Slim and Templer stared down at me with all the weight of history from the wall of my new office. The portraits of my illustrious predecessors as professional heads of the Army reminded me of the historical significance of my appointment, and focused my thoughts on my current responsibilities and expectations. From 28 August 2006 – my first day as Chief of the General Staff – it was up to me to tackle those issues which I knew were confronting the Army and its people. In a different era those illustrious predecessors had sat in the oak-panelled splendour of the old War Office and had held the appointment of Chief of the *Imperial* General Staff. Today there is nothing oak-panelled or imperial about the utilitarian main building of the current Ministry of Defence; but, despite the functional surroundings, I was acutely conscious that I was now at the top of the Army tree, and immensely proud and privileged to be there. There was vital work to be done.

However, on that first day I was yet to discover that within weeks of my appointment critics would be circling in an attempt to shake me from my lofty perch – or at least to remind me that, the higher you climb, the greater the exposure and the further there is to fall. Earlier that summer, and with the agreement of my hugely respected predecessor, Mike Jackson, I had tried to begin to address the concerns that had been growing within the Army about our overall capability to do all the things that were being asked of us. Having used my final conference as Commander in Chief and an article placed in a Royal United Services Institute journal to flag up my views, I now hoped that as Chief of the General Staff I could really begin to shape the agenda and influence key decisions. I was very aware, however, that outside the top end of the Army – including within the Government and among the other services – my views would be challenging. Admittedly, my perspective was an Army perspective; but it was the Army that was doing most of the heavy lifting, the fighting and the dying. And with the prospect of an impending 'perfect storm' of overlapping deployments in Iraq and Afghanistan I was determined to alert both Tony Blair's administration and my fellow chiefs of staff to the pressure building on our Army. I also needed to reassure those under my command that I not only knew what was going on, but was doing something about it. It was a task which I knew would require me to argue my case within Whitehall, but also to articulate it more publicly so that it would be heard by all the people I needed to reach. I was also concerned that service personnel were beginning to think it was necessary to form an independent organization – the British Armed Forces Federation – to lobby for improved living accommodation, better medical care and enhanced compensation claim limits. In my book, looking after individuals should naturally be a principal duty of the chain of command, and I was determined to make the group's existence superfluous. If I, and my senior colleagues, did our jobs properly there would be no need for a federation or a union. I was determined that such a movement was not going to gather momentum on my watch.

My first move as CGS came on 31 August when I sent a long letter – which I had drafted in the month before I got to London – to Des Browne, the Secretary of State for Defence, in which I outlined my key concerns. I copied the letter to the MOD's most senior civil servant, the Permanent Secretary, Bill Jeffrey; to the Chief of the Defence Staff, Jock Stirrup; and to the heads of the Royal Navy and Royal Air Force, Jonathon Band and Glenn Torpy. I felt strongly that they needed to be the first to know what I was worried about. I began the letter by expressing my general uneasiness with 'the pace of life and pressure on our people at present' and described the Army as 'running hot'. I was keen to stress our continuing positive attitude and flexibility, but argued that 'the demands of the organisation are currently greater than our ability to provide satisfactorily for the needs of the individual – and it is individuals who are at the heart of our success on operations'. I was worried that the tempo of operations, short intervals between tours and gaps in our ranks meant that our overall manning ran a 'severe risk akin to a cliff-edge experience'. If our manning levels were to go into free fall, then our operational problems would expand exponentially. My letter went on to reveal my disquiet about certain aspects of essential equipment, such as the utility and safety of some of the patrol vehicles we were using in Iraq and Afghanistan, and the availability of helicopters.

Our troops deserved the best, and I was not convinced that they were receiving it, either at the fighting front or at home, where the standard of single and family living accommodation was extremely poor in too many parts of the Army Estate. I was also concerned that we were not paying a fair day's pay for a fair day's fighting in Iraq or Afghanistan. Clearly, greater spending on defence would go a long way towards solving these problems, but I recognized that a significant increase in funding was unlikely and so in my letter I suggested efficiency savings – which included the reduction of our troops in Germany and the consolidation of our major headquarters and staffs – and a reprioritization of resources within the Army and more widely within defence. I reasoned that provision for possible future conflict, of an unknown nature, needed to be moderated in order to provide properly for what we could see and needed now for current operations. This, of course, would have meant a rebalancing of resources between the three services, which would clearly not be popular elsewhere but would probably – to those prepared to be objective – seem logical. Furthermore, I also criticized the way in which single-service decision-making had been diluted by the inefficient, ineffective bureaucratic process of creeping centralization within the Ministry of Defence. I had seen this developing during my three tours of duty in the

MOD over the previous twenty years. So I put it to Des Browne that responsibility – including moral responsibility – for decisions was becoming detached from the single service chiefs, who are the individuals who have ultimate responsibility for the effectiveness of their own services. Furthermore, knowledge of this trend was undermining the confidence of our subordinates – after all, if they think, 'Well, the boss understands but cannot actually do much about it,' then we are in a bad place.

I ended what was effectively my manifesto with a declaration that as Chief of the General Staff I fully intended not only to lead the Army 'but to inform and explain to soldiers, their families, and the wider population . . . so that they understood what we were doing, why we were doing it'. Accordingly, I stated that I required the freedom to interact with the media without constantly seeking ministerial clearance. As I put it to Des Browne: 'Losing popular support at home is the single biggest danger to our chances of success in our current operations.' I knew we had to get the message out, and widely.

I hoped that my letter would prove to be a primer for a serious discussion with the Secretary of State in my initial office call with him, which had been arranged for early September. In the meantime, while my letter was being digested, I decided that on my first weekend in the job I must visit Afghanistan, to demonstrate some leadership as the new boss, to show solidarity with our people, to bring myself up to date and to get a first-hand feel for things. Helmand had really hotted up since I had last been there a few weeks before, as Commander in Chief. On that original visit in June 2006, 16 Air Assault

Brigade had had their first major engagement with the Taliban when a strong patrol had been involved in a major firefight in the town of Now Zad. At the time we had hoped that this was a one-off encounter with – well, we were not sure whom – and that the focus of our efforts could remain on the wider reconstruction and development elements of our mission. After all, that was what we had apparently gone to the south of Afghanistan to do. Yes, the 3 Para battlegroup was trained and prepared to fight; but that was not the expectation, only the worst-case scenario. By the time I returned in early September, things were very different. Skirmishes, known in the trade then as TICs – troops in contact – were frequent and intensive, often resulting in casualties on both sides but disproportionately so for the enemy – which was both good news and bad news, as we were there to try to win the hearts and minds of the people to the government side, not to blow their hearts many yards away from their minds.

That early visit in the dust and sweltering heat of an Afghan summer typified what was always a somewhat surreal experience as a senior visitor going to an operational theatre: one day you are in London in a suit arguing policy, the next day you are in combat kit and body armour in Basra or Sangin talking to a soldier who has just lost a mate in a firefight or killed his first insurgent. And sometimes the temperature difference – 15 degrees Celsius in London and 45 degrees in theatre – could be quite testing, especially when one is nearer sixty than twenty-one! From 2004 to 2009 I made very frequent such visits to Iraq and Afghanistan. The pattern would be similar – usually flying overnight with British

Airways to Bahrain, Kuwait or Muscat in the Gulf, then connecting with a small RAF communications jet and flying on to Baghdad or Kabul. My preferred format for a visit to either country was to go to the capital city first for a day of briefings and discussions with our ambassador and senior coalition, NATO and British commanders, and then to go south to the front line. That final leg of travel was usually by RAF Hercules transport aircraft, often sitting with the aircrew on the flight deck, and finally in whatever RAF or Army helicopters were available. I would then spend twenty-four hours with our commanders and troops on the ground before heading back out the same way, via the little RAF jet to the Gulf and via BA, now back in civilian clothes, to London, usually arriving a bit dog-eared! But with two overnight flights and a following wind I found that I could achieve all I needed to achieve in a three-day period. Visits like that were long enough to get a good feel for how things were going, but not too long to be a burden to the troops on the front line. I made about a dozen such trips to Iraq and the same to Afghanistan in five years.

On that first trip to Afghanistan as CGS in early September 2006, I took two journalists with me. One was Sir Max Hastings, the very experienced war correspondent, editor and journalist; the other was an in-country writer from the much-respected Associated Press. This was a deliberate move on my part to start to establish a better understanding among the British public, and indeed our own service families, as to why we were in Afghanistan at all. I think it is fair to say that at that time Iraq was a deeply unpopular war, but Afghanistan was a misunderstood one and in real danger of being erroneously tarred by the Iraq brush as 'another of Tony Blair's bad ideas'.

Whatever were the merits of our contribution to the intervention in Iraq, I have always been firmly of the view that Afghanistan was much more important to the United Kingdom. It was from Afghanistan that Al-Qaida had launched a succession of attacks on the West, culminating in 9/11. It was from Afghanistan that Osama bin Laden, with Mullah Omar's acquiescence, was orchestrating his highly politicized Islamist agenda to recreate the historic caliphate of Islamic hegemony. Furthermore, it was from Afghanistan that a threat was directed at our own country, through attempts at extremist radicalization among our entirely welcome post-colonial Muslim population, particularly in some of our inner cities. And, putting the political manipulation of an ancient religion to one side, it was from Afghanistan that a very high proportion of the drug rubbish on our streets came. So from the outset, our reasons to be in Afghanistan were sound; but if our mission was supposed to be about reconstruction and development, why were we now engaged in so much fighting? Had we miscalculated?

On that first visit as CGS I had some very frank discussions with many key people, but especially with two bullish officers, Brigadier Ed Butler, the Commander of 16 Air Assault Brigade, and Lieutenant Colonel Stuart Tootal, the Commanding Officer of 3rd Battalion, the Parachute Regiment. 3 Para was the single battlegroup that the initial planning had deemed it necessary to deploy; or – and one began to wonder – was it just all that was calculated to be affordable, given our presence in

Iraq? It had been deployed, moreover, with the stated intention of undertaking reconstruction and development work, a task the former Defence Secretary, John Reid, had publicly hoped could be completed in three years 'without a shot being fired'. I have since discussed this point with him, and I agree that his comments were widely quoted out of context; but I am afraid the yawning gap between the peaceful intent of the mission as articulated by Dr Reid and the more violent outcome is a legacy that an otherwise much respected politician and Secretary of State for Defence will have to carry.

That outcome had involved the largest number of British military casualties in any operation since the Korean War. Stuart Tootal lost fifteen men dead and forty-six wounded during his battlegroup's six-month tour. Although our concept of operations had been to develop pockets of stability and expand them like growing inkspots on a page, as our classic counter-insurgency experience and current doctrine taught us, President Hamid Karzai and Provincial Governor Engineer Doud had both insisted on the garrisoning of the principal, but vulnerable, district centres right across Helmand Province. On the face of it, protecting these district centres – each one an Afghan version of a town hall – was understandable from their perspective. Nevertheless, this soaking up of our limited resources and the denial to the small British force of the opportunity to spread itself more widely and encourage the Helmandi people to support their elected government robbed us of the chance to succeed in the critical 'hearts and minds' bit of the operation. The result was that, by the time of my visit, the district centres had become the focus of intense fighting. There were many acts of great heroism – after all, when did British soldiers last throw grenades at the enemy only feet away and fire thousands of rounds in a single engagement? As a result, the district centres became magnets for concerted and fierce Taliban attacks. How many fighters they lost in those battles, history and our intelligence fail to record, but what was supposed to have been a proactive mission to bring a new future to Afghanistan became a reactive one to prevent a vicious, militant return to the country's oppressed past.

Unaware of the high-level decisions being made, and in the best traditions of the British Army, the troops just got on with the business in hand. On my visit they expressed themselves frankly and I immediately registered their determined, but uncomplaining, attitude, which strengthened my own resolve. Much has been written about the experiences of 16 Air Assault Brigade on that tour, which have been well documented in a number of books – including Tootal's own memoir, written after he resigned in November 2007, citing the 'appalling' and 'shoddy' treatment of our troops, illustrated by the poor pay of junior soldiers, lack of training equipment, and shortcomings in housing and healthcare. His brigade commander, Ed Butler, resigned in June the following year, repeating the claim that the Government was risking soldiers' lives by failing to fund troops and equipment. Stands by such accomplished officers revealed the ongoing strength of feeling in the Army about such matters and kept the issues in the public eye. They both know that I was sorry that they felt they had to resign – both had excellent careers ahead of them – and by then I was on the case that they had made to me; but perhaps I was not vocal enough for their liking.

On the long flight back to London I thought deeply about my ability to *really* make an impact on the many issues that I wanted to confront. Although charged with responsibility for the overall fighting effectiveness of the Army, today the Chief of the General Staff – as a result of the centralization which so vexed me – owns so few of the decision-making levers pulled and pushed by his predecessors. Alanbrooke and Templer would have shaken their heads at my inability to determine and decide. But, if arguing and influencing was what it was about today, then I was determined to make myself heard, and equally determined to make a robust contribution in the formal decision-making bodies of the Ministry of Defence.

As a single-service chief of staff, you have three opportunities to make your voice heard. The first is through the Chiefs of Staff Committee, which comprises the three single-service chiefs, the Vice Chief of the Defence Staff and (in the chair) the Chief of the Defence Staff. These five men give advice to the Government – either directly or via the Secretary of State for Defence – about the military practicalities of possible future missions in response to world events, and then monitor at high level the conduct of whatever current operations are in hand. In August 2006 Iraq was in full flow and we had just committed, at an increased level, to Afghanistan. Within the chiefs' committee, therefore, I saw my task as being to ensure that sufficient priority was placed on achieving overall success in Iraq and Afghanistan, both of which were predominantly land forces operations.

Throughout my time as CGS I saw our land forces as being not only those of the Army but also those drawn from the Royal Marines (who, historically, are part of the Royal Navy) and from some parts of the Royal Air Force, especially their ground protection, helicopter and troop transport forces. Rightly or wrongly, I felt responsible for *all* our land forces during my time as head of the Army – especially as the Chief of the Defence Staff, Sir Jock Stirrup, was a fast jet pilot who, although brilliant at what he did, could not have been expected to understand the sights, sounds and smells of the battlefield. You don't have time to pick up body parts and decide who lives and who dies when you're in a cockpit flying at the speed of sound. This is no criticism, but at that speed you don't have time to weigh up the wider options. In the air environment action is instinctive; conducting land operations, especially countering insurgencies, is anything but instinctive.

I suppose at the end of the day it is all about professional background and experience. I learnt a lot of theoretical stuff at Sandhurst about decision-making and leadership, but it is at the school of hard knocks in the operational field that a young platoon and company commander lays his foundation for high command. In difficult ground operations, among the civilian people you have gone to help and among your own soldiers who depend on you, there is no substitute for experience. Of course, no one has a monopoly on wisdom; but, at the top level, wisdom comes from practical, often harsh, experience, not just from textbooks, military academies and the Staff College. That said, Jock Stirrup had been one of the top students on the Higher Command and

Staff Course when I had been responsible for running it some years before, and of course had great experience of air–land cooperation gained from the Dhofar War in the 1970s; still, that was experience gained from the cockpit not the slit trench. Conversely, I am sure I could never have made much of being a fast jet pilot, or planning a complex multi-aircraft sortie. Each to his own, and perhaps that is the issue.

Away from the operational perspective, the second way to influence decision-making as CGS is as a member of what is now called the Defence Board. This is chaired by the Permanent Secretary and composed of the five members of the Chiefs of Staff Committee plus other assorted senior military officers and civil servants. It also included three civilian non-executive members, on the basis that their board-level experience should contribute to balanced and impartial decision-making. Paul Skinner, the Chairman of Rio Tinto Zinc, and Ian Rushby, late of BP, were particularly impressive when their busy diaries allowed them to attend what were often hastily arranged but important meetings. Their presence was particularly important because the Defence Board deliberates over and decides upon the major resource allocation and equipment procurement decisions – in other words, who gets what money and what kit. So it is critical that within this highly centralized process the Defence Board's discussions are crisp and well-informed and its decision-making is timely. With such responsibility, effective chairmanship is vital. A single service chief's role today is therefore very much to argue, influence and persuade. This is fine provided logic rules the day. But, despite the political desire in recent years not to have a public fuss in defence over spending, the MOD has this awful knack of keeping the aspirations of the three robber barons – the three single service chiefs – in some kind of unholy, unspoken balance. Again, this is fine if the threats to our security come equally from the sea, land and air, which in the days of the Cold War they probably did; but that is not the case today. It is our land forces, broadly defined, that are under intense pressure in this, the first decade of the twenty-first century, as they do their best to protect our freedoms, values and interests – and, rightly or wrongly, I took my responsibility for them personally.

The third way a head of service, like CGS, seeks to exert influence sits in counterpoint to the first two ways, for he has to look after the interests of the Army, Navy or Air Force as its overall tribal chief. Logic might suggest the priority should go to one service or another depending on the nature of existing operations. In the current climate, this would point towards the land forces; but if your people are looking to you in the maritime environment to protect the aircraft-carrier, destroyer or submarine programmes, or in the air environment to maintain the number of fast jets in the front line, then it takes a very brave man to take the hits where it hurts when budgets are tight. To Jonathon Band's great credit, over the last few years as First Sea Lord he graciously accepted, after due protest, quite a reduction in resources going to the current fleet; but the future aircraft-carrier programme still found its way through the funding jungle and the submarine programme was always going to be protected within the higher politics of our independent nuclear deterrent. Fast jet numbers for the Royal Air

Force have always been wrapped up in a mathematical calculation that only staff officers from that service really understand. To put it bluntly, fast jets are very, very expensive and absolutely vital when we need to contest and control airspace over the United Kingdom or over our deployed forces; on the other hand, what today's operations desperately need from the air are helicopters and transport aircraft to move our people around the battlefield and take them back and forth to and from conflict zones. All this means that the tribal chief function inevitably sits at odds with a service chief's more corporate roles. Reconciling these conflicting elements of the job is a huge ask for any individual, and probably an unfair one. In my view, the reconciliation can only come from proper debate and discussion at high level, strong leadership at Board level in determining and then owning those decisions, and clear communication of the matters decided. Looking back, I am not convinced that we collectively rose to those challenges well enough in the critical years of our double commitment to Iraq and Afghanistan, or indeed, perhaps, thereafter.

My office call with Des Browne duly took place in September 2006 and focused on my letter. It was scheduled for forty-five minutes, and he did me the courtesy of extending it to an hour and a quarter; but how much of my letter he understood I never really knew. He had not been in the department many weeks, and if he accepted my argument about the centrality of our current operations and the critical need to succeed, he kept this well disguised. I think the wider issues passed him by completely. That is not to be taken as undue criticism of our then Defence Secretary. Frankly, unless you have some background or acquired interest in defence then, superficially exciting as it is to take on as a Cabinet minister, the responsibilities attached when the nation is fighting two demanding wars while only organized, funded and equipped for one make it a poisoned chalice of some potency. Perhaps the fact that no fewer than five apparently well-meaning individuals have sipped from this cup in recent years and succumbed makes the point – especially when Des Browne was given Scotland to look after as well in one of Gordon Brown's hasty ministerial reshuffles! To put the point bluntly, it took me thirty-seven years to be ready to command the Army; I am the first to recognize that it is a terribly tall order to ask very competent lawyers like Geoff Hoon or Des Browne to grasp the essentials in thirty-seven hours. At least John Hutton had a genuine interest in defence, even if he had no background in it; and when he – at the time, inexplicably – jumped ship in June 2009, Bob Ainsworth had the advantage, when the chalice passed to him, of having served an apprenticeship as Minister of State for the Armed Forces, effectively the No. 2 ministerial post.

Back in that autumn of 2006, the question of MOD priorities was not clarified until the Defence Board held an 'away day' of discussions in late October, which enabled it to conclude that the primary focus of the department was 'strategic success in Iraq and Afghanistan in the context of countering global terrorism'. Wonderful! But it was little short of a blinding glimpse of the obvious, and begged the second-order question of why this conclusion was not reached and announced until our operations in Iraq were in their fourth year and our major reinforcement of Afghanistan was in its sixth month. To some of us this defied logic. The sad reality of that time was that much of the MOD, in its byzantine way, was conducting business as usual, with equipment procurement and assessments of priorities continuing in a cocooned environment far distant from the harsh reality experienced by our soldiers on the front line of Helmand or Basra Palace. Sadly, the protection of vested interests within and between the services, others relating to industry and others with a political flavour seemed to rank higher than the need to succeed in the field.

That said, the inter-service bit and the industrial bit I could understand, but the political override was very difficult to come to terms with. The nation's finances were tight, and in a couple of years' time they would get dramatically worse; there was no appetite to increase defence spending then in real terms, despite our participation in two wars. So it was expected, indeed assumed, that the armed forces would get on in their usual 'can do' manner and do what needed to be done: there was certainly to be no rebalancing of the defence budget that might lead to an embarrassing public fuss over jobs. 'Muddling through', something I have thoroughly disdained since Belfast in 1972, was to be the guidance. With what result? No big decisions taken to rebalance the defence budget, just year-on-year action to make sure we could pay next year's bills. The longer-term consequences therefore became even more pressing, with the soldiers and marines on the front line getting simply what was left over after 'higher departmental priorities' and whatever we could persuade the Treasury was a cost directly consequent to our operations in Iraq and Afghanistan, under the 'Urgent Operational Requirements' protocol – a statutory obligation on the Treasury to pay to the MOD the additional costs of operations.

Yet the deliberations of the Defence Board, for better or worse, were not for the eyes and ears of those to whom we needed to send out a strong message: the soldiers, their families and the British population more generally. The Army desperately required better public relations to restore its image after the accusations that recruits were bullied at the logistics training unit at Deep Cut and the apparent abuse of Iraqis in Basra in 2003–4. These were shameful events – the work only of a tiny minority, but very damaging. However, when I took over as CGS, the chiefs were still under the media communications embargo put in place by one of the former defence secretaries, Geoff Hoon. He had seemed to believe that all the negative and leaked stories about defence issues had come from the single services fighting their turf wars. As a result Hoon disbanded the single services' media relations offices (a decision that had really irked my pre-decessor, Mike Jackson) and replaced them with another centralized, civilian-led, staff which imposed a pretty draconian and restrictive regime. Hoon may have been right about the source of leaks – I don't know – but as far as I was concerned there was an overriding need to get our message out more widely. As I have already explained, I felt very strongly about this. But the basic issue from my point of view was a rather more pressing one. If I was to have an impact in getting our message out, I would need to increase my public profile, because

Right: As the general responsible for operations throughout Bosnia, I could not have done my job without aviation support. I spent countless hours in the back of a Lynx helicopter provided by a small Army Air Corps detachment.

Below: As a firm believer in the increased momentum that helicopters can bring to the battlefield, I was delighted to be invited to become Colonel Commandant of the Army Air Corps. Here I learn to fly a Gazelle at Middle Wallop in October 2002.

Below: In my final three appointments, wherever I travelled on duty by helicopter, I invariably flew the aircraft as second pilot – surely a saving to the defence budget!

Daily Mail

FRIDAY, OCTOBER 13, 2006 · www.dailymail.co.uk · 45p

MARY WESLEY

The Vacillations of Poppy Carew

ALL NEW COLLECTION

FREE ROMANCE DVD

Pick up the latest in our FREE 14-DVD Romance Collection today

COLLECT FROM WHSMITH OR WE CAN POST THEM ALL TO YOU

EXCLUSIVE: General warns our military presence is making things worse and says moral vacuum at home breeds Islamic extremism

WE MUST QUIT IRAQ SAYS NEW HEAD OF THE ARMY

Left and below: Like most headlines, this one was rather more exciting than the story that followed. The *Daily Mail* put its own emphasis on my remarks about Iraq, rather overlooking the significance of getting out of that country some time soon in the context of the pressure on the Army and the importance of Afghanistan. I spent much of the next day emphasizing the context of my remarks – but retracting nothing.

Below: Some chose to portray my remarks as an attack on No. 10; in fact they were designed to ensure that the Army could do properly all that the Government was asking of us.

Above: Those who missed the point of what I was saying, or thought I was acting unconstitutionally, believed that I would be Out Some Time Soon!

They're not called insurgents, mister, they're called generals'

To Sir Richard,
with all good wishes
MATT

Left: Matt of the *Daily Telegraph* caught the mood, in his inimitable style!

Below: Frustrated by the way the media were reporting events in Afghanistan, I abandoned the family holiday in Cornwall in August 2007 and flew out to try to turn the coverage around.

Below: Although the BBC carried a very fair report in a live interview, I bowed my head to wipe the sweat off just before going on air, and provided the *Daily Telegraph* with a front-page photograph.

Right: Many readers saw the photograph for what it was and complained. The *Telegraph* produced this one a few days later.

Is this better? Gen Sir Richard Dannatt

A wily general who stands up for his men

'Y ou weren't doing him any favours using that picture," he told me.

Above: On 13 October 2006, while I was explaining my remarks about Iraq to the media in London, Pippa stood in for me at the passing-out parade for naval recruits at HMS *Raleigh* in Cornwall. She did a brilliant job!

Left: Oman has been a very strong ally of the United Kingdom since the Dhofar War in the 1970s. Here I am inspecting a guard of honour in Muscat in September 2007.

In South America, Chile is another key ally. The ceremonial battalion marches past after their defence minister had presented me with their Cross of Victory in February 2009.

Above: The stability of Pakistan is vital to the overall security of the South Asia region. I made several visits to Islamabad and Peshawar. Here I return the salute of the guard of honour at Army Headquarters with my opposite number, General Ashfaq Kayani, in February 2008.

Below: Close relations with India are just as important as those with Pakistan. I pay my respects at the National Memorial in New Delhi in December 2008, accompanied by my opposite number General Deepak Kapoor.

Above left: In October 1996 King Harald V of Norway, our Colonel-in-Chief of the Green Howards, unveiled a memorial to all Green Howards who fell in the Normandy campaign. The memorial is in Crépon, where Stan Hollis of 6 Green Howards won D-Day's only VC.

Above right: An unexpectedly high tide caught the band between the sea and the sea wall during the drumhead service prior to the unveiling.

Right: King Harald and I discuss the dilemma of the band's soggy socks!

Left: I became a Knight Commander of the Order of the Bath in the Queen's Birthday Honours in June 2004.

Below: Representing Her Majesty at the Sovereign's Parade at Sandhurst in December 2008 – a huge privilege.

Above: We failed to get Prince Harry to Iraq in 2007, but he deployed to Afghanistan the following year after we had reached an agreement with the British media. He served in Afghanistan for ten weeks, doing all the jobs expected of a young officer – including carrying the water for his crew (right).

Above: At my investiture as Knight Grand Cross of the Order of the Bath in 2009, I was accompanied by (from the right) my daughters-in-law Emma and Lucinda, Pippa, and my god-daughter and niece Flora Scott-Barrett.

Above: With over fifty-four years' service between them, my driver and my orderly, colour sergeants Paul Simpson (left) and Steve Crighton, were made MBEs in the New Year's Honours 2009.

Above and right: To demonstrate the close links between the county and the armed forces, I was invited to become President of the Royal Norfolk Agricultural Association for 2008. I was delighted that Prince Harry, even though he was not long back from Afghanistan, came to the Royal Norfolk Show in June that year.

Below: For the finale in the Grand Ring on the last day of the show, I changed into uniform to thank the county for its support.

in August 2006 I was extremely worried that most people outside the close circle of the Army and the keen but small band of Balkan-watchers would have little or no idea who Richard Dannatt was.

It was critical that what I said was listened to, and that it carried weight on behalf of the Army – particularly as I knew that one of the first things I would have to do as CGS was to address a problem which had deep implications not just for the reputation of the Army, but for the legitimacy of our role and future in Iraq. I would have to explain to the public the outcome of the court martial in which the commanding officer of 1st Battalion, the Queen's Lancashire Regiment and six of his subordinates were being tried on a variety of charges relating to abuse in Iraq. Whatever the outcome of the trial, the fact would remain that an Iraqi civilian, Mr Baha Musa, had died in the Army's custody as a result of over ninety injuries to his body. This tragic episode came on the back of a further, but thankfully small, number of high-profile cases relating to abuse of Iraqi civilians by soldiers in southern Iraq in 2003 and early 2004. So when it was proposed that an informal introduction to the British media over drinks be organized for me one evening in my first fortnight in post, I accepted, seeing this as an ideal way to let the public put a name to a face before I had to perform the difficult task of explaining the court martial, and probably apologizing on behalf of the British Army.

It was at that informal gathering, held in mid-September 2006 in the Cavalry and Guards Club and attended by most of the mainstream media, that I took the opportunity to sow the seeds of a couple of important issues that were to become recurring themes over my three years as CGS. I asked the assembled journalists two, largely rhetorical, questions. The first was: given all that was being asked of our armed forces in Iraq and Afghanistan, and of the Army in particular, was the 5 per cent of total Government spending being allocated to defence sufficient? While I hoped that might prompt something of a more general public debate on the size of the defence budget, the second question was more immediate. On the back of my very recent visit to Helmand, and echoing concerns put to me by a number of very hard-pressed and tired paratroopers, I asked the assembled company, after a couple of drinks in one of London's finer military clubs: did they think that about £1,150 take-home pay was enough reward for a month's hard fighting by a young soldier in Helmand or Basra City? Some struggle to believe in miracles; but, to give credit where it is due, it was perhaps not surprising that, after some journalistic pressure and keen discussions with the Treasury, the Ministry of Defence announced on 10 October a tax-free uplift of nearly £2,240 for every soldier who completed a six-month tour of duty. The point was not lost on me that a combination of logic, British fairness and media pressure, coupled with a well-argued internal case, could have results. Noting this development, Alison Steed wrote in the *Daily Telegraph*: 'It is amazing how quickly the Government can be shamed into action once it becomes clear to the population just how badly our troops are treated.' Was it enough? I don't know, but it might pay for a holiday at the end of six months in Helmand or Basra, and it was a start in my campaign to improve the soldiers' lot.

I had suggested to Richard Norton-Taylor of the *Guardian* before my Afghan visit that, as I had also put it in my letter to Des Browne, the Army was 'running hot', and that the only way to deal with this was to restore some balance in the informal covenant between the nation and its Army. The operational allowance was an early success, and I felt encouraged. But before I could go much further in my campaign I had to deal not only with a vast array of routine matters, but also with the un-expected. Into this latter category fell a pressing need to untangle a tricky inter-service Gordian knot relating to Afghanistan that was neither welcome nor on my radar. A company commander in 3 Para in Helmand had chosen to send a series of very graphic and in many ways important emails to a number of colleagues at home. His missives were important because one of the issues con-fronting 3 Para at the time was its involvement in heavy fighting about which the public knew very little, because of a Government embargo which restricted reporting to their supposed humanitarian efforts alone. The story of the fighting had to get out. Over time, and once the stance on the media had been revised, it did; but in the meantime the Parachute Regiment major's own account talked about a lack of manpower, the need for more helicopters, the morale-sapping impact on the men of daily casualties, and the death of Corporal Bryan Budd – the soldier who was later awarded a posthumous Victoria Cross.

Such stories would not generally have been par-ticularly newsworthy had it not been for the inclusion of some rather unfortunate, and unfair, references to the Royal Air Force's close air support capabilities, brought to my attention in a roundabout way by the Chief of the Air Staff's office. The criticism was that the RAF was not supporting the ground operation adequately – that it was, in the words of the Parachute Regiment major, 'utterly, utterly useless'. The net result was the potential for an embarrassing public row which honour demanded and leadership required that I sort out. So, on the morning of Saturday, 23 September, I appeared in an almost deserted BBC studio near my home in Norwich to explain to John Humphrys on the *Today* programme that, far from being 'utterly, utterly useless', the RAF was more than pulling its weight in what was very much a team business. Trying to provide some much-needed perspective to the criticism of our Air Force colleagues, and emphasizing the collegiate nature of operations, I said that

> if the odd person has had a disappointment in that an air strike that they have called in has not identified the target, or has identified the wrong target, that's under-standable in the fog of war and the heat of battle and it is disappointing that some members of the team have seen fit, in a private email, to criticize other members of the team. We don't need that. This is difficult and dangerous work. We're doing it success-fully because we're doing it as a team.

John Humphrys, the consummate interviewer, then cleverly used the issue as an entrée to a wide-ranging inquisition into our mission in Afghanistan. Given the restrictions on reporting at the time, his questions and comments were entirely fair, and the interview allowed me to make a robust case for why what we were doing in

Afghanistan was really important. I used words then that I was still using three years later:

> We went there to carry out a wide-ranging mission whose eventual purpose was to put the rule of law properly from Kabul right across Afghanistan and for that country to have a legal and sustainable economy. To do that, you need to have a security environment where these things can happen. The first thing is to try and get the security issues sorted. The Taliban have opposed us because they support the drug warlords whose illegal economy lines their pockets. We've got to deal with that issue and we're dealing with it resolutely. When that is settled, or settled sufficiently, we can then get on with the other main parts of our mission to bring the rule of law and a legal economy into that country. Of course it's going to take time.

Later in my term as CGS I refined my line on Afghanistan in the light of our subsequent experience, but the essential rationale has remained: that our operations are important not just for the people of Afghanistan and the region, but for the security and the people of the United Kingdom and the West more generally.

In a sense, the need to deal with the fallout from those emails, though unexpected, provided me with a useful opportunity to press home some important points I really wanted to make on the Army's work in Afghanistan. This was a theme that I was determined to underline in an interview that I gave to Sarah Sands of the *Daily Mail* on 10 October in my attempt to further stimulate a public debate. I chose Sands because I knew her by reputation – she'd conducted a very fair interview with Mike Jackson during his farewell visit to Afghanistan before retirement, and she had a son serving with the Irish Guards at the time. I chose the *Daily Mail* as the conduit for my views not, as it was later alleged by some, because I had decided to attack the Government, but because it spoke to middle England, the constituency with which I wanted to engage.

The hour and a half that I gave Sands was to prove a watershed in the ongoing debate about the Army and, for better or worse, set the tone for my time as CGS. Sarah Sands came to my office in the MOD and we talked in the presence of an MOD press officer. The interview successfully covered the issues I wanted to raise – those I had outlined in my letter to Des Browne – and a bit more. Perhaps, in retrospect, I regret having given her too much material on too many subjects in that interview, as the focus on the importance of Afghanistan in comparison with Iraq and the pressure on our soldiers became obscured. With some curiosity I awaited the publication of the interview, which had been slated for the Saturday edition, wondering how she would write it up. One lesson that I had learnt over the years was that any engagement with the media has the potential to have a dynamic of its own. If something you have done with the media comes out in your mind at 6 out of 10 or better, then that's a good result.

I didn't have to wait until the weekend. Two days after the interview, I travelled down to HMS *Raleigh* in Plymouth, where I was due to take the passing-out parade of naval ratings from their basic training the following morning. After a very good dinner the evening before, I was just concluding a round-table discussion that I had found myself leading on Iraq and Afghanistan when a staff officer rushed into the dining room and suggested that we might want to watch the ten o'clock news. The *Daily Mail* had brilliantly ambushed the other media by producing its Friday edition just before 10 p.m. The front page headline announced: 'WE MUST QUIT IRAQ SAYS NEW HEAD OF THE ARMY' and offered an exclusive under the rubric: 'General warns our military presence is making things worse and says moral vacuum at home breeds Islamic extremism'. It was accompanied by a photograph of me taken in Norwich three weeks earlier, when I'd been defending the RAF's integrity from the Parachute Regiment! The timing of the publication of the piece, along with its advertised content, gave the television channels no option but to run with the story – unverified and scarcely analysed – on the main evening bulletins.

I watched with fascination. The quotes were all recognizable, the points were all ones I had made, but the journalistic weighting and interpretation were distorting. The *Mail* cast me as a surprise package for speaking out as I had – all the more surprising as I had been expected to be 'a managerial, John Majorish figure, keen to do the Government's bidding' (news to me) but had turned out to be 'A Very Honest General'. Sands portrayed me as being far braver than I believed I was being by giving a journalistic slant to the words: 'I am going to stand up for what is right for the Army. Honesty is what it is about. The truth will out. We have got to speak the truth.' Casting me as the good guy, willing to stand up and be counted, the article proceeded to provide information about my background, beliefs and family and detail my various concerns. The issue which subsequently caught the media's imagination, however, was Iraq and my opinion that we needed to 'get ourselves out sometime soon'. 'Let's face it,' I had said, 'the military campaign we fought in 2003 effectively kicked the door in. That is a fact. I don't say the difficulties we are experiencing around the world are caused by our presence in Iraq, but undoubtedly our presence in Iraq exacerbates them.' All these comments were fairly reflected, but my purpose of emphasizing the priority of Afghanistan over Iraq and the longer-term health of the Army had been largely missed. In my own scoring terms I was below 6 out of 10 initially, and disappointed.

It was not long before my office called to say that No. 10 was up in arms and that Des Browne wanted to talk to me urgently. I took the view that everyone knew where I was and waited for the phone to ring. In the event, I didn't speak to anyone from No. 10: having decided to make a courtesy call to the Prime Minister's people, I found that no one senior was around to take it. After a while Des Browne rang. 'Why didn't you talk to me first?' he demanded. I was a bit stuck over that one, because I recalled writing a long letter about precisely these issues and then discussing it with him a month before. But in the spirit of helpfulness I suggested that as I had started all this, then it should be I who should face up to radio and TV interviews the next morning. Browne seemed relieved at the suggestion, so that was decided. I took the offer of a car from Plymouth to whisk me back to London through the night, leaving the commodore in charge of HMS *Raleigh* to worry about who would take his parade the next morning. Always one for a challenge and ready to save the day, my wonderful wife, Pippa, agreed to stand in for me and take the parade, which – by popular acclaim – she did rather better than I did on a subsequent occasion.

During the long car journey back to London I had ample opportunity to think about the situation. To me, the comments that I had made were not as explosive as had been made out, but the *Daily Mail* had put its own editorial twist on them, while missing the essential (from my perspective) point about Afghanistan and Army pressure. Of course, Iraq was an extremely important issue in its own right, but as far as I was concerned it sat within the overall strategic context of Afghanistan, the huge pressure on our forces, and the wider security and moral issues that all this posed. But what did everyone else, Des Browne and No. 10 aside, think? Well, it takes six hours to drive from Plymouth to London, and I listened to all the radio stations as they went around their news loops. Common themes began to emerge. Yes, there was a degree of surprise that I, as head of the Army, had said what I had said; but I detected a rapidly developing consensus on the various radio shows that, constitution-ally proper or not, my views had struck a chord with public opinion and that I was on the right track. They were themes which would dominate the media's rapidly developing feeding frenzy. Whether, in agreeing that I would handle the media the next day, Des Browne had thought that I would retract all the exciting bits that had hit the headlines I do not know, but my car ride told me that my intentions for the Army and the nation's instincts were not a million miles apart. I resolved that in the morning my focus would be on consolidating the points made about the need to conclude our operations in Iraq as soon as possible, and on providing more context and explanation about the importance of Afghanistan and the need to alleviate some of the pressure on the Army and our families.

On my arrival back at our apartment in Kensington Palace, there was just time to shower, shave and pick a suitable uniform before heading off to the MOD, where the first interview was scheduled for the *Today* programme. Sleep was off the agenda that night, but a trust that I was doing the right thing sustained me. That first interview was with Jim Naughtie, who homed straight in on my comments about Iraq. I endeavoured to rebuild a context to the brief quotes which had appeared in the *Daily Mail* and clarify my points, emphasizing: 'I'm not going to allow a piece of paper, however thin, to be placed between myself and Des Browne, or indeed the Prime Minister ... I'm a soldier speaking up for his Army.' Thirteen minutes on *Today* was just the start of the various media obstacles to be negotiated that morning. I next spoke to *GMTV*, then to BBC1's *Breakfast*, reiterating the same points and appreciating the opportunity to speak to such a wide audience.

I had not expected – or indeed intended – the Sands article to make such waves, though Max Hastings suggested in the *Daily Mail* on 14 October that 'The storm which has followed the general's comments was inevitable' because I had stirred up a political hornets' nest with my candour. Yet I felt that nothing which I had said was new; indeed, one might even say that the issue of a withdrawal from Iraq, in the context of the new operation in Afghanistan, was distinctly old hat. Not only had senior ministers and their military colleagues been discussing the subject for months, but *three years earlier* the Chief of the Defence Staff, Admiral Sir Michael Boyce, had declared that the armed forces could not fight another war for eighteen months because they were 'overstretched' by Iraq. In his last days as Chief of the General Staff, Mike Jackson was reported as saying in response to a question about when British troops would be withdrawn from Iraq: 'The sooner, the better – for everybody. But not sooner than it's right to do, and it is so important that that is understood.' It was not *what* I had said, but the fact that *I*, a newly arrived CGS, had said it, that had made headlines. My words had been pounced on by journalists who neither had access to the full transcript of my interview with Sarah Sands nor were aware of my previous correspondence and discussion with Des Browne. While some of the subsequent column inches that appeared in the press helpfully developed the public debate that I had been so keen to initiate, it was clear that most editors were also extremely happy to use my words as means by which to score some political points. That was their business, not mine.

The result was that press reaction to my recent words was mixed, but largely supportive. Of those generous in their praise for my 'plain speaking', it was not entirely surprising that retired senior officers rallied to my side. Major General Patrick Cordingley, for example, told a journalist that he agreed with my comments and thought them 'very brave'. Cordingley's words, in common with those used by many others, indicated to me that observers regarded what I had said as courageous, which in turn suggested that what I had done had put me into some sort of peril. I did not feel in peril, and I did not consider my interview in any way 'brave'; but with the publication by the *Daily Telegraph* of an article headed 'General's Quit Iraq Remarks Leave Blair Feeling Isolated', I became inadvertently caught up in a political tempest. Although some commentators understood that my comments had not sought to make political points, others suggested that my interview had strayed into the political sphere, criticizing Government policy and causing a dangerous rift between the Army and the Government. Charles Moore argued in the *Telegraph* that I had 'charged into the no-man's-land of politics without much covering fire', while some colleagues suggested that I should have pursued the points in private and, if dissatisfied, resigned. Yes, of course, I could have resigned; but in doing so I would have left my sudden successor with exactly the same problems. And if I was minded to resign after two months, having thought about these things for the previous two years, I should never have taken the job in the first place. Matthew Parris, whom I have never met, went as far as to pen a piece for *The Times* which began: 'I agree with every word that Dannatt said. But he has got to be sacked' because 'the Armed Forces are there to implement policy, not attack it'. Former Tory Defence Secretary Michael Portillo was in agreement, opining: 'It is not acceptable really, that Generals intervene in the way of political matters. I think that it probably has been naivety.' Well, everyone is entitled to their view, but I do not think there is very much naivety in trying to lead an Army that is fighting two wars at the same time and not being properly funded for either, while at the same also making sure that there is an Army there to meet the nation's needs in ten years' time.

From my perspective, I was not being naive. I knew exactly what I was doing, and did not back-track during the interviews I conducted the morning after the story broke. I knew that things had to be said, that the Army could not go on as it was, and that the events of the summer had raised the stakes in Afghanistan. Besides, we were already locked into a policy of extraction from Iraq under General George Casey's plan for accelerating a handover to the Iraqis. But, as he handed over command of coalition forces in Iraq to David Petraeus, the surge in US troop levels looked conspicuously at odds with our extraction and drawdown plan. As it happened, and as I will discuss later, both were right. Baghdad and the north and west of Iraq needed properly sorting out, but the south was always different, more susceptible to political manoeuvres and heavily influenced by Iran, which had its own axe to grind over the West's opposition to its nuclear programme. I also truly felt that our remaining in Iraq *was* exacerbating our security problems, and so I said it. I firmly believe that our extended presence there, as a result of poor post-conflict planning, had turned the attitude of the people successively from welcome to consent, then from tolerance to intolerance, and finally to hostility – a trend fuelled by the Iranians' own agenda.

I remain convinced that it is much less likely the bombings of 7 July 2005 in London would have happened had the UK either not joined the US attack on Iraq in 2003 or been able to withdraw from the country much more quickly, enabled to do so by proper post-conflict planning. Moreover – and this is a point I raised in the Sarah Sands article but have not subsequently reiterated in depth – our national drift towards a multicultural society in the UK, while laudable in many ways, has loosened the links with what has traditionally given this country much of its strength, its character and its confidence – namely the Judeo-Christian tradition – and this liberal environment has provided the backcloth on which other religions and cultures have been able to assert themselves, some for political rather than religious reasons. Islam, as one of the world's major religions, with many common and ancient links to the Old Testament of the Judeo-Christian Bible, has a proper place in the family of religions; but its manipulation in the hands of Islamist extremists, whose agenda is more political than religious, presents the possibility of communities being changed in their character, culture and beliefs without the population at large realizing what is happening. Probably, as the head of the Army, and as a believing Christian, albeit simply a mainstream member of the Church of England, it was not my job to opine on these things. But if, as a leader in any sphere, you do not stand up for what you believe, then frankly your pool of moral courage is emptying pretty fast.

So did I stray into the political sphere in 2006? I do not think so, because I was *reinforcing* Government policy for a phased withdrawal from Iraq, not criticizing it. If I had attacked the Prime Minister's policy or refused to launch a specific operation, then that would have crossed the constitutional line and calls for my resignation would have been warranted. In retrospect perhaps I was being, as Richard Norton-Taylor commented on my interview, 'unconventional' rather than unconstitutional. A month after the interview, Rear Admiral Richard Cobbold, the Director of the Royal United Services Institute, provided some useful perspective in an article, reflecting that I had gained almost universal approval for my comments from the Prime Minister down and arguing that some journalists had thrown up their hands in 'faux-horror' at what I had said. It seems likely that this was the reason why I had not been 'summoned' to see either Des Browne or Tony Blair. On the morning that the story ran in the *Daily Mail*, as I concluded the series of radio and television interviews, all was quiet from No. 10. I believe they were assessing the prevailing wind. It blew my way, and I was officially supported. Indeed, I did not meet the Prime Minister personally until some six weeks later, when he came across to the MOD for a working lunch. He hardly spoke to me. I think he was embarrassed.

To this day, I still maintain that the substance of the *Daily Mail* article was not in itself worthy of a front-page headline. I am still not sure whether Sarah Sands realized at the time that she had a scoop; her editorial colleagues, working to their own political agenda, provided that dimension to the story, as was explained in a very accurate analysis in *Private Eye* the next week. But, of course, in the context of the politically charged atmosphere which had suffused the Whitehall village since Tony Blair's commitment of British forces to the coalition operation to remove Saddam Hussein, any remarks by a service chief of the kind I made were going to spawn headlines. The thing that worried me was not the furore per se, but the fact that the political veneer applied to what I had said would blur the core message and put off those who felt I was making wider points that they could otherwise support. I was, after all, simply trying to generate support for the Army, as it did what the Government was requiring of it, and at the same time to tell the nation of the importance that I attached to eventual success in Afghanistan and the need to keep the British Army as a force in being to face whatever the future had to bring. I felt strongly that burning ourselves out in Iraq and Afghanistan would do neither us, nor the country, any favours in the long term.

When the fuss died down, I decided I had met or even exceeded my own 6 out of 10 pass mark. Whether I was right in that or not others can decide; but it meant that men and women who served in the Army, or who belonged to the wider Army family, or just cared about the Army and more widely about some of the things that make this nation tick, knew that I was not going to allow drift and muddle to characterize my time as Chief of the General Staff during these uniquely difficult years.

9

The Military Covenant

There is probably no more poignant moment in a
service chief of staff's tour of duty than laying the
wreath on behalf of his service at the Cenotaph in
Whitehall on Remembrance Sunday. As Chief of the
General Staff I did this three times. It was a huge
privilege, but not one that I enjoyed in any respect. I felt
the weight of history very deeply on my shoulders. The
First and Second World War generations had always
defined the Remembrance weekend. The presence of the
Sovereign at the Cenotaph, as well as most of the Royal
Family and, through live television, the nation, combined
sharply with one's personal emotions. I always think of
Tapper Hall, shot dead beside me in 1973, and of Peter
Willis, Gus Garside, Sam McCarter and Calvert Brown,
blown to eternity just in front of me in 1975. I think of
them as the bugle sounds the Last Post; and, as Chief
of the General Staff while we were fighting and dying in
both Iraq and Afghanistan, I could not help but think of

the families for whom remembrance was now a source of both pride and very deep hurt. Ever since my stroke in 1977 I have hated standing still in public for very long, and on each occasion I could not wait to get back inside the Foreign and Commonwealth Office whence we had marched out, bearing our wreaths. Personal remembrance aside, if there is ever a moment when the covenant between the nation and its armed forces is best exemplified it is Remembrance Sunday. In 2006 that covenant was badly out of kilter. As I saw it, my challenge was to restore it to balance.

By Remembrance Sunday 2006 I had already made a fuss about pay, resulting in the awarding of an operational allowance to troops serving in war zones, and Sarah Sands of the *Daily Mail* had catapulted many of my wider concerns very prominently into the public domain. But what to do next? As a single-service chief of staff, my ability to influence the conduct of operations on the ground was quite properly very limited, confined to discussions of higher strategy and advice to the Government within the context of the Chiefs of Staff Committee in London. As service chiefs, we were all very conscious of the impropriety of trying to run the war from the far-off heights of Whitehall: this was the task of the operational commanders in the field who reported to the Permanent Joint Force HQ in Northwood. Instead, I saw my primary task as focusing on the Army's core and most important asset, its people. After all, without properly recruited, trained and motivated people the Army would be nothing, and the remarkable successes achieved over many years by our highly committed and professional armed forces would run into the sands. That this personal commitment of every single person in the Army continued to be as strong as it had ever been was vital not just to the future of the Army, but to its success on operations today. My task was to ensure that the Army remained worthy of the commitment made to it on a daily basis by our young men and women on the front line. As I saw it, and as I repeatedly said to anyone who would listen, there was a litany of issues that demanded attention, in addition to those associated with the provision of equipment on operations – including, among others, 'people' issues, such as housing, pay, and medical provision for our wounded.

I decided that the appropriate strategic move as Chief of the General Staff was to convene a conference of all those involved in the wider provision of welfare support to the Army. At first glance this seemed a relatively straightforward thing to do, but the further my staff got into the preparation for this, the more complicated it seemed to become. So many armed forces and defence personnel issues had become tightly woven into the centralized processes of the MOD that it was politely pointed out to me that to plan a purely Army welfare conference was an impossibility. Much of the welfare support given to the Army as a whole was now provided on a tri-service basis. If there was to be a worthwhile conference it would need to be a defence-wide event that dealt with the needs of all three services. Equally, if I wished to chair the conference it would not be appropriate for me to do so as the Chief of the General Staff, but I could as a representative of the tri-service Chiefs of Staff Committee. I was startled to discover that such bureaucratic sensitivities threatened to stand in the way of doing the right thing for the Army. I was very pleased, however, to learn that Derek Twigg, the Under Secretary of State and Veterans Minister, wished to be present. Nevertheless I impressed upon him that if he was to come then he needed to allocate the whole day to the event. I had witnessed the previous year his predecessor, Tom Watson, turning up to the Army Families' Federation Conference for just twenty minutes, giving a short scripted speech, and then disappearing before the delegates could get stuck into the difficult issues of housing, childcare and education. Derek Twigg needed to face the music. We agreed that he would give the opening address and take questions, and that I would conclude the conference. In the event, a lot of issues were aired, and although no major decisions were taken, all those present were left in no doubt that those of us at the top of the organization knew what the problems were, understood them, and had a determined commitment to attack them.

Another initiative that was more directly under my control was my decision to call together all the unit commanding officers from across the Army, both Regular and Territorial, to one of four regional conferences. The purpose was to allow them to hear from me and the Adjutant General, Freddie Viggers, our perspective on issues as we saw them from the top of the Army. At each of these conferences we spoke for about an hour, giving our perspective on the way operations in Iraq and Afghanistan were developing, explaining the implications of the pressure that this sustained activity was having on the Army, and setting out what we were trying to do to restore some balance into people's lives.

Perhaps more importantly, we built into the programme time for the commanding officers to have an opportunity to give Freddie and me their views. As far as I was concerned the Army was 20 per cent about strategy – that was Freddie's and my job – and 80 per cent about delivery at the tactical level or on the shop floor – which was the commanding officers' job. What bound the two together was trust, and proper communication between us was an important way of cementing this bond. This was the primary function of the conferences: to provide us with a chance to hear from the chalkface of the Army, and to offer commanding officers direct access to us and then to send them away reassured that in these tumultuous times, under unprecedented levels of stress, the Army, its people and its future were in safe hands.

I found that a useful by-product of these meetings was to render needless any thought of an Armed Forces Federation. If anyone was to be the Army's shop steward, it was to be me. Only if I failed would the clamour return from men and women across the Army for more effective leadership than they believed they were getting on the issues that most concerned them. The prize was to get the Military Covenant back into balance, which meant ensuring that those brave young men and women who volunteered in their country's service would be fairly looked after during their time in uniform and, if wounded, afterwards. Equally importantly, we needed to ensure that their families back home received civilized levels of support and care. The Army had always known that if soldiers were confident that their families back home were being looked after properly, they would put their minds fully to the task in hand without worrying unduly about their loved ones. It seemed to me that in recent years this fundamental truth had been forgotten. Only with the Military Covenant restored could we honestly claim to be doing all that the nation, through the elected Government of the day, was asking of us. In mid-2006, I judged the pressure on our people, through a combination of intense operational commitments and poor quality of life, to be intense and our morale fragile.

As 2005 gave way to 2006 the situation in Basra and in southern Afghanistan had become more hostile, and our fatalities and casualties rose sharply as a result. In Iraq, the Iranian-backed Shi'a militias had perfected the art of constructing the triple EFP – a row of three explosively formed projectiles, or 'roadside bombs' in media parlance, to which most of our patrol vehicles were vulnerable, especially the much-criticized 'Snatch' Land Rovers. In Afghanistan, gun, grenade and rocket battles with the Taliban and the effect of legacy minefields left over from the time of the Soviet occupation exacted their almost daily toll. The increasing number of casualties, many suffering complex wounds with which in previous conflicts they would not have survived the battlefield, placed a renewed focus on our medical and welfare provision. What we found was not good.

A particular problem was the arrangements for the care of our seriously wounded. We had begun to store up a problem for ourselves from the mid-1990s when, as part of the downsizing of the military after the Cold War, it was decided to close the armed forces' dedicated hospitals. In much of the unreasoning euphoria that followed the collapse of the old Soviet Empire, many assumed that the conventional conflicts that traditionally caused large-scale casualties would become extinct, and that those casualties caused by the few limited wars that might confront us could be provided with secondary-level care by the National Health Service. In theory, the decision to use the NHS was not an unreasonable one, but it was nevertheless extremely risky in practice, as it was entirely predicated on the basis that the wars we would fight in the future would not require any dedicated resources to deal with the specialized nature of military casualties, or indeed to deal with the high numbers of wounded who might find themselves being repatriated to the UK for treatment. It seemed to me that the entire gamut of our experience in this area from the First and Second World Wars, which had led to the establishment of the old military hospitals, had been swept aside in the excitement of securing a 'peace dividend' from the ending of the Cold War. As it turned out, the relatively light casualties we sustained in Kosovo, during our early deployment to Afghanistan in 2001–2 and even from the initial intervention in Iraq in 2003 did not seriously test the new arrangements. The Royal Centre for Defence Medicine had been established in Birmingham to train our military medical staff for work in the field, with secondary care at home to be provided by a number of Ministry of Defence Health Units, established in regional hospitals up and down the UK. Similar arrangements were made in Germany and Cyprus. The result of these decisions was that, while field hospital provision for our people deployed on operations was good, provision in the UK for those returning home injured was poorly prepared for the number of casualties it was called upon to care for. Importantly, in retrospect, it was apparent that little or no consideration had been made for the care of families at these hospitals while their loved ones were undergoing treatment.

Once the Iranian-backed Shi'a militias had begun to step up their pressure on our troops in southern Iraq from mid-2005, and especially when casualties began to mount in southern Afghanistan from mid-2006, the fragility of the new arrangements for our seriously injured became painfully apparent. Press criticism focused on the NHS, but this was wrong. The clinical attention that our wounded received in Birmingham, particularly at Selly Oak Hospital, was second to none in the country. Selly Oak had been chosen as one of the best poly-trauma hospitals in the country, if not the best, and the medical and nursing staffs were brilliant. The issues were all on the periphery, but they were important – very important – and the solution to them lay in the hands of the military, not the NHS. However, despite the best efforts of some individuals, the military medical staffs in Birmingham and London did not seem to realize we had a problem. We needed an institutional shake-up.

What we increasingly saw from mid-2005 onwards was a marked increase in cases where a young soldier, shot or blown up in battle in Iraq or Afghanistan, would wake up in the pristine environment of an NHS ward in Selly Oak Hospital. His, or her, sudden translation from a military environment on operations, in the company of friends and colleagues, to a civilian one came as a profound and unwelcome shock. From being with a bunch of mates in Basra or Sangin to being surrounded by a wardful of civilians who might not even know where

Basra or Sangin was, or what the Army was doing there, was itself a substantial further trauma. Many of us with an operational background realized that this situation was unacceptable, but initially the hierarchy of the military staffs in Birmingham and London could not, or would not, see the problem. What was worse was that we had made very little provision for the families of wounded soldiers. In our rearrangement of the Army Medical Services earlier in the decade we had seemingly entirely ignored the truth that wounding always had a profound impact on a soldier's immediate family and friends, whose needs – both psychological and physical – also had to be recognized. While the Army's casualty notification system worked pretty well in a formal sort of way, and arrangements existed to get close family members of wounded soldiers to the hospital, little effort had been made to consider the impact on families thereafter. The Army had made nowhere near sufficient provision for them. They needed somewhere decent to stay, and they needed to be kept in the picture as to what was happening to their son, husband or partner. Furthermore, it had to be realized that their involvement as part of the wider patient group was a key element in their wounded relative's recovery, especially if he or she had suffered profound or cataclysmic trauma injuries of a spinal, neurological or internal nature or, of course, had lost limbs or eyesight. The families of some of our wounded in 2005 and 2006 had very sad tales to tell.

It was against this background that the great British public began to play a role in supporting our wounded servicemen and their families, in what I contend has always been the British way. Of course, the Government of the day has an absolute responsibility to look after those of its soldiers, sailors and airmen who go into battle and who are subsequently injured in the nation's name; but it has always been our practice for the public, private and charitable sectors to come together to contribute to the care that is then needed. After all, as I have often said publicly, without the extraordinary support of the public at large we would never have had the Royal Hospital Chelsea in London or the Erskine Hospitals in Scotland, all of which have played key roles in the care of our injured and veteran servicemen for many generations. So when our service charities began to get stuck into our medical and welfare problems in 2007, this was not a challenge thrown down to the Government, merely evidence that the nation was beginning to get behind its soldiers and their families. Persuading veterans minister Derek Twigg, and then Kevan Jones, of the normality of and historical precedent for this private and charitable support was not an easy task.

The most successful, and high-profile, charity that emerged from the Iraq and Afghanistan conflicts was Help for Heroes. Its origins were modest, but its contribution to service welfare has been immense, and in the spirit of the traditional British approach it has been non-critical and determinedly non-political. As Bryn Parry, who founded Help for Heroes, always says, he just wanted to do something for our 'blokes'. Great things often have small beginnings, but to succeed they need vision and drive. Bryn, and his wife Emma, provided both. They had been moved to do something after a visit to Selly Oak Hospital. Their initial contact had been with Sarah-Jane Shirreff, whose husband Richard was commanding the 3rd Division at the time and who was closely involved in operations in southern Iraq. Richard and Sarah-Jane felt equally strongly that we could and should be doing better for our wounded and their families. At about the same time Pippa and I had visited our rehabilitation centre at Headley Court. In conversation Pippa had astutely asked the commanding officer, Lieutenant Colonel David Minden, what, if he had a 'dream list', he would like to improve in the quality of care for his patients. He replied wryly that he would not mind some tins of paint to improve the look of the staff living quarters, but what he really wanted was a good swimming pool. The paint was quickly fixed, but it was incredible that at our principal rehabilitation centre there was not a proper swimming pool on site – just a small hydrotherapy pool – so that the commanding officer was forced to bus his patients to a local swimming pool and fight for time among all the other legitimate users of this public service. He felt that he needed such a pool for the exclusive use of recovering servicemen and women to build up their stamina, restore muscle strength and give them some relaxation too. But, he said, he could not see this ever getting high enough on the list of other funded priorities for spending at Headley Court, so he was not pushing the issue. Pippa told me she felt otherwise, and very strongly.

At this point enter Bryn Parry, a former soldier and a very successful cartoonist. Sarah-Jane asked Pippa and me to meet Bryn and Emma Parry over lunch. In conversation, the issue seemed pretty straightforward. We had identified a need for a swimming pool at Headley Court that the MOD, because of many other competing priorities, was unlikely to fund, and the Parrys had the vision, determination and drive to get something done. It was agreed. A new charity would be set up, its first and primary target being the funding of a swimming pool. We thought that we would need to find about £2 million. I am happy to admit that this figure seemed almost unattainably high, and we all took a deep breath as work got under way. Bryn began by designing brilliant logos; the necessary administration was gone through with the Charity Commissioners, a loan secured from the Army Benevolent Fund to float the project and a team of volunteers recruited by Sarah-Jane to man an office in Tidworth Garrison. With Jeremy Clarkson on side as a patron, invitations were sent out for the launch.

Help for Heroes was officially launched on 1 October 2007 in our apartment in Kensington Palace in the presence of about sixty supporters. Bryn and I both made short speeches and, as they say, the rest is history. Not £2 million but £50 million was raised in the charity's first two and a half years. A state-of-the-art specialist swimming pool and gymnasium rehabilitation complex costing £8 million was opened on 4 June 2010 at Headley Court by Prince William. A major programme of third-stage recovery centres, giving a launch pad to a new life for our wounded, was put in hand with the collaboration of the Ministry of Defence and other service charities from 2009, and significant grants were made to other provider charities such as, among many others, Combat Stress, working with the psychologically injured, St Dunstan's, working with the visually impaired, and Battleback, working with the physically injured. Not by design, but by circumstance, Help for Heroes stirred up the entire service charity sector, and also provided a brilliant way for the population at large to get behind its servicemen and women, and their families. All the service charities in their various areas benefited from the upswing in support for the services and found new ways to develop their work. Many members of the general public who had not previously supported service charities now put their hands in their pockets to do so. The Royal British Legion, with its famous annual Poppy Appeal, broke its own fundraising records in 2007, 2008 and 2009.

One of the charities that rose particularly quickly to the challenge was SSAFA, the Soldiers, Sailors, Airmen and Families Association. They were quick to see the urgent need for good-quality accommodation for the families of wounded soldiers spending time supporting their sons or husbands at Selly Oak or Headley Court. Up to that point the MOD had only provided the most basic accommodation. Something really good was needed. The experience of the Norton family brought the issue home most starkly. In July 2006 Pippa had found herself talking to Peter and Sue Norton at the Victoria and George Cross reception in London. They told her their story. Captain Peter Norton, an explosives disposal expert, had been very badly injured in Iraq in 2005, losing an arm, one leg and most of the use of his other leg. He was very fortunate to be alive. The George Cross he was awarded, while hugely justified, was scant compensation for the injuries he suffered. Within a very short time after the incident in which he had so nearly lost his life, and during which he had inspired those around him with his extraordinary courage, he had been evacuated by air to the United States Army hospital near their huge airbase at Ramstein in Germany. Peter's life had been saved by the medics at the US hospital in Baghdad; but he remained critically ill, and in order to give him the best chance of survival he needed to be kept stable on his journey home. His wife Sue and their youngest son, Toby, were flown out to be with him at Ramstein in Germany, where his medical condition demanded a stopover. For Sue and their two small children, virtually everything that they had known before pretty much stopped. Life would never more be described as 'normal'. But in one respect Sue was lucky. During her time at Ramstein she was accommodated by the Americans at the Fisher House, a charitably funded home-from-home for families sited adjacent to the US hospital. Here she was provided with every comfort she needed, including space of her own and support when required. As she was to say later, living in this beautiful place surrounded by forests of tall trees was her 'pine-scented haven' at this dreadfully difficult time. Americans always do these things so well – we can take a leaf out of their book.

It was when Peter returned to Selly Oak that Sue's problems really began. There was next to no provision for her and her two little boys: only minimal welfare support and no childcare available at all. She chose to commute daily to Birmingham by car, as there was nowhere suitable for her and the children to stay. She farmed the boys out with friends and family as best she could, but Toby was still being breastfed and was not allowed on to the hospital ward. Meals were taken – when they were taken – in the hospital canteen. Somehow she managed to juggle Toby's needs to be regularly fed around her need to be with her severely wounded husband. Not surprisingly, she later described the experience as a 'nightmare blur of misery and exhaustion . . . I simply don't know how we survived it.'

Sue Norton was not alone in those days: there was also Tom, a young lance corporal, whose parents preferred a ninety-mile daily trip rather than stay in the ghastly accommodation offered to them. They were self-employed and ultimately lost their business because of the physical, mental and financial strain they were under. Diane Dernie, the mother of Lance Bombardier Ben Parkinson, probably one of the most severely injured soldiers ever to have survived the battlefield, found herself staying, as Christmas 2006 approached, in a small hotel in Birmingham that was due soon to close. The owners felt so sorry for Ben's family that they were prepared to let Diane have the keys of the hotel rather than see her move on again. Some Christmas that was for the Parkinson family. Another mother writing to my wife put it most starkly: 'Pippa, those families are bleeding, and are bleeding hard.'

The mother of a young marine wrote:

We were fortunate to be lent a car for the first six weeks or I really don't know how we would have coped – taxis are so expensive. It was so lonely too, and it would have really helped if we could have met some of the other families going through what we were going through. Sometimes people made us feel we were trying to get a free ride when all we wanted to do was just be near our son. I don't think we will ever forget how we were made to feel then, and I still feel angry and let down just thinking about it now.

And a letter written to Pippa from the mother of one of our South African soldiers, Private Rory McKenzie, who had lost a leg in Basra, reads:

When we arrived in Birmingham with Rory still unconscious at the time, we were informed that the Welfare Services could only house us for the first two weeks, thereafter we would be on our own. That first night we were given a hostel room with two single beds, and although it was quite awful, with the Rand at over 14 to the Pound, we were just so grateful for anything at all. Subsequently we were moved to a small flat which we shared with two other families which gave us some privacy. Privacy is so important because believe me, Pippa, in those early days there are a lot of tears to be shed . . .

Again it was the charitable sector that stepped in to help. Pippa and I discussed the situation between us, concluding that with so much going on we should divide our efforts: she would focus on SSAFA Forces Help while I concentrated on Help for Heroes. Pippa and a senior SSAFA staff member, Liz Sheldon, drove out to Germany to visit the Fisher House in Ramstein that had been of such fundamental importance to Sue Norton and her boys. Pippa and Liz were convinced that homes such as these were exactly what our families needed. So, in September 2007 SSAFA, with the enthusiastic support of its President, Prince Michael of Kent, launched an appeal for £5 million to build two Fisher-style homes at both Selly Oak and Headley Court. There were many who doubted it could be done. Several people told Pippa that the money simply was not around and that we should be looking for cheaper options. Fortunately neither Pippa nor Commander Paul Branscombe at SSAFA Forces Help agreed. They were determined that our troops and, perhaps more importantly, their families should have only the very best, as did their American counterparts.

And so began an extraordinary time for us all. Pippa, always a supporter of better conditions for Army families, was usually happy to remain in the background but now found herself giving talks and making appeals wherever she was invited. One day, at the invitation of the Chairman, Lord Levene of Portsoken, she addressed the Lloyd's of London charity board; the next she spoke to SSAFA supporters in a Masonic Hall in Harrow. Where it was did not matter, but getting the message out and the money in did. And in only nine months the £5 million was raised. The first house was opened in February 2008, despite the rather sad and ill-judged opposition from some local residents near Headley Court. Fittingly, the first guests were a 22-year-old Royal Marine, who had lost both legs and an arm in Afghanistan on Christmas Eve, and his nineteen-year-old fiancée, now his wife. The second house in Selly Oak was opened at the beginning of 2009. Both houses are impressive modern homes with large en-suite bedrooms and fully equipped reception rooms and kitchens – everything that Pippa and Sue Norton had hoped for. Appropriately, both are known as Norton Houses, a tribute as much to Sue, who was forced to experience entirely unnecessary stress in addition to the trauma of dealing with her husband's injuries, as to Pete, who has to live with the injuries brought about through his remarkable service to the country. The charitable sector had most decisively stepped up to the mark.

But support from the general public was not to be confined to those who had been wounded and their families. One of the most anguished comments made to me by the young soldiers of 3 Para in Afghanistan in July and September 2006 was their worry that their civilian mates back in England had no idea what they were going through. The focus of the Government's media effort was on the reconstruction and development aspects of the mission, so fighting and dying did not fit the pre-ordained narrative. Their worry was that on returning home their friends would say something along the lines of 'Had a good few months in the sun, then?' with little or no appreciation of the intensity of what they had been through. Perhaps a greater worry to commanders in the field was the widely negative view taken by the public at large of the mission in Afghanistan. If Iraq was an unpopular war that few national leaders seemed prepared to speak up for, then Afghanistan was in real danger of being tarred by the same brush, as another of 'Blair's wars' that no one seemed to understand or support.

By the summer of 2007, our second in southern Afghanistan, this negativism was palpable. My family and I went to Cornwall for our usual summer holiday – minus Bertie, who was with his battalion in Afghanistan. I had only been in Cornwall a couple of days when I became really fed up with the intensely negative reporting of the operation and decided to do something about it. Somewhat to his surprise, my Military Assistant, Lieutenant Colonel Alistair Aitken, took a phone call from me just a few days into his leave:

'Alistair, I have had it with the way that the media is reporting Afghanistan. We are going out there to set the record straight, and we are going tomorrow.'

Ever the dutiful staff officer, he replied immediately: 'Right, sir.' Then there was a pause, and then the observation: 'Tomorrow . . . I will do some planning.'

For the family, my sudden decision to go to Afghanistan was a big surprise, but one with which all agreed. Normally the two weeks of beach cricket – to our own rules – surf, golf, sailing and just unwinding were sacrosanct, but not that year.

Alistair was as good as his word, and the following day we found ourselves in the air on our way towards Afghanistan. In the event it was an excellent short visit that got me around most of the units in Helmand, allowing me to put over on television and in parts of the print media what the Army and RAF were actually doing in Afghanistan and why we were there. A television interview with Alastair Leithead of the BBC was particularly useful except that, while waiting in the open in 40 degrees to do the interview, I bowed my head to wipe off the running sweat before going on camera. Some snapper snapped. The picture appeared on the front page of the *Daily Telegraph*, suggesting by my apparent attitude that we were in despair. Newspapers! However, to that publication's credit, and amid some popular protest, the same newspaper carried a more upbeat photograph a couple of days later under the caption: 'Is that better?' And there were two other postscripts to the visit. I appeared with virtually no warning in the forward operating base where Bertie was deployed, throwing him somewhat, but a cup of tea behind a sangar gave us a few minutes to chat. Slightly cheekily, at the same time I also took the opportunity to challenge the Royal Mail over postal charges for parcels to the troops. Alan Leighton, then chairman of Royal Mail and someone I knew reasonably well, very quickly agreed that parcels up to two pounds in weight could go free of charge to troops on operations. I heard the news as I was coming off the golf course back in Cornwall a couple of days later. Welcome as it was, I knew deep down that the whole issue of recognition for our troops abroad needed its own proper strategic focus, entailing more than my simply popping up in Helmand during the quiet summer news period.

I had agreed to make a major speech to the International Institute for Strategic Studies in early autumn 2007. Since my public comments on Iraq and Afghanistan the previous year there was some nervousness in the MOD about this speech. However, at that moment I had no particular axe to grind in public, just a desire to spread a better understanding of what we were trying to do and why, and so I instructed my staff to put together a speech that gave a fair summary of where I thought we were in terms of our operations in both Iraq and in Afghanistan and made some favourable comments about progress we were beginning to make on restoring balance to the Military Covenant, including important steps to improve the effectiveness and appropriateness of battlefield equipment. Alistair

Aitken, however, perhaps fearing for his summer leave the next year, persuaded me to include a forthright section on the relationship between our troops and the population at large. This echoed the sentiments expressed by 16 Air Assault Brigade and Stuart Tootal's 3 Para the previous autumn. Perhaps I could see what was coming, as on my way to work that morning I commented to Colour Sergeant Paul Simpson, my driver for twenty years, that I did not wish to be in the news headlines that evening. The subjects with which we were engaging were genuine issues for the Army, and needed tackling in a cool, dispassionate way. I hoped that there would be little of the hype we had seen in 2006. I was to be disappointed.

I suppose that, given the noise and heat generated the previous year, it was only natural that the news media would retain a close interest in this outspoken general, especially to see whether I might say anything that would embarrass the Government. They duly picked up on the final point I made in the speech, my comments becoming second lead that evening on BBC Radio 4's *Six O'Clock News*. In the lecture I referred to

a growing gap between the operations that we, as an Army, are conducting and the attitudes and understanding of our own people. Soldiers are genuinely concerned when they come back from Iraq or Afghanistan to hear the population that sent them there being occasionally dismissive or indifferent about their achievements, because if they ever did, they now no longer approve of the campaign. We are in danger of sapping our volunteer army's willingness to serve in such an atmosphere again.

These words seemed to strike a chord with many listeners across the country.

Generally in life, if you throw a pebble into a pond the ripples die away after a few moments. On this issue of public recognition for what our troops were doing, the opposite was the case. There was a remarkable effect. The ripples seemed to go on endlessly, rolling into a vast wave of public support that resulted in Help for Heroes, the SSAFA Norton House Appeal, and so much more. At the same time the general public began to get behind our troops in a very demonstrative way. Many towns and cities began to lay on homecoming parades for their own regiments. Football clubs began to invite soldiers to be celebrities at their home matches, and the remarkable town of Wootton Bassett near RAF Lyneham in Wiltshire began to honour our dead as they returned home. All these public demonstrations, whether for returning units marching ten feet tall amid ringing applause through their home town, or for the fallen who were carried in silence under the tolling bell of Wootton Bassett church, came together to reassure the Army that the people were behind them. It made the sweat, the blood, the sacrifice and the tears, at the very least, tolerable. This demonstration of public support and affection was of incalculable benefit to the Army and the armed forces – and also, I think, to the Government, though I am not sure they realized that.

I felt that by the middle of 2008 the Military Covenant was coming back into balance – at least the people of this country were solidly behind us.

Even though an army comprises a large group of people,

there are some members who are more prominent than others, be they generals, second lieutenants or private soldiers. At this time we had two very special young officers serving, Second Lieutenants William and Harry Wales. Both were in the Household Cavalry Regiment and eager for active service. Early on, Prince William had accepted that a deployment to Iraq or Afghanistan would be out of the question, given his position as first in the direct line of succession to the throne. That said, and to his great credit, he later volunteered for helicopter training with the Royal Air Force in order to become an air–sea rescue pilot. Having done some flying myself, I know that no one should be in any doubt about the bravery and commitment of that decision. Helicopters are a bit like bucking broncos; to be prepared to fly one in a storm-force wind is most unusual, and requires very real courage. However, his younger brother, Harry, was understandably very keen to be deployed on Army operations overseas just as soon as possible. My predecessor, Mike Jackson, had begun the process of drawing up protocols with all the interested parties whereby either of the princes could do precisely this. By the summer of 2007 there was the very real prospect of Prince Harry deploying with his regiment to Iraq. In the circumstances at the time, and given where his regiment was likely to be based and what his likely tasks were to be, I judged the risk to be acceptable. After consultation, all parties concerned were in agreement. Of course, beyond the benefit of personal development through operational experience for Prince Harry, there was the very real prospect of cementing the Royal Family even more solidly to the armed forces and the nation through one of the

Sovereign's grandchildren deploying and sharing the risks of operational service along with the rest of the Army. But then the British media began to play a role.

Over the course of my Army service the media have always been a significant presence, with a constantly changing and developing role. From my earliest days in Northern Ireland, the lesson was stark: whoever got their story into the public domain first tended to win the public argument. This is a vitally important consideration, especially in a counter-insurgency campaign, where the battle is as much for public opinion and perception as it is for terrorists killed or captured. In the early days of the Northern Ireland operation the Army was not very smart about this, despite the many lessons it had learned in the 'small wars' that had characterized the withdrawal from Empire following 1945, where information operations had played a central and even defining role. Too often the IRA managed to turn a tactical defeat for themselves into a propaganda victory by getting their version of a shooting or bombing into the media first. It took some time for the Army's message to develop the sophistication for which it was later to become renowned; but when it did, it boasted an agile press office that was able to get verifiable facts out into the public domain very quickly.

The Falklands conflict of 1982 took this management of the media to a new level. Journalists could not get anywhere near the action without the full support of the armed forces, as without us they could not even get to the battlefield. And, as often in the pre-satellite communications era, they relied on us to transmit their copy or film. Even so, it proved impossible to prevent the premature reporting of 2 Para's advance on Goose Green. However, by the time of the first Gulf War in 1990–1, and after many Ministry of Defence and Staff College seminars had examined the issue of relations between the media and the armed forces nearly to death, a policy was developed that accredited journalists to units on an official basis. Those who refused accreditation took their own chances in the desert as free-runners, at huge personal risk. Accredited journalists were by contrast attached to units, properly protected and given an agreed level of access to commanders and soldiers. It was at this time that Kate Adie realized the significance of being referred to by her assigned unit as a PONTI – a 'person of no tactical importance'. If push had come to shove, she might have found herself very low on the pecking order!

This process of accreditation encouraged the military to believe that it could, in some measure, exercise a degree of control over the media. However, the operations in the Balkans from 1992 onwards rapidly demolished this comfortable assumption. However bloodthirsty the environment, the Balkans were in Europe, and access to satellite and near-instant communications were readily available. Journalists did not need the acquiescence of the military to get the coverage of events that their editors demanded. The military had to work out low-level understandings with journalists operating in their areas of responsibility. Personally, I found a policy of complete openness the best way to gain this cooperation. If, within the bounds of sensible security, journalists were given the information they needed, then they would be satisfied and we would, in all likelihood, get the story told as we wished it. Martin Bell sat in on my Orders Group for the move into the Serb-held part of Bosnia in December 1995. He knew the plan. We got him to the right places. In the event the story was reported faithfully and factually, to the mutual satisfaction of the BBC and the 4th Armoured Brigade!

By the time of the second Gulf War, relations with the media had moved on further. The illusion of control by the military, exercised well in the Falklands and the first Gulf War, albeit less smoothly in the Balkans, resulted in a policy in 2003 that entailed journalists being formally 'embedded' with units – for all practical purposes, each being taken onto the strength of that unit. The outcome of this was that journalists were able to present some of the most graphic reporting ever seen from battlegroup level of local battles and engagements. This was useful, but it entailed the loss, in my opinion, of a proper portrayal of the wider context in which the operation was being conducted. Editors now seemed to be much more interested in the blood and guts of the action than they were in the tactics and strategy of the war. I am still not sure whether this was a failure of editors or, maybe, a reaction against the armchair generals of the Falklands era who had previously dominated television screens at home.

In any event, by the time I found myself responsible for decisions relating to Prince Harry, the media was very prevalent, by design, at unit level. Nothing was going to be kept secret for very long. Too soon, and too quickly, the media's speculation as to his likely deployment area, his tasking and the vehicles he would be operating in became public knowledge. The situation was not helped by the Iranians' detention of a party of sailors and marines from HMS *Cornwall*. The prospect of a senior member of the Royal Family falling into hostile hands in similar circumstances was unthinkable. Prince Harry would not go to Iraq in 2007. He and I were very disappointed, as we agreed over a drink shortly after I had reluctantly taken the decision to cancel his deployment.

The sea-change in support for the military by the autumn of 2007, however, seemed to present a new opportunity to deploy Prince Harry, and Afghanistan was quite a different prospect from Iraq, with journalists once again enjoying much less access to the action if they did not have the military's support. In conjunction with Prince Harry's private secretary, we resolved to try again to deploy him on operations. Managing the media was going to be the main problem, as his deployment, if widely and publicly known, could endanger both his own safety and that of his comrades. After lengthy discussions among ourselves I came to the view that we could not try to work around the media: the answer was to talk to them. The editors of all our main UK media – daily, Sunday and regional newspapers and periodicals, radio and television – were invited to a meeting in the Ministry of Defence. The Director of News had agreed that I would lead the discussion with the editors. For the first twenty minutes or so everyone just talked around the problem. It seemed too difficult. I then put my finger on what I felt was the issue.

'Look, the way I see it is that you want to report Prince Harry on operations and I want to get him there. What is stopping me getting him there is that whenever you get a sniff of a plan you begin to speculate – usually correctly

– so I cannot deploy him. So why don't I tell you where he is going and when, you keep quiet, and we will give you the access you need to him throughout. You get your stories and Prince Harry gets on operations.'

At that point metaphorical pennies seemed to drop all around the room. The tone of the conversation changed immediately as discussion began to focus on whether we could all trust each other enough to make it work. The foreign media were identified early on as the weak link. However, it was agreed by the assembled editors that they would nominate representatives to sit down with the MOD media staff to see if a scheme could be devised. Some intense discussions took place over the next few weeks, resulting in an understanding agreed by all parties.

And so, in late 2007, with the Household Cavalry Regiment in the process of deploying to Afghanistan, the British media were told that Prince Harry would also be deploying. The understanding we had reached provided for a pool of print, radio and television journalists being given access to Prince Harry before, during and after his deployment. The media selected the members of the pool themselves, and the material would be available to all those who kept within the understanding. Anyone who broke ranks would get nothing. The eventual release of the pooled material was designed to satisfy the needs of all. Over and above the media, the small number of very senior people who needed to know the plans were briefed, Prince Harry flew out to Afghanistan – and I waited to see what would happen.

Reports from my staff came back that he had arrived, moved into his operational location and begun work as a forward air controller – the essential interface between the troops on the ground and the aircraft operating in support. Christmas 2007 came and went. The Royal Family was shown at church at Sandringham, without Prince Harry; those who might have speculated why not knew the answer, so there was no speculation. Less edifying were a couple of incidents reported to me in which two soldiers home on leave had contacted one of the tabloids with an 'exclusive' about Prince Harry. I was very disappointed at this lack of loyalty. The soldiers concerned were equally disappointed that the tabloid in question did not bite their hands off, and then extremely surprised when they were sorted out in no uncertain terms when they returned to their units. Thirty days of deployment passed, so Prince Harry qualified for his medal, as is standard practice in any operational theatre, and then the weeks began to tick by. My personal definition of success was for the understanding to have held for a month. We got into the third month and the end of his regiment's tour of duty began to appear on the horizon. At the tenth week, I was in Pakistan visiting the Pakistani Army and Jock Stirrup was in Australia when both of us got telephone calls saying that a US website had picked up an article in an Australian magazine revealing that Prince Harry was in Afghanistan. I spent most of the night watching Sky and CNN television: it was quite clear that the cat was out of the bag and there was no alternative to pulling Prince Harry out. Jock Stirrup, as Chief of the Defence Staff, was in overall operational command of all British servicemen deployed while I, as Chief of the General Staff, retained full command over all soldiers. The decision was taken and Prince Harry flew home, very gallantly hailing the seriously injured marine Ben McBean, who had lost an arm and a leg in an explosion, as the real hero of the hour.

The media coverage of Prince Harry's return was huge, and rightly so. Yes, as a young officer he was just doing his job, and as an individual his life and safety were no more or no less special than those of any other soldier; but everyone felt at once that his deployment was really significant. It was a brilliant personal experience for him, it reinforced yet again the close bonds between the Royal Family and the nation, and it brought Afghanistan into everyone's home via television coverage that not even Ross Kemp could equal. I also firmly believe that his presence in no way jeopardized the security and safety of the other soldiers around him, something which had always been one of our major worries. When the dust settled, Prince Harry wrote a charming letter of thanks to me. And Des Browne, still Secretary of State for Defence at the time, was gracious enough to say, 'Well done, I didn't think you would get away with it!' Perhaps inevitably, there was some soul-searching by elements of the media about where their responsibilities lay, but with the exception of Jon Snow of Channel 4, the mood prevailed that this had been a move in the national interest and that professional journalistic consciences should be clear. Of one thing I am certain: the episode will be debated at Staff College media seminars for years to come. Was it a one-off? Time will tell.

As a postscript to these events I invited Prince Harry to be the royal guest at the Royal Norfolk Show in 2008. Since Pippa and I married in 1977, Norfolk has been my home, and since the death of her father in 2004 I have run the family arable farm just south of Norwich. It was for neither of these reasons that I was asked to become President of the Royal Norfolk Agricultural Association for 2008. Instead, Henry Cator, the then Chairman, made the suggestion as a way for Norfolk to show its solidarity and support for our armed forces. The Royal Norfolk Regiment was a very proud part of the county, its traditions now taken forward by the Royal Anglian Regiment, whose 1st Battalion had just completed a gruelling but very successful tour in Afghanistan in 2007. In the county we also have the Light Dragoons based at Swanton Morley near Dereham – armoured recon-naissance soldiers recruited from the north-east, but very much part of Norfolk, and honoured by the county whenever now they go away and return from operations. We also have RAF Marham, once commanded by Jock Stirrup, from where some of our fast jets have deployed in support of land forces in Afghanistan. The Territorial Army and the Sea, Army and Air Cadets are all very well represented in the county. So Norfolk felt, and feels, very much part of our military fabric and family, and it was for that reason I was asked to preside over the Royal Norfolk Show in 2008. We were all delighted that Prince Harry came as our guest in the year that marked the centenary of the show becoming the *Royal* Norfolk Show. Attendance was over 100,000 – with a marked increase in young girls, it was noted!

Having toured the show with Pippa for two days, I changed from my grey suit and bowler hat into uniform for the final evening event in the Grand Ring. It filled with military bands, pipes and drums, the King's Troop

Royal Horse Artillery, a detachment from the Light Dragoons, the Royal British Legion, all the Blue Light Services and the RAF Falcons Parachute Display Team. As a climax, by total coincidence, three Apache attack helicopters of the Army Air Corps appeared above us, on a training flight from their base at Wattisham just a few miles away. Bertie, not long back from Afghanistan, was heard to remark: 'Dad, in Afghanistan you can't get an Apache for love or money; come to the show and you get three!'

10

War on Two Fronts

When I became Commander in Chief, Land Command in March 2005, the assumption given to us by the Ministry of Defence as the basis for planning force levels in Iraq was that by autumn 2006 we would have reduced our commitment to a small task force of between a thousand and fifteen hundred soldiers. We were also told to assume that we would have a medium-sized task force of about three and a half thousand soldiers in Afghanistan. These deployments were to be found, of course, over and above our residual commitments to Northern Ireland, Bosnia and Kosovo. However, when I became Chief of the General Staff in August 2006, the reality was that we had eight thousand soldiers still deployed in Iraq and little prospect of reducing that number. The force deployed in Afghanistan was, as predicted, about three and a half thousand strong. Resilient supply lines from both Iraq and Afghanistan back to the United Kingdom were required for support, transport and medical evacuation, but having two lines of communication placed huge additional demands on us.

By 2006 this war on two fronts had locked us into a 'perfect storm' of commitment over and above our resourced capability, a predicament which we had long feared. The problem was not so much the total numbers involved as that we had to continue to provide them indefinitely. The planners in the headquarters always quipped: 'Plan for the worst case, and you will never be disappointed,' but this assumed that we would be asked to do only what had been planned. Fighting a sustained war on two fronts had never been one of our planning assumptions. Now, facing this reality, we were really struggling to find the resources we needed to meet both requirements. I reflected ruefully on the parsimonious wishful thinking that allowed politicians to send their citizens to war while refusing to provide the money necessary to ensure the success of the deployment. Despite this, on the ground our people got on with the tasks magnificently.

We had always said that in Iraq we would draw down our forces when the conditions were right, rather than to any pre-ordained timetable. In theory this was absolutely the correct approach, but the complication for the British effort in Iraq was the 2004 decision to do more in Afghanistan from mid-2006. The result was that we had no choice but to reduce our force numbers in Iraq in order to increase our numbers in Afghanistan, regardless of whether the conditions on the ground in Iraq justified it or not. I feared that it was rather assumed that the situation in Iraq would inevitably improve. It did not.

Under the plan put forward by General George Casey,

the overall US coalition commander in Iraq, we would hand over our four provinces in the south of the country to Iraqi control, progressively reduce our forces and ultimately withdraw. However, the rising tide of violence in Baghdad, as well as in northern and western Iraq during 2004 and early 2005, coupled with the covert Iranian intervention in the south, meant that the American talk in 2006 was no longer of force reduction but, under the new US commander General David Petraeus, of substantially increasing force levels in a new 'surge'. Unfortunately, this came at a time when we were desperate to reduce our commitments in Iraq, for the reasons I have just given. This, however, did not fit the plans of our coalition partners. Nor, in truth, did it allow us the opportunity to do everything we needed to do to remain sufficiently in control of our region in southern Iraq.

Nevertheless, despite the pressure on our numbers and resources, and notwithstanding the criticism subsequently directed at us, it remained our firm intention, just as it had been when we had last controlled Iraq in the 1930s, to leave southern Iraq, and Basra in particular, a better place than we had found it. I returned to Iraq for the first time as Chief of the General Staff in September 2006, a few days after my visit to 16 Air Assault Brigade in Afghanistan. Discussions in Baghdad centred on the effectiveness of the Maliki Government. After the woeful performances of the coalition-backed interim and transitional governments that had gone before, hope, if not expectation, was high that Nouri al Maliki would turn out to be the kind of Prime Minister that the fledgling democratic Iraq so desperately needed. He had the

advantage that he had not been elected as the representative of one of the large power blocks; he was his own
man, not a mouthpiece for one faction or another. The
challenge facing him was to turn this political weakness
into a real strength, and to do this would require wily
leadership and astute management of the varying competing interest groups and factions. This would have been
a task beyond the competence of many a mature
democrat; however, in the new Iraq there was optimism
that he could rise to the daunting task. His overriding
problem was security – but not, as Lieutenant General
Graeme Lamb, the senior British officer in Iraq at the
time, told me, 'how to deliver security' so much as 'how
to secure the oil and electricity'. It was clear to those who
were thinking about these things that resentment, hatred
and violence were all feeding off poverty. The trick was
to find a formula that would improve oil extraction and
power infrastructure in order to improve people's quality
of life, increase state revenue and attract foreign investment. Only then would the new Iraq have a chance. It
seemed to me from discussions I had with our ambassador
in Baghdad, together with senior members of the
coalition, that there was no shortage of plans to do these
things, merely an inability to implement them.

Three and a half years on from the invasion of the
country, it was a serious indictment of our lack of pre-
invasion planning that we were in this position. Now, as
a result of the democratic process that we had put in
place, the future was to be placed firmly in Iraqi hands.
Was it at all reasonable to expect the young democratic
Iraq to succeed where we had struggled? Handing over to
them was the correct thing for us to do, but it remained

one of a series of large gambles we were forced to take over the coming months. It stands as a tribute to the maturity and strength of character of the new government, as well as to the effectiveness of Petraeus' surge, that the gamble eventually paid off.

When I got down to Basra on that visit I was briefed on the operations that we were conducting on the ground. The overall aim under General George Casey was to hand over to properly constituted Iraqi authorities. Our task was to prepare Basra for this eventuality. Major General Richard Shirreff had put in place a plan – Operation 'Sinbad' – which entailed going systematically through the districts of Basra to re-establish policing and to do what was possible to rebuild the civil infrastructure. On the premise that education was the key to the future, his civil focus had been on schools. I went with some of his soldiers to see our people refurbishing classrooms and sports pitches, as well as visiting army and police training sites as usual. Sadly, as on previous visits, Basra had the air of somewhere that had enjoyed good times in the past but was now in decay. Rubbish was everywhere, sewage ran down the streets and too many people were standing around not doing very much. Now that a measure of security had been provided, what was really needed was inward investment to provide clean water, clean streets and jobs. This was the substantive challenge. Still, as always, the British troops were enthusiastically engaged in doing whatever they could. They were watchful of their own security, of course, but very conscious that they were making a difference – all of which was a sharp contrast to a year later in Basra, when we were fighting for our lives.

While Richard Shirreff and his troops were doing what they could on the ground, elsewhere wider issues were being played out. In the United Kingdom the Government remained blind to the urgent requirement to fund our operation properly. Of the three classic counter-insurgency ingredients – muscle, money and message – it was still money and message that were lagging behind. Frankly, the strategic message to most of the British population, among whom the war in Iraq was hugely unpopular, was always going to be difficult; but although the lack of money in Iraq was fully within our gift as a country to fix, for reasons that still elude me our Government and its Treasury persisted in its state of myopic dysfunction with regard to the need to fund its campaigns properly.

The initial frustrations over some of our military equipment paled into insignificance when contrasted with our reluctance to part with money to get reconstruction and development going in southern Iraq. In 2006 the British Government earmarked just £24 million for our entire civil and military 'Better Basra' policy, in contrast to the $86.7 million which the Americans gave to our British commanders in Basra to spend on projects as they saw fit. Of course, getting the money spent properly was a major issue, but at least the Americans were prepared to take a risk to make that part of the gamble pay off.

Our embarrassing dysfunctionality stemmed in part from the fact that we failed to organize ourselves properly. The relationship on the ground in southern Iraq between the Foreign and Commonwealth Office, the Department for International Development and the

Ministry of Defence was, to say the least, ambiguous. The theoretical solution lay in close coordination of both policy and implementation, but the real problem lay in actually achieving practical consensus on the ground. I would go further, and suggest that it reflected a profound lack of leadership on the part of the organs responsible for delivering UK Government and coalition policy. We failed to organize ourselves properly in a single, transparent chain of authority, with the result that internecine squabbling over roles, resources and responsibilities dangerously damaged the combined effect we were trying to achieve. Various cross-departmental bodies had been put in place with the aim of facilitating this combined effect, but none of them had enough teeth to be effective. In Iraq, as elsewhere, we espoused a so-called 'comprehensive approach' in these situations, but the rhetoric and the action did not add up. Any future Government that really wants to make a difference on the world stage has got to find a way to solve this problem – which is essentially one of leadership. The problem is not confined to areas of conflict, but is also evident in those parts of the world where investment and development could act to prevent conflict in the first place. When I was CGS I repeatedly observed a vast chasm between what we said at home, for domestic political consumption, and what we were actually managing to achieve on the ground. We must do better, not just in Iraq and Afghanistan, but in Africa and elsewhere. Prevention, when properly funded, is far better than the expensive cure – military intervention.

By the time of my next visit to Iraq, just before Christmas 2006, Operation 'Sinbad' was in its final stages. It was having a beneficial effect in Basra prior to our handover to the Iraqis and our planned withdrawal from the city. However, under David Petraeus the campaign plan was changing. He had successfully argued for a significant force uplift to confront Sunni Muslim violence, especially as it moved to the support of Al-Qaida in Baghdad, and in the north and west of the country, on the basis that 'my enemy's enemy is my friend'. As Thomas Ricks has recounted in *The Gamble*, much of the ideological impetus for this new US policy had come from a retired US Army officer, General Jack Keane, who had worried in retirement that the Army he loved was in danger of defeat.

I had first met Jack in Washington when he was Vice Chief of the United States Army Staff and I was Assistant Chief of the General Staff, visiting shortly after 9/11. I knew that if he felt strongly about something then he would not rest until it was seen through. However, Jack's vigour in lobbying in Washington would have had no purpose had it not been for the intelligence and determination that David Petraeus brought to the campaign. Petraeus had already served two tours in Iraq before he was appointed to run the US Army's Command and General Staff College. While there, he set about surrounding himself with some of the best young, but battle-hardened, brains of the US Army, developing a new counter-insurgency doctrine relevant to contemporary times. This was a brilliant move by the United States Army, which throughout its history has been at its most formidable when it has been able to adapt to change.

However, in late 2006 our concern in southern Iraq

was that increased US pressure in Baghdad and elsewhere could have an adverse effect in Basra, especially if
the Americans chose to put pressure on the Shi'a militias
in Sadr City in Baghdad. It could result in a Shi'a backlash in Basra just at the time when we were hoping to
reduce our force levels. It made our drawdown aspirations, when contrasted with the American 'surge', look
badly out of line – and they were. It also renewed the
pressure on us to get investment and development going
in Basra as part of our 'comprehensive approach'. We
believed then that development, not security, was the
pressing issue in Basra. However, the prospects for a
'New Deal' for Basra increasingly now seemed rooted
more in fantasy than reality, especially when our joint
FCO/DfID Provincial Reconstruction Team removed
themselves from Basra to the safety of Kuwait City, as
rocket attacks on our bases had increased. Richard
Shirreff had argued for a Joint Inter-Agency Task Force
in Basra, but his call fell on deaf ears, just as it had when
Major General Bill Rollo had raised the same idea a year
before. So, on my return, I told Jock Stirrup that our
track record with regard to inter-departmental cooperation in south-east Iraq was poor and that, in my
judgement, we were facing the last safe moment to get
our house in order and retain the initiative before it was
snatched out of our hands by our enemies.

By the time I returned to Iraq two months later in
February 2007, there was, nevertheless, a palpable feeling
of optimism in Baghdad. Significant United States troop
reinforcements were on their way and new reconciliation
and outreach programmes were beginning to show
positive results in some areas of the country. Even more

encouragingly, the Government of Nouri al Maliki was showing itself to be responsible and fair. On the ground in the south, however, our problem remained. While the Americans in their growing numbers were now improving their tactical awareness through a deployed presence in all their difficult areas, we in Basra were on the point of withdrawing from all our 'downtown' sites prior to full handover to the Iraqis. By the time of my visit in February only Basra Palace remained in our hands – and it was clear that in pursuing this policy we had given ourselves a real problem. It was right that we should at some stage withdraw from Basra City to let the Iraqis run their own lives: they knew that was the policy and that we were going. The crucial issue was timing. The steadily growing Iranian presence in Basra, backing the Shi'a militias, was increasingly becoming a serious political and security issue.

On the face of it, Iranian support for the militias made no sense. Although nearly all the people in the region are Shi'a Muslims, there are ethnic differences: the Iraqis are Arabs, while the Iranians are Persians. There is no love lost between them, especially because of the very bloody eight-year war fought between the two countries in the 1980s. But the Iranians had their own reasons for confronting the West, not least the international pressure being applied on them to curtail or close their nuclear programme; and one way of putting pressure on the West was for the Iranians to put pressure on the British in Basra City. This they did. Basra Palace became the focus. Rocket and mortar attacks on Basra Palace increased in intensity, while routine resupply convoys turned into tactical battles, invariably only getting through after a major firefight. We won all these battles, but not without human cost.

Over a quick bite of lunch on a visit to the 2 Rifles battlegroup in Basra Palace that February, I found myself perched next to a young lance corporal in the Duke of Lancaster's Regiment. I asked him how it was going, and he replied, 'Shit.'

'Why?' I persisted.

Quietly he told me that his best mate had just been killed, and that in a subsequent firefight he thought that he had shot someone he shouldn't have.

Fighting takes an unprecedented toll on our service-men and women, both physically and mentally, as these tough battles around Basra demonstrated to me once again. (Interestingly, I met the same young man about eighteen months later on a promotion course. He seemed to have come to terms with his circumstances and was happy to talk to me again.) Immediately after lunch I was due to go out on patrol with a platoon of riflemen when a salvo of rockets came smashing in, delaying our departure for a while.

The visit illustrated the dilemma we were in. We intended to leave Basra Palace and the city so that the Iraqis could run the place themselves. This had always been the policy, and it had seemed to make sense in the south. Indeed, previously the Americans had been look-ing to us to see what lessons could be learned from us as we handed over. For their part, however, the Iranian-backed Shi'a militias were determined to make it look as though the British were being chased out of town, lick-ing their wounds, their tails firmly between their legs. So while we portrayed our exit as a planned withdrawal, they saw it as a significant victory, claiming that we had been forced out. The men and women first of 2 Rifles and then of 4 Rifles fought very brave battles in those closing months of our presence in Basra. By the time of my visit in February 2007, 2 Rifles had had over four hundred contacts – battles by another name – and in the first three months of their tour they had taken over sixty battle casualties, including eight killed. They were living under constant threat from artillery, rocket and mortar fire when in camp, and from IEDs, rockets, machine-gun and rifle fire when out on patrol. In a speech I gave soon after this visit I observed that

in the face of all this I found their resilience and morale remarkable – testament to good small unit cohesion, offensive spirit and very strong leadership at all levels. Back home their families are finding it hard, especially so since 2 Rifles averaged two weekends away from home per month for the seven months prior to this seven months tour. A strong regimental net-work and a proactive rear party looking after the families are helping enormously, but I judge that we are spending the capital of our people's goodwill faster than we are replenishing it.

It is perhaps worth recording that in my last weeks as Chief of the General Staff in 2009 I visited 2 Rifles again, this time on their next operational tour in Afghanistan, and later, with Pippa, I visited their rear party at their base in Northern Ireland. In Afghanistan they lost thirteen soldiers killed, but yet again they never lost a tactical battle.

The intensity of these campaigns is perhaps best illustrated by the large number of gallantry awards made, not least being the Distinguished Service Order given to Lieutenant Colonel Rob Thomson, the commanding officer of 2 Rifles. Nevertheless, I worry for these extraordinary brave men and women, like my young Lancastrian lance corporal, and trust that the nation as a whole will never forget the debt of gratitude it owes them, and will continue to do its duty by them. I hope that in this regard public memories will not fade.

I next visited Iraq in September 2007, shortly after a series of calls on my opposite numbers in the US armed forces in Washington. There was an increased sense of optimism throughout the country. The combined effects of the US troop surge, the reconciliation between large numbers of Sunni Muslim fighters and the Government, and the somewhat unexpected ceasefire by the Sadrist Shi'a militias were proving beneficial. Prime Minister Maliki was being given some breathing space. While in Baghdad I spent some time in the West Rashid district of the city with a US Army task force of about a hundred men. They were living in a joint security station with a unit of the Iraqi National Army, just next to the local Iraqi police station. What had been one of the most dangerous parts of the city was now almost peaceful, at least by Baghdad standards. The statistics seemed to prove the theory that, once an area had been cleared of insurgents, it needed to be held in sufficient strength to maintain security. It was a false economy to think that the 'hold' part of an operation could be trimmed down once the fighting had ended. In May, before the troop surge, there had been seventy-one IED attacks in that area, but by August the figure had dropped to just 16. The monthly total of all kinds of attacks – small arms, grenade, rocket and IED – had fallen from 368 in May to 88 in August. Although one is wary of the US obsession with statistics, there was no getting away from the clear evidence that things were now better in Baghdad, and markedly so. David Petraeus and Ray Odierno, the US corps commander, recognized that over and above the troop surge, the reconciliation of the Sunni people to the government was a key element in their success and that the Shi'a ceasefire had presented another opportunity. The debate now focused on the extent to which the Iraqi Government could manage to do deals with the Shi'a, in the same way that it had with the Sunni.

While the situation in Baghdad had changed enormously for the better, that in Basra remained poor. We had now completed our withdrawal from Basra Palace. Taking over the mantle from 2 Rifles, their sister battalion, 4 Rifles, under the command of Lieutenant Colonel Patrick Saunders, had literally held the fort until the date of withdrawal was reached. Gritty battles to resupply the Palace had been commonplace, lives were lost and medals won, but on the day of withdrawal the Last Post was sounded and the battalion withdrew in good order, unopposed by the militias. The mortar and artillery attacks on our base around Basra airport had also reduced markedly. This prompted some soul-searching. Had we done an inappropriate deal with the enemy? In a counter-insurgency this will always be a moot point; but, given that the purpose of the operation is to win the hearts and minds of the people and not simply to kill insurgents, imaginative tactics should always be considered. The situation now was that Basra was in the hands of the Iraqis and we were standing off in what we described as 'over-watch', prepared to re-enter the city if there was a major breakdown in law and order. Some criticized us for just hunkering down in our main base by the airport, but the future had to lie with the Iraqis, and we had returned their city to them. Major General Graham Binns, who had taken over from Richard Shirreff and four years before had commanded 7th Armoured Brigade when it had liberated Basra, saw our mission now as one of military assistance to the Iraqi Army, and of encouraging infrastructure reconstruction and economic development. The question now was whether we, supporting the Iraqi authorities, would make the most of the opportunity that had been presented. With British forces now out of the city, thus denying the Iranian-backed militias easy targets to attack for their own political purposes, the ball was firmly at the feet of the civil authorities, whose responsibility it now was to ensure rebuilding and reconstruction. For our part, the civil side of the British 'comprehensive approach' also had to step up to the mark to help the Iraqi authorities begin to transform their city. I was not alone in worrying that, whatever their strength of will, they simply did not have the resources to do what was necessary.

The situation was still hanging in the balance four months later when I returned in January 2008. Relatively minor issues exemplified our inability to improve things. For example, those who needed to get into the city could not do so in safety because of the lack of suitable vehicles in which to travel. A military convoy would inevitably risk attracting attack, while using a soft-skinned vehicle was plainly stupid. The previous autumn a request had been made for civilianized armoured vehicles to be supplied to move our senior officials around the city. But in January 2008 such vehicles were not expected to be delivered until May, nearly a year later and now far too late to exploit the window of opportunity we had had. We were simply far too slow, far too bureaucratic and far too unresponsive to immediate needs to achieve what we had set out to do. I was deeply frustrated that while our young men and women were fighting and dying on the front line of two of our country's wars, those of us who understood what needed to be done were still failing to bring sufficient attention to resolving even some of the most minor issues that would enable us to succeed, and bring the troops home. The phrase that came to mind was 'spoiling the ship for a ha'pennyworth of tar'. I often asked my staff what the problem really was – was it money, industrial capacity, leadership or energy? I invariably concluded that while more money would help, the real lack was in leadership and drive at the highest levels.

Another impression I had was that, if our military posture was one of over-watch, we had precious few assets to do any watching. In withdrawing from the downtown sites we had lost our situational awareness on the ground, so we needed more capability to watch from the air. The Americans often referred to their 'unblinking eye' capability, whereby an unmanned aerial vehicle (UAV) – a 'drone' in popular parlance – could watch a target for days on end, establish the pattern of life and provide the real-time links for ground operations.

These things are very expensive, however; so I had often argued for not just fast jet, satellite and UAV or 'drone' surveillance, but for the man-in-the-loop capability that helicopter surveillance could provide. This helicopter capability had, to my certain knowledge, been a football kicked around the MOD for at least five years, with no definitive result. One suspected that inter-service rivalry lay at the heart of the problem, but I could not forget the hugely beneficial value of the helicopter-mounted surveillance capability we had enjoyed for decades above Belfast and Londonderry. Of course, there was the threat of a surveillance helicopter being shot down above Basra – indeed, we had lost a Lynx and its crew earlier in the campaign – but we had the technology to provide effective measures to counter this threat, albeit at a cost. Cost seemed to be the usual problem. One of our allies in southern Iraq, Denmark, saw the same need, adapted some of its helicopters and deployed them within three months. For a variety of reasons, which I could never fully accept, we couldn't even do this. And while we demonstrably failed to exploit the opportunity before us, the governance of Basra increasingly fell into the hands of Shi'a extremists and corrupt profiteers. The Iraqi-controlled 'Basra Security Committee' was weak and falling increasingly under the thumb of the militias. After the investment we had made with commitment and blood over five years, matters were now moving out of our control again. The risk of Basra imploding had always existed, but the likelihood of it doing so increased as our very limited resources began to be switched away from Iraq to Helmand.

In addition to these problems, we also missed a major

trick in another area: namely, to trust the newly emergent Iraqi forces, and to put cooperation with them above the imperatives of force protection. Early in the campaign, in 2004, it had been agreed by the chiefs of staff, as a matter of policy, that our training of the Iraqi Army was to be done in barracks, and that we would not deploy on operations with them. It was held that there were real issues of security for our people if they were to be sent out in small groups with Iraqi units. This policy was in sharp contrast to the American practice in Iraq, and to our own approach to training and mentoring in Afghanistan from 2006. It may well have been the right decision early in the campaign in Iraq, but by late 2007 it was badly out of kilter with what was required. Unfortunately, it never seemed to cross the mind of anybody senior in the chain of command, including myself, to change our approach. To know what was going on we needed to be very close to the Iraqi units we were training, but we missed this opportunity. The problem was exacerbated by an Iraqi decision to replace the locally raised 10th Division, with whom we had been working for several years, with the newly formed and only semi-trained 14th Division. If ever there was a time to embrace the mentoring, monitoring and training role it was then. I blame myself as much as anyone for not realizing that the situation had changed and that we should have been embedding our training teams with the Iraqis. We all failed on this issue. We had missed the moment and were to be horribly embarrassed by this failure a few months later in Operation 'Charge of the Knights', as will become apparent. Perhaps we should have all understood our cultural differences better, and could have done so, had we spent more time

together. On one visit to Iraq, I was due to have lunch
with 10th Iraqi Division, but, because I was short of
time, suggested we had a 'stand-up' lunch, so I could talk
to more people. In the event, we did indeed have a 'stand-
ing-up' lunch, but it wasn't quite what I'd had in mind: a
beautifully laid table, wonderful food – just no chairs!

Seeing that Basra was increasingly falling under the
influence of the Iranian-backed Shi'a militias, we knew
that this issue was going to have to be confronted at some
stage. But we had gone through the process of handing
control to the Iraqis, so it was their problem – essentially
a political one – to solve, albeit with the coalition in
support. Outside Basra we were training up the new 14th
Division. Our judgement was that they would be ready
for operations against the militias in about June. The very
ebullient Iraqi commander in Basra, General Mohan al-
Furayji, agreed, and was working to the same plan. He
envisaged a phased operation during which the Iraqi
security forces gradually but decisively asserted control
over Basra and squeezed out the militias and other lawless elements. The British commander in southern Iraq
by this time was Major General Barney White-Spunner,
a hugely competent and talented Household Cavalry
officer. What happened next surprised Barney, David
Petraeus and the entire coalition hierarchy, as well as,
probably, General Mohan. In late March 2008 Mohan
briefed Prime Minister Maliki on the situation in Basra
and the developing plans to deal with the situation later
in the summer. But Maliki, with more than half an eye
on the forthcoming elections, decided instead that the
operation to clear Basra should be mounted immediately,
regardless of our advice that most of 14th Division was

not yet ready for combat operations. David Petraeus tried to stall the Prime Minister, but the latter's mind was made up. Maliki and most of his Government accordingly decamped from Baghdad to Basra to direct Operation 'Charge of the Knights'.

Against his better judgement, but in accordance with his orders, General Mohan began the first moves on 23 March. Unfortunately, the result was as he and Petraeus had predicted. The newly formed units of the 14th Division proved no match for the well-armed and confident militias. Many police and soldiers either switched sides or just melted away. Reinforcement was required urgently. The Iraqis moved the headquarters of their 11th Division, together with two well-trained brigades, into Basra. Fortunately, both brigades came accompanied by their embedded United States training teams and mentors, known in the trade as MiTTs. The entry of the MiTTs gave General Mohan immediate access to unparalleled American surveillance capability and firepower. The US MiTTs had a rapid effect on the battle, coordinating precision strikes by fast jets, attack helicopters and artillery, the evacuation of casualties and the movement of supplies, especially ammunition. Barney White-Spunner's headquarters immediately sought and received permission from London to do the same, reversing the long-standing but now seriously outdated policy of not embedding our training teams with Iraqi units.

From a standing start, British teams were formed to embed with the three brigades of 14th Division. This included the deployment of joint terminal attack controllers or JTACs, who carried out the same functions as the US MiTTs. All these efforts succeeded in turning around what had initially been a very unpromising operation, and by early April the situation in Basra had been stabilized. Fourteen phases of Operation 'Charge of the Knights' during May cleared the city and province of the Iranian-backed Jaysh Al-Mahdi (JAM) militias, loyal to the volatile Muqtada Al Sadr. Al Sadr was the son of a leading Shi'a ayatollah who had been murdered several years before by Saddam Hussein's regime, but the son had little of the leadership talent of his father. Confronted by well-trained and equipped Iraqi troops, supported by coalition firepower and logistics, the JAM militias melted away, Al Sadr himself opting to spend much time in Iran.

Senior officers turning up in the middle of battles are never welcome by those doing the business on the ground, so I waited until the middle of April to see how Barney and his people were getting on. It did not surprise me in the least to see that they had reacted in exemplary fashion to the demands of the new situation posed by Nouri al Maliki's decision to advance the date of the clearance operation. I had been extremely nervous about the situation in Basra, given the extreme paucity of our military capability on the ground relative to the growing threat of Iranian-inspired insurgency, so I went straight into the centre of Basra to see for myself, and to meet up with General Mohan and the new Iraqi general who was about to replace him, Mohammed Aziz. It had been agreed that I would meet the commanding officer of 1 Scots – the Royal Scots Borderers, 1st Battalion the Royal Regiment of Scotland – whose battlegroup was providing the British JTACs to the 14th Division. We had arranged to meet at a particular road junction before the

Iraqi generals arrived, but we had to change our rendez-vous as the chosen crossroads was under mortar fire when we arrived. Mohan and Aziz arrived a little while later at the new location. They were an interesting contrast in styles. The confident Mohan turned up in a highly pressed combat suit with no body armour, surrounded by an enormous entourage of close protection soldiers, while Aziz, who was about to replace him, looked and talked like the professional soldier he was, an experienced fighter and veteran of battles in Ramadi and elsewhere.

Sensing whose trust I had to win, and with an eye to the future of our cooperation with the Iraqis in Basra, I took off my helmet and waved away my escort as I sat down in a rubbish dump to talk to Aziz. Flies swarmed everywhere and the place stank appallingly. He was quite clear what he needed to secure Basra for the future: an intensive period of training for his troops to prevent the militias coming back, and an effective headquarters from which to run things himself. I said that I would see what I could do to help him achieve both objectives. He stressed that he needed a modern headquarters with computer screens so that he knew what was going on. I noted the request for computer screens; but of course the real challenge was to deliver an experienced short-term training team to teach the Iraqis the finer aspects of modern command and control. This we did: within weeks we provided a strong team from my old head-quarters, the Allied Rapid Reaction Corps, now commanded by Richard Shirreff.

If I was encouraged by some aspects of this visit, I came away with a heavy heart over others. The battle for

Basra had been turned by the advent of huge US capability, but it had to be remembered by those who were quick to criticize that we were in a coalition led by the Americans: if they chose to switch their main effort to Basra from elsewhere for a period to meet a newly developing situation, then that was what happened. This was not a national virility competition, and in any case we were running on something of a shoestring in resource terms, midway through our redeployment to Afghanistan, and could never have supported the Iraqi offensive in the way that the Americans did. Perhaps we should have, but as was clear to all involved in the operations at the time it was simply not possible to stretch resources planned for a single campaign over two very demanding operations, in different countries, at the same time.

The elastic could only stretch so far, and the message we had been assiduous in presenting to our political masters at the time was that if it was pulled any more, it would break. I made this abundantly clear in the Chiefs of Staff Committee and in my periodic meetings with whoever was Secretary of State for Defence at the time. Despite the pressure, our contribution had been significant. As part of the coalition we had guarded the southern flank of Iraq since 2003 and now, in a wider strategic move, had agreed to reinforce Afghanistan so that the United States could focus on its parts of Iraq, where the main problems had been hitherto. Throughout we were doing our best, as the junior partner in the coalition, to dance to the tune of the organ-grinder, who had himself changed the tune after it had started. After all, the original military plan, espoused by George Casey and followed by us in handing over to the Iraqis early, might well have been the overture to the whole performance of eventual US withdrawal. It turned out not to be so. Anglo-American relations are fundamental to the security of our country, but we need to remember that we haven't called the shots in military affairs between our two countries since July 1944, and since Normandy we have been the junior partner in our joint military endeavours. This is not a problem, but it is something that armchair critics need to remember before they criticize our role in the 'Charge of the Knights'.

This operation proved to be the beginning of the end for the United Kingdom's involvement in Iraq. With its success Basra was very much in the hands of the Iraqis, and rightly so. International effort was now needed as never before to get some significant external investment not just into the infrastructure of the city, but also into the port and the airport, to equip them as conduits for trade and the future wealth of Iraq. Factional politics between Shi'a, Sunni and Kurd made tasks like passing a Hydro-Carbons Bill through the new Iraq parliament – to agree the split of oil wealth – major obstacles to progress; but they were Iraqi obstacles in the way of Iraqi solutions to Iraq's future. Chilcot and the passage of time can offer judgements on whether we should have changed the course of their history, but the future of Iraq is firmly in their hands now. A flourishing economy and a stable polity are the objectives, and the opportunity to achieve them is theirs.

I made three more visits to Iraq before we finally pulled our remaining troops out, on the basis of a difficult job well done. After a visit in June 2008 I rang

Michael Crocker, the head of Shell for the Middle East, to tell him that I felt we had got southern Iraq to as stable a condition as could be attained, and that now was the time to invest. Flying into Basra airfield over the years, every time at night, and seeing the amount of gas being burned off from inefficient oilfields, told me that here was a huge economic opportunity for Iraq to grasp, to the betterment of their people. If Kuwait, just a hundred kilometres away, could be such a success, then why could not Basra become so, too? This was the question I posed to Michael Crocker – and anyone else who would listen, for that matter. Of course, this dimension was picked up by our Government and given some momentum, so in recounting my personal involvement I claim no credit; I use it merely to illustrate that we, as soldiers, know only too well that the solutions to these complex interventions are military in part, but in the main are political, economic and social.

My final visits to Basra, in late 2008 and early 2009, were bizarre in many ways. On one of them I took James Harding, the editor of *The Times*, because I was concerned at the time that the stance of that important newspaper was more critical than a fully informed opinion could justify. He came, he saw, he listened and the tone of that influential newspaper changed.

I was always pleased to meet and talk to as many of our soldiers in Iraq as possible and to tell them, with entire sincerity, what a tremendous job they were doing. Having come and gone for over five years, I had built up a wider and longer perspective on the subject than most of the men and women I spoke to, many of whom were on their first tour of duty in a combat environment.

What happened years or even months before was ancient history to some of them, and I was conscious of trying not to sound too much like a latter-day dinosaur. The advantage of age, of course, was that I could see the issues they were facing on the ground in a slightly broader perspective. However, I remembered what it was like to be a young soldier. When I was commissioned I was keen to get to Belfast before it was all over. I was not to know that the 'Troubles' would rumble on for thirty-eight years – nearly my entire military career. On the other hand, the Falklands conflict, although a deadly affair which cost 255 British lives, was time-limited. It was solved by a resolute Government acting determinedly in the political arena, together with professional, motivated and well-trained armed forces, and it was over in a matter of months. Campaigns like Iraq and Afghanistan, however, take time and are solved not in weeks but over years. They place a premium on continuity of direction at the higher levels of Government and demand a proper understanding of the need for strategic patience and dedicated investment. Northern Ireland has taught us this, at least. So it felt truly bizarre to be back in Basra Palace in March 2009, remembering how two summers before our soldiers had been ducking and weaving around the base to avoid incoming mortar shrapnel while preparing to go outside the gates to fight bitter battles in the city. Being able quietly to chat to locals along the banks of the Shatt al-Arab waterway was an experience in odd contrast to the intensity of the battles of Operation 'Charge of the Knights' only a year before. The Memorial Wall in front of the British headquarters with its 179 names stood as a stark reminder of the human cost of our endeavour.

I commented in a speech following my last visit to Basra that

> we will not be universally praised for what we have achieved and some will be overtly critical, but we have done what we set out to do and we leave Basra in good shape, secure and confident about the future. But it is also essential that we learn lessons from this campaign and transfer them effectively to Afghanistan to ensure success there.

When I said in October 2006 that we should get out of Iraq 'sometime soon' it was so that we could focus on the more important campaign in Afghanistan. That had been British Government policy from the moment Tony Blair announced it at the NATO summit in June 2004. When he said it, we recognized that we could support Iraq or Afghanistan in a sustained way, but not both. Our commitment in Iraq would need to end before that to Afghanistan was ramped up, which was the simple reality of the force levels and structure handed us by the Strategic Defence Review in 1998. In the event, through the dedication and commitment of our people, we did enough in Iraq against the odds. But taking a gamble over Iraq will only have paid off if we do indeed succeed in Afghanistan.

At the time I was writing this memoir in 2010, our operations in Afghanistan remained very much within the 'work in progress' category. The early battles by Stuart Tootal's 3 Para battlegroup in 2006 had been followed by increasingly large deployments by a sequence of ever bigger brigade groups. In 2007–8, as the British Task Force endeavoured to expand its influence within Helmand Province in support of the Afghan authorities, so the Taliban intensified its opposition. Helmand Province is the vital ground in southern Afghanistan. Control Helmand and you control Kandahar, itself the southern end of the traditional avenue of influence to controlling Kabul. Helmand was, and is, key. Whether we fully appreciated that in 2004 I do not know, but we know it now. However, General David McKiernan, the US general in command of the NATO deployment to Afghanistan in 2008, described the situation in the south of the country as a stalemate. It seemed that we could win every tactical battle, but without making progress towards the strategic goal of placing the elected government of Hamid Karzai firmly and fairly in control, and with the people's support. Killing Taliban fighters was not the solution, but winning the hearts and minds of the people of Helmand and Kandahar was. Within a campaign design of 'clear, hold and build', we could not succeed if we could not properly handle all three parts of the equation – but this is where it becomes expensive; and we don't do expensive, particularly in the midst of a recession.

On the ground, as 2007 gave way to 2008, the nature of the military fight changed. Initially the Taliban had taken us on with small arms, machine guns and rocket grenades, but as they tired of being killed in large numbers they resorted to the classic insurgent tactic of avoiding direct combat and attacking us instead with IEDs, in exactly the same way that the Iraqi militias and the Provisional IRA had done before them. This was vividly demonstrated in 2009 when, having concentrated our forces for Operation 'Panther's Claw' in central Helmand, we had stripped out our troops in northern Helmand in order to provide reinforcements further south. 'Panther's Claw' was a significant success, bringing eighty thousand people into the Government-controlled area in time for the presidential elections; but in order to provide the necessary mass of troops for that operation, previously secured areas had to be weakened. The result of this economy of force move was that in the Wishtan area of Sangin, for example, where there had been two hundred NATO troops the summer before, there were only thirty in early summer 2009, the rest having redeployed south for 'Panther's Claw'. The Taliban saw this as an opportunity and reoccupied the Wishtan district, lacing it with IEDs to the fatal cost of the 2 Rifles battlegroup deployed there.

Within an operational design of clear, hold and build, the 'hold' phase is in many ways the most important. If the areas cleared of the enemy cannot then be held in sufficient strength, there is no prospect of a better life being built for the people for whom the campaign is being fought. Of course, huge efforts have to be made by bringing in international and local civilian officials and experts to begin the vital consolidating process of offering the people a brighter future. Infrastructure – schools, roads and wells – is important; but even more so is the opportunity to conduct economic activity that is legal. In southern Afghanistan, the growing of the opium poppy must be replaced by traditional crops such as wheat, saffron and pomegranate. Without an economy based on legal activity there is little or no prospect of building a society where corruption is not the norm and the police are not bent on extorting illicit fines and payments from the local population rather than protecting them.

This comprehensive approach to operations is expensive in terms of both resources and military manpower. It is not possible to build a better life for the people, and thereby win their 'hearts and minds', without providing security. That is a military matter, and requires sufficient boots on the ground to be successful. It is a false economy to reduce force numbers during this phase of a campaign in an attempt to save money, because the inevitable consequence will be increased cost of blood and treasure later on. This has been the bitter experience of virtually all British counter-insurgencies, but I remain staggered by the vast numbers of policy-makers who forget this in their urge to cut costs. My view is that the short-term cost of a counter-insurgency deployment needs always to be considered as part of a long-term investment (like that in Northern Ireland); and this, as Northern Ireland demonstrates, requires real political courage and leadership.

As planned, once we had got our Army numbers in Iraq down to the minimum level adequate to achieving our residual tasks, it became possible for the Army to deploy more troops to Afghanistan. On the basis that we only do what the Government of the day wants us to do, it was quite clear to the Chiefs of Staff Committee in 2008 and 2009 that there could be significant troop uplift in Afghanistan in 2009, if for no other reason than to fulfil Tony Blair's intent as set out in 2004.

Communicating this to the new Prime Minister, Gordon Brown, turned out to be something of a challenge. To his credit, having exhibited very little interest in defence during his years as Chancellor of the Exchequer, Gordon Brown invited all of the chiefs to a working dinner in No. 11 Downing Street in early 2007, while he was still at the Treasury. We put our heads together before going and agreed that not only would we welcome the invitation, we would act as if we hoped to be invited again. We agreed not to talk about money. Come the evening, we had a most interesting round-table discussion about foreign and security issues which, of course, included Iraq and Afghanistan. As an aside, I had my only one-to-one meeting with Tony Blair in his office in No. 10 Downing Street five weeks before he handed over to Gordon Brown – a meeting that was never going to move anything from an Army point of view. But with Gordon Brown in the chair, things started brightly. Almost against the odds, I felt an apparent desire on his part to want to understand what our concerns were. During the first nine months of the Brown premiership, the Chiefs had three working breakfasts in No. 10, along with the Secretary of State for Defence, Des Browne, and the Permanent Under Secretary, Bill Jeffrey. A rapport seemed to be achieved. More personally, the Prime Minister and I corresponded about a book he was writing on wartime courage; indeed, he included additional material at my suggestion, acknowledging my contribution in his foreword. But, ominously, we did not seem to make much progress on the subject of Afghanistan, and then he became distracted by the financial recession. The breakfasts at No. 10 stopped.

Perhaps, inadvertently, I changed my own dynamic with Gordon Brown. A year into the life of Help for Heroes I agreed to give Tom Newton Dunn of the *Sun* an exclusive interview, by way of rewarding that newspaper for the remarkable support it had given to our service people over the last year, and to Help for Heroes in particular. I told Tom when he came to my office in the Ministry of Defence that I was more than happy to discuss anything but that I had no issues on which I wanted to unburden myself, and that this would be a very boring background interview. I wished to make no headlines. We talked for about an hour until he got around to the issue of soldiers' pay. Tom was keen to push the case for more pay for our troops. How much is enough is a great question, and in 2006 we had argued successfully for an operational allowance, giving all ranks an extra payment of £2,240 tax-free for a six-month operational deployment. More generally, the Armed Forces Pay Review Body has always faithfully researched and represented the case for a fair comparative deal for soldiers, and in recent years its recommendations have been accepted in full by the Government. Comparability across different sectors of employment is one of the issues considered by the review body, which is probably why Tom brought the issue into our conversation. In answering the question whether our soldiers were paid enough, I responded by suggesting that Tom should do his own research comparing the pay of soldiers, policemen, firemen and traffic wardens, and draw his own conclusions.

He did. Traffic wardens are paid more than private soldiers. Traffic wardens do not fight in Basra or Helmand. Returning from a visit to Iraq a few days after the interview with Tom, I was met at Heathrow by a rather worried Captain Toby Glover, my ADC, with a copy of that morning's *Sun*. 'Traffic wardens are paid more than soldiers' was the story. It was correct, but unhelpful. I like to fight my battles on ground of my choosing, not on that chosen by other people. In a narrow sense I had given Tom the story, and I took responsibility for that; but I was annoyed with the way Tom had made political capital out of it, in such a way that it looked as though I was making the political point. I was not, but I could see that appearances were otherwise. I was critical of myself, and told Des Browne so, as he and I shared a car on our way to Rupert Murdoch's summer drinks party. 'Why not write to the PM to put the record straight?' suggested Des. Later that evening I did so, and a few days later I received a cordial handwritten reply from Gordon Brown in which he agreed that the media always misrepresents us all at some stage. To return to my earlier formula with regard to the media, according to which a score of 6 out of 10 or above represents success, in this episode I gave myself a score of no more than 4. I remain grateful to the *Sun* for its unwavering support of our troops; but at a personal level I was deeply disappointed with that particular episode, though I take responsibility for it.

As we approached the summer parliamentary recess of 2008, we all expected the Government to decide the succession at the top end of defence before the break. So it was no great surprise when Des Browne, still Secretary of State for Defence, made appointments to see Jonathon Band, Glenn Torpy and myself, respectively the current heads of the Royal Navy, the Royal Air Force and the

Army, to discuss the future. In the event, the conversations with each of us were quite short. As all three of us would retire the following year – an almost unprecedented situation – Air Chief Marshal Sir Jock Stirrup would carry on as Chief of the Defence Staff until some time after the next general election. Tim Granville-Chapman, Vice Chief of the Defence Staff, was also due to retire, and no sooner had I left Des Browne's office than Jock Stirrup asked me which general I wanted to nominate to replace Tim as Vice Chief, as he was keen to avoid the Chief and the Vice Chief coming from the same service. I told him that my preferred candidate was Nick Houghton, who at that time was the Chief of Joint Operations and uniquely qualified for the post. It was clear from my brief conversation with the Secretary of State that the Government did not believe that I had any future in the Army (the only job I could be promoted into was, after all, Chief of the Defence Staff), and retirement, whether I liked it or not, beckoned. The 'Very Honest General' had ruffled too many feathers to be allowed to stay.

11

What About Tomorrow?

There is always a temptation for those responsible for strategy to meddle in the day-to-day detail of operations, involving themselves in business that should be of no immediate concern to them. This is probably inevitable, given that even the most senior general starts his professional life at the sharp end with rifle, grenade and bayonet, and it is probably impossible ever to remove from the military brain the abiding fascination with the tactical details of operations, no matter what rank is eventually attained. But right from the beginning of my tenure as Chief of the General Staff I was determined that I would resist this temptation, relying on the chain of command to exercise its responsibilities unimpeded by an interfering busybody from Whitehall. I saw my job as concerned primarily, although not exclusively, with ensuring that the Army was prepared in the best possible way for the challenges that the future was to present. So I decided I would promote a widespread debate from the top down, and right across the Army, about the utility of military force, and what the British Army had to do to ensure that it was fully prepared not just for all current challenges but for those of the future. It was clear to me that, with an Army so heavily committed to current operations, it was inevitable that our day-to-day tactical actions (especially in Iraq and Afghanistan) would have a significant effect on shaping our strategic development. Indeed, I often said that were we to fail today, tomorrow would be a very much more uncertain place. However, I was also certain that when looking towards the future it also made sense to look back at the past, in order fully to understand the trajectory of development that would take us from that past through the exigencies of the moment and into the future.

When I became CGS in 2006, so much had happened in global affairs, defence and security since 9/11 that some were arguing that we were in the midst of a Revolution in Military Affairs, a once-in-a-lifetime event (like the invention of rapid-fire, rifled artillery, for example) that changes the face of warfare for ever. I was not convinced. It seemed to me that what we were going through was less a revolution than a rapid evolution. In 2006 I was certain that this process of change was in full swing and now, as I write in 2010, it is obvious that it continues unabated, and shows little sign of stopping: the Defence Review scheduled for later this year, and those that follow, must capture the essence of this change and incorporate it in forward policy. But interestingly, the direction of travel has not been that which we first predicted at the time of the fall of the Berlin Wall in 1989, nor that mapped out during the New Labour Strategic

Defence Review a decade further on, nor even that envisaged in the aftermath of 9/11. I am certain that so far as defence and security are concerned, the challenge facing this generation is as great as any that have faced its predecessors in the last century. Unless we analyse today's problems from first principles, in order to understand the character and nature of future conflict, we will end up preparing for – and, even worse, fighting – the wrong war.

Whether we like it or not (and many seem to have their heads in the sand on this issue), the world's democracies are deeply committed to a battle of ideas, fought in both words and blood, against an intransigent ideological totalitarianism ironically made even more dangerous than Soviet communism by virtue of its lack of state systems and structures. Islamist terrorism grows within states and moves between them, regardless of boundaries, because it appeals to those who are easily, but wrongly, persuaded that their world and values are threatened by the West. Its operating environment has been the airliner, the airport, the bus and the underground train of the developed world; its home bases have been in the lawless environment of the failed states of the less developed world. Consequently, the battleground will continue to be unpredictable and the task of our land forces, in particular, will be both complex and multi-faceted. We need to be prepared for a very wide range of tasks, from high-intensity war-fighting operations to low-level combat, both conventional and irregular, within a complex environment, and to conduct them all simultaneously. And at the same time we must maintain the support of our own population, in whose name we operate. We must also, as an Army, maintain our own values and reputation: the ends do not justify the means.

The only way we can prepare for the challenges of the future is to be flexible and agile, and willing to adapt, while remaining robust in the defence of the standards that set us apart from others. Under one of my predecessors as CGS, General Sir Roger Wheeler, the Army set out for itself six core values: selfless commitment, courage, discipline, integrity, loyalty and respect for others. I felt that although all six were highly important, perhaps the most important was the last one, respect for others. If we imbue ourselves with an understanding that we treat everyone as individuals who have a right to be respected, then we are attacking the culture that sees bullying as no problem, sexual harassment as fun and the abuse of civilians in whose country we might operate as acceptable. I stressed the importance of respect for others most vigorously during my years as CGS – after all, no one who is bold enough to volunteer to join the Army should be bullied in training, and when we deploy to a far-away country to help people build a better life, what can be worse than abusing their human rights through inappropriate behaviour? As I often said, if we do that, we fall from the moral high ground to the valley in an instant; and in an age of the ever-present media, we do so in a very public way.

During my time as Assistant Chief of the General Staff in 2001–2, the then Chief, Sir Michael Walker, and his immediate predecessors had been assisted in their strategic development responsibilities by a second major general, the Director General of Doctrine and Development. After a long-running cost-cutting battle with the Central Staff, this post had been cut and the incumbent's residual staff rolled into a tri-service 'Concepts and Development' staff, headed by a particularly free-thinking sailor, Rear Admiral Chris Parry. By the time I took over as CGS our capacity as an Army to evaluate the present and prepare for the future had been much diminished. The primary task of helping me focus on tomorrow fell to my Assistant Chief, a position occupied in turn by Major Generals Bill Rollo, Simon Mayall and James Bucknall. My best opportunities to get debate going about the future of the Army and defence more generally lay in making major public speeches from time to time. I also set up a series of senior Army leadership away days, known as 'Salad Days', when all the serving generals and lieutenant generals had the chance to come together to thrash out issues relating to the future size, structure, doctrine and modus operandi of the Army. We badly missed the dedicated post of the Director General of Doctrine and Development, and I was delighted when my successor, David Richards, saw the chance later to recreate an equivalent of this role.

On Monday, 30 April 2007, and in the spirit of keeping forward thinking going, I had the opportunity to rehearse some of my developing views in front of an audience at All Souls College, Oxford. During the lecture I reflected on the nature of campaigning in the context of the post-Cold War world, and concluded that we still had much to learn about how best to use the armed forces to secure the country's national interests in an era lacking the strategic certainties provided by the confrontation in Europe between NATO and the Warsaw Pact. What were our armed forces for, now that the threat of a violent confrontation with the Soviet Union and her allies on the central German plain had happily receded into history?

The 1997–8 Strategic Defence Review had formulated part of the response to this question, but I had grown increasingly nervous that the SDR was already a decade old, and in need of serious revision. Underlying this unease was the feeling that we, in defence, needed to be far fleeter of foot, particularly with regard to equipment procurement, in grappling with today's problems, rather than focusing unduly on tomorrow's *potential* problems or – even worse – on yesterday's. During the lecture I wondered aloud whether in fact we should have seen 9/11 coming, and done more, if not to prevent it, then at least to prepare for it. It seemed to me with the benefit of hindsight that we had been guilty of sleepwalking: the heavily centralized bureaucracy of the MOD had created an Army to deal with what we had *hoped* would be the strategic realities of the post-Cold War world, rather than to deal with what was *likely* to emerge. We wanted to believe that this was, to steal Francis Fukuyama's phrase, the end of history.

The West had triumphed in the global battle over Communism, and the 'bright sunlit uplands' of universal tranquillity – this time to steal Churchill's famous wartime expression – beckoned. The swords could be beaten into ploughshares, peace dividends were there to be taken and the likelihood of war – hot or cold, declared or undeclared – had receded. I well remembered the sense of euphoria that had swept the country and its decision-makers at the time. Former Warsaw Pact countries joined in the apparently unstoppable move to global demo-cratization; Nelson Mandela saw off apartheid in South Africa; by the end of the millennium, well over half the world's governments were democratic and, in theory at least, pacific by definition. This apparently declining prospect of major inter-state war, coupled with the growing economic interdependence of nation-states and the ubiquity of the international media, led to moral consciences being more readily pricked, which itself led to a marked increase in smaller military interventions. But, looking back, I was certain that there had been plenty of indicators to suggest that the world would not be as benign as we had persuaded ourselves to expect if only we had been alert enough to see, then, a crescent-shaped shadow looming over Fukuyama's shoulder.

It was difficult at the time to judge precisely what had happened to the global polity. For some, the first Gulf War at the start of the 1990s was an aberration, a throwback to the proxy politics of the Cold War; for others it was a signpost to an emerging pattern of conflict dominated by failed and rogue states. I tend to the latter view. However, before we could really confront that issue, a year or two later we began our involvement in the Balkans, where we agonized not about war-fighting, but about how to keep a peace within someone else's war. This seemed to point to a future where chaos, rather than carefully choreographed conventional conflict framed against a backdrop of nuclear deterrence and the threat of mutually assured destruction, would be the defining characteristic. But during this decade we also grew to think, rather complacently perhaps, that liberal intervention of the type that gave effect to New Labour's 'foreign policy with an ethical dimension' was easy, and could be conducted on the rather blasé basis of 'go first, go fast, go home'.

Indeed, the post-Cold War optimism of the early 1990s (and the narrative it produced in which the West had won the Cold War and, with the defeat of Communism, history was now dead) seemed to be re-inforced militarily by the outcome of our swift interventions in Macedonia, East Timor, Kosovo and Sierra Leone, and even by our initial experience in Afghanistan, where we were in and out of Kabul within six months in 2001, under the expert guidance of Major General John McColl. 'Security', with its softer impli-cations, seemed to have replaced the harder imperative of 'Defence' as the currency of engagement for military forces. Looking back, one can also see that the SDR in 1997–8 had helped fuel this complacency. Nothing much had seemed to change. The UK's armed forces, while busy in Bosnia and Northern Ireland, had been broadly in balance: balanced in our relationships with Europe and the United States; balanced between the aspirations of the maritime, land and air environments; and at ease about Britain's role in the world under the New Labour Government, which seemed content for the country to remain one of the permanent five members of the UN Security Council and of the G8 group of top industrial nations, while heading the Commonwealth and being the leading European partner in NATO.

Set against this comfortable view of the world was a contrary narrative according to which the seeds of the violence that erupted in 2001 had in fact been quietly growing in hothouses far from public view since at least 1979, when the Cold War still had a decade to run. That year is redolent with foreboding. It was in 1979 that the then newly elected Polish Pope John Paul II began to suggest that religion and nationhood mattered more than Lenin or Stalin would have cared to admit; it was the year when Ayatollah Khomeini in Iran turned the flamethrower of Islamic anger and jihad against the West; the year when Teng Sia Ping began to bring China back into world politics; and, perhaps most critically, the year when Osama bin Laden, still at that time a Saudi playboy, discovered after the Mecca uprising and the Soviet invasion of Afghanistan that he had a vocation in promoting Holy War.

The drama of 9/11 brought all these diverging imperatives together into those ghastly fireballs. The conflict between Capitalism and Communism in the Cold War had been swept aside in a new hot war, fuelled by passion and deeply held religious sentiments that took the supposedly rational western world unawares. We should not have been surprised. The West had for years during the 1980s deliberately stoked the fires of righteous Islamic anger against the Soviet occupation of Afghanistan. It was these passions, building on long years of grievance in the Middle East among the militarily dispossessed and the historically humiliated – grievance sustained today by the ongoing Israeli–Palestinian conflict – that were now circling back, seemingly uncontrollably, to burn the hands of those who had fuelled them. It is also worth recording that an unintended consequence of the CIA's arming of the *mujahedin* was the breakdown of traditional Afghan tribal structures – another factor contributing to the vacuum of governance within that country into which others could move for their own purposes. So the threat from the politically motivated Islamists, who have manipulated one of the world's great religions for their own ends, should have come as no surprise to the West; but it did.

The Ministry of Defence's response to the shattering impact of 9/11 was to revisit the outcome of the 1997–8 Strategic Defence Review. As I have suggested in an earlier chapter, our response to 9/11 was poor and had profound long-term consequences for the Army. The problem was that we, and the United States, instinctively interpreted 9/11 as a terrorist issue and made revisions to the defence planning assumptions or DPAs (which dictate what we are and are not resourced to do) which focused on the visible symbols of the problem. These included placing a renewed emphasis on countering global terrorism through the use of Special Forces and precision attack, together with anything that had a high-technology edge as a means of finding terrorists and destroying them. All this would have been laudable as part of an overall policy, but instead it became *the* policy. It was also cheap. For the Army, the 'double medium' planning assumptions established by the SDR, which provided for the ability to deliver two medium-scale deployments simultaneously, were swept aside in a rapidly conceived and delivered 'New Chapter' to the SDR based on the assumption that henceforth the UK would only ever be called upon to provide a single medium-scale six-month war-fighting commitment, together with two small-scale or battalion-sized operations. This led to a de facto reduction in the size of the Army to five combat brigades, precisely at the time that we began to address the possibility of joining the United States in the attack on Iraq. As with many decisions that are made in haste, we were to repent this unfortunate one at leisure.

The development of these ideas came together in an unhealthy confluence in 2002 with the scandal of the 'dodgy dossier' in the lead-up to the Iraq War, political ambivalence towards the detail of defence and a clear bias within the Ministry of Defence away from the Army, if not on inter-service grounds, then certainly on cost grounds. The result, in February 2003, was an Army ill-prepared and ill-equipped for the *sustained* war-fighting task demanded of it in Iraq, a task decided on and authorized very late in the day. Our logistic procurement system was by now based on the 'just in time' principle, which assumed that we only ordered stock when it was required; rather than keeping large quantities of stores and equipment in our own storage facilities, we reduced our stock after the Cold War, and relied on industry to provide it for us when it was required. Unfortunately, we had not considered the fact that industry needs time to produce what is needed, and time is not always on our side. In the days of the Cold War the system was based on the principle of 'just in case', with warehouses and depots full of expensive equipment which might be needed. By 2003 all these warehouses, and their contents, had gone. The British Army that went into Iraq in 2003 was still largely equipped and shaped by the legacy of the Cold War, which was fine for the initial stages of the operation but left it badly unprepared for the demands of the long years of the conflict that were to follow.

The problem was that we had not considered whether 'go first, go fast, go home' actually offered us anything more than a cliché that reflected our hope that all the problems we would face in the future were ones that we could solve with a rapid intervention and an equally rapid exit. It did not, for instance, allow any consideration of the need for a follow-up plan to stabilize Iraq once Saddam Hussein and his henchmen had been removed. Nor indeed did it allow for any consideration of the true nature of the campaign we would have to construct to win over the newly conquered Iraqi people to their new Government. Aside from this failure to prepare to support the peace, the newly re-juggled defence planning assumptions simply did not provide us with the capacity to deliver a proper war-fighting capability beyond the first six months of a deployment. To believe that dealing with the *causes* of 9/11 would require merely a high-tech or a Special Forces response was, frankly, naive, and the meddling with the DPAs left us structurally unable to deliver what was required beyond the initial high-profile arrival of the troops in a trouble spot. Going down from six fully formed ground manœuvre brigades to five does not sound much of a reduction to the uninitiated, but it had a dramatic effect on the sustainability of the Army.

Then, to compound the by now systemic difficulties posed for the Army by the revised DPAs, Tony Blair pledged us at the Prague NATO summit in June 2004 to a substantially increased commitment in Afghanistan from mid-2006. By the time I was speaking at All Souls College in 2007, that commitment had steadily grown into a fully fledged medium-scale deployment, far beyond that for which we had planned. I considered at the time, given the sudden and violent response to our deployment into Helmand Province, that we would need to continue this commitment to Afghanistan for the next five years, at least. This was far beyond anything that the SDR and its DPAs had ever envisaged, and far beyond anything the Treasury was prepared to pay for or to which the policy at the time was prepared to admit. Structured, equipped, manned and funded for one enduring medium-scale/brigade-size deployment, we were now committed to two enduring operations with no realistic end-point in view. In a further complication, one of these operations was in a region perched precariously above a large proportion of the world's remaining supply of oil, and both were to be conducted in the face of extremism and jihad. And, so that we don't forget, it is worth noting that at the time we also remained extensively enmeshed in the post-communist Balkans as well as post-colonial Sierra Leone and the Falkland Islands.

What was to be our response to Tony Blair's over-commitment of his country's armed forces? It certainly was not to renege on our promises to the United States and to pull out of the coalition in Iraq; nor was it to renege on our commitment to NATO and to pull out of Afghanistan. We had to cope, somehow, despite the fact that we were now 'running hot', with no expectation that the situation would ease, or cool, in the short term at least, and with no expectation that our Government would honour the oft-stated public commitments to provide the additional resources to get the job done properly. Unfortunately, the oratory of our politicians with regard to financial support for our commitments abroad was heavily nuanced. When the public were told that money was being allocated for Iraq or Afghanistan, for example, it was more often than not a reference merely to the obligatory funding required under the Urgent Operational Requirements (UOR) agreement that existed between the MOD and the Treasury to provide cash for the *additional* costs of operations. The endemic underlying underfunding of defence going back to 1998 was never addressed.

My job, therefore, was to make our commitments to both Iraq and Afghanistan work, despite the impediments I have described. In 2007 this involved ensuring that we could achieve tactical success in Iraq and Afghanistan on a daily basis; arguing for operational coherence in both theatres in a campaign sense (that is, defining why we were there, establishing attainable objectives, and getting our commitment resourced accordingly); ensuring in a strategic sense that the pervasive extremist Islamist challenge to our wider values and interests was stemmed; and ensuring that in five or ten years' time there would still be a British Army worthy of the name, not just the memory of one that had expended itself, exhausted and empty, in the middle of the current decade. I considered this last task to be probably the most important I faced. At its heart was the health of the bond of trust that needs to exist between the Army and the people – the Military Covenant, about which I have already written – without which our success on operations would be put in doubt, and the long-term effectiveness of the Army would diminish.

I had the chance a couple of months later, within the context of the annual Future Land Warfare Conference hosted by the Royal United Services Institute over two days in June 2007, to take the argument further. How

As the incumbent Chief of the General Staff, you always have your predecessors there keeping an eye on you!

Below: Des Browne and I did not always see eye to eye, but we got on better than many people thought.

Above: Boris Johnson and I watch a flag being raised to mark the first Armed Forces Day in 2009.

To Sir Richard Dannatt,

In the hope the Army gets the resources it needs, and with best wishes,

MrBill

HOWARD McWILLIAM 2009

PLEASE GIVE GENEROUSLY

Left: My final visit to Afghanistan raised the issue, once again, of resources for our troops. It was remarked that I was coming home with quite a shopping list. The front page of *The Week* said it all.

Above: Fishing on the River Spey has always been a great joy. David Cameron put an interesting proposition to me on 30 September 2009; perhaps I should have paused for thought a little longer before I gave him an answer.

Below: On 7 October 2009 I was installed as the 159th Constable of Her Majesty's Fortress and Tower of London – a huge privilege, even if the occasion was slightly diluted by the torrential rain!

THE PARACHUTE REGIMENT FREEFALL TEAM

Above: Richenda and her Red Devil.

Below: By summer 2010 Help for Heroes had raised £60 million to help our wounded from Iraq and Afghanistan. The Norfolk Dog Day, masterminded by Fee Sharples, attracted 15,000 people in August 2009 and raised £87,000.

Top and above: Having avoided parachuting throughout my military career, there was only one answer I could give when asked if I would do a jump for Help for Heroes. I thought two and a half miles up was a long way to come down, but as next out of the door was Richenda, followed by Bertie's wife Emma, and our great friend Jo Edwards, there was no alternative.

Above: Sue Norton and her sons, Toby and Tom, whose experiences inspired the SSAFA Norton Houses for the families of the injured at Selly Oak and Headley Court. Captain Peter Norton was awarded the George Cross.

Left: With Major Phil Packer, injured in Iraq, who has inspired many to overcome their injuries and resume a purposeful life.

Below: Veterans of all ages need our support. Here I am in 2007 with Henry Allingham, then 111 years old and the oldest surviving soldier of the First World War.

Left: Pippa, who has followed the drum for thirty-two years, with her two Norfolk terriers, Bumble and Hebe.

Below: In addition to his business in London, Tom started Street Child of Sierra Leone in 2008. In its first two years, his programme has benefited over a thousand youngsters in that poorest of countries. Here his football team of street children, resplendent in out-of-date Norwich City shirts, get ready to take part in a competition organized by his younger brother Olly.

Above: Bertie followed his grandfather into the Grenadier Guards, and in 2008 I went up to the Infantry Training Centre, Catterick, to take a passing-out parade for recruits whom he had trained.

Left: On my unscheduled visit to Afghanistan in August 2007, I spent a few minutes with Bertie in Forward Operating Base Price, Gereshk. Bertie is wearing his grandfather's embroidered cap badge.

Below: Four legs, three blokes. Olly, working in Verbier, organized a fundraising ball which raised £100,000 for Help for Heroes in March 2009. Several wounded soldiers came out for the event – here Olly is on the chairlift between Trooper Stevie Shine (left) and Lance Corporal Rory Mackenzie.

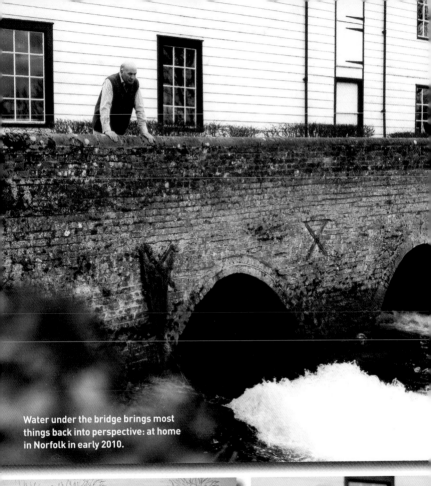

Water under the bridge brings most things back into perspective: at home in Norfolk in early 2010.

Above: From a sketch drawn by Major Tim McMullen as he waited patiently for a pheasant to be flushed out of the maize around Keswick Church.

Above: The future is in the hands of the next generation: with my eldest grandson, Arthu the dumper truck at Keswick.

could we transform the Army from one that was continentally based and facing a single threat into one that was genuinely expeditionary, and do this while simultaneously fighting two wars abroad? How could I ensure that the Army was able to cope with today's requirements while at the same time ensuring that it remained balanced for tomorrow's unknowns? The series of three annual Future Land Warfare Conferences that I co-chaired with the Directors of RUSI, first Rear Admiral Richard Cobbold in 2007, and then Professor Michael Clarke in 2008 and 2009, provide milestones by which to gauge the development of our thinking. I concluded in June 2007 that if the problem was the triple need to counter global terrorism, the Islamist agenda (not Islam, but the political manipulation of its teachings) and the vaguely expressed objective of the re-establishment of an extended caliphate, then we were certainly looking at a conflict that would last a decade or two, perhaps a whole generation. This would be a contest of ideas and values on a global scale, not just among the people of Iraq and Afghanistan, but among the people in London and Washington and elsewhere, as we struggled to maintain their security, and their support.

Did this mean that inter-state conflict was a thing of the past, an anachronism in our more sophisticated age? No. We would be foolish to rule out the possibility of inter-state conflict at some point in the near future. Geopolitics has a see-saw motion, I believe, in which the balance between pressures for inter-state fighting and those for fighting 'among the people' varies over time. The very long periods between Waterloo and the Crimean War, for instance, and between Sebastopol and the Somme, were consumed by small, asymmetric wars, when a conventional army like Britain's fought irregular troops in an unconventional way. The same story can be told of the British Army in the twentieth century: intense conflicts between the wars, and after 1945 only a single year – 1968 – in which a British soldier has not been killed on active service. No one, for example, who is knowledgeable about Iran, or North Korea, would ever consider that the possibility for inter-state warfare is dead. It just so happens that the UK's primary war-fighting experience today is that in Afghanistan, in which fighting 'among the people' predominates; but this does not rule out the prospect of a more conventional type of conflict in the future. It was important for us as an Army to understand how to shift our thinking between these paradigms; to be able to prepare for other options and alternatives while building on the base of today's reality of the bloodstained earth in Iraq and Afghanistan.

Four months later, in October 2007, all the formation and unit commanders not currently deployed on operations came together for our first 'Army Conference', which I co-chaired with my close contemporary General Sir Reddy Watt (who had succeeded me as Commander in Chief, Land Command). Our purpose was to ask ourselves how we were to make the important journey towards 'One Army', a single, unified organization made up of both Regular and Territorial Army elements, led by a single chain of command and supported by a single Army staff, capable of rising to all contemporary challenges. My theme had been developing over previous months, and had three elements. First, we had to succeed in Iraq. Second, we had to put the elements in place to be successful also in Afghanistan over the long term. Finally, we needed to ensure that we did not ignore the possibility of one day having to conduct high-intensity operations again, either as part of a discrete campaign or as one strand of a complex one. In 2007 it seemed important that we should make every effort to do that, albeit as the third priority after Iraq and Afghanistan, but nevertheless as an important hedge against anything unexpected the future might throw at us. No one in the Army now had any illusions that Afghanistan would be anything other than a long-term commitment for the UK, but I never ceased to be amazed by those, in politics and the media, who worried about a seemingly open-ended commitment to nation-building in that devastated country. Counter-insurgency, done properly, has never been quick, or easy. Nor would this campaign be; but one day it would end, and then what next?

It was at the same Army Conference, in October 2007, that I first publicly argued the case for an increase in force levels in Afghanistan so that we could extend our success in Helmand more widely across the whole southern region – a case which the Government would accept only reluctantly, and only in part, in 2009. I presented my plans to keep the British Army as balanced as possible between the demands of today's 'wars among the people' and the possibility that we might have to fight something more conventional in the future. In all this I was realistic enough to recognize that our ability to deliver these imperatives was determined to a large extent by how much money was available to us, and just how much of our effort and energy was going to be consumed by Afghanistan in the years ahead. Any hope of rebuilding a fresh capability for use elsewhere would always be constrained by when the Afghanistan commitment could finally be reduced or ended. However, I was also clear that the issue for defence was as much about priorities as it was about the amount of cash available. The view I articulated in October 2007 – and hold even more firmly today – is that we must resource what defence really, really needs, and not dissipate our budget on things that we would simply like, or that suit other agendas.

Prior to the RUSI Future Land Warfare Conference of 2008, I held the first of the 'Salad Days' – the gathering of the senior Army leadership in order to hammer out our views about the future. I felt we all needed to buy into the debate and take collective ownership of the eventual decisions. The Army has often been criticized for holding a multitude of different views at any one time. By the middle of 2008, the argument that we needed to restore a measure of conventional war-fighting capability as soon as possible to be ready for the future still held considerable sway. However, the pressures of Afghanistan and our greater understanding of what eventual success there might demand lent much more weight to the school of thought that said Afghanistan was not only the present, but illustrated and defined the future, suggesting that our plans for the future should be geared to that form of conflict and warfare.

After our in-house discussions I believe there was a wide understanding – and certainly a consensus – at the top end of the Army about what we considered the likely shape of the land environment would be in ten years' time and how we need to adapt to meet these new challenges. So where did I, and my fellow generals, want to see the Army go over the next ten years? We all agreed that the starting point of this journey was firmly rooted in the present. We would not be setting our aspirations for 2018 in a far-flung technological age or in an ill-defined strategic context. In a break from traditional defence planning, I said that we would like to see planning start with *today* and work forward. This may have seemed slightly at odds with the current practice, but I felt we must be flexible enough to take account of shifting current operations and to veer and adjust our capabilities and resources accordingly. We needed to get away from 'blue skies thinking' and from programmes that took a generation to introduce: current pressures did not give us that luxury, and the experience of many such procurements demonstrated that by the time the equipment arrived the requirement had changed.

Our key conclusions were that the Army of tomorrow must retain the capability to fight major combat operations *and* stabilization operations, both simultaneously *and* sequentially, and perhaps as part of the same campaign. There were no binary choices between this course of development or that one; the future was looking increasingly complex, and future conflict could resemble elements of everything that we had known in the past. Indeed, we believed that we had reached the point where the most likely operations were among the most demanding because of their complexity. Moreover, our operations in Afghanistan and Iraq had clearly demonstrated that even with integrated technology and systems, the mass and footprint afforded by *numbers* constituted an essential element of the future Army: in other words, we could not get any smaller. Indeed, I would argue strongly that we need to be bigger, and to fully integrate our Regular and Territorial manpower in focusing on the most likely tasks.

Although we needed to maintain our ability to be expeditionary, defence had to move away from the idea that all campaigns would be short in duration. 'Go first, go fast, go home' had had a very short shelf-life as a policy aspiration. We needed to have an increasing capacity to endure, which implied not only greater numbers of people, but enough depth to enable us to operate in this environment for longer. In order to do this, I said, we needed a structure that was capable of the wide range of tasks in great numbers, which meant that we would not be going down the path of a two-tier, specialized Army. We might need thirty thousand troops for a major combat operation at the start of a campaign, but equally the stabilization operations which were likely to follow might require even more manpower at certain stages. Furthermore, I also observed that some stabilization operations could be greatly shortened if larger numbers were deployed in the first place. One striking lesson I had learned from the past five years of conflict was that too much economy in the initial operation was ultimately false economy, for it meant that it took far longer to reach the end-state.

It was also important that the Army retained its ability to 'manœuvre' on a large scale. The term 'manœuvre' has connotations far beyond those of physical movement on the battlefield. In British doctrine it means 'to gain a position of advantage relative to the enemy', which is not just about armour outmanœuvring other armour. History is replete with examples of military success being delivered by outmanoeuvring the other side as much by thought as by force, from Troy to the German blitzkrieg through the Low Countries in 1940 to Slim's outmanœuvring of the Japanese around Mandalay in 1945. It is of critical importance to the Army, I argued, that it retain senior deployable head-quarters capable of the command and control of manœuvre operations within a variety of environments. In my experience it was only at the level of the division – the level of command exercised by a major general – that planning and conducting of both major combat oper-ations and stabilization operations could be managed simultaneously: anything below that was simply too small and under-resourced to undertake the tasks neces-sary to outmanœuvre our enemies in thought, time and space.

The argument about retaining a coherent divisional HQ structure also extended upwards to the next level of command capability, that of the 'three star' or 'corps' level of operational command. For the UK this capabil-ity resides within NATO and in particular in the Allied Rapid Reaction Corps. The ARRC is a capstone capability for the UK. Not only does it provide a NATO-assigned, national HQ that is able to operate routinely at the operational level of command on NATO, European Union, coalition or even stand-alone UK operations, it allows us to nurture future generations of officers in the higher levels of manœuvre. As our Army diminishes in size, we run the risk of losing the ability to command at corps level. The Reichswehr in Germany kept the flame alive in the 1930s, and we need to do likewise as we focus almost exclusively at the present time on highly intensive counter-insurgency and stabilization operations in Iraq and Afghanistan. Once a capability is lost, it is extremely difficult to relearn.

To foster the retention of our knowledge of how to operate and to command at this level, in October 2008 I sponsored the first ever Army-level study period held in modern times to examine the 'War that Never Was'. This was a consideration of the planning of the 1980s under-taken by the Soviets' 3rd Shock Army and NATO's Northern Army Group, using the experience of retired officers who had operated at the higher levels of command at that time. At my direction, Major General Mungo Melvin put together an excellent week-long study which reminded the present generation of up-and-coming senior commanders, who had won their spurs in Iraq and Afghanistan, that the skills of major campaign planning and high-intensity operations might still make their return to the field of conflict. Those who chose to criticize the time and effort put into that study period had clearly not understood the point; nor had they been watching their television sets when Russia had invaded Georgia earlier that summer.

By the time of the RUSI Future Land Warfare Conference of 2009, it had become quite clear to me that our shift in conceptual thinking, driven by events on the ground, needed to be reflected in our organization and equipment planning. The process of so-called 'trans-formation in contact' needed to have some practical embodiment. The Army Board took the view that the days of our ground manœuvre brigades specializing as either 'armoured' or 'mechanized' might have to end. The concept of homogeneous, or identical, brigades would enable us to develop brigades of a sufficient size and mix of capabilities either to operate on their own in a stabilization operation or to come together as a division to fight a high-intensity operation. By not chopping and changing units between brigades we would have the advantage of being able to train as we fought. Furthermore, I argued the case at the Defence Board that we must start to equip our brigades routinely with the new capabilities that they use on current operations in Afghanistan and not just issue special new equipment in the days before they deployed. Once soldiers had seen a glimpse of the future in Afghanistan, it was unaccept-able, in my view, to take this new equipment away from them when they got home. As I would often say, we cannot 'un-invent' the future. This sort of behaviour was intensely demotivating to professional soldiers. On one occasion, when visiting a training ground in Canada in summer 2009, I asked a Royal Engineer major why he did not have a modern night-sight on his rifle. 'I had one in Afghanistan,' he said, 'but I had to hand it in when we got back.' This is unacceptable. If we are to continue to keep our people committed to an operation like Afghanistan, and gain their commitment to whatever might come next, it is axiomatic that we will have to increase our investment in our land forces to ensure that we have coherence between the Army on operations and the Army at home and in training.

In our 'Salad Day' discussions, we also came to the view that there will be a requirement for specialist capabilities among our land forces that cannot be assigned to any one major combat formation. For instance, it was clear that we must start to develop capabilities to perform what the MOD was beginning to call military assistance, security and development tasks. This was a new, emerging task for the British Army, and would involve carrying out better the softer, or less kinetic, tasks in the new environments in which we find ourselves. Experience in Iraq and Afghanistan has demonstrated the effectiveness of small units that specialize in the training and mentoring of indigenous forces, not just in military tasks but in providing an enduring cultural and educative link between us and those whom we seek to assist. Alongside combat operations, the availability of a multi-disciplined and inter-agency organization, capable of both fighting alongside local forces and delivering reconstruction and development tasks in areas where the civil agencies cannot operate, is extremely attractive. I believe we should develop a career path that would see an officer spending a tour with indigenous forces, followed perhaps by an attachment to the Department for International Development overseas, or a local authority at home or a police force in Africa or elsewhere. Perhaps this is where we start to embed our deep language and cultural training, not just for our current areas of operation, but in potential future conflict zones. This is the stuff that was second nature to our grandfathers and great-uncles; as I have argued, I believe we are in a continuum, not a new paradigm, and so these skills still remain very relevant to the modern Army, potentially operating far from its home shores.

These aspirations for the Army of the future were the logical deductions that we drew from our current experiences; but because of the highly centralized nature of defence, they were largely beyond my ability as CGS, or even that of my 'Salad Day' colleagues, to implement. Nevertheless, the exercise had done much to enable us to prepare ourselves fully for the Defence Review that was to follow the general election of 2010. As I write, no one yet knows what deductions will be drawn in the review about the character and nature of future conflict; but my years as CGS made it absolutely clear to me that Afghanistan was both a challenge and an opportunity, not just for the British Army but for NATO and the United Kingdom. In Afghanistan, we must succeed. Given the right commitment – from our Government, from the United States, from NATO and its partners in the region, most notably Pakistan – we will do so. My task was to ensure that the Army was configured – mentally as well as physically – to do so over the long term, despite the fact that our own Government seemed unwilling to conceive of this as a potentially very long-term commitment, or to fund it adequately. An important step for the British effort was the recognition that this was far from being purely a military campaign. Perhaps for the first time – after many false starts in Iraq and the Balkans – we had truly begun to understand that these must be, increasingly, joint and inter-agency campaigns.

In Afghanistan the entire campaign is led by NATO, but nevertheless many areas of Whitehall have an important part to play in its execution. To achieve the effect we require necessitates a comprehensive approach in which high-level unity is the first and most important element. If we do not achieve a strong and enduring national, political, industrial, cross-Whitehall and inter-departmental commitment to delivering success in Afghanistan, and elsewhere if the need should arise, it is unlikely we will achieve it on the ground.

What is required now – indeed, has been required, but lacking, since 2006 – is the need for Britain to conceive of its involvement in Afghanistan as what it is; namely, to accept that the country is at war. This requires of us a degree of seriousness of intent and commitment that I believe for years has been absent from our Government. The current situation requires the same sort of War Cabinet-type commitment that Margaret Thatcher established during the Falklands War. As an aside, it is interesting to observe that her War Cabinet had no representative from the Treasury. She had the leadership qualities to say, first as Prime Minister and also as First Lord of the Treasury, to the Chancellor of the day: 'This is important to the Nation: fund it properly.' Such firmness stands in stark contrast to the weak relationship that existed between Tony Blair and Gordon Brown in Downing Street during these past years. In effect, we had the absurd situation where the occupant of No. 10 said, 'We will do this or that,' while his neighbour said, 'Fine, Tony, but I am not going to pay for it.'

The campaign in Afghanistan from 2006 to 2009 was waged in large part from within budgeted MOD resources, which is unique in our history, and is an indictment of the lack of importance accorded to the campaign by the Government of the day. In my view it was only in mid-2009 that Gordon Brown fully appreciated his responsibilities towards the funding of defence, and perhaps the consequences of the earlier underfunding. Those of us close to the issues, first of Iraq and then after 2006 of Afghanistan, were never under any illusions: we were at war. If we wanted to succeed, which we must, then we had to get onto a war-like footing, which meant that we needed to change our entire approach – from the top down – to the securing of ultimate success.

A little while later, I had the chance to underline that message in public. In December 2008 I was privileged to represent Her Majesty the Queen at the Sovereign's Parade at Sandhurst – the climax of the year-long leadership development course for our young Army officers. I said to the officer cadets being commissioned that chilly day into the Field Army – all of whom would be in Afghanistan at some point in the next two years – that they were entering an Army that was at war, even if not everyone in the country, not even everyone in Whitehall, realized that sobering fact. I concluded that address, deliberately, with the words 'God bless you'; as I did so, I felt a rising emotion – quickly dispelled by the hectic nature of the next few moments of that wonderful day for the cadets and their families.

12

Tomorrow Starts Today

If my comments at the Sovereign's Parade at Sandhurst caused surprise to some of the assembled spectators, they helped nevertheless to contribute to the growing realization among many that not just the armed forces, but the nation as a whole, had a major interest in our succeeding in Afghanistan. Of course, what we were doing would benefit the Afghans and the whole South Asia region; but facing down the Islamist challenge there, at arm's length, was very much in the interests of the security of the West more generally, and our own country in particular. Notwithstanding that I was to retire in August 2009, I knew it was right to put maximum effort into moving that operation as far forward as possible. I also knew that the principal strategic threat to our success was the loss of popular support at home.

We needed to get the message out very clearly as to why we were in Afghanistan and what we were doing there; so I was more than happy to take Rebekah Wade, then the editor of the *Sun*, and Matthew Harding, a senior News International executive, on my next visit to Afghanistan. As on previous visits, I held discussions in Kabul and then flew down to Kandahar and on to Camp Bastion, Lashkar Gah and Task Force Helmand. As ever, my travelling companions were hugely impressed with what the soldiers were doing, their morale and motivation, their evident sense of purpose and understanding of why they were there. It was just before Christmas 2008, and on one evening we had a working supper with the Deputy Governor of Helmand. Rebekah knew she had to dress appropriately and appeared looking rather like a biblical character, complete with headscarf and shawl. The rations on offer were fairly biblical, too. But the key impression taken away from the evening was the determination of the Deputy Governor to get across to the people that the growing of poppy for opium production was contrary to Islam and the teaching of the Qur'an. I felt that if that was stated as the official, and religious, position, there was real hope. The News International team came away with the same view too.

Back in London, as the new year of 2009 began to unfold, the fundamental difference of opinion within Government began to become clearer. The chiefs of staff had reached the view that a force level in Afghanistan of nearly ten thousand British troops was both necessary and sustainable, especially now that the drawdown in Iraq was all but complete. I was strongly of this view. Within an operational design of clear, hold and build, the critical element was having enough boots on the ground to hold the areas we had cleared in order to begin the process of building a better life for the people.

Without the guarantee of security, people would remain too scared to trust our promises; so we needed sufficient men on the ground to ensure this. The Taliban repeatedly claimed to villagers that we wouldn't be there for ever, whereas they would, so it made sense to trust them for security, rather than us. Unfortunately, given our limited numbers on the ground, the Taliban claim was all too often true. Only by having sufficient troops available to guarantee security could we have a realistic chance of winning the hearts and minds of the people, persuading them to support their district and provincial governments, and through them the Government in Kabul. Of course, the reality in Afghanistan is that it has never been, and probably never will be, a centralized state; still, there needs to be enough government from Kabul to give guidance to the provincial and district governors, who really call the shots. But enough boots on the ground implied more British soldiers deployed, and that costs money, especially in terms of the mission-specific equipment that was needed. To try to take the sting out of the issue, but to reinforce the basic point, I invariably said in radio and television interviews that while more boots on the ground were urgently needed in Helmand, it did not matter whose feet were in those boots; they could be British, American or Afghan, but more boots on the ground there had to be. It was only that way that we could secure the population and gain their confidence and support. But in the context of a national financial meltdown, with unprecedented amounts of money going to prop up the banking and financial sector, there was never going to be any more money for defence, despite the fact that we were fighting an increasingly bloody war on behalf of, and in the clear interests of, the country.

As the national and international financial crisis really began to take hold, Gordon Brown's focus understandably became fixed on this issue, to the apparent exclusion of all else. After all, that was his area of expertise. But the cost was paid by defence, in particular the war in which we were engaged in Afghanistan. The working breakfasts with the chiefs of staff at No. 10 had stopped. By early 2009, I had not spoken personally to the Prime Minister for over six months, and was alarmed to learn from John Hutton, who had followed Des Browne as Defence Secretary, that his record of one-to-one conversations was not much better. I had to assume that Jock Stirrup was putting our case cogently to the heart of Government.

For better or worse, I saw an opportunity to put my point of view to Gordon Brown in the middle of Horse Guards Parade one bright morning in early 2009. The first formal event of any state visit by a foreign head of state is the arrival ceremony. The President of Mexico was visiting and we – the Government, including the chiefs of staff – had assembled on Horse Guards Parade to await Her Majesty as host, and then the President of Mexico as the visitor. Having arrived in good time, I noticed the Prime Minister and Foreign Secretary walking across Horse Guards Parade from Downing Street, and decided that this was a good moment for an ambush. Intercepting the Prime Minister, I excused myself for interrupting their conversation on account of Afghanistan – 'General, I would not have expected anything less' – and briskly made the case for a troop uplift there and then, stressing not only the need from an Afghanistan point of view, but that we had got away with short-changing the Americans in Iraq because of our emphasis on Afghanistan, so we really needed to get this one right. 'Ah, well, I am seeing President Obama this week, and we will talk about these things,' was the evasive answer I got. During the conversation David Miliband stood there looking puzzled. Later that week Gordon Brown and Barack Obama did indeed talk about Afghanistan. As the Foreign Office telegrams were reporting that the United States was looking for more support in Afghanistan from its European partners, including us, the President's pitch to our Prime Minister was entirely predictable. I am reliably told that when Brown and Obama did meet, an early part of the conversation was along the lines of: 'Hey, Gordon, couldn't you do a bit more in Afghanistan?' For whatever reason, Gordon Brown announced a troop uplift of five hundred soldiers that week! While the uplift was welcome, it went only part of the way to bringing the force level up to that recommended by the chiefs of staff.

In my last months as Chief of the General Staff, Operation Panchai Palang – 'Panther's Claw' – was planned and executed by Task Force Helmand, with the aim of increasing the proportion of Helmand that was under Government control before the presidential elections in midsummer. As the operation was in full swing in July 2009 I broke my own rule about non-interference to visit the troops involved and, to deliver on a longstanding promise, I took Sarah Montague of the BBC Radio 4 *Today* programme and her team with me. Again, it was one of those opportunities to try to change our strategic messaging. Of course we need to win the hearts and minds of the people in Helmand, but we also need to win, or retain, the hearts and minds of the people in this country. If Iraq was unpopular, Afghanistan was misunderstood, and it was vital to get a clear explanation out of what we were doing and why. Losing popular support at home is the one guaranteed way to lose a counter-insurgency campaign, as the Americans discovered to their cost in Vietnam. Throughout a comprehensive visit programme Sarah produced some very good and, from our point of view, helpful reports. For years I have believed in taking a chance with the media, on the basis that the better informed they are, the greater their understanding and the better the reporting. On one occasion, as Sarah recalled afterwards, as I was heading into a briefing from which she assumed she would be excluded, I said, 'Come on, Sarah, you will find this interesting.'

We had one bad day on the visit. The plan was to fly from Camp Bastion to Lashkar Gah for breakfast with Gulab Mangal, the Governor, and then on to visit 2 Rifles in Sangin. The previous day a Ukrainian contract helicopter carrying stores had been shot down as it approached the town. All six on board had been killed. We were going to the same place, at about the same time of day, but I was reassured by the thought that we would be in the very capable hands of the RAF. Standing on the flight line at Camp Bastion early in the morning waiting for our helicopter, I was less than impressed when, rather than an RAF Chinook with an Army Air Corps Apache as escort arriving to pick us up, a pair of US Army Black Hawk helicopters landed. 'These are yours, today, General!' yelled the ground crewman, and in we climbed. I looked at Sarah Montague and she looked at me. 'Aha,' she thought. 'Oh dear,' thought I. We were in for fun and games. With the previous public discussion about the quality and quantity of our equipment in Iraq and Afghanistan very much a live issue, the image of the head of the British Army being conveyed around southern Afghanistan in an American rather than a British helicopter was going to excite all sorts of people back at home, for all sorts of reasons. Not surprisingly, in a live broadcast to the *Today* programme from Sangin later that morning, Sarah asked me about our helicopters for the day. I was fairly non-committal about the issue, leaving her to offer the explanation that in a coalition operation everyone pooled their resources, so we had been given an American helicopter that day. Slightly unfairly, I replied: 'It seems you have taken the brief well.' She had answered her own question, but the damage was done.

Before I had got back to the United Kingdom after that visit, the issue of General Dannatt's helicopter was doing the rounds in the media. A few saw it for what it was, or was not, but others saw it as a wonderful chance to have a real go at me. Add to that a comment that I would have quite a 'shopping list' of equipment on my return, and Afghanistan was quite rightly back in the news, irrespective of Operation 'Panther's Claw'. The 'shopping list' was a phrase of Sarah's, but fair enough so far as what we needed to win the campaign against IEDs was concerned. It was quite clear to everyone that the biggest tactical problem we faced in Afghanistan at that point was how to defeat the Taliban's use of IEDs. These were their weapons of choice, so we needed to counter them rapidly. We had the technology to do this – not just to wrap our soldiers in bigger and better armoured vehicles and in body armour and helmets, but to observe, strike and destroy those who were laying these devices. It was expensive, however. Had we made the case sufficiently for the Government to understand the nature of the problem and to provide the money necessary to pay for it? I had weeks left before handing over to my nominated successor, General Sir David Richards, and I did not want him to have to continue the endless head-banging that had characterized my time as Army Chief. He needed the opportunity just to focus on success in Afghanistan and the forthcoming Defence Review, which would hold its own challenges, without endless acrimony left over from my tenure.

When I returned to London the atmosphere in Westminster was even more febrile than usual. The shock of the revelations about MPs' expenses were daily head-lines. I made a speech at Chatham House about the future of defence. Interviewed by Eddie Mayer of the BBC *PM* programme afterwards, I was somewhat taken aback by his final question: 'General, with all this focus on MPs' expenses, isn't it time for a coup?' What a question to be asked on live radio! I replied that my hope was that Parliament could put itself back into a position of national leadership, in the best interests of the country. But after that, and my last visit to Afghanistan, it was open house for some politicians on Dannatt. Bob Ainsworth, then the new Secretary of State for Defence, whom I admire considerably for his honest, no-nonsense approach, put a note around his ministerial colleagues advising against criticizing me in public. However, that did not stop a campaign being run to investigate my expenses. These people did not appreciate that as public servants our recoverable expenses are very heavily monitored and relate solely to the cost of entertaining various categories of guests in the public interest. We do not enjoy the same opportunities as MPs to benefit from our expenses. It is worth in particular recording the regulation that, of the total cost of an official social function, no more than one-third should be for alcohol, it being assumed that guests will only be offered three units. In over twenty years of official entertaining I have never been able, within the bounds of common courtesy, to contain the costs to within the public budget. I have no idea by how much over the years Pippa and I have subsidized the public purse. Most of my colleagues are in the same position. It was with some amusement, then, that at the Oval cricket ground on the day that we regained the Ashes from Australia, Olly, my youngest son, showed me a story on his mobile phone in that day's *News of the World*. Contrary to the somewhat offensive assumption that I had taken the public purse for a ride, it had been revealed by the MOD accountants that I was in fact a very frugal entertainer. On occasions, my receipts showed that I had served wine at £1.49 a bottle and that Pippa had done some of her shopping for official functions at Lidl and Tesco. Shortly after that I was asked by Tesco whether I would be prepared to sponsor a range of low-cost official entertaining menus. I was amused, but chose not to.

But much more to the point, after a long silence between the Prime Minister and the head of the Army, whose service was doing most of the heavy work on behalf of the country in Afghanistan, Gordon Brown wanted to talk to me. In my last month in office we had a long conversation on the telephone, Pippa and I had lunch at Chequers during which Gordon Brown and I talked in the margins, and I had a one-to-one meeting with the Prime Minister in No. 10 Downing Street, preceded by an extensive conversation with Jeremy Hayward, Gordon Brown's private secretary responsible for defence and other related issues. Whether it was wishful thinking on my part, or the performance of a consummate politician, I came away from that series of encounters with Gordon Brown thinking that perhaps, at long last, he understood what was important about Afghanistan, and that he completely recognized that it was most definitely in our national interest to prevail. As Chancellor he had failed to understand or fully fund defence, and in his early days as Prime Minister he had appeared to want to understand; but I believe it was only in his last year in office that he really began to appreciate the full extent of his responsibilities towards the armed forces, and the extent of the gap he had created between the requirements of defence and its actual resourcing: a gap in the amount of high-quality equipment needed by our people, and a gap of £35 billion over the next ten years in the defence budget itself. This was some legacy that he would pass on to his successor.

On 28 August 2009 I handed over as Chief of the General Staff to David Richards. I was very confident in my selection of successor. I had handed over to David on three previous occasions, and our thinking was broadly on the same lines. As my personal staff took Pippa and myself, together with our immediate family, on a very special boat ride, at their very generous personal expense, down the Thames from Westminster Pier to Tower Pier via the Thames Barrier, I had no qualms about passing the baton to David. But it is very difficult to feel passionately about issues of national security in the middle of a war one day, and walk away completely the next. My motivation has been and remains to act in the best interests of the defence of the realm, the safety of our citizens and the well-being of our armed forces. My personal challenge, I reflected as the Chief Yeoman Warder of the Tower of London came to meet me at Tower Pier to escort me to my new lodgings as Constable of Her Majesty's Palace, Fortress and Tower of London, was to work out how to continue to act within that motivation in retirement. I shall comment a little more on my thinking in the epilogue to this book.

Looking back on my last few months as CGS, I realized that high among the concerns I had was that, although support for our armed forces among the British public was as high as I had ever known it to be, the level of public understanding and awareness of the nature and extent of the threats we faced, now and in the future, and the role of the armed forces in tackling those threats, was probably as low as I had ever known it to be. One of the reasons for this seemed to me to be that many in our political classes had succumbed to the dangerous illusion that in our post-Cold War world issues of security and defence are no longer as important as they used to be. Looking back, I realized that the public discussions and debates on these issues which used to fill pages of newsprint every week had almost entirely disappeared. We seemed now to be cocooned in a false sense of security. The historian Niall Ferguson captured the essence of the challenge we faced in an article he wrote in *The Times* in March 2009, in which he argued that 'economic volatility, plus ethnic disintegration, plus empires in decline are about the most lethal combination in geopolitics. We now have all three. The age of upheaval starts here.' Ferguson's comparison of the West's strategic complacency now with the situation in the 1930s might appear alarmist to some, but in my view his analysis was right on the button. Ignorance and complacency, it seems to me, are far more dangerous than the threat of 'alarmism'. Instead, we needed to take the debate about security and defence far more seriously, and develop the dialogue much more widely across the country, than perhaps we had managed to do for the better part of a generation. Deciding our vital spending priorities has become all the more urgent against the background of what George Osborne has repeatedly described as the inevitable 'age of austerity'.

By 2009 it was absolutely clear to me that the starting point for this discussion had to be an assessment of the character and nature of future conflict – the threats we face as a country now and those we are likely to face in the future – for without this understanding we cannot hope to ensure that the roles and capabilities of our armed forces remain relevant to the UK's needs. If there was an underlying theme in my thinking, to which I came back time and time again in my own mind and in discussions with others, it was that of *relevance*. As CGS I was forced to conclude that much of our planned investment in defence was at the very least of questionable relevance to the challenges we faced now and will face in the future.

I entirely accepted – and accept now – Professor Sir Michael Howard's warning that 'No matter how clearly one thinks, it is impossible to anticipate precisely the character of future conflict. The key is to not be so far off the mark that it becomes impossible to adjust once that character is revealed.' Clearly, strategic shocks happen, as 9/11, the Falklands in 1982 and Kuwait in 1990 all attest. Yet it remains equally true that the character of future conflict is being revealed in conflicts across the globe right now. Even conflicts arising from unforeseen events will share many of the characteristics of those in which we are engaged today. As General Jim Mattis, Commander of US Joint Forces Command, told the US Senate Armed Services Committee in 2009: 'Simply put, much of what we see in the cities of Iraq, the mountains of Afghanistan, and the foothills of southern Lebanon, I believe we will see again in the future.'

In attempting to assess the type or quality of future conflict, we must not fall into the trap of considering war or conflict in isolation as functions of force, or simply activities in their own right. As Clausewitz reminds us in *On War*, conflict is above all a political activity and must always be placed in its political context: 'War cannot be divorced from political life,' he argues, 'and whenever this occurs in our thinking about war, the many links that connect the two elements are destroyed and we are left with something pointless and devoid of sense.' The critical assessment one has to make relates not so much to descriptions of our potential adversaries and how they may choose to fight us, but rather to the strategic drivers that will dictate the 'how and why' of the conflicts we may face in the future. This brings me back to the conclusion that had been forming in my mind and among my colleagues throughout my time as CGS: our starting point when considering the future must be to take account of where we are now – tomorrow starts today. This is the inescapable context of the conversation: the present is the area where we have the greatest clarity and the least discretion and, given the imperatives of the electoral cycle, also the dimension that will have the greatest impact on policy-makers.

For the UK this starting point, it seemed to me, was defined by a context that had at least four elements. The first is the fact that 'Blair's wars' have spawned a political generation nervous of the potential costs – political, financial and human – of military intervention abroad. Indisputably, war is a nasty business, expensive in both treasure and the blood of our servicemen and women. During the years since 9/11 hundreds of our soldiers, sailors, marines and airmen have given their lives in the service of their country, and our wounded can be counted in four figures. Many will carry the disabilities and bear the physical and mental scars for the rest of their lives. Inevitably, these being land campaigns, the Army and the Royal Marines have borne the greatest burden. Nevertheless, I see no inclination on the part of political leaders today to pass by on the other side when crises emerge. Doing the right thing will always be the right thing to do. So we should not assume that this 'age of uncertainty' will give us the discretion we might hope for to avoid the international entanglements that come our way as a country. What is clear to me, however, is that our political leaders need to do much, much more than ever before to explain the imperative, legitimacy and rationale for the use of force, in terms of a clear and compelling narrative, both to Parliament and to the public. It must fall to those at the top of the defence establishment to participate in this process, explaining the utility of force as an instrument of national power. Above all it is essential that those in defence do in fact ensure that the military instrument continues to have utility, and to do this we must constantly adapt to remain relevant.

In the second place, the country faces the most severe economic downturn for seventy years. In this context it is inconceivable that we will be able to fund everything we might wish for in order to maintain a 'balanced force' against all possible contingencies. Put bluntly, it is questionable whether we can afford a first-division Navy, Army and Air Force with the current broad range of capabilities – including the nuclear deterrent – and do all this on about £35 billion a year. It is inevitable that some rebalancing will be required if our armed forces are to remain relevant and not simply to represent – as Max Hastings recently put it – a 'balance of inadequacies'. As Niall Ferguson argued, this economic crisis may also serve as a catalyst of global instability, increasing the threats to us. So, precisely at the point where we need to invest more in our defence and security, we may actually be forced to spend less. We must, therefore, spend wisely. To paraphrase a British Government official speaking a hundred years ago, 'We are running out of money – we're going to have to start to think.'

In the third place, our current defence capabilities – and those we will field over the next decade – are largely a legacy of decisions taken twenty years ago, rather than a true reflection of what we need today. We have done much in recent years to invest in the things that we need to fight and succeed in Iraq and Afghanistan, and defence has been adapting, often very rapidly, to meet these challenges, but it is also true that few of these investments have come from the core defence budget. The balance of investment in our defence budget remains heavily skewed towards equipment and capabilities that are optimized for what General Sir Rupert Smith described in his book *The Utility of Force* as 'industrial warfare'. To me as head of the Army over the years from 2006 these capabilities looked increasingly tangential – some even irrelevant – given the challenges and threats the Army *actually* faced. The principle of a balanced force, able to meet all contingencies, is a good one; but it appeared to me to be entirely *un*balanced if the bulk of our defence resources were focused on areas that we would probably never use.

The fourth critical element in the current context for defence is that success in Afghanistan is not discretionary. If there is anything I have stressed repeatedly it is this. When he was Secretary of State for Defence, John Hutton made clear Afghanistan's link to our national security and indeed the challenge we face, arguing strongly in an address to the International Institute of Strategic Studies in November 2008 that while 'the First and Second World Wars were the defining conflicts of the last century . . . it may be that Afghanistan will be the defining conflict of this century. It does strike to the heart of our interests as a nation. And the preservation of the values that all of us today hold most dear.' Nevertheless, it is wrong to believe that success will come either quickly or easily: we should expect to be there for years to come, and to sustain a significant effort. But succeed we must: our own national security, our credibility and reputation, our strategic partnership with the United States and the future of NATO are all bound up in Afghanistan. We must ensure we do enough to succeed and not simply enough not to fail.

If this is our starting point, we need next to agree the nature of the threats that are most likely to face us in the future. Three stand out for me. The first is that the UK is unlikely to be targeted militarily by another state for the foreseeable future, either with nuclear weapons or other weapons of mass destruction, or with conventional forces. If this is the case, as I believe it is, the implications are profound for a set of armed forces still largely equipped, trained and structured for a particular view of conventional state-on-state war-fighting. It is difficult not to conclude that our focus on preparing and equipping for a particular type of conventional state threat has left us unbalanced. We appear to have walked into a situation where a contradiction exists between what we believe the threat to be, and the way in which we are equipped. In other words, we are equipped to fight a war we do not believe will happen. It is important that we do not fundamentally weaken our capabilities and expertise for dealing with a resurgent conventional existential threat, no matter how remote; but it seems to me self-evident that we also need to get the right balance between the near term, where there is much more certainty, and the long term. At present I see our balance of investment as being too heavily weighted towards the future and too lightly towards the present: this is the part of the equation that, in my view, we have miscalculated in recent years.

The second key point concerns the threat to the UK from failed or failing states in an era of global inter-dependence. Key drivers of instability such as climate change, poverty, population growth, the global economic downturn and energy competition combine to under-mine weak states, leading to regional conflict and instability. Depending on what measure you use, there are between forty and seventy potentially failing states across the world, and they threaten the very fabric that holds the international community together. Consequently, we now recognize failed and failing states as the principal threat to our national interest. To his credit, Gordon Brown got this right when he described both the challenge and our response succinctly in his Kennedy Memorial Lecture of April 2008: 'Once we feared rival nations becoming too strong; now the worst threats come from states that are too weak. Failing states . . . are a problem for us all. We must respond not by walking away . . . but by engaging as hard-headed internationalists – through diplomatic, economic and yes, when necessary, military action.'

So, if defence is to remain relevant, continuing to benchmark our forces predominantly against con-ventionally equipped hypothetical enemies is now of limited usefulness. For the foreseeable future, the prin-cipal and most common threats to Britain's national interests will arise from global instability and from non-state groups. It is precisely in this arena that the traditionally 'soft levers' of diplomatic and economic power often have limited effectiveness, as the examples of

North Korea, Zimbabwe, Iraq and Burma, to name but a few, demonstrate. On the other hand, Sierra Leone is just one striking example of where timely military intervention can have a decisive and lasting effect, for the benefit of the country, the region and the UK. Military force will often be required, and when it is, its purpose will be to prevent or pre-empt instability or to restore stability. Stabilization operations will therefore be our most likely and most demanding task. And because stability is a human condition, the object of our operations will primarily be the local population rather than purely the opposing armed forces.

Sierra Leone, for me, is an example of what I would call the post-post-colonial era. We had previously been the colonial power and developed Sierra Leone; it had then quite rightly gained its independence, but had subsequently descended into an appalling civil war. It plummeted into chaos, as fighting to control its mineral resources intensified, with many children becoming child soldiers. At the height of the mayhem, the British Army Spearhead Battalion was deployed to evacuate the British nationals; but on their arrival they were greeted as saviours and invited to stay, receiving a very warm welcome. What had been intended as a short evacuation operation became a peace support intervention, and we have helped stabilize the country through building up the population's own capacity to run things themselves. It has been a real success story. On a personal level, I keep a close eye on Sierra Leone as in 2008 Tom, my eldest son, founded Street Child of Sierra Leone, a charity that sets out to take children off the streets of this poorest of countries, reunite them with their families where possible, give them education and hope, and thereby reduce the likelihood of their becoming the child soldiers of future conflict. In a cycle of prevention, intervention, stabilization, Tom's charity work, benefiting some one thousand children, is very much in the prevention category, and thus completely on the right lines.

The third and final point relates to the proliferation of non-state groups. States no longer have a monopoly on strategically significant violence, as the Israeli Defence Forces found to their cost in Lebanon in 2006, and the example of the global franchise established by Al-Qaida has led to a sharp increase in the incidence of transnational violence perpetrated by a bewildering array of terrorist groups, state proxies and militias, and for a variety of ends. These predatory non-state actors thrive and proliferate in conditions where there is a disintegration of state authority, spreading insurgency and disorder: either commercial insurgency (such as drug trafficking or transnational organized crime), or most potently a spiritual insurgency, as some commentators have described it. It is this latter category that poses the greatest threat to our own security and way of life. The threat posed by Al-Qaida-inspired Islamist extremism operating from within failed and failing states is pervasive, global and deadly. This is probably the struggle of our generation – perhaps our 'thirty years war' – but it is not one we wish to fight on our own soil. Nor is it one that we would wish to fight with the tools of conventional interstate warfare. In this respect John Hutton was spot on when, speaking to the Institute for Public Policy Research in April 2009, he called for 'a rebalancing of investment in technology, equipment and people to meet the challenge of irregular warfare. If a country like the US, with all its vast resources and military strength has decided to prioritise, I think the UK should do the same.'

So how should we respond to these complex threats? There are of course those who would wish to walk away from today's reality and make the case for a less ambitious, lower-profile role, akin to that taken by many of our European partners, or even an isolationist stance. This view, arising in part from the political costs of the campaigns in Iraq and Afghanistan, and from the financial pressures of the global financial crisis, cannot be ignored: for some, it is a legitimate reflection of contemporary domestic political concerns. But I do not agree. This approach is flawed on at least two counts. First, it does not adequately recognize the globalization of our national security interests. Trotsky's veiled warning that 'You may not be interested in this war, but this war is interested in you' is as relevant to today's threats as it has ever been. It would represent a radical departure from our inherent British 'strategic culture'. Our history and the inescapable demographic legacy of our Empire, status, trading interests, geography, transatlantic ties and responsibilities as a P5, G8, NATO and Commonwealth member have hard-wired international activism into our political and national DNA.

A couple of years ago Tony Blair remarked in his foreword to *Building on Progress: Britain in the World 2007* – correctly, in my view – that 'Britain has always produced a strongly activist foreign policy . . . Britain is an island nation whose role in the world has, for centuries, been global. We recognise that what happens beyond our borders can have a dramatic impact on our citizens and national interests.' Moreover, a non-interventionist stance is not consistent with the policy of any major political party. Indeed, speaking to the International Institute of Strategic Studies in Opposition in July 2009, William Hague expressed the view that he sensed no appetite within this country for what he described as 'strategic shrinkage'. Any significant reduction in our defence posture would significantly diminish the influence our armed forces allow us to exert in Europe, in NATO and above all with our principal ally, the United States.

Let us also be clear about the United States. Closely linked to Britain's activist foreign policy, and pivotal to our defence and security, is the transatlantic connection. Professor Colin Gray put it typically colourfully in a presentation to the Royal United Services Institute in November 2008: 'Drunk or sober, the US is a huge net positive security provider for Britain. The US alliance/connection – in all dimensions – is by far the best deal the UK can hope for . . . The US alliance is mandatory, it is not discretionary.' Having been involved in the British–American Project and for many years a member of the Anglo-American Society – The Pilgrims – I was delighted to see that William Hague's first overseas visit as the new Foreign Secretary in 2010 was to Washington.

Britain's calculation has long been that maintaining its status as the United States' military–strategic 'partner of choice' offers a degree of influence and security that has been pivotal to our foreign and defence policy. This relationship nevertheless can only be sustained if it is founded on a certain 'military credibility threshold', as Professor Michael Clarke, Director of RUSI, put it in an article for the *RUSI Journal* in 2009. So, if we wish to preserve this relationship and status, then determining the capabilities we need to sustain this threshold of military credibility with the United States is at least as important as determining those that flow from our own nationally defined military priorities. But credibility is more than a function of capabilities. Credibility with the USA comes from a relationship in which we can be relied on to state clearly what we can and will do, and then to deliver. In this respect there is recognition that our national and military reputation and credibility, unfairly or not, has been called into question in the eyes of our most important ally as a result of our strategic conduct in Iraq. It is vital that steps are taken to restore this credibility.

Let me now turn to address the question as to the utility of force as a national instrument of power in the context of these threats. What I am most certain about in this context are in fact the limitations of force. Clausewitz's most enduring and valuable contribution was to remind us that 'war is an extension of politics by other means'. It follows therefore that conflict resolution can only ultimately be achieved by politics, not by force alone. This is all the more the case in the highly complex stabilization campaigns in which we will continue to be engaged for many years to come. Though much of the burden in these campaigns will fall on those in uniform, success will only be achieved if their efforts are fully integrated with those of other Government partners – the Foreign and Commonwealth Office and Department for International Development, for instance, together with all the other instruments of national power – within what has been described as an overall 'comprehensive approach'. I am not sure that this approach has yet to be properly embraced across Whitehall. Until we get better at integrating all our efforts, we will continue to fall short of our aims. Indeed, without much better integration, force alone may have very limited utility in today's conflicts, and may even prove counter-productive.

In the same vein, it seems to me self-evident that prevention retains a powerful relevance today. It is certainly preferable to intervention. I am not talking here about the narrow military aspects of power projection, but rather about building the capacity of indigenous governments, security forces and their regional partners to provide the conditions of security and stability conducive to good governance, essential services and the rule of law. This 'strategic partnering' can achieve exponential effects if implemented in a timely fashion. It can prevent crises and conflict from arising (in the long run saving money and lives), restore stability, and strengthen the United Kingdom's influence significantly in regions critical to our national interest. On long-term stabilization operations, such as we face in Afghanistan, partnering has the potential to transform the strategic geometry of a country in a way that force itself cannot ever hope to achieve. We must never be beguiled by the temptation to rely exclusively on the use and threat of force. When it is used, in my experience, it is more often because we have left it too late to use the soft instruments of power that could have made a significant difference to a situation if deployed early enough.

But prevention will sometimes fail; and in these circumstances military intervention will continue to have enduring utility. When global security and Britain's national interests are threatened, and where conflict prevention has failed, military intervention to restore stability will remain an essential, and sometimes the only, policy option available to the Government. We should not assume that the experience of the campaigns in Iraq and Afghanistan makes intervention less likely. I agree with what US Secretary of Defense Robert Gates said in a speech to the National Defense University in September 2008: 'We are unlikely to repeat another Iraq or Afghanistan anytime soon – that is forced regime change followed by nation building under fire. But that doesn't mean we may not face similar challenges in a variety of locales.' If we do, we must respond to them. It is my belief, from all that I have experienced in a lifetime of soldiering, that intervention and stabilization operations will be the pattern for the future, and will occur with increasing frequency. Nevertheless, prevention remains a far better option, if it can be achieved.

We need to be conscious of the reality that intervention will rarely be an end in itself. We must divest ourselves of the comfortable delusion that we can go in quickly and return just as fast. The purpose of any military intervention is likely to be the restoration of stability. As the US general Charles Krulak warned us over ten years ago, giving testimony to Congress in September 1998, 'instead of the beloved son of Desert Storm, Western Militaries are confronted with the unwanted step-child of Chechnya'. All our previous assumptions about what is decisive in these operations have been overturned. In these scenarios, the intervention itself can only be an enabling activity. As both Iraq and Afghanistan have demonstrated to our cost, and some embarrassment, it is the *stabilization* aspect of the operation that is decisive. We now know that enduring stabilization operations on land, often involving intense combat, but focused on securing the population rather than exclusively on defeating the enemy, will be the experience that the bulk of our armed forces are most likely to face for the foreseeable future. And the adoption of 'military assistance to stability and development' as a new military task recognizes this reality. If defence is to remain relevant to these types of operation and to the needs of the Government, we must ensure that we now resource this new task, prioritizing our investment in the capabilities, equipment, skills and training needed to optimize our armed forces for the demands of these operations.

We should not be surprised by this discovery. Indeed, the position in which we find ourselves as an Army is nothing new. Both times I met General Masood Aslam in his role as Commander XI Corps of the Pakistan Army, operating in the North West Frontier Province and in the Federally Administered Tribal Areas, he said to me, 'We have learned the lessons of your fathers and grandfathers – have you?' At the time, I was not sure that we had. Aslam had a point, and a very pertinent one. From the 1880s the British Army had been structured to operate as a colonial police force, involved in the so-called 'small wars' of the Empire, while simultaneously maintaining a smaller continental standing army to be able to meet major contingencies. Prior to the 1930s it was entirely clear that the resources would go to the imperial tasks first, as these were the current operations in the national interest that could not be lost. However, one of the lessons of the First World War was that the balance had swung too much in favour of the colonial force and that, as a result, a great deal of understanding of the higher levels of warfare had been lost over the generations. Later, as we withdrew from Empire, two developments took place that still have resonance today. The first is that during the Cold War the balance of capabilities between fighting high-intensity warfare and conducting low-intensity campaigns of the counter-insurgency type became skewed, concentrating on the need for defence in a possible war of national survival. Insurgencies still occurred as we withdrew from Empire; but, as the Army became smaller, so these operations (except for Northern Ireland) took a definite second place as far as national defence priorities were concerned. Our policy was to disengage and return from East of Suez. As a result even residual 'out of area' capabilities became dual-roled. Additionally, I sense that, in a desire not to be considered still attached to the colonial past, we lost the mindset and skills across Government that our fathers and grandfathers instinctively understood: as a result there developed – and still exists in some quarters – a reluctance to do anything that appeared to be colonial in nature.

Furthermore, the type of conflicts for which we need to prepare now are different in many ways from those for which we have trained in the past. In contrast to the position in which defence policy-makers found themselves during the SDR of 1997–8, when the uncertainty and lack of clarity about the new context for security forced us to adopt a capability-based approach to defence, it is clear to me that we are now witnessing some clear signals to the nature of future conflict. Iraq and Afghanistan are not aberrations; instead, they are signposts, which have forced us to adopt a more threat-led, or circumstance-led, approach to defence planning. Some of the language used in the current debate about future conflict has been radical. Rupert Smith has described it as a 'paradigm shift'. Others, as I noted earlier, have spoken of a Revolution in Military Affairs. I have some sympathy with an evolutionary spirit, if not the substance of this revolutionary approach, for, as Basil Liddell-Hart observed rather acerbically in his *Thoughts on War* of 1944, 'The only thing harder than getting a new idea into the military mind is to get an old one out.' I certainly think that we in defence have been guilty of clinging steadfastly to an old idea, the Cold War paradigm of interstate industrial war – Krulak's 'beloved son of Desert Storm' – for too long, and guilty too of assuming that the capabilities required for this type of war would be fit for all. The force we have now, with its emphasis on high-end technology and platforms optimized for defeating conventional opponents, is simply a reflection of this view.

My conclusion is that, instead of there being such a radical 'paradigm shift' in military affairs, what we see today is the inevitable reaction of our adversaries and potential adversaries – state or non-state – to the overwhelming conventional superiority of the United States and its allies. We should not assume that all our enemies will be as eccentric or compliant as Saddam Hussein.

How, then, should we set out to describe the challenges we will face? In the past, our tidy military minds have inclined us to categorize conflict and warfare into discrete, well-defined frameworks: peacekeeping, peace enforcement, counter-insurgency, irregular warfare and war-fighting, all neatly arranged in a linear fashion along a spectrum of conflict. What we face today, and will I believe face for the foreseeable future, will be much more akin to a kaleidoscope of conflict. The only thing we can be sure of, as Colin Gray tells us in *Another Bloody Century*, is that 'We can predict with confidence that there is going to be a blurring, a further blurring, of warfare categories.' The most apt term I have heard to describe this condition is 'hybrid', which the *Oxford English Dictionary* tells us means 'a thing combining two or more different elements or species'. Frank Hoffman, in an article for *Joint Forces Quarterly* in 2009, described it like this:

> Instead of separate challengers with fundamentally different approaches (conventional, irregular or terrorist) we can expect to face competitors who will employ all forms of war and tactics, perhaps simultaneously ... conflicts will increasingly be characterised by a hybrid blend of traditional and irregular tactics, decentralised planning and execution and non-state actors, using both simple and sophisticated technologies in innovative ways.

I am not yet persuaded that it will be helpful to apply the label 'hybrid conflict' to describe the nature of future conflict; we should treat attempts to categorize this evolving type of warfare with caution, for doing so may condition and constrain our response. We do not need another catchphrase for the intellectually idle. I do, however, believe that it is helpful and accurate to describe the challenges we face in terms of hybrid circumstances and hybrid adversaries.

What do I mean by these? In the first place I believe the term 'hybrid circumstances' captures the complexity of the environment in which conflict will occur, and here there are two trends worth highlighting. The first significant trend is that we are in an era of persistent conflict. This implies persistent engagement, though not necessarily perpetual warfare. This arises from the variety and range of threats and causes of instability we face, above all from the threat of Islamist extremism inspired by Al-Qaida – perhaps, as I have suggested, the struggle of our generation. This is not to say that individual conflicts might go on for ever; but what is clear is that both the frequency and duration of conflict have increased to the extent that there is unlikely to be a discernible gap between conflicts. For our armed forces this implies persistent engagement, rather than the episodic, brief operations for which we are structured: no longer can we expect to 'go first, go fast, go home'. The implications are clear – we need forces capable of sustained campaigning, rather than one-shot use; and we need to place and sustain defence on a campaign, not a peacetime, footing.

The second trend is complexity, above all the complexity of the terrain, in which I include physical, human and informational geography. Our enemies will seek out physical terrain – ground by another name – that neutralizes our surveillance and targeting capabilities. We will find that operating in coastal regions, swamps and estuaries, jungles and mountains, and above all in urban areas will become the norm. The human terrain will be highly complex as numerous population groups will coexist and compete. As the population will be the object of our operations, we will require sophisticated cultural and linguistic understanding, which was a second-nature skill to our grandfathers and great-uncles. And the complexity of the information environment can only increase, exacerbated by the likely expansion of conflict and competition into space and cyber-space. In operations where we compete for influence among the people, we must invert our current understanding and view these operations first and foremost as information campaigns supported by wider military operations, rather than the other way round.

Adding to the complexity of these hybrid circumstances will be the challenge posed by hybrid adversaries: a combination of state, non-state and proxy forces. There is nothing new about irregular forces. But globalization and the fragmentation of state authority in unstable regions have enabled these non-state groups to extend their impact beyond the single country or region to a global reach. Moreover, the diversity and proliferation of these groups is a new phenomenon: consider the array of insurgents operating in Iraq a few years ago. Increasingly we are seeing the rise of truly capable non-state forces, exploiting ready access to technology and weapons, often through state sponsorship. This is epitomized by forces such as Hezbollah, the Taliban and, in terms of global reach and lethality, Al-Qaida. Nor are these non-state groups and proxy forces the only hybrid adversaries we may face: we know that several potentially hostile states such as Iran have developed and practised extensively with asymmetric tactics and cooperation with irregular forces.

And what of the strategy these hybrid adversaries are likely to employ? It seems to me that their ends are far less likely to involve the defeat of adversaries' armed forces or territorial expansion and much more likely to concern control or influence of the local population – either for ideological or commercial reasons – at the expense of the legitimate state authorities. Thus future conflict will fundamentally involve a competition for people: for their loyalty, support and security. So I would extend Rupert Smith's pithy and much-quoted phrase: we are engaged not just in war *among* the people but fundamentally in war that is *about* the people. People are no longer just the environment; they are the object itself: it is their hearts and minds that are at stake. What is inescapable to me as a soldier for forty years is that competing for the will of the people and establishing security can only be achieved by operating among and alongside the people. This will take time, and it will be manpower-intensive. Of course, technology will enable, but it cannot replace manpower and the human dimension. So, if the object of our operations is the people, we should be pretty sceptical about concepts that suggest that war *around* the people can deliver our objectives. Such a notion misses the target, both literally and figuratively. To conclude, my view is that war *among* the people is the context, and war *about* the people is the object.

Our hybrid adversaries will have access to means across the full spectrum of capabilities. This is inevitable, given that these adversaries include both legitimate armed forces of potentially hostile states and non-state groups. But what is a new and threatening trend is the increased lethality and capability of non-state groups and the greater agility they show in exploiting emerging technology. Whether it is Hezbollah's use of anti-ship missiles, sophisticated signals intelligence, UAVs and anti-armour missiles, or the pervasive and ubiquitous threat of IEDs – sophisticated and simple – or the potential exploitation and use of chemical, biological and nuclear weapons, we must assume that this trend will continue. Non-state groups will be our most likely opponents, and their access to technology and to state sponsorship will make them increasingly capable. If we are to remain ahead of our adversaries we must ensure that we too can adapt as quickly as they.

Finally, we can expect the ways of fighting employed by hybrid adversaries to test our agility and adaptability. Hybrid tactics, irregular warfare, asymmetric approaches – call them what you will – are not new. Avoiding an opponent's strengths and exploiting his weaknesses are the acme of fighting: think back to David and Goliath, or, if you don't want to go that far back, to General Slim on the Irrawaddy. If the tactics employed by our adversaries today and in the future seem new, it is perhaps because we in the West have been slower to adapt than our enemies. In Kosovo the Serbian forces learned from the costly experience of the Iraqi Army in 1991 and neutered NATO's overwhelming air superiority by dispersion, deception and camouflage, largely avoiding destruction. And in 2006 Hezbollah, a decentralized mix of irregular forces employing a combination of regular state-like capabilities and irregular swarming insurgent tactics, were able to inflict a strategic defeat on the Israeli Defence Forces. These conflicts, and the tactics they reveal, are signposts for the future. The sophistication and complexity of tactics employed by these hybrid adversaries are striking. In Iraq and Afghanistan we are seeing true 'all-arms' manœuvre by our enemies, in complex ambushes for example. Moreover, these hybrid adversaries have also become highly adept at using and integrating all the levers of power available to them – ironically, some are much more effective at the comprehensive approach than we are. Hezbollah's strategy of integrating employment, medical care and social welfare with military action, and its sophisticated use of information operations, exploiting the media environment, is a case in point.

We should expect that future conflict will not be confined to a single theatre of operations, but may be waged at home as well as through diasporas. The 7/7 bombings in London in 2005 are a stark example. We should also expect to be confronted by multifaceted threats: terrorism, piracy, insurgency and major combat with a hostile state's armed forces, all simultaneously. We must expect that our opponents will attempt to neutralize our superior standoff surveillance and targeting capability by dispersing among the people and by operating in complex (most likely urban) terrain. And we should expect our dependence on space-based systems and cyberspace to be attacked and exploited. There is no panacea or single solution to these hybrid threats. But in confronting them we can and must do better to restore our balance.

So what are we to do? We must not delude ourselves

that our ability to be flexible and to adapt does anything to address the deeper structural imbalance that characterizes our defence capabilities. It does not. The trick surely is to identify the right balance, and that varies over time, in relation to threats that we might face. The further out one looks, the less clear the future is, and therefore the more one needs a balanced force to hedge against future uncertainty within a twenty-year time horizon. The first Secretary of State for Defence in the coalition Government of 2010, Liam Fox, observed in a speech to the UK Defence Conference the previous year that 'the main challenge here is between equipping our forces to succeed in our current conflicts and preparing for any future contingencies'. For as many decades as I can remember, defence has over-invested in the far future at the expense of relevance for the threats it faces today and in the immediate future. Across the current planning horizon, during which timeframe the country will have been engaged in two medium-scale stabilization campaigns on land, a mere 10 per cent of the MOD's equipment programme will have been invested in the land environment.

How do we address this discrepancy? My view is that we need to replace the idea of a 'balanced force' with something more akin to a 'relevant force'. The judgement that defence has to make in this context concerns the balance of investment between relevant capabilities designed to face the known challenges of today and tomorrow and the spread-bet capabilities designed as a hedge against the uncertainties of the longer term. Across the Army, Navy and Air Force we need *relevant* capabilities: support helicopters, surveillance platforms and strategic lift, to name but a few. Seeking a 'relevant' force does not mean becoming unbalanced in favour of the present. Far from it. Equipping the armed forces correctly for the conflicts of today will provide it with the capabilities needed to engage hybrid adversaries of the future.

We must also get our own house in order, and demonstrate that we can adapt quickly to new strategic realities. This is one of the greatest strengths of the British armed forces – of the Army in particular – and of which I am very proud. In recent years the Army has undergone a radical transformation. It is almost unrecognizable as the Army that formed up in Kuwait in 2003. It is better equipped, better structured, better trained, better balanced, better led in the field and with a generation of hard-won experience. Its force structures are changing all the time to meet new requirements. The British Army is working to retain its ability to conduct divisional manœuvre in major combat operations as part of NATO or a US-led coalition. At the same time, far-reaching measures are being made to optimize the Army for the most likely prevention and stabilization tasks, with sufficient capacity to operate for the long term, well after the major fighting has died down. And, of course, elements of the Royal Navy and Royal Air Force have adapted too. Iraq and Afghanistan have been entirely joint endeavours for the armed forces.

But in addition to these structural issues, I am convinced that the Army's entire culture has to change. We need to provide systemic and systematic support for the unconventional capabilities the Army requires in order to succeed in the kind of operations in which we are currently engaged and to which we are likely to remain committed for many years to come. Stabilization and counter-insurgency tasks must not be regarded as part-time or peripheral operations, subservient to high-intensity war-fighting in terms of the intellectual, practical and emotional effort we give to them. I was struck by Bob Gates's remark to the National Defense University in 2008 that 'In the end, the military capabilities we need cannot be separated from the cultural traits and reward structure of the institutions we have: the signals sent by what gets funded, by who gets promoted, what is taught in the academies and staff colleges and how we train.' If we were to apply those criteria to our own armed forces, many would agree that we still have a fair way to go in this business of transforming ourselves to remain relevant. This process of transformation needs to be wide-ranging, and to deal with each aspect of 'fighting power', encompassing physical, conceptual and moral imperatives. Clearly, it must go well beyond our deploy-able structures and speak directly to us in terms of our fighting culture, our thinking, our leadership, our train-ing and, of course, our war-fighting doctrine.

In the physical component, the army took the ground-breaking decision in 2008 to optimize its deployable ground manœuvre brigades for the most likely, medium-scale, enduring stabilization operations (in other words, like Afghanistan), while ensuring that it retained the capability to conduct large-scale intervention should this be required, although at longer notice. This decision demands two fundamental changes of the Army: first, to rebalance capability across all our ground manœuvre brigades; and second, to ensure that we have enough of them, of sufficient size, to meet current operational demands while at the same time satisfying the requirement for a reserve for contingency tasks. At a time when our people have been operating at an almost unsustainable tempo, a structure of six ground manoeuvre brigades will also offer the very welcome fringe benefit of delivering an interval between tours of 30 months (divided into recuperation, training, high readiness for other operations and training for operations in Afghanistan) in each 36-month cycle.

The job of the Army is to provide the necessary capability to defend our nation, no matter what form that threat may take. We would be foolish to close our eyes to the uncertainty of the future or the rise of other strategic actors. In our drive to learn these new ways of war – if indeed they are new – we must not forget how to conduct the old ways of war. To that end, it is incumbent on all involved to seize every opportunity to keep alight the intellectual (and practical) flame of formation-level and higher-level war-fighting skills. We need to retain our ability to provide formation-level training, because if we don't, because we are focusing exclusively on the immediate needs of low-level training to ensure success in Afghanistan, these skills will erode. I was shocked in this regard to see the bitter experience of the Israeli Defence Forces (IDF) in southern Lebanon in 2007. They had structured themselves since the late 1990s to deal with a particular counter-insurgency campaign. Their soldiers were used to receiving detailed target packs that gave them perfect situational awareness about which window to go in through on a raid, and where the insurgents would be. Divisional headquarters were static and used to conducting their operations on a campaign basis. When the IDF had to conduct operations in southern Lebanon, they found that they were unable to cope with uncertainty, with an enemy who could not be seen, and to respond with the flexibility of mind demanded by a mobile and intense campaign, especially at the higher tactical level.

More widely, in the physical component, the Army is also fundamentally re-examining the role, purpose and structure of a variety of elements of what might be described as the 'Institutional Army' – the traditional or 'inherited' Army. It is also reconsidering the issue of regular versus reserve balance from first principles. My own view is that we need not an Army made up of separate Regular, Reserve and Territorial components, but a single Army – of, say, 140,000 men and women – consisting of soldiers and officers serving with varying degrees of commitment and readiness – 'part-time/ full-time' better describes the concept. One of the key lessons I have drawn from our experiences in Iraq and Afghanistan is that within that Army we must have a structure robust enough to cope with the pressure of intense operations. It would seem entirely logical that we need a bigger Army in order to cope with the known pressures of the next few years. I am talking here not about more infantry battalions, but about battalions with more robust establishments, so that they can absorb casualties without unduly diminishing their operational capability, as well as maintaining sufficient non-deployable elements. With the casualties we have been sustaining in Afghanistan, the six-month operational tour length is essential to allow us time to repair and retrain. Indeed, given that the MOD's principal aim is to achieve strategic success on current operations, in the context of global counter-terrorism, the need for adequate manning levels is pressing. Interestingly, the US Army recruits to 107 per cent in battalions to account for the non-deployable element, and all our major allies are making significant and rapid increases to the size of their armies: the US Army by over 13 per cent; the US Marine Corps by 15 per cent; the Australian Army by over 18 per cent; New Zealand by 25 per cent; and Canada by 28 per cent. What about us? If the past is anything to go by, we will continue to buy fast jets, submarines and large surface naval vessels in numbers that do not address the requirements of today's wars, while the weary foot soldiers, and those who support them, continue to bear the brunt – and bloodshed – of fighting today. It cannot be right.

In the conceptual component, we have some intellectual catching up to do. We need to regain agility in our ability to learn rapidly from operations and embed what we learn in our tactical doctrine. We have also concluded that the demands of current and future operating environments require a much greater emphasis on education than on training. We need to look particularly closely at how we can re-invest in education for this generation of officers, if we wish to identify the next generation of military thinkers. The Americans have done well in this area: consider men such as McMaster, Nagl, Petraeus, Abizaid, all of whom benefited from a mid-career spell at an Ivy League university. Where will our next Bagnall, Kitson, Liddell-Hart or Fuller come from without this level of investment? As security rises in importance relative to defence, and the attractions of preventing conflict grow as opposed to conducting costly intervention and stabilization operations, there is an important opportunity for one of our major universities to offer a comprehensive study programme, not just for soldiers, but for the myriad of Government and non-Government civilians with whom they are likely to work. In getting the 'comprehensive approach' to conflict resolution to work properly, studying for a master's degree or conducting research in a multi-disciplinary academic environment is more likely to produce the right results than it is – as seems to be the norm at the moment – meeting one's colleagues from other institutions for the first time at the airport on the way to a hot spot abroad.

And finally, in the moral component, we have frankly been asking too much of our people. We need to give substance and meaning to the rhetoric that is often employed. Our ability to attract and above all retain high-quality people needs very careful consideration. This is about much more than financial inducements, though they will be important. It is about the quality of the whole Army experience, through life, including excitement and opportunity, healthcare, pensions, educational opportunities and housing. It all depends on people. I am incredibly grateful for the increase in popular support for the armed forces and the interest in the welfare of our men and women that has been evident since the autumn of 2007. All of our men and women who have returned from Iraq or Afghanistan have been honoured and moved by the reception they have received. Who would have thought that in early 2009 we would have seen thousands line the streets of Belfast to honour a marching regiment, as we did on the return of 1st

Battalion, the Royal Irish Regiment from Afghanistan? The fantastic public response to appeals not just by Help for Heroes, but by all the service charities, has exceeded all our expectations, and this is also testament to the high respect and sympathy felt by the people of this country towards our soldiers. But I would like to think that alongside this increase in public empathy with soldiers' welfare, there is also a desire to empathize with what these soldiers actually do, particularly on operations. The ability to provide humanitarian assistance, to converse with those of another culture and background with a view to gaining their trust and respect, and to fight with controlled aggression and determination – all on the same day – is something we frequently ask of our people. It doesn't take a special kind of person to do this; just a willingness to work hard as part of a team, to think of others before yourself, to live by an agreed set of values and observe certain standards of behaviour, and above all, to wish to be able to take a degree of pride in your work and in those around you.

To many, the Army may seem a distant and somewhat aloof organization. Indeed, today only 7 per cent of 17–24-year-olds have a family member with any military experience at all; but I hope that a greater understanding of what we do and who we are will engender a willingness by more of our young people to serve for a time in this demanding but honourable profession. The experiences, skills and qualifications gained are unlike those offered by any other walk of life, and while there are undoubtedly challenges, the overall reward of job satisfaction and personal development is considerable. Anyone who has the honour and privilege to wear the Queen's uniform does so with a degree of pride and self-worth that I believe is unrivalled anywhere in civilian life. It is my contention that it is indeed a fine and honourable thing to be a British soldier; and in contrast to Kipling's 'Tommy this and Tommy that' we must not take the commitment of today's 'Tommies' for granted. They and their Army have been transformed by today's wars, but the nation needs them for tomorrow's challenges, too. Looking to the future, there is no shortage of work for soldiers to do; just something of a shortage of soldiers, and of the money to recruit, train, equip and deploy them.

Over the years, the character of the environment in which our forces operate has changed, and the enemy and his tactics have definitely changed. It remains a fundamental principle of our approach to warfare, however, that we must outmanœuvre our enemy in speed of thought and action. If we are not structured, resourced, trained and educated for today's and tomorrow's conflicts, then it is we who will run the risk of being defeated. I am convinced that we have the wherewithal to ensure that this does not become reality. A lot has happened within the Army in the forty years between 28 August 1969, when I joined, and 28 August 2009, when I gave up my post as its professional head. Enemies have come, and enemies have gone; Governments have come and Governments have gone; but the British Army endures. It does so because of its people: the men and women who serve in its ranks, and the families who sustain them. My family has sustained me throughout my service, for which I will always be immensely grateful. The challenge for the future is to ensure that the nation properly values and sustains its Army, and never takes its soldiers or their families for granted.

Epilogue
Last Post?

All my friends told me, in completely unequivocal terms, that in my first few months – perhaps, even, for a year – after stepping down as the Chief of the General Staff, I should try to do nothing, and certainly accept no significant invitations. I completely failed to follow this advice.

As a family, we have always tried to go to Scotland in September to fish on the River Spey. It is a huge privilege to be able to spend time every year on one of the most attractive salmon rivers in the British Isles. We fish the Brae Water, which is that section of the river just upstream from Fochabers in Morayshire. Like everything in life, the river has had its ups and downs. On 27 September 1995 I was hugely excited to catch four fish within an hour, all over 15lb in weight and all hooked at the same place on the river; but 2009 was to see no repeat. Virtually all salmon rivers have struggled in recent years, for a series of not altogether agreed reasons.

Explanations, like nets scooping up the fish in the river estuaries, deep-sea fishing off Greenland, climate change generally and any number of frustrated fisherman's theories, have been offered and debated in the last decade, but the jury is still out. I suspect that our Creator is the only one who really knows what is going on in our often poorly conserved world.

On Wednesday, 30 September 2009, which was the last day of our fishing – and of my first complete week on the river for many years – I was somewhat surprised to get a telephone call from Edward Llewellyn, David Cameron's chief of staff, who had tracked me down to the banks of the River Spey, asking if I would be willing to take a call from his boss later that day. Not knowing what he wanted to talk about, but curious as to why the Leader of the Opposition wanted to call, I said I would be willing to talk to him at about 4 p.m. However, 4 p.m. came and went and, as this was the last day of the season on the Spey and of our holiday, I gave up waiting on the bank and waded back into the river. For the uninitiated, salmon fishing is very much a battle between man, fish and river, with no quarter given or expected from any party. On that day I had waded up to my chest in a fairly fast-flowing part of the river, just keeping my balance in the strong current, and had cast about 40 feet of line from my 15-foot rod, when my BlackBerry in the pouch at the top of my waders began to ring. My initial thought was to ignore it, but then I remembered the previous arrangement with David Cameron.

'Sorry, I am late calling; is it OK to talk?' he asked.

'Yes, it's fine,' I replied, 'but I am in the middle of the River Spey, and if I get into a fish, I will have to break off.'

As throughout the rest of the week, I did not get into a fish; but the conversation that ensued concentrated my mind not a little and changed my personal dynamics for the next few months.

In essence, David Cameron asked me whether I would be willing to give some advice over the coming months to him and his team on defence matters. He explained that in Opposition it was difficult to get first-hand and current operational advice, and so was asking for my help in providing this. Furthermore, he said, after a long time in Opposition he might be looking, should his party win the general election, to bring some specialists into Government.

We discussed matters for a while before I said that in principle I would be willing to assist. To most people it seemed very likely that his party would come to power at the forthcoming election, and I felt it was in the national interest for them to have as full an understanding of current defence matters as possible, especially given our involvement in Afghanistan and the importance of the Defence Review which would inevitably follow the election.

From my point of view, the conversation was helping to resolve a personal dilemma with which I had already begun to struggle. Having just spent three years heading an army that had been locked into two difficult conflicts, and believing that Afghanistan was a mission that we absolutely had to get right, I was finding it difficult to have been totally involved on 28 August 2009, but then to accept it was not my business at all on 29 August. David Cameron's telephone call seemed to offer a solution to my problem. However, in that conversation of

30 September, I pointed out that although I had stood down as Chief of the General Staff the month before, I did not come off the Army payroll until 20 November and could do nothing until then. I do not think David had appreciated that point before our conversation, but he now acknowledged that in the intervening period there was a danger attached to our conversation becoming public knowledge. In the event that it did leak out I predicted there would be a considerable fuss, but we concluded if that did happen, we would have to take it on the chin.

I reeled my line in and headed back through the river to have a think. Unfortunately, I picked a slightly different route out of the water, going nearly up to my armpits at one stage and totally submerging my BlackBerry. It has never been the same since, emitting more of a grunt when someone calls rather than a polite ring tone. Back on the bank, I reflected on our conversation. Clearly a role advising the Opposition would be controversial, but it would be an informal and pro bono arrangement, and anyway would not start until November. Moreover, I was aware that a lot of people were quietly talking to the Tories, in anticipation of their forming the next Government. I think that is a perfectly legitimate aspect of our democracy and our predominantly two-party system. However, I had to deal with the political angle in my own mind. I have never belonged to a political party, nor do I now, and my loyalty as a public servant is to the national interest. I decided that in this case what I had agreed to, while potentially controversial, was in principle right. I clarified in my own mind that my motivation was, as before, simply to act in the best interests of the defence of the realm, the safety of our citizens and the well-being of the armed forces. That, I felt, was an honourable position to take, and over the last year I have stated that motivation to the point of boredom – one interviewer even finishing the sentence for me. What might or might not happen if the Conservatives won the election was an issue that I felt could be addressed nearer the time; for now it remained in the realm of the hypothetical. So, with a waterlogged BlackBerry and no fish, Pippa and I left Scotland and headed south.

Events were to move faster than I expected. The following week, on 7 October, I was to be installed as the 159th Constable of the Tower of London. To become Constable was a huge honour and I would be following in many eminent footsteps, not least those of the great Duke of Wellington himself, who had been Constable for twenty-six years in the mid-nineteenth century. In more recent times the term of office had been fixed as five years, but even so, for a variety of complicated reasons, there had not been an installation ceremony in the Tower for eight years. Although the ceremony itself is private and held within the Tower, Historic Royal Palaces, which is the charitable trust that runs the Tower, was keen to raise the profile of the event. So we planned a number of initiatives with local schools in Tower Hamlets and arranged some media coverage, including interviews with several newspapers, radio and television. It was in a Radio 5 Live interview on the Victoria Derbyshire programme that I began to smell a rat and suspect that my conversation with David Cameron was unlikely to remain private. A phone-in caller, who described himself as an ex-soldier, was effusive in thanking me for what I had done for the Army while I had been Chief, and then asked me if there was any way that I could stay on and continue to contribute to defence and public life. I tried to dodge the question by replying that I was about to become Constable of the Tower of London, and as that was my next job it was the one on which I would be focusing. To my surprise the caller persisted and asked me whether, hypothetically, I could be more formally involved in public life, perhaps even become a minister – after all, Lord West, a former Chief of the Naval Staff, was now a minister in Gordon Brown's Government. I said that yes, I supposed it was possible, hypothetically. He then asked directly whether I had been invited to be involved. Few things in interviews usually throw me, but this question from the 'ex-soldier' did. Momentarily I hesitated – searching for the honest answer – before replying that I had not been asked that question, publicly. At which point the conversation ended, and I wondered if the answer I had just given had closed the issue.

It did not take Nick Robinson of the BBC long to track David Cameron down at the Conservative Party Conference in Manchester and put the same question to him. Was General Dannatt going to be joining the Conservative Defence team? As a man of proven integrity, Cameron had little option but to confirm that he had indeed asked me to help – and the story immediately began to attract media attention. In an attempt to make a virtue out of necessity, Cameron referred in his Party Leader's end-of-conference speech to the fact that I would indeed be advising the Conservatives.

There was a very mixed reaction to the news. My close

family and friends, and very many members of the public who wrote to me, thought that it was a positive and public-spirited thing to do; not so the majority of the media. Most of the reaction was negative, some pretty strident, and one or two pieces quite uncomfortably personal in their criticism. Much of it seemed to assume that I was to go straight into some paid advisory role, prior to becoming a minister after the election, and although most of that was speculation, wishful thinking or just plain wrong, when an idea gains currency the momentum is fairly unstoppable. I had predicted a fuss, which we were duly having. As it happened, on the day of David Cameron's speech to his party conference, I was giving the annual lecture to the Windsor Leadership Trust in London. I spoke to the title 'Leadership in Turbulent Times'. The address was on the record, as was part of the question-and-answer session that followed. My fellow Windsor Leadership Trustee, the former ITN anchorman Martyn Lewis, was in the chair and could not resist giving rein to his journalistic instincts in putting some searching questions. It all made for a very interesting afternoon and evening.

Over the next few days and weeks, I chose to ignore what was being said publicly and get on with the other things that I was doing – chief among which was starting to write this book. Come late November, I was able to offer such advice to the Conservative Party as was requested, but my involvement was always fairly peripheral. Some tried to keep the story in the shock-horror category, including those involved in one rather excited exchange on the BBC *Question Time* programme, but frankly I chose just to get on with life. It was quite clear to me that whatever merit there might have been in someone like me joining a future Conservative Government, there was no public appetite for the move – at least, not in that part of the public represented by the majority of the media. As the general election approached, I explained to David Cameron that, whereas I was quite content to give such advice as was useful as he prepared for Government, when or if his team were elected my role would cease, as his proper source of military advice should then be the Chiefs of Staff Committee. My former colleagues would not have thanked me for second-guessing them. Any thought of a ministerial role within Government was clearly out of the question, and I certainly had no intention of becoming a 'special adviser'. I have deprecated for some time the rise of the salaried special advisers within Government in recent years, and I certainly had no intention of joining their ranks. Since the formation of the Coalition Government shortly after 6 May 2010 that has remained my position, and I have chosen to express my views subsequently in articles, interviews and speeches, when invited to do so.

Reflecting on that whole episode, I criticize myself in the first instance for agreeing to become an adviser too quickly. As the older man in the original conversation I should have counselled less haste and more time for reflection; but I think David Cameron was acting on his own concerns that, while he knew Afghanistan and the upcoming Defence Review were big challenges, he did not feel completely on top of those subjects, and so was looking for help. For my part, I was well aware of the issues and very willing, perhaps too willing, to provide whatever advice was deemed useful. I think there were salutary lessons to be learnt all round – certainly, the next time I retire I shall follow the advice of my friends more closely. That said, I respect someone who is willing to admit what they do not know and ask for help. In the last few months, since the formation of the Coalition Government, I have been impressed by David Cameron's confidence on defence and security issues. Chairing a new National Security Council on day one in Government sent all the right messages, and his handling of the publication of the Saville Inquiry into Bloody Sunday was very well judged. I am optimistic that we have a pragmatic Prime Minister with the character and integrity to lead the nation well; but it is early days and the future is notoriously difficult to predict.

As my comments above and the latter chapters of this book have already indicated, the Security and Defence Review of 2010 was always likely to be a most significant new codification and blueprint for the future development of British foreign, security and defence policy. I have already made my views clear on these matters. However, for the avoidance of doubt, I believe that a proper analysis of the nature and character of future conflict, in particular pointing to the instability of failed or failing states, will reveal that the likely threats to our security in the near to medium term will be complex – some would call them 'hybrid' – and therefore likely to demand a response more akin to the kind of operations we have conducted in Iraq and Afghanistan than to the more conventional state-on-state warfare for which we prepared, trained and equipped ourselves over the previous forty years of the Cold War. Our response is more likely to be kaleidoscopic than singular. Moreover, despite the financial pressures, our historic, institutional and traditional legacy continues to place us as a nation in a position such that 'strategic shrinkage', as William Hague has put it, is not a serious policy option for a responsible British Government. However, the experience and the expense of our interventions in Iraq and Afghanistan will not only make future governments wary of involving our armed forces in operations that are anything other than manifestly non-discretionary, but point towards the importance of correctly identifying future trouble spots and preventing conflict, as opposed to intervening in, containing or stabilizing a conflict situation. I tried to draw attention to this in my speech at Chatham House in May 2009, and have been delighted to see that my old university, Durham, has picked up the significance of prevention rather than intervention and plans to invest significant energy and ideas in this hugely important concept.

More immediately, the trick to be taken in late 2010 was to work out how to fill the £35 billion black hole in defence spending that had opened out over the previous five years, while not only succeeding in Afghanistan but ensuring that we had some high-readiness capability to respond to new crises and challenges in the short term and remained able to invest sufficiently in protection against the uncertainties of the future. Achieving all these objectives in the financial climate of 2010 is a very tall order. The solution is the strict application of priorities, and the guiding principle is relevance. What we spend our resources on must be relevant to the threats and challenges facing us. The challenges of today and the near term are very clear and, by definition, the highest priority. To succeed in Afghanistan we need a modest increase in expenditure on our land forces, which as I have said repeatedly include not just the Army, but the Royal Marines and the helicopter and transport parts of the Royal Air Force too.

For those who worry that such an increase will unbalance our ability to protect ourselves against the broad range of unknown threats in the future, I would point again to the growing consensus that Defence Reviews should be conducted by statute every four or five years, and not just when the Government of the day decides. Not only does this preserve future flexibility of response, it should take the party politics out of the higher issues of defence, which themselves are so important that they should be governed by national interest and not party point-scoring. In four or five years' time, should our involvement in Afghanistan have been largely scaled down, and should other threats with different characteristics have emerged, then another Defence Review at that time can change the priorities. I accept that such changes in priority will present a huge challenge to the defence procurement process, but the way we currently buy equipment for our armed forces is in any case too protracted, expensive and bureaucratic for the current age of austerity. The procurement process must become quicker, cheaper and more responsive; the pace of our current and future transformation makes such change axiomatic.

Put bluntly, these arguments translate from the general to certain specifics. The Army should reduce its holdings of main battle tanks and heavy artillery and its presence in Germany; the Royal Air Force should reduce its numbers of fast jets and its number of main operating bases, while increasing its helicopter and transport aircraft numbers; and the Royal Navy should think long and hard over whether the nation's best interests are served by such a large investment in two fully capable aircraft carriers with the associated complement of fast jets. Given the uncertainty over the intentions of a number of states that hold nuclear weapons, unilaterally dispensing with our independent nuclear deterrent is not, for now, a discussion topic, but it should not remain off the agenda indefinitely.

Should decisions be taken that reflect my conclusions, these will produce an army and an air force properly configured for today's challenges but retaining the capability to adapt to the future, and a navy with the greater flexibility that a larger fleet of smaller ships can bring to protect our shipping and trade routes, in contrast to putting most of our national maritime eggs into two huge and very expensive baskets. How to provide air power over deployed land forces was never properly debated in the 1997–8 Strategic Defence Review and should be considered now. The aircraft-carrier project was a very eye-catching announcement in 1998, but not the product of detailed debate. A more rational conclusion would be the provision of such air power from land bases in friendly states, with aircraft range extended by a fully reworked air-to-air refuelling capability. Unlike the United States, we are no longer a global power, and should not pretend to be so. The aircraft carriers run the risk of over-reaching our ambition, our capability and our pocket. To return to the guiding principle of relevance, we should emerge from this Defence Review with capabilities that are relevant to the highest priorities of today, relevant to our principal allies – chief among which remains the USA – but able to adapt, over time, to future needs.

Equipment is important, but our armed forces are ultimately constituted by their people – our servicemen and women and their families. For today and into the future we must ensure that we have the right number of them, and that they are properly looked after. Napoleon said that in war 'the moral is to the physical, as three is to one'. He was right. All the ideas, plans and equipment will be rendered marginal if either the leadership of our people or their own will to win – their morale – is anything other than of the highest order. Earlier in this book I have pointed out the dangers of a loss of balance within the Military Covenant, of a failure to match the amount of work faced by our people with adequate care for their legitimate individual needs and those of their families. In the last few years we have made some significant advances in operational equipment, medical care, welfare, pay and allowances, and accommodation. Nevertheless, despite the huge upsurge in public support for the armed forces that we have seen in homecoming parades and donations to the service charities, the morale of our people could be seriously eroded by a rowing back on some of the progress made. Cuts to 'soft' areas like training, allowances, and building and refurbishment programmes would reverse the balance in the Covenant that has been achieved. In these financially stringent times, cuts in these areas may seem very attractive; but the damage they would do would be out of all proportion to the savings possible – savings that are tiny in comparison to those that would flow from the bold readjustments to our force structure and equipment programmes that I have summarized in the section above. We tinker with our people's lives at our peril.

Rudyard Kipling understood the British soldier well, and understood him in the context of a difficult campaign in Afghanistan. In 1892, reflecting on a soldier struggling to be served a drink in his local pub, he concluded his famous poem 'Tommy' with the words:

For it's Tommy this, an' Tommy that, an' 'Chuck 'im out, the brute!'
But it's 'Saviour of 'is country' when the guns begin to shoot;
An' it's Tommy this, an' Tommy that, an' anything you please;
An' Tommy ain't a bloomin' fool – you bet that Tommy sees!

And Tommy does not just see for himself; he sees for his family and his colleagues as well. He wants a fair deal for his family and himself, but he also knows there need to be enough soldiers too. He knows that we struggled in Iraq because we did not have enough troops, because the budget was tight and because we had committed ourselves to a second operation in Afghanistan. He knows that we struggled for too long in Afghanistan because we could not hold the areas we cleared of Taliban in sufficient strength to begin to build a better life for the people, and thereby win their hearts and minds. He knows that in the complex and hybrid security environment of today and tomorrow there will be value inherent in the numbers of 'boots on the ground', because he knows that today's and probably tomorrow's wars are being fought among the people – they are the operational environment – and about the people – it is their hearts and minds we have to win. It is for this reason he is now puzzled that our recruitment has slowed to a trickle and training depots are nearly empty, because apparently the money has run out. He finds this particularly difficult to understand when he sees holes in the ranks in his unit as a result of the sustained pressure on individuals over the last ten years and from the casualties taken during his unit's last tour in Afghanistan.

Tommy also looks to his leaders in these turbulent times, to set matters on a sensible course. But he is choosy about whom he follows with confidence. He will determine for himself what really gives a potential leader their authority – the right to lead – and he will probably conclude that, at the end of the day, it comes down to the leader's personal qualities: the nature of their character and the degree of their integrity. From his experience he knows that character defines the person, and answers the question as to whether this is someone to emulate or to follow, and with what degree of enthusiasm. Moreover, he knows that integrity establishes the moral baseline of leadership. He will ask himself: Is this someone who can be trusted? Is this someone whose instructions are honourable? Is this someone to commit to? Do they really have legitimate interests at heart, or is this person simply a self-seeker, or purely interested in the bottom line? These are all judgements in any walk of life for the subordinates, the employees, the followers, the voters to make. Within the military, Tommy's judgements will ultimately define success or failure in the enterprise – perhaps not in the short term, but certainly in the medium and long term.

The British soldier, sailor and airman is a citizen, too. He or she was born somewhere in this country or in the Commonwealth, or perhaps in Nepal or in the Republic of Ireland, and after a period of service will go back, perhaps with a family, to the civilian community. He or she will take back the sights, sounds and experiences of many challenging years – sometimes dangerous, sometimes boring, but very different from the experiences of those classmates at school who followed other walks of life. The Army in which I served for forty years exhibits many of the characteristics of a family that you never fully leave. Military service is less a job, far more a way of life, and you cannot turn your back on a way of life. It was my decision in 1969 to join the Army; it was Pippa's decision in 1977 to marry a soldier, albeit one who thought he was about to leave; and, of course, Tom, Bertie, Olly and Richenda had no choice about being born into an Army family, my having decided on a full career in khaki. For Pippa and me, life in the Army involved twenty-three house moves; for the children it meant numerous primary schools before boarding school gave them some continuity of education; and for my two daughters-in-law, Lucinda and Emma, and two grand-sons, Arthur and Freddie, it meant joining a family characterized by uncertainty and focused on issues that passed most of the population by, even if the two little boys were far too young to realize this. But it is within the overall notion of family that I have been so indebted to Pippa. Once our own children were a little older, she trained as a counsellor with Relate – the old Marriage Guidance Council – working wherever our postings took us. Ultimately, of course, combining the role of general's wife with that of a very busy and skilled relationship counsellor took chameleon skills of a high order, but she juggled the demands superbly.

It is on the importance of families, reflecting the dedication at the beginning of this book, that my final words should therefore dwell. Families bring stability and families constitute home. For a soldier, sailor or airman constantly on the move, often in difficult or dangerous circumstances, belonging to a family and enjoying its support is vital. For some, the Army provides that family, and this is a responsibility that needs to be acknowledged right through active service and on into retirement. For others, there is the support of wives, husbands, partners, mothers, fathers and children. Such support provides enormous strength in the dark times, but it comes at a cost to the family back at home, who are watching, waiting and worrying whether their soldier, sailor or airman will come home and when, and wondering whether they will be fit and well, or physically or mentally disabled, or perhaps coming home in a cortège through Wootton Bassett. That last tragic possibility is at the heart of the unlimited liability implicit in our life of service, and at the heart of the Military Covenant. For myself, I am most grateful to all my family for putting up with me during the difficult times. Nevertheless, I cannot escape from the knowledge that I am part of something even bigger – of my regimental families and indeed of the whole Army family, to whom I owe so much.

Across the fields from our house in Norfolk is a very small Saxo-Norman round tower church that sits on a small hill overlooking the River Yare. It was probably built originally to keep a watch out for Danish raiders, but over the years this little church, just large enough for a family baptism, has come to symbolize for me the physical embodiment of a much larger family whose head is, of course, our Creator, with whom I struggled to come to terms all those years ago. I do not think He minds that we drive our pheasants from the copse around the church on family shooting days; and I think that He must be pleased that that little church has stood for nearly a thousand years as a symbol of Himself – the God who understands and inspires and sustains. It is my hope that over the next thousand years we, as a nation, will not neglect our Christian heritage, any more than we neglect to remember those who gave their lives in war, and whose names are written on the small memorial in our graveyard: those who gave 'their Today for our Tomorrow'. What we, as a nation, have chosen to do with 'our Tomorrow' is a very big question, of course. Have we used our time, our energy and our resources in a way that they, our forefathers, would have seen fit to approve? How responsible as a people have we been with our heritage, and how seriously have we taken the ultimate sacrifice they made for us? These are, I suggest, uncomfortable questions that at times we all need to ask of ourselves. When the history of the end of the last century and the beginning of this one come to be written, will the 1970s, 80s, 90s and this decade – the four that spanned my Army service – be thought to have fulfilled the expectations, hope and promise looked for in 1918 and 1945?

Inscribed on a stained glass window at the east end of our little parish church are the words 'In Sure and Certain Hope'. These words also form Pippa's family motto. For me, hope is not chance, but the expectation of better things to come. In the 1970s we could not see the solution to the Troubles in Northern Ireland, but there was a fierce hope that peace would return to the Province. In the 1980s we could not see the solution to the Cold War, but we hoped that one day the Iron Curtain would come down and Europe would be reunited. In the 1990s there seemed to be no logic or end to the vicious civil wars in the Balkans, but we hoped that one day common sense would eventually prevail and the killing stop. Today other challenges in Iraq, Afghanistan and elsewhere surround us, and the future is by no means certain. But in whatever field of human endeavour we put our hand to the plough, hope has to be there as the headmark at the end of the furrow. For two years at Sandhurst, I, along with countless others before and since, wore the motto of the Royal Military Academy – 'Serve to Lead' – as part of my cap badge. Perhaps we have never needed more than we do today a full understanding of the twin concepts of service and leadership: serving others in order to earn the enormous privilege of leadership.

Picture Acknowledgements

Most of the photographs in this book are from the author's collection. Those that are not, or that require further acknowledgement, are listed below. Every effort has been made to trace copyright holders; those overlooked are invited to get in touch with the publishers.

First section
Pages 4–5: all images except for the group photograph: courtesy of the Green Howards Museum Trust
Pages 6–7: Guard of honour, Berlin, 1977; Green Howards march through Pickering, 1981: both courtesy of the Green Howards Museum Trust

Second section
Page 1: FRD announces that there will be no amalgamation for Green Howards, 1991: courtesy of the Green Howards Museum Trust
Pages 2–3: FRD and Sanya Stankovic: courtesy of the Green Howards Museum Trust
Pages 4–5: FRD and General Talic: courtesy of the Green Howards Museum Trust
Pages 6–7: FRD talking to the press via satellite, Pristina, 14

June 1999: TopFoto.co.uk; *The Bank Job – Operation MAGPIE – Mostar – Bosnia – 18th April 2001* by David Rowlands: commissioned and owned by the Warrant Officers and Sergeant Mess of 2nd Battalion The Princess of Wales's Royal Regiment

Third section

Pages 2–3 (clockwise from top left): Daily Mail front page, 13 October 2006: Daily Mail/Solo Syndication, including photo of FRD: Big Agency; FRD outside Ministry of Defence 13 October 2006: Getty Images; Matt cartoon: Matt/Daily Telegraph; FRD in Afghanistan, August 2007: courtesy of the Green Howards Museum Trust; *Daily Telegraph* cutting, 25 August 2007: Daily Telegraph, including photo of FRD in Afghanistan, 18 August 2007: Andrew Parsons/PA Wire; FRD in Camp Price, southern Afghanistan, 18 August 2007: Andrew Parsons/PA Wire; cartoon by Holland, *Spectator* 21 October 2006: Holland/Spectator ; 'The soldier who took on Blair' cartoon by David Smith, *The Week*, 21 October 2006: David E. Smith

Pages 6–7 (clockwise from top left): three images of the ceremony at Crépon, 1996: all courtesy of the Green Howards Museum Trust; Prince Harry on patrol, Garmsir, February 2008: © John Stillwell/Pool/epa/Corbis; Prince Harry, Helmand, 18 February 2008: Corbis/WireImage; FRD at the Sovereign's Parade, Sandhurst, 2008: Tempest Photography

Page 8: FRD and Prince Harry, Royal Norfolk Show, 2008: Mark Cuthbert/UK Press/Press Association Images; FRD in bowler hat, Royal Norfolk Show, 2008; FRD at the finale of the Royal Norfolk Show, 2008: both Eastern Daily Press

Fourth section

Page 1: FRD as Chief of the General Staff: Gill Shaw/www.gill-shaw.co.uk

Pages 2–3 (clockwise from top left): FRD and Des Browne, Edinburgh Castle, 11 April 2008: David Cheskin/PA Archive/Press Association Images; FRD and Boris Johnson, London, 22 June 2009: National Pictures/TopFoto; FRD's installation as Constable of the Tower, 7 October 2009: News Team International; 'Short-changing the Army', cartoon by Howard McWilliam, *The Week*, 18 July 2009

PICTURE ACKNOWLEDGEMENTS

Pages 4–5 (clockwise from top left): Red Devil freefall team, Netheravon, 9 September 2008: Cpl G. Moreno/Army News Team; FRD and Red Devils in freefall: © Crown Copyright/MOD. Reproduced with the permission of the Controller of Her Majesty's Stationery Office/Steve Tan; Sue, Toby and Tom Norton: Heathcliff O'Malley; FRD and Henry Allingham, 10 July 2007: Stefan Rousseau/PA Archive/Press Association Images; Norfolk Dog Day, August 2008: Colin de Chair; Richenda Dannatt and Red Devil: Cpl G. Moreno/Army News Team

Pages 6–7: Tom Dannatt in Sierra Leone: both Jo Edwards; Stevie Shine, Olly Dannatt and Rory Mackenzie, Verbier, March 2009: Scott Hornby

Page 8: FRD at home: Derek Tamea; FRD with Arthur Dannatt: Jo Edwards

Index

INDEX

INDEX

INDEX

INDEX

INDEX

INDEX

INDEX

INDEX

INDEX